REVOLUTION
IN PRINT

REVOLUTION IN PRINT

THE PRESS IN FRANCE
1775-1800

**ROBERT DARNTON AND
DANIEL ROCHE,** *Editors*

UNIVERSITY OF CALIFORNIA PRESS

BERKELEY   LOS ANGELES   LONDON

IN COLLABORATION WITH

THE NEW YORK PUBLIC LIBRARY

University of California Press
Berkeley and Los Angeles, California
University of California Press, Ltd.
London, England
© 1989 by
The New York Public Library, Astor, Lenox and Tilden Foundations
Printed in the United States of America
1   2   3   4   5   6   7   8   9

For illustrated items not included in the Exhibition Checklist, the legend
includes full citations and French titles. In legends for items included in the
Exhibition Checklist, citations have been abbreviated and cross-references
to the checklist have been provided.

Unless otherwise indicated
in the legends, photographs were provided by
the institution credited. All photographs
of items from The New York Public Library
are by Robert D. Rubic.

Library of Congress Cataloging-in-Publication Data

Revolution in print : the press in France, 1775–1800 / Robert Darnton
and Daniel Roche, editors.
        p.   cm.
    ISBN 0-520-06430-5 (alk. paper).   ISBN 0-520-06431-3 (pbk. : alk. paper)
    1. Printing—France—History—18th century.   2. Publishers and
publishing—France—History—18th century.   3. Press—France—
History—18th century.   4. France—History—Revolution, 1789–1799—
Literature and the revolution.   5. Books and reading—France—
History—18th century.   6. Revolutionary literature—Publishing—
France—History—18th century.   7. Revolutionary literature, French—
History and criticism.   I. Darnton, Robert.   II. Roche, Daniel.
Z144.R5   1989
686.2'0944—dc19   88-20744

CONTENTS

Foreword
vii

Acknowledgments
xi

Introduction
ROBERT DARNTON
xiii

PART ONE
PREREVOLUTIONARY CONDITIONS

Censorship and the Publishing Industry
DANIEL ROCHE
3

Philosophy Under the Cloak
ROBERT DARNTON
27

Malesherbes and the Call for a Free Press
RAYMOND BIRN
50

PART TWO
REVOLUTION IN THE PRINTING TRADES

Economic Upheavals in Publishing
CARLA HESSE
69

CONTENTS

Printers and Municipal Politics
PIERRE CASSELLE
98

Agitation in the Work Force
PHILIPPE MINARD
107

A Provincial Perspective
MICHEL VERNUS
124

PART THREE
THE PRODUCTS OF THE PRESS

Journals: The New Face of News
JEREMY D. POPKIN
141

Pamphlets: Libel and Political Mythology
ANTOINE DE BAECQUE
165

Books: Reshaping Science
JEAN DHOMBRES
177

Almanacs: Revolutionizing a Traditional Genre
LISE ANDRIES
203

Prints: Images of the Bastille
ROLF REICHARDT
223

Songs: Mixing Media
LAURA MASON
252

Ephemera: Civic Education Through Images
JAMES LEITH
270

Exhibition Checklist
291

Notes
313

Contributors
349

FOREWORD

Few events in human history have affected not only the course of the nation that initiated them but also the lives of virtually every people of the globe. The French Revolution was one of those events, for it espoused for the first time in the history of the West a truly universal civilization, transcending cultural, national, ethnic, social, and racial boundaries by proclaiming the fundamental and inviolable rights of all peoples of the world to freedom and equality. Insofar as it translated these ideals into a living reality, the French Revolution can be said to have founded the modern era, to have given shape for the first time to the principles and institutions by which we now define our purposes and measure our achievements in public life. For these reasons it is an event whose bicentennial is worthy of commemoration, not only by the nation of its origin but by all the world, particularly that young nation, our own, which shared so intimately in the formulation and realization of its ideas and ideals.

The New York Public Library takes great pleasure in sponsoring *Revolution in Print: The Press in France, 1775–1800* as part of its efforts to commemorate the Bicentennial of the French Revolution. The book, and the exhibition with which it is associated, would not have been possible without the generous and enlightened assistance of Professor Robert Darnton of Princeton University. In the summer of 1986 I met with him to discuss an appropriate way for the Library to participate in the international celebration of the French Bicentennial. Professor Darnton recalled that in the 1960s as a graduate student researching political ideology in the prerevolutionary period, he had had the good fortune to become acquainted with an enthusiastic member of The New York Public Library staff who kindly granted him access to the Library's vast collection of uncataloged pamphlets from the period of the French Revolution. Darnton had been impressed by the range and depth of the collection, which included a substantial number of items not available in other repositories, including the Bibliothèque Nationale. We agreed that the Bicentennial offered a unique opportunity to make the riches of the Library's revolutionary collection known to the public.

Our meeting concluded with the decision to mount a major exhibition, "Revolution in Print: France, 1789," which would celebrate the freeing of the press and the role of printing in the French Revolution. Professor Darnton saw the exhibition and this companion book as an opportunity to share recent scholarship in French cultural history of the revolutionary period by American, French, and other international scholars and to stimulate interest in the extraordinary holdings, both cataloged and uncataloged, to be found in almost every division of the Library. Under his guidance, the original proposal for an exhibition and accompanying book has expanded to include related exhibitions by the Schomburg Center for Research in Black Culture and the Music Division and Dance Collection of the Performing Arts Research Center; a series of public programs; and, in conjunction with the American Library Association, a condensed traveling version of "Revolution in Print," which will tour nationally to major urban libraries. The Library owes Professor Darnton a debt of deep gratitude for his vision and effort, which have informed every aspect of our institutionwide celebration of the Bicentennial of the French Revolution.

Professor Darnton's first step in organizing the project was to invite Professor Daniel Roche of the University of Paris, the distinguished French scholar of eighteenth-century culture, to collaborate with him as co-curator of the exhibition and co-editor of this book. The Library is grateful to Professor Roche for his contribution. Carla Hesse, Assistant Professor at Rutgers University, has also performed an invaluable service as the Research Curator for the exhibition. An advisory committee of eminent American and French historians and scholars was formed to refine the intellectual content of the exhibition, and I wish to thank them for their participation: Keith Baker, Raymond Birn, Elizabeth Eisenstein, Lynn Hunt, Darline Levy, Henri-Jean Martin, Linda Nochlin, Robert Palmer, Jeremy Popkin, Michel Vovelle, Isser Woloch, and Denis Woronoff.

Diantha D. Schull, Manager of Exhibitions, has shaped and directed the Library's overall program to commemorate the Bicentennial of the French Revolution. Without her leadership such a comprehensive program of international collaboration would not have been possible. The staff of the Exhibitions Program Office deserve strong recognition for their efforts on behalf of the exhibition and this publication, and in particular Jeanne Bornstein, Research Coordinator.

It is our hope that this exhibition will facilitate research and the exchange of information and materials between American and French repositories. I wish to thank both the former and present directors of the Bibliothèque Nationale, André Miquel and Emmanuel Le Roy Ladurie, for their willingness to permit the loan of twenty-five key objects from their institution. We also want to express appreciation to the following French, Swiss, and American institutions and collectors who have generously lent objects from their collections to the exhibition: Archives Nationales, France; Archives de Paris; Imprimerie Nationale, Paris; Musée de la Révolution Française, Vizille; Bibliothèque Municipale de Lyon; Musée de l'Imprimerie et de la Banque, Lyon; Bibliothèque Publique et Universitaire, Neuchâtel; American Antiquarian Society, Worcester, Massachusetts; Rare Book and Manuscript Library, Columbia University, New York; Arts of the Book Collection, Yale University, New Haven, Connecticut; Clinton Sisson; and the Albert Field Collection of Playing Cards, Astoria, New York.

Many individuals at The New York Public Library assisted Professors Darnton, Roche, and Hesse in planning and organizing both the exhibition and book, including staff of the Special Collections, the General Research Division, the Science and Technology Research Center, the Jewish Division, the Oriental Division, the Slavic and Baltic Division, the Map Division, the Music Division, the Schomburg Center for Research in Black Culture, the Conservation Division, the Office of Public Affairs and Development, the Public Relations Office, the Publications Office, the Graphics Office, the Public Education Program Office, and the Donnell Media Center.

The project has been made possible by a generous grant from the National Endowment for the Humanities, Washington, D.C., a federal agency. Additional assistance has been provided by the Florence J. Gould Foundation, Inc.; this gift made it possible, among other things, to commence a major project to catalog French revolutionary materials in the Library's collections. Finally, the Library owes its deepest gratitude to Mr. and Mrs. Saul P. Steinberg for their generous gift in support of the exhibition.

Vartan Gregorian
President and Chief Executive Officer
The New York Public Library

ACKNOWLEDGMENTS

To produce a major exhibition and a volume such as this is to incur debts—
intellectual and personal obligations that are as important as the fiscal support from great public institutions such as The New York Public Library
itself. Behind the exhibition and behind this book lies the labor of dozens of collaborators and self-effacing individuals who beaver away in the
various divisions and collections of the Library, far from the public's eye,
making sure that books get to readers and that the printed word remains
alive.

Our thanks go to all of them, and first of all to Carla Hesse, who as Research Curator spent the better part of two years assembling the pieces of
the exhibition and organizing them into a coherent whole. She also selected
the photographs and wrote the captions for this book. Catherine Hodeir
assisted Carla Hesse from France, where many items had to be culled from
a variety of libraries and museums. As Manager of the Exhibitions Program,
Diantha Schull oversaw all our efforts with skill and charm. As Assistant
Manager, Susan F. Saidenberg organized the traveling version of the exhibition, which will go to thirty libraries, and the video production. Jeanne
Bornstein, Research Coordinator, served as research assistant to Carla
Hesse and coordinated all aspects of the exhibition and preparation of the
catalogue manuscript with unfailing good humor. Barbara Bergeron helped
edit the catalogue and other interpretive material for the exhibition. Myriam
de Arteni, Exhibitions Conservation Specialist, handled the conservation of
New York Public Library material in the exhibition requiring preservation
and restoration. Jean Mihich, Registrar, assisted by Melitte Buchman,
Caryn Reid, and Sandra Spurgeon, made all the loan arrangements and
coordinated the inventorying of objects from the Library's own collections.
Lou Storey, Installation Specialist, designed both the Gottesman and travel-

ing versions of "Revolution in Print" and, with the assistance of Tracy Fell, supervised the installation of the exhibition. Suzanne Stallings and Edward Rime, Exhibitions Assistants, provided clerical support for the entire project. And Clinton Sisson generously agreed to loan us the replica eighteenth-century press so that we could print copies of the Declaration of the Rights of Man and of the Citizen in the Library's Astor Hall.

Francis O. Mattson, Head of Special Collections Cataloging, deserves special mention for his help in locating material. Under his supervision, cataloger Gina Fisch-Freedman brought several very special items to our attention for this exhibition. We also want to thank those in the other divisions of the Library who cooperated in the effort to select the most important items from its vast collections: Elizabeth Diefendorf, General Research Division; Robert Rainwater, Spencer Collection; Roberta Waddell, Miriam and Ira D. Wallach Division of Art, Prints and Photographs; Leonard Gold, Jewish Division; Alice Hudson, Map Division; Edward Kasinec, Slavic and Baltic Division; John Lundquist, Oriental Division; Betsy Bentley, Science and Technology Research Center; Jean Bowen, Music Division, Performing Arts Research Center; and Howard Dodson, Schomburg Center for Research in Black Culture.

For help with the exhibition, we want to thank Richard De Gennaro, Director; Donald Anderle, Associate Director, Special Collections; Lisa Browar, Brooke Russell Astor Librarian for Rare Books and Manuscripts; Bernard McTigue, Curator of the Arents Collections and Keeper of Rare Books; Paul J. Fasana, Andrew W. Mellon Director and Associate Director for Preparation Services; John Baker and the staff of the Conservation Division; Gregory Long, Harold Snedcof, Susan Rautenberg, and Carolyn Cohen, Development Office; Betsy Pinover and Lauren Moye, Public Relations Office; Marilan Lund, Graphics Office; David Cronin, Public Education Program Office; Myrna Martin, Volunteer Office; Walter Mintz and Stanley Kruger, Stack Maintenance and Delivery Division; and Marie Nesthus, Media Center, Donnell Library.

Finally, our thanks to those who helped create this book: Sheila Levine, Barbara Ras, and the staff of the University of California Press; Richard Newman, Manager of Publications, The New York Public Library; Robert D. Rubic, who photographed all New York Public Library objects; and Pamela Selwyn, who translated the essay by Rolf Reichardt; Sonja Haussmann, who translated the essays by Pierre Casselle, Michel Vernus, and Lise Andries; and Maxwell R.D. Vos, who translated the essays by Philippe Minard, Antoine de Baecque, Jean Dhombres, and Daniel Roche.

Robert Darnton
Guest Curator

INTRODUCTION

ROBERT DARNTON

THIS BOOK CONFRONTS a question that has never been squarely faced, though it has tickled many imaginations: What was the role of printing in the French Revolution? Historians generally treat the printed word as a record of what happened instead of as an ingredient in the happening. But the printing press helped shape the events it recorded. It was an active force in history, especially during the decade of 1789–1799, when the struggle for power was a struggle for mastery of public opinion. By examining the world of print, we hope to open up a fresh view of the Revolution as a whole.

The point may seem self-evident, but for all our preoccupation with the media, we have never attempted to understand how the dominant means of communication in the most powerful country of the West contributed to the first great revolution of modern times. Imagine a world without telephones, radio, and television, in which the only way to move opinion on a national scale is by movable type. Imagine that world exploding. It fragments in a thousand pieces. A group of men attempt to put together a new order, beginning with a Declaration of the Rights of Man and continuing with new designs for a constitution, an administration, the church, the currency, the calendar, the map, weights and measures, forms of address, and language itself. At every stage in this process, they use the same basic tool: the printing press. Without the press, they can conquer the Bastille, but they cannot overthrow the Old Regime. To seize power they must seize the word and spread it—by journals, almanacs, pamphlets, posters, pictures, song sheets, stationery, board games, ration cards, money, anything that will carry an impression and embed it in the minds of twenty-six million French people, many of them bent under poverty and oppression, many sunk deep in ignorance, many incapable of reading the declarations of their rights. When the revolutionaries grasped the bar of the press and forced the platen down on type locked in its forme, they sent new energy streaming through the body politic. France came to life again, and humanity was amazed.

After two hundred years the amazement has dissipated. Weary of manifestoes, good intentions, and the cycle of revolution and reaction, we tend to treat the great explosion of 1789 as something laid to rest in textbooks—a historical curiosity. This book sets as its ambition a reawakening of that curiosity and a reappraisal of the power of the press. It seeks to speak to ordinary readers and at the same time to challenge scholars with a fresh set of questions.

The questions may be "academic," but they cut deep into the forces that have transformed life for everyone. Consider the freedom of the press. What did it entail when it came into existence—first, in practice, with the fall of the Bastille; then, in principle, with the Declaration of the Rights of Man and of the Citizen? What did it actually mean, not just for readers but also for authors, publishers, booksellers, and the thousands of persons who depended on the printing press for their living? Could anyone print anything after 14 July 1789, including works that might look seditious, libelous, or pornographic to the new men in power? What was the nature of literary property when property rights in general were redefined by revolutionary legislation? What was literature itself, as a system involving patronage and power as well as artistry with language?

France under the Old Regime was a crazy-quilt of overlapping units—provinces, intendancies, municipalities, judicial territories, bishoprics, taxation zones, and customs areas—many with their own laws, weights, measurements, and dialects. How could the authorities in Paris weld them into a single nation? The printing press served as the main instrument in the creation of a new political culture. But how did it function under the conditions of revolutionary government, and how far did its products penetrate into the everyday lives of ordinary people? These are some of the questions addressed in this book and in the exhibition behind it. They are raised not out of antiquarian curiosity or from a pious respect for the principles of 1789 but because culture and communication have become a critical area of concern in 1989. The French Revolution provides us with an opportunity to explore this area when it first emerged as a vital ingredient of public life.

The book is divided into three parts. Part One describes the publishing industry under the Old Regime. It shows how printing was embedded in a complex set of social, economic, and political institutions so stifling in their effect that a vast underground industry developed, undermining the ideological foundation of the regime. Part Two examines the effect of the Revolution on the way publishers, printers, and booksellers conducted their business. It takes up such previously uninvestigated questions as the economic consequences of the destruction of the printers' and booksellers' guild, the organization of work and the agitation of workers in the new printing shops, and the lobbying for jobs and political influence after the dismantling of the old apparatus for administering the book trade. The profusion of new authorities with new demands on the printing press makes it extremely difficult to sort out the politics of printing, so we have limited our account to Paris and one example of revolution and counter-revolution in the provinces. Part Three deals with the products of the press. Instead of concentrating on the most familiar objects—books and journals—it discusses a broad range of printed material, from the most refined treatises to the rawest pamphlets. It shows how printing intersected with other media, such as songs and pictures, and how the ephemera turned out by the press—almanacs, stationery, playing cards, board games, paper money—carried revolutionary messages into the sphere of everyday life.

In order to cover so much ground, we have had to work as a team; and to make the book cohere thematically, we have had to coordinate our contributions, neglecting some subjects and emphasizing others. We would have liked to include more on reading, both as a form of revolutionary sociability and as a mode of making sense of the Revolution. We had planned to examine libraries, public and private. We wanted to discuss writers and writing, reviewers and advertising, typography, book design, paper making, pamphlet peddling, subscription collecting, and a dozen other subjects. But we ran out of time and space. A great deal remains to be done, for we have only begun to explore the history of the printed word, and we can only hope, in consigning our own work to print, that we have captured that history at one of its most dramatic moments.

PART ONE
PREREVOLUTIONARY CONDITIONS

CENSORSHIP AND THE
PUBLISHING INDUSTRY

DANIEL ROCHE

IT IS TRUE that in our own time there are governments that restrict free expression. It is true that from time to time we hear of episodes that perplex us and that cast a stark light on the limitations of free speech, even in democratic countries. Even so, it is not easy to believe that, from the sixteenth century until the Revolution, censorship of speech and writing was official policy in France; the existence of a "thought police" was the normal state of affairs. There was no freedom of the press under the Old Regime, because from the earliest days of its power the Crown established surveillance of printers and booksellers and a mechanism for controlling the dissemination of ideas.[1] Different instruments were employed to this end, and the policy was justified by a variety of arguments in which the economic and the ideological were always nicely balanced: The rights of the privileged publishers of Paris and the inviolable values of an inegalitarian society had to be defended. The royal power also intervened at both ends of the chain that links creative writers to their public: readers and other authors. Before publication came a skillful exercise in censorship, applied through a policy of selective privilege that involved the prepublication inspection of manuscripts for content and the rewarding of publishers who, in return for their cooperation with the established order, enjoyed the advantages of a monopoly. After publication, control was further applied by the police.

The existence of these two parallel mechanisms—one of preventive censorship, the other to prohibit forbidden and clandestine transactions in printed matter or infractions of the rules governing booksellers—clearly indicates the keen awareness of the absolutist state and its rulers of the importance of the printed word. They, too, saw it as the principal vehicle of knowledge and thought, the medium of all political and religious discus-

3

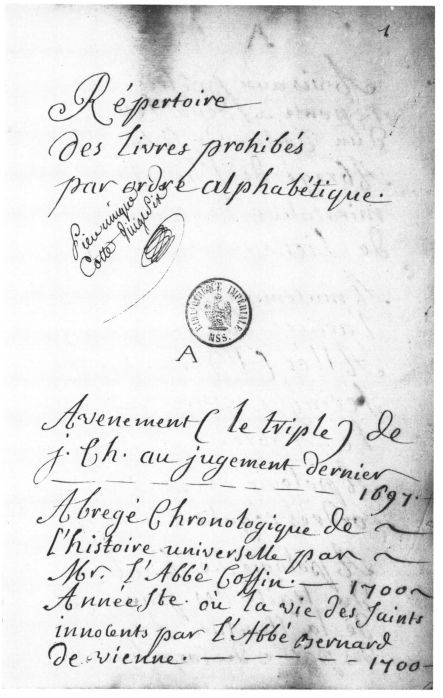

Archives de la Chambre syndicale de la librairie et de l'imprimerie de Paris. "Catalogue of Prohibited Books in Alphabetical Order." N.d. Bibliothèque Nationale, Cabinet des Manuscrits.

The book guild of Paris kept lists of prohibited books like this one in order to ensure that none of their members printed or sold them (cat. no. 119).

sion, the instrument for the expression of subversive criticism as well as intellectual obedience and acquiescence. Censorship existed to modify (or forbid) written material before it was published. The officers of the book police and the representatives of the publishing industry had the job of tracking down dangerous, prohibited, or clandestine works, and to this end they oversaw printers, booksellers, workers, and peddlers. The system did not always work perfectly: From Richelieu to Colbert in the seventeenth century and from Pontchartrain to Maupeou in the eighteenth, the royal government was not fully in control of the situation. It was never able wholly to prevent the circulation of forbidden or condemned books, antimonarchist booklets, the innumerable pamphlets that floated around Paris and the provinces, writings, songs, satires—in fact, a whole body of printed criticism and controversy. But the political situation and the widening dissemination of "philosophical" works (a term eventually applied to all dangerous writing, all "bad books") distinguish the last decades of publishing under the Old Regime, and confer on them a character of their own. Never before had it been so clear what was at stake; never before had the internal contradictions of the censorship system, in its dealings with the publishing industry, become so evident. While booksellers pushed increasingly to expand their businesses, the inspectors of the book trade increased their efforts to keep it within the bounds of legality. The widening influence of the ideas of the Enlightenment in government circles made life easier for the bold and harder for the censors. Tugged as they were from repression to tolerance and back again, the censors and the book police never succeeded in keeping publishing and bookselling in chains.[2]

Censorship and Publishing

Although we have not yet arrived at a full understanding of censorship under the Old Regime, recent scholarship has succeeded in tracing the main tendencies in the practices and policies of the book police. The period 1660–1680 stands out as a turning point.[3] Under some key officials—Jean-Baptiste Colbert and Nicolas de La Reynie; Louis Phélypeaux, comte de Pontchartrain, and the abbé Jean-Paul Bignon—the increasingly close supervision of printed matter was accompanied by an increasingly active prosecution of illicit, counterfeit, or controversial publications, periodicals from abroad, pictures considered immoral—in short, of all "bad" printed matter.[4] In these years the foundations were laid for a carefully run, centralized censorship and an efficient, hard-nosed police—a tradition that lasted more or less until 1789.[5]

THE CENTRALIZATION OF CENSORSHIP

The author or printer/publisher could reach the public either by the official route of controlled printing and distribution, or by the illegal, clandestine route over which censorship had no power, except *a posteriori*—although if books and leaflets fell into the hands of the censors or the book police, they would be caught up in the machinery of repression. Prepublication censorship could be applied only along the official route, and the royal censors were, by the end of the seventeenth century, firmly in control of the situation, because the Crown had established its authority over anyone who claimed any right of press censorship: the church, the universities, and the parlements (higher law courts). Universities, especially the Sorbonne, lost their accustomed monopoly of censorship after the seventeenth century.[6] The church, and especially the bishops, who expressed themselves vigorously at General Assemblies of the Clergy, retained the right to approve only works of piety and theology, and to condemn published works deemed unacceptable, whether printed with or, more often, without official authority. In any case, as the eighteenth century opened, censorship had been declericalized and had become an instrument of the absolute state.

The state tolerated the intervention of its officers of justice for a long time, provided that their intervention was exercised in a royalist fashion. As the power of the parlements was increasingly contained, however, they were restricted to supervision, condemnation, and repression. Under the Regency, the parlements, expecially the Parlement of Paris, failed to recapture an autonomous censorship role. The courts and the church in the eighteenth century no longer intervened, except where an example had to be set or a spectacular condemnation handed down. The case of Father Hardouin's *Histoire des Conciles* in 1715; the denunciation of Claude-Adrien Helvétius's *De l'Esprit,* which provoked a flood of subversive works in 1759; and the appeal for the suppression of the *Encyclopédie* each presented an opportunity for the parlements to proclaim, and thus assert, their right to approve or condemn a work before it was published. The Sorbonne and the French clergy (which still hoped to recapture some of its old authority in the field) sought mainly to pressure the secular power, which paid little heed, except for granting a handful of condemnations. Publishing had fallen, once and for all, under the authority of the state.

Censorship and the Politics of the Book

The effectiveness of the state's system of control was established by 1699, when the abbé Bignon became director of the book trade. Under the supervision of the chancellor or the keeper of the seals, the Office of the Book Trade (known as the Direction of the Book Trade after 1750) entrusted to its censors the examination of all works destined for legal publication; to be legal, all books had to be registered. After examination, they received either "privileges" (the exclusive rights of publication and sale) or "tacit permissions" (authorization given to works the state could not sanction openly yet did not want to condemn). If works were refused, the reasons had to be stated. Some books and leaflets, which in or outside Paris could be printed with the approval of police chiefs or even provincial governors, escaped this filtration process.[7] The strengthening of controls made it possible to contain the sharply increased flow of printed matter, which grew from five hundred titles a year in 1700 to more than a thousand in 1771—a level that, in turn, was greatly exceeded in the period from 1789 to 1790. It is important to recognize, however, that increased intervention was not only an attempt at closer ideological control (as is too often asserted of all official activity in connection with books) but was also the sign of an important stage in the evolution of the monarchical state.

The transformation of the state from a system concerned primarily with law to one occupied above all with finance entailed the supersession of the chancellor and the officers of justice by the controller-general of finance and his commissioners.[8] The censorship established under an earlier philosophy of government was now to function in the shadow of mercantilism and a strictly directed economy. The state now intervened to suppress foreign publications not only in order to prevent subversion but also to protect the monopoly of Paris's publishers. But the book-trade administrators never meant to stifle production and were constantly torn between their ideological and economic responsibilities. Guillaume Lamoignon de Malesherbes, after 1750, simply strengthened and implemented what had already evolved under his predecessors: a nicely balanced, qualified, and pragmatic system of freedom—adapted first and foremost to the needs of commerce, and then to the religious and philosophical controversies of the day. Thus, after Louis de Chauvelin, J.-B. Paulin, abbé d'Aguesseau, J.-P. Bignon, J.-F. Maboul, and C. G. de Boze, who had overseen the production of printed matter under Louis XIV and Louis XV,[9] censors began to define the limits of acceptable illegality and to classify books submitted for their approval according to the official categories that determined what channels of distribution books could enter. They also decided which books were to be approved at once or after a given delay, and whether they would receive a privilege, a tacit permission, or some other kind of authorization. In this manner the state encouraged the production of books and also rescued and legitimated part of the flow of printed matter that otherwise would have slipped into clandestine channels.

750. *narration d'omaï*   Milcent   —

751. *Du Domaine et de l'utilité*   l'auteur   Coqueley   P. du 3 Juillet
     de son aliénation a perpétuité   de   1789.
     par ch. de Sergy Censeur royal   Champigny

752. *Mémorial historique des*   Poinçot Lib. Le V.te de P. du 26 juin 1789
     états généraux pendant le   Fontarin   d
     mois de mai 1789; reçu un
     depuis du 3.e Ordre

753. *Le nouvel égoïste, comédie*   Moyer Lib.   Dudin   P. du 3 Juillet
     en deux actes   1789

754. *Dela Dignité du commerce*   V.e Tillard de fainville —
     et de l'état du commerçant   et fils Lib.
     par M. anquetil Duperron

755. *exortation à tous bons françois*   l'auteur   Dombcieu   Rayé du
     relativement aux états généraux   3 Juillet 1789
     adressée particulièrement aux
     habitans de la paroisse d'aroma
     en bresse, par M. Olivier des
     fourines

756. *Esprit de mably et de soudillan*   artaud
     par M. Beranger Censeur
     royal

757. *Le Couteau* —   Laporte   Perrin de
                                        imp. Lib.   Cayla

Archives de la Chambre syndicale de la librairie et de l'imprimerie de Paris. "Register of Privileges and Simple Permissions for the Book Trade." 1788–89. Bibliothèque Nationale, Cabinet des Manuscrits.

This register allowed the Paris Book Guild to keep track of the legal status of a book. From left to right the register lists the title of the work, the person permitted to publish it, the censor who reviewed it, and the decision of the royal administration. No. 755, for example, is a work on the Estates General that the royal officials suspended from circulation on 3 July 1789 (cat. no. 118).

In enunciating these principles for all the world to hear, C.-M. Lamoignon de Malesherbes, director of the book trade from 1750 to 1763, became the symbol of the monarchy's ambiguous policies. A man of the law owing allegiance to the chancellor, he became the instrument of centralized executive action; a man of merit and talent, he devoted himself to the embarrassing defense of privilege and regulation; a liberal and enlightened friend of the philosophes, he represented a technocratic, or at least utilitarian, authority. Under Malesherbes, censorship defined the forbidden zones of literature as God, king, and morality. Beyond that, judgment was left to the public; the autonomy of the intelligent reader as well as the responsibility of the author were both recognized. Finally, suppression was carried out by negotiation and by tacit agreement between writers/publishers on the one hand, and royal officials on the other. The royal power left itself room to adapt policy to circumstances and to extricate itself in the event of accident or error—which accounts for some serious incidents, such as the scandals surrounding *De l'Esprit* and the *Encyclopédie*.

Malesherbes defined his liberal philosophy in a way that set the tone of cultural policy at the height of the Enlightenment.[10] He favored limiting arbitrary power in enforcing the boundaries of religious and political orthodoxy, and beyond those boundaries he tried to make prohibitions effective by reducing them to a minimum. In his view, censorship could succeed only if it were tolerated and accepted, within reason, by all parties (the works of Voltaire, Rousseau, Diderot, and others confirmed that point because they generally aimed at a gray area between the lawful and the unlawful). Malesherbes also favored a policy of rewards, which would win the loyalty of printers and authors and would promote work that exalted the glory of the monarch. After 1750 this strategy became more difficult because the boundaries of the forbidden were no longer clearly defined and because the bastions of the monarchy—the academies as well as the censors—were besieged by the partisans of new ideas.

Censors and Society

Before 1660 there were probably fewer than ten censors. At the time of the abbé Bignon, there were sixty or so (thirty-six of them working on religious matters), and more than 130 worked under Malesherbes. On the eve of the Revolution more than 160 censors were employed by the state. True, the trend is partly explained by the increase in printed matter, but it principally reflects the success of the policies developed at the beginning of the eighteenth century. Authors, recognizing the state's tactic of qualified tolerance, acquired the habit of visiting the censors and accommodating

ALMANACH ROYAL,

ANNÉE

M. DCC. LXX.

PRÉSENTÉ

A SA MAJESTÉ

Pour la première fois en 1699.

A PARIS,

Chez LE BRETON, Premier Imprimeur ordinaire du ROI, rue de la Harpe.

AVEC APPROBATION ET PRIVILEGE DU ROI.

4io
CENSEURS ROYAUX:

Bailleron, *à Beziers.*   Caqué, *à Reims.*
Hugon, *à Arles.*   Le Blanc, *à Orleans.*
Charmetton, *à Lyon.*   Butter, *à Etampes.*
Willius, *à Mulhausen en Alsace.*   Sarrau, *à Montpellier.*
Flurant, *à Lyon.*   Brouillard, *à Marseille.*
Hoin, *à Dijon.*   Pouteau, *à Lyon.*

CENSEURS ROYAUX.

Theologie, MESSIEURS,

DE Lorme, en Sorbonne.
Le Seigneur, au Collége de Lizieux.
Coterel, Curé de S. Laurent.
Foucher, Principal du Collége de Navarre.
Le Mercier, en Sorbonne.
Buret, dans la maison des Docteurs de Navarre.
Dupont, rue du Cimetiere St André.
Riballier, au Collége Mazarin.
Genet, au Collége Mazarin.
Chevreuil, en Sorbonne.
Du Sauzet, Grand-Maitre de Navarre.
De Loriere, en Sorbonne.
Adhenet, Bibliothécaire de Sorbonne.
Bouillerot, Curé de S. Gervais.
Aubry, Curé de S. Louis en l'île.

Jurisprudence, MESSIEURS,

Saurin, rue neuve des prs Ch. vis-à-vis la rue de Louis le Grand.
Gallyot, rue Hautefeuille.
Courchetet, rue des Rosiers.
Maignan de Savigny, cul-de-sac de la rue Férou.
Terasson, rue du Battoir.
Coqueley de Chaussepierre, rue des deux Portes S Severin.
Moreau, rue Vivienne.
Marchand, rue Bourglabbé.
Mouflier, rue des Fossés S. Germain, cul-de-sac Sourdis.
Roussélet, Cloitre Notre-Dame, près le Puits.
Regnard, rue Hautefeuille.
Cadet de Saineville, rue des vieilles Audriettes.
De la Laure, cloître S. Benoît.
Bouchaud, rue des Lavandieres, Place Maubert.
De Lignac, rue Caffette, Faubourg S. Germain.
L'Abbé Piole, à Vienne en Dauphiné.
Du Châtel, à Reims.

Histoire Naturelle, Médecine, & Chymie, MESSIEURS,

Cazamajor, rue S. Thomas du Louvre,

"Royal Almanac, the Year 1769. Presented to His Majesty for the First Time in 1699." [1769]. The New York Public Library, Rare Books and Manuscripts Division.

Each year the Crown issued a directory of all its administrators and officers, including the royal censors. Shown here are those assigned to particular cities and those specializing in theology, jurisprudence, natural history, medicine, and chemistry (cat. no. 115).

themselves to their requirements[11]—the more eminent conducted such negotiations at or near the top, as did Voltaire with Germain Louis de Chauvelin, the keeper of the seals, and René Hérault, the lieutenant-general of police; Boisguilbert with Michel de Chamillart, the controller-general of finance; Diderot with Malesherbes; and even Rousseau when it came to the publication of *Emile*. The officials in the Office of the Book Trade intervened constantly in the ordinary business of the republic of letters; and if criticism intensified after the departure of Malesherbes, it was because authors had become less inclined to censor themselves and more bold in straying from the path of legality.

The increased number of censors was accompanied by a tendency toward specialization, although it never became completely inflexible: Theologians inspected works of philosophy, and men of letters evaluated works on aesthetics or morality. There was never an explicit division of subjects; rather, a series of choices progressively defined those on whom the authorities could rely, of whom, in turn, a small core assumed constant duties more regularly than their colleagues. Being a censor was not a full-time occupation, carrying its guaranteed pension after twenty years of service. It was a function generally disparaged among men of letters, and was, moreover, one that could involve embarrassment through the assumption of some degree of personal responsibility. Helvétius's *De l'Esprit* was read by Jean-Pierre Tercier, first assistant in the Department of Foreign Affairs. Only a theologian could have appreciated the free-thinking implications of the manuscript, and Tercier signed an authorization to publish without too close an examination. The scandal of this irreligious text appearing under a royal privilege produced an uproar, and despite patronage at the highest levels, Tercier lost his position.[12]

Between the end of the seventeenth century and the Revolution, however, censorship began to offer something more like a career, but one not devoid of risk. Louis-Pierre Manuel in *La Police de Paris dévoilée*[13] and Marie-Joseph Chénier in his *Dénonciation des inquisiteurs de la pensée* were to impress the less creditable aspects of censorship on public opinion—and on their literary colleagues who had succumbed to the blandishments of power and place.

> Can my readers contemplate, without peals of mirth, a Voltaire, a Jean-Jacques Rousseau, a Buffon, a Destouches, a Piron, a Gresset, indeed all men of letters in all fields, forbidden to proffer their ideas to the public without seeking the permission of Armenonville, Chauvelin, Hérault, Berryer, Lenoir, De Crosne, Desentelles, Villequier, Marin, Suard, *et hoc genus omne*? My imagination cannot couple those

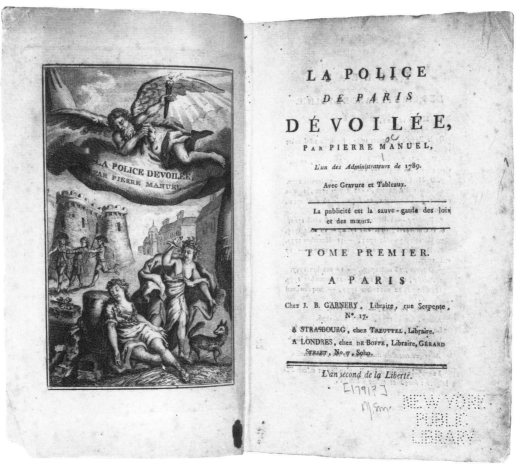

Pierre Manuel. "The Police of Paris Unmasked." [1791?]. The New York Public Library, General Research Division.

Pierre Manuel's "Police of Paris Unmasked" was one of the most famous revolutionary exposés of the corruption of the police of the book trade under the Old Regime (cat. no. 153).

who hold the rod and those who suffer it, without thinking of a flock of eagles submitted to the governance of turkeys.[14]

Thus Chénier, from the viewpoint of a new age, imposes on us a revised image of a past that we must examine more carefully.

Censorship and Compromise

Censors were recruited from among the ranks of the privileged and talented alike—a fact that underlines the inherent contradiction in the censorship system and that also facilitated the establishment of bonds between the Enlightenment and the absolutist monarchy. The world of censorship was peopled by clergy without parishes, mostly academics and intellectuals connected with the university and thus subject to ecclesiastical discipline. At the turn of the century, they generally held official posts, serving as professors at the Collège Royal, librarians, or secretaries of government departments. They included some noblemen, almost all holding administrative positions in the judiciary or the military. But most of the censors were men of some education and talent: doctors like Lassonne, lawyers like Terrasson, officials like Tercier. Censors, as a group, resembled members of learned societies: they were united by common intellectual pursuits and by common links to the established powers. Forty percent were members of an academy, and about the same proportion had edited a periodical (in 1757, of ten editors of the *Journal des savants,* nine were censors). They were to be found in all the agencies the royal government used to influence public opinion; at the same time, however, they demonstrated how the heirs of the Enlightenment used the structure erected by Colbert and Bignon to their own advantage. By taking over cultural and administrative positions in the royal service, they could exert leverage even over the machinery of surveillance. Like the members of the academies, censors affirmed an ideology of compromise, half-philosophical and half-absolutist, tolerating new ideas and favoring a reasonable degree of intellectual daring.

The offices of the censorship facilitated the meeting of men of power and men of intellect on the common ground of an ideal of utility and progress. In their daily decisions to forbid or permit publication, their activities expressed the ambiguity of their position and their often-divided loyalties: on the one hand, an overt respect for church, king, and morality, as well as a defense of conformism; on the other, some speculative daring—mostly dissimulated but sometimes openly expressed, as in the example of Fontenelle. This ambiguity was imposed by the very nature of their work, which brought them into close contact both with the director of the book

13

trade and with authors, booksellers, printers, and publishers. They had mastered a technique of screening and filtering—one that was rigorous in principle (examination of written works and inspection of the finished product) but flexible in application, allowing for dialogue between writer and censor, concessions by both parties, and gradations of permission to publish.[15] Censorship worked well thanks to competent officials, but only within the limits set by the administration from the days of the abbé Bignon and Malesherbes.

Prohibitions and Conventions

As the flow of printed matter increased, the task of inspecting it became enormous.[16] From year to year, and from subject to subject, proscriptions fluctuated, ranging from 10 to 30 percent of the works examined. The important thing was not so much the number of new manuscripts rejected as the reasons for the rejections. To censor is, first and foremost, to establish criteria for the acceptable, and the reasoning that underlay the Old Regime's criteria was not always clearly stated. Each censor could discuss the criteria with each author, and the decisions were not cloaked in anonymity. If a problem arose, it might engender delays, which could choke the system and require the intervention of the director of the book trade. Prohibition was designed to block anything that could impugn received religion, established power, or accepted morality. But these principles increasingly came into conflict with the evolution of society and with other principles, both economic (French publishing must be encouraged) and ideological (the state must forbid as little as possible) promulgated by the government whose task was to preserve the old order.

The reports of the censors reveal assumptions that are diametrically opposed to those of free thought. A graduated scale of disapproval can be traced from "agreement with no problem" through "I don't want to know about it" to the fairly rare categorical rejection. The selection process also shows the traces of personal relationships among members of a closely knit society conditioned by interests and influence.[17] Beyond the fundamental taboos, the vague and flexible criterion of "public interest" allowed easy passage to uncontroversial innovations. The censor Piquet, for example, made twenty-three alterations in the text of the *Nouvelle Héloïse*—twenty-one of them involved no more than slight modifications of language so that an idea would be purified of potentially disturbing overtones; the other two required outright suppression of passages that openly questioned the authority of the church and the king. The censor was working from the original, unauthorized Amsterdam edition, and it fell to the bookseller-printer

Censors took their work seriously, and no subject was beneath their scrutiny. These two censors' reports are from the eve of the Revolution (1788). The one on the left is quite critical of a new edition of the works of the philosophe d'Alembert. It received only a "tacit permission," indicated by the "P.T." in the right-hand corner. The other is a review of a pamphlet describing the virtues of Benjamin Franklin's new stove design (cat. no. 117).

Guérin to incorporate his changes, with or without the author's consent, for the French edition. Here we can discern the dubious effectiveness of censorship: The main current of innovation in literature often flowed outside the law in the form of illicit publications. The legal branch of publishing adjusted to this anomaly as best it could, while the book police faced the task of suppressing pirated and clandestine works.

The Book Police

From the end of the seventeenth century onward, publishers and booksellers had to reckon with an efficient and alert "book police,"[18] whose apparatus of rules, orders, observation techniques, and inspection methods persisted right up to the Revolution, owing to the activity of its few but zealous officers. Between the police and the reading public (ever more eager for dangerous innovations) emerged a group of cultural intermediaries who operated in a no-man's-land between the legal and clandestine publishing industries. The group included booksellers and printers in search of a quick profit, as well as distributors, peddlers, small tradesmen, and writers both salaried and free-lance. All of them were under surveillance.

THE PRINCIPLES OF COMMISSIONER DELAMARE

The system of state intervention, so typical of all branches of government under Louis XIV, can be found in the book trade also. In the second half of the seventeenth century, when the foundations of the modern, absolutist state were being laid, the control of men and ideas called for more subtle modes of intervention and more flexible procedures. It was Lieutenant-General Nicolas de La Reynie and Commissioner Nicolas Delamare, the senior officers of the Paris police, who devised and imposed the system that, after 1699, was applied to the rest of the kingdom as well. Repressive action, coordinated by the lieutenant-general of police in Paris, was placed under the authority of the chancellor and the director of the book trade. It was their function to apply it more or less restrictively, and to implement the decisions of the King's Council for the ordering of local distribution of printed matter.

Under Bignon and Malesherbes, the office of the director of the book trade had assumed responsibility for a wide range of business, from routine administrative supervision to decisions charged with the utmost literary significance.[19] The consistent tendency of the royal power was to unite inspection and enforcement; thus, the responsibilities of the director of the book trade and those of the book police were entrusted to the same hands, as with Antoine de Sartine, Jean-Charles-Pierre Lenoir, and Joseph-François Albert from 1763 to 1776. When they were separated, as under Malesherbes (director, 1750–63), Le Camus de Néville (1776–84), Laurent de Villedeuil (1784–85), Jean-Jacques Vidaud de la Tour (1785–88), and Poitevin de Maissemy (1788–89), prevention and repression did not always march in step. For one thing, one always had to reckon with the provincial intendants; in police matters their authority was absolute, and they often intervened in book-trade matters. How extensively they did so seems to have varied greatly, from what little we know about it. In Normandy the intendant virtually took over responsibility for the book trade, organized the industry and saw to surveillance. By about 1730, however, he was compelled to share his powers with the first president of the Parlement of Rouen, whose authority seems to have been imperfectly defined. Because of such ambiguities, the position of inspector of the book trade was established in Rouen at the middle of the seventeenth century, as in Paris, and had the effect of both supporting and circumscribing the actions of the local authorities.[20] At Montpellier, the intendant, Bernage, obtained a general authorization to be apprised of all important matters related to the sale and circulation of prohibited writings, although he left routine cases to the lieutenant-general of police "as happens every day in Paris."[21] Centralization carried the day, in government administration as in industry.

Throughout the country self-regulatory bodies were established within the industry, after the Parisian model. They took the form of *chambres syndicales* of the local booksellers' and printers' guilds, as well as representatives of the royal authority in the persons of the local inspectors of the book trade. Parisian authorities still intervened in the book trade of the provinces and even of foreign countries. Because the effectiveness of the machinery depended in great part on the zeal of the provincial officers, the lieutenant-general of police in Paris often sent emissaries to inquire about, search the records of, or arrest or dismiss those who were delinquent in their duties. The punitive expeditions of the Parisian inspector Joseph d'Hémery consigned to the Bastille a score of such provincial offenders apprehended at Rouen, Caen, Troyes, Noyon, Auxerre, and Orléans.[22] The Paris police often coordinated their measures with the provincial intendants: The marquis d'Argenson and Pontchartrain, for instance, persuaded the Orléans intendant to search the premises of Jean Bordes, a local bookseller, and to arrest him for extradition to Paris in 1710. In 1732 C. H. Feydeau de Marville asked Pontcarré, intendant of Rouen, for his assistance in keeping watch on shipments from Paris and Normandy of *Dom Bxxxx, portier des Chartreux,* one of the best-sellers in the forbidden

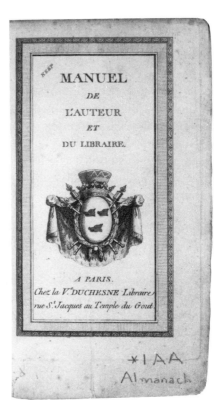

"Authors' and Booksellers' Manual." [1777]. The New York Public Library, General Research Division.

Manuals like this one provided authors, publishers, printers, and bookdealers with a ready reference to all the regulations of the book trade and the registered printers, booksellers, guilds, royal administrators, and censors. The pages below include a list of provincial cities with booksellers' guilds (p. 34) and the beginning of an alphabetical list of the printers and booksellers of Paris, with their specializations noted (p. 35) (cat. no. 77).

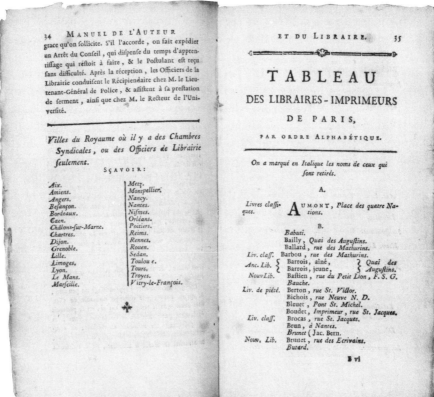

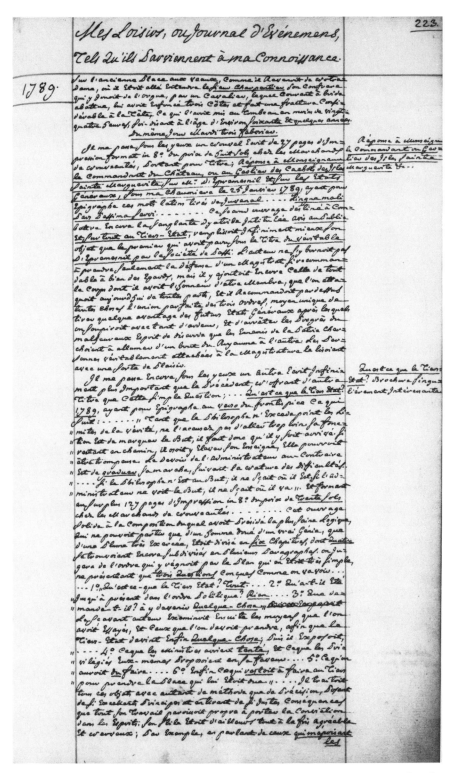

Siméon-Prosper Hardy. "My Leisures." 3 February 1789. Bibliothèque Nationale, Cabinet des Manuscrits.

On this page of his personal journal, the Paris bookdealer Hardy takes note on 3 February 1789 of the appearance of Sieyès's famous pamphlet, "What Is the Third Estate?" The journal shows how even the official guild bookdealers kept abreast of the illicit book trade (cat. no. 56).

literature.[23] Thus, centralized inspection and local action usually went hand in hand.

The office of inspector of the book trade developed at the beginning of the eighteenth century as a special branch of the Paris police when Commissioner Delamare was appointed to work with the Parisian *Chambre syndicale* on confiscations of illegal books; "inspection" grew from there. D'Hémery, appointed in 1748 and inspector for nearly forty years, gave the job its definitive shape. As the right-hand man first of Malesherbes and then of Sartine, d'Hémery was well-acquainted with the printers, booksellers, and authors of the capital. From 1750 to 1769 he kept a diary that shows he was remarkably well-informed about clandestine publications.[24] Similar positions were created in the 1730s in Orléans and Rouen, and in 1767 Sartine created or revived them in Lyons, Rheims, Nancy, Orléans, Bordeaux, Montpellier, Toulouse, Nîmes, and Sedan.[25] In 1776 Marseilles was furnished with an inspector, who was very ill received by the Provençal printers. Louis-François-Claude Marin, also a censor, and editor of the *Gazette de France* as well, discharged the office with considerable harshness from 1785 to 1789;[26] his conflict with Beaumarchais made Marin both notorious and detested. With their local jobs keeping them in close touch with regional booksellers, the inspectors were often effective agents and dedicated supervisors of the publishing industry as well as of the book trade.

INSPECTION PROCEDURES

The inspectors worked directly with the officers of the *chambres syndicales*, who were responsible for inspecting crates and packages of books arriving in their towns. Their principal duties were to detect fraud and to enforce the rules governing printing and bookselling, rules that had been developed in a series of general ordinances in 1686, 1723, and 1777. Their zeal in confiscating pirated and prohibited books was more apparent than real: They were solicitous of the goodwill of their colleagues "who, eventually succeeding them in positions of authority, would be in a position to retaliate."[27] But, in any case, there existed institutions and procedures to control the publishing industry and to prevent the printing and sale of any book that did not have an official privilege or permission. In practice, these local-police activities took three principal forms.[28]

First, the police oversaw the production and distribution of virtually all printed matter. Working with the local booksellers' and printers' guilds, they kept track of typographical equipment such as presses and type fonts and tried to prevent the setting up of clandestine printing shops. Second, they examined and inspected work in the licensed printing establishments.

From the time of de La Reynie, the number of booksellers, printers, and peddlers had been fixed and a particular district set aside for the production and sale of books. In Paris it was the university quarter, the precincts of the Palais de Justice, the approaches to the quais of the Seine, and the Pont Neuf. Careful preparation was given to the election of officers of the guild, the bold and unruly being excluded.

Thus, throughout the eighteenth century people in the book trade enjoyed little freedom outside the system of privileges and permissions of which they were at once the operators, the beneficiaries (particularly in Paris), and the victims.[29] Infractions usually drew heavy penalties: For example, a fine of 500 livres (for the first offense) for lending one's name as owner of a printing shop or bookstore, for violation of the rules limiting the time when the printing shops could be open, or for selling pirated or forbidden books. Repeated offenses could result in the loss of master's status, the stocks, whipping, banishment, prison, or the galleys.

Third and finally, the lieutenant-general of police, the intendants, and the inspectors did their best to control the entry of books into the kingdom and its principal cities. Even before 1660 the syndics of the printers' and booksellers' guild had been given right of inspection of bundles, chests, and packages of books; the ordinance of 1723 restricted points of entry to Paris, Rouen, Nantes, Bordeaux, Marseilles, Lyons, Strasbourg, Metz, Amiens, and Lille. Shipment to any other point was forbidden on pain of confiscation and prosecution. Any private person to whom books were shipped had to undergo the formality of a visit to the offices of the local government. Bales and packages could be opened only in designated locations, and the police kept track of shippers, by land or water, who had to have special certificates (*acquits-à-caution*) inspected and stamped with the shipments. In Paris, anything arriving at the city gates was taken to the customs by a *commis des aides*, inspected, resealed, and taken to the office of the guild's syndics. If it was determined that an infraction had occurred, the books were confiscated. Commissioners of police and directors of the book trade had worked together since the system was first established; they foresaw and provided everything it needed to function smoothly. During d'Hémery's time, the role of the inspectors widened, until in the eyes of the public they came to represent a fundamental constraint of liberty: the control of the press. But, harsh and precise though they were, the rules could be evaded and the inspectors hoodwinked. That the system was fallible under Louis XIV and Louis XV is demonstrated by the subterfuges employed by various offenders in order to print, distribute, or import "bad books."

Illegal imports into the kingdom, clandestine impressions in Paris or the provinces, pirated editions successfully printed and launched, a well-organized domestic traffic in printed contraband—all this was enough to satisfy, and indeed enrich, those who traded in books on the wrong side of the law. Diderot said as much in his *Lettre sur le commerce de la librairie:*

> The more stringent the proscription, the more it raised the price of the proscribed work, the more it stimulated people to read it, the more it was bought, the more it was read. How often might the publisher and the author of an authorized book have said to the magistrates—had they only dared—"Gentlemen, of your kindness, vouchsafe us a little ordinance so that our work may be torn up and burnt at the foot of your great staircase!" When the crier went around announcing that a book had been proscribed, the printers said, "Good, another edition!" [30]

Following the era when police officers were hunting down the clandestine printing shops set up in Paris by Madame Fouquet, wife of the imprisoned superintendent of finance under Louis XIV, the authorities assumed more pragmatic surveillance practices. The state sometimes shut its eyes to the distribution of controversial works that circulated at first clandestinely and then in the open, because the book police avoided interfering with commerce. In 1731 Chauvelin, in his instructions to the inspector of publishing at Orléans, wrote: "Nothing is more deleterious to the trade in books than an excess of severity." [31]

The policing system was intended to defend the same orthodoxy as was preventive censorship: church, king and morality. Its significance lay less in the effectiveness of its repressive measures than in the affirmation of its willingness to enforce the public unity of faith, law, thought, and action. After being proclaimed under the absolutist monarchy of the seventeenth century, this mission was reiterated with ever-increasing laxity and ambiguity during the relatively tolerant age of the Enlightenment.

The Publishing Industry and Surveillance

Nevertheless, the repressive practices should always be examined with attention inasmuch as they are a part of the ordinary conduct of the Old Regime toward the publishing industry. The police files allow us to do this, even though they show only the successful incidents of repression and thus obscure the doings of the great foreign producers of "bad books" described by Robert Darnton, drawing on the rich archives of the Société typographique de Neuchâtel. [32] At the bottom of the pyramid of police action lay regular inspections of printing shops and bookstores, which were sometimes effective and resulted in the confiscation of pirated or forbidden works. The best results were obtained when the book-trade inspector was able to dismantle an entire network of offenders. Whether dealing with clandestine Jansenist presses or with the contraband writings of the philosophes, the police could achieve their aims only by sharp-eyed spying and an adroit use of the internal enmities of the trade.[33] Stool pigeons, blackmail, lightning raids all played their part in sending offenders to the Bastille.[34] But if informers and spies were an indispensable auxiliary of the police effort, there was another side to the coin. The solidarity and complicity cut right across the book trade and extended into the censorship itself. The most carefully prepared police raid could be foiled if it came up against a sufficiently weighty convergence of interests.[35]

Almost a thousand offenders went to the Bastille between 1659 and 1789 for offenses related to the book business, a figure that represents about 17 percent of all those imprisoned there. The rate of convictions was not constant: It was high around 1660, for instance, but slowed down as Delamare and La Reynie exerted a firmer control over the industry and were able to display a degree of tolerance.[36] It picked up again when Jansenism was proscribed, and attained its peak under Malesherbes between 1750 and 1759.[37] Thereafter, the activity of the book police, like that of the censor, diminished. These figures are interesting because they permit us to distinguish among the prisoners from the publishing industry: Printers and booksellers who had committed minor offenses or had undertaken low-risk pirating of authorized books made up the majority of arrests, and the activist minority had fallen into the hands of the police because they had accepted the dangers of or acquired a taste for (or simply needed the profits from) such high-risk activities as printing or trading in unorthodox religious, philosophical, political, or pornographic books (Table 1). The big fish slipped through the net, particularly toward the end of the Old Regime, either because they were well protected at high levels or because they were safely outside the country.[38]

Within the universe of prisoners, the gradations of professional standing, offenses, and penalties highlight the fundamental inequality in the incidence of repression. True, more than two-thirds of the offenders came from the book trade, but those who suffered most were journeymen, peddlers, and lowly distributors rather than the master printers.[39] The former, in general, spent more time in their cells than the latter, except for some hardened recidivists. Authors, more than three hundred of them and not the least distinguished, were sedulously kept under lock and key; Voltaire spent eleven months in the Bastille, and most of the authors appear in the

TABLE 1
Offenders Against the Book Laws in the Bastille, 1659–1789

Year	Number of Prisoners	Percentage*	Booksellers/ Printers	Journeymen	Distributors	Authors/ Pamphleteers	Total (excl. authors)	Total
1659	65	6	—	—	1	3	1	4
1660–69	419	19	21	7	14	40	42	82
1670–79	319	8	6	3	1	16	10	26
1680–89	584	5	5	2	2	22	9	31
1690–99	232	4	6	—	1	2	7	9
1700–09	459	4	1	—	5	12	6	18
1710–19	406	12	19	5	16	8	40	48
1720–29	645	16	39	16	32	20	87	107
1730–39	472	19	25	34	22	11	81	92
1740–49	513	19	19	12	50	19	81	100
1750–59	339	40	21	22	41	52	84	136
1760–69	354	35	19	9	51	47	79	126
1770–79	296	41	26	3	50	42	79	121
1780–89	176	23	11	3	11	16	25	41
TOTAL	5,279	17.8	218	116	297	310	631	941

SOURCE: The calculations are based on the data in Frantz Funck-Brentano, Les Lettres de cachet à Paris, étude suivie d'une liste des prisonniers de la Bastille, 1658–1789 (Paris, 1903).

* Offenders against the book laws as a percentage of all prisoners.

prison records as having stayed between six and twelve months. In short, the economics of the publishing industry determined the degree of repression, and the fear of scandal outweighed all other considerations.

Toward the end of the Old Regime, the government officials began to question the effectiveness of their own actions. When the decisions of the censors diverged too far from public opinion, they lost their effectiveness. Redefinition of what was appropriate for the public, for the times, and for authors had in less than a century altered the meaning of censorship. Censors themselves began to look like prisoners of the system and to forbid the publication of works that, as readers, they approved of. The principal thrust of the censorship in the seventeenth century was against any obstacle to the triumph of the monarchical ideal or to the Counter-Reformation, which was reaffirming the unity of Catholics. By 1700 the abbé Bignon's group of learned men and clerics was proffering a vision of the world, religion, and society that was already enlightened in some respects but which was hostile to all forms of popular culture and to the spirit of criticism— that is, to any form of learning that was unconventional and therefore dangerous.

By the end of the eighteenth century censorship was attempting at one and the same time to hold a line and to be flexible. The force of new ideas was subjected to the restraint of a tolerant judgment, which became less effective and less useful with the passage of time. Economic and ideological imperatives were taken into account: It became as important to sustain the activity of the printing trades as to prevent the circulation of "bad books." But control and commerce became increasingly uneasy bedfellows, particularly when the disciples of the Enlightenment gained a foothold in the royal government. By 1789 the censors had lost their bearings. The book police hung doggedly onto their role, for what it might have been worth. By exercising surveillance and moderate repression—as the gap between the sanctions provided by law and those actually applied grew ever wider—censors did what they could to keep the book trades in conformity with the established order and to check the growing appeal of "bad books" for the reading public. Whatever the effectiveness of the repressive measures, the men in charge of them did not believe in thoroughgoing repression. Malesherbes, who permitted the printing of some daring books and protected the *Encyclopédie,* illustrates this point. But it was he, even more than his predecessors, who threw the printing trades' little men and petty offenders into prison. Police activity under Louis XIV, Louis XV, and Louis XVI did not prevent the circulation of forbidden works or the distribution of pirated editions; indeed, for some of them it served as the best possible advertisement. As Tocqueville observed, complete freedom of the press would have been less dangerous.

The Revolution did not put an end to the book police or to censorship. Article II of the Declaration of the Rights of Man points in two directions. It provides a ringing proclamation of freedom: "Free communication of thought and opinion is one of man's most precious rights: therefore, every citizen may speak, write and print freely." And it leaves to lawmakers the task of defining infractions: "except that he must answer for the abuse of that freedom in such circumstances as the law may provide." This was to legitimate, at one and the same time, total tolerance and the possibility of judicial intolerance. In 1989 just as much is at stake, for we have learned how frail our liberties are.[40]

PHILOSOPHY
UNDER THE CLOAK

ROBERT DARNTON

WHEN THE PUBLIC hangman lacerated and burned forbidden books in the courtyard of the Palais de Justice in Paris, he paid tribute to the power of the printed word. But he often destroyed dummy copies, while the magistrates kept the originals—and they were less profligate with their autos-da-fé than is generally believed. Knowing that nothing promoted sales better than a good bonfire, they preferred to impound books and imprison booksellers with as little fuss as possible. According to one estimate, the authorities condemned only 4.5 books and pamphlets a year, on average, during the 1770s and 1780s, and publicly burned only nineteen of them.[1] While those works went up in flames, however, thousands of others circulated secretly through the channels of the underground book trade. They provided the basic diet of illegal literature for hungry readers throughout the kingdom. Yet no one knows what they were.

What was the size and shape of this body of literature, the ordinary variety sold "under the cloak" by peddlers everywhere? The regime itself had no idea. Despite some attempts at bibliographical police work, it kept no complete list of all the books that could be considered illegal, even though they had never been formally condemned.[2] The very notion of legality in literature remained fuzzy, because the authorities in charge of the book trade constantly fudged the line that separated the licit from the illicit. On the legal side, they issued *privilèges, permissions tacites, permissions simples, permissions de police, simples tolérances,* and casual authorizations that went without a name or appeared in registers with circumlocutions such as "permitted only for persons who are very well known."[3] On the illegal side, they confiscated pirated editions of legal books (*contrefaçons*), legal books that were imported by an individual who did not go through an official bookseller, books that were not offensive but that lacked any kind of permission

27

(often imports of books authorized in other countries), and books that caused offense in the three standard ways specified by royal edicts and censors' reports: by undermining the authority of the king, the church, or conventional morality.

One could not even determine the degree of iniquity among the "bad books" (as the police called them) in the last category—and such distinctions mattered, because some books, if confiscated, might be returned to the bookseller and some might be grounds for sending him to the Bastille. Between 1771 and 1789, officials of the booksellers' guild in Paris filled a series of registers with the titles of all the books confiscated in the Parisian customs. At first they classified them under three rubrics: "prohibited books" (to be sequestered or destroyed), "not permitted books" (to be returned in some cases to the sender), and "pirated books" (to be sold for the profit of the bookseller who owned the original privilege). But as the entries accumulated, the distinctions disintegrated into a confusion of overlapping, inconsistent terms; and in the end, the classification system collapsed into an undifferentiated mass of 3,544 entries with only one characteristic in common: all smelled somehow of illegality.[4]

When it came to fine distinctions, the officials could not trust their sense of smell. For who could keep up with the literature pouring off the presses? Who could tell the difference between a quasi-legal book and a moderately illegal one? Shipping agents were supposed to have this ability, because they could be fined for forwarding illegal literature. Yet Jean-François Pion, an agent in Pontarlier, confessed himself incapable of recognizing forbidden books. When he asked for guidance from a customs officer at the Swiss border, he received the following reply:

> I cannot tell M. Pion positively which books are prohibited. In general, everything that is opposed to religion, the state, and good morals cannot enter. There are specific proscriptions against some books, such as a pirated history of France, the *Encyclopédie*, and others. But the quality of books doesn't much concern the customs office. It is a matter for the booksellers' guilds.[5]

Booksellers, of course, were better informed. They ordered the shipments, and the syndics of their guilds inspected them, accompanied in principle by a royal *inspecteur de la librairie*. But most booksellers had only an approximate idea of what books were actually in circulation, especially those that traveled through the underground. Literary journals were censored and were not supposed to review such works, though they sometimes did so. One could not even judge a book by its title. Of course, title pages gave off many clues. Anything with the standard formula "with approbation and privilege from the king" printed at the bottom was likely to be legal, though it might be pirated. Anything with a flagrantly false address ("Philadelphia," "At the sign of liberty," "A thousand leagues from the Bastille") made no pretense of respect for the law. But there was plenty of room for confusion between those extremes. Booksellers often ordered from catalogues or even from rumors passed through the trade grapevine, and they often got the titles wrong. Some could hardly spell. When Poinçot of Versailles asked for twenty-five "nouvelles des couvertes des ruse," his Swiss supplier realized he wanted a travel book, *Nouvelles découvertes des russes*. The Swiss also correctly read his remark on "la bes Raynalle" as a reference to the abbé Raynal's *Histoire philosophique et politique des établissemens et du commerce des européens dans les deux Indes*.[6] But they badly bungled an order from Veuve Baritel of Lyons, which seemed to concern some innocent-sounding "Portraits des Chartreux" but, in fact, referred to the pornographic and anticlerical *Histoire de Dom B*****, Portier des Chartreux*.[7]

Such mistakes could have serious consequences. A bookseller caught with *Histoire de Dom B****** in his shop could be imprisoned or disbarred from the trade. A wagoner transporting it could be fined and forced to surrender everything on his cart. A peddler selling it could be branded with the letters GAL (for *galérien*) and shipped off in chains to row in the galleys. Such punishments actually occurred.[8] The Old Regime in its last years was not the jolly, tolerant, laissez-faire sort of world imagined by some historians, and the Bastille was no three-star hotel. Although it should not be confused with the torture house invented by prerevolutionary propagandists, the Bastille ruined the lives of many people engaged in literature— not authors so much as publishers and booksellers, the professionals who made literature happen even if they did not create it. Such persons had to distinguish between legal and illegal books every day in the course of their ordinary business. By studying the way these professionals coped with that difficulty in the eighteenth century, one can move toward a solution of it as a problem that has plagued historians two centuries later—that is, the problem of identifying the dangerous element in the literature actually circulating in France on the eve of the Revolution. One can hardly survey all the literature in a single essay, but one can try to trace its boundaries by showing how it was handled by the people who made a living from it: how they talked about it in the jargon of their trade; exchanged it among themselves; marketed, ordered, packaged, shipped, and sold it throughout a vast system for getting books to readers outside the limits of the law.

The problem of demarcating forbidden literature appears at first as a question of language. When the police interrogated one of their prisoners in the Bastille, a bookseller named Hubert Cazin who had been caught with all

29

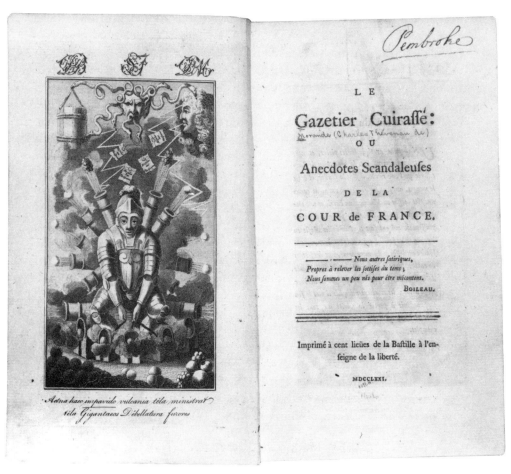

LE

Gazetier Cuiraſſé:

Morande (Charles Théveneau de)

O U

Anecdotes Scandaleuſes

DE LA

COUR de FRANCE.

—————————— *Nous autres ſatiriques,*
Propres à relever les ſottiſes du tems ;
Nous ſommes un peu nés pour être mécontens.
BOILEAU.

Imprimé à cent lieües de la Baſtille à l'en-
ſeigne de la liberté.

MDCCLXXI.

Charles Théveneau de Morande. "The Armor-plated Journalist." 1771. The New York Public Library, General Research Division.

"The Armor-plated Journalist" was an extremely illicit book describing the lewd life-style of the court. It flaunted its outlaw status by employing the fictitious printer's address, "A hundred leagues from the Bastille" (cat. no. 102).

kinds of forbidden books and compromising papers in his shop in Reims, they asked him to explain a puzzling term that cropped up often in his correspondence: "philosophical articles." Cazin defined it as a "conventional expression in the book trade to characterize everything that is forbidden." [9] The police had heard other terms: "clandestine books," "drugs," "miseries," and, as already mentioned, they had a favorite expression of their own: "bad books." Printers used another one in their craft slang: "chestnut" (a forbidden book); "to chestnut" (to work on a clandestine job). [10] But publishers and booksellers preferred a more elevated term, "philosophical books." It served as a signal in their commercial code to designate books that could get them in trouble, books that had to be handled with care.

The terminology of the trade can be studied best in the papers of the Société typographique de Neuchâtel (STN), a major publisher and wholesaler located in the Swiss principality of Neuchâtel, on France's eastern border. Like dozens of similar houses, the STN faced the daily problem of matching supply and demand, and that involved formidable problems of communication. Aside from the difficulties of transporting heavy crates of fragile, unbound sheets over primitive roads to the right person in the right place at the right time, the publishers had to make sense of the letters they received, and their customers had to get the message straight when they sent in their orders. The directors of the STN received letters from booksellers they did not know, in places they had never seen, requesting works they had never heard of. The titles were often inaccurate, misspelled, or illegible. And the books themselves were frequently dangerous: To send the wrong work through the wrong channel was to court disaster. But how could one tell right from wrong in the unbound ocean of French literature and the confusion of the daily mail?

The publishers relied on their code. "Philosophy" signaled danger. When the directors of the STN first went into business, they did not stock many forbidden books and did not favor the jargon of the trade: "From time to time there appear some new works that are called quite improperly *philosophical*," they wrote to a bookseller. "We don't carry any, but we know where to find them and can supply them when we are asked to." [11] But they soon realized that "philosophical" works were a vital sector of the trade for many of their customers. P. J. Duplain in Lyons informed them that he was eager to do business, "especially in the philosophical genre, which seems to be the one favored in our century." Manoury wrote from Caen: "N.B. Would you have any philosophical things? It's my main line." Letters from every corner of the kingdom contained variations on the same theme: "philosophical merchandise" (Le Lièvre of Belfort), "philosophical works" (Blouet of Rennes), "books of philosophy" (Audéart of Lunéville), "philosophical books of all kinds" (Billault of Tours). [12]

31

Because the code was shared by everyone in the trade, the booksellers assumed their supplier would know what they were talking about when, as in the case of Patras in Bar-sur-Aube, they issued blank orders for "three copies of all your newest philosophical works." The same assumption underlay their requests for information. Thus Rouyer of Langres: "If you have something good, something new, something curious, something interesting, and some good philosophical books, please let me know"; and Regnault le jeune of Lyons: "My line is all philosophical, so I want almost nothing except that kind." The supplier was expected to know what books belonged to that category, and in any case the orders often made the point clear. In an order for eighteen titles, Regnault marked all the "philosophical" books with a cross, explaining that they should be carefully hidden in the crate. There were six: *Le Compère Matthieu; Dom B*****, Portier des Chartreux; La Fille de joye; L'Académie des dames; De l'Esprit;* and *L'An 2440*—a typical selection, which ranged from pornography to philosophy in the form of a theoretical treatise.[13]

"Philosophical books" could not be handled in the same way as legal works or even mildly illegal ones, the kind that were merely pirated or uncensored but not offensive enough to run much risk of confiscation. The STN did not print many hard-core forbidden books. Having run afoul of the town officials for publishing an edition of the *Système de la nature* in 1771, it preferred to procure such works by means of exchanges with specialists in the genre: Jacques-Benjamin Téron, Jean-Samuel Cailler, Pierre Gallay, and Gabriel Grasset in Geneva: Gabriel Décombaz in Lausanne; and Samuel Fauche in Neuchâtel itself. Exchanges were common in all kinds of eighteenth-century publishing. By swapping the works he printed against assortments from the stock of other houses, a publisher could diffuse his editions rapidly, thereby reducing the risk of piracy or counterpiracy while increasing the variety of his own list. Publishers balanced their exchange accounts (*comptes de changes*) by calculating the number of sheets that changed hands. Except in the case of unusual formats or illustrated editions, a sheet of one book would be taken as the equivalent of a sheet in another. But "philosophical books" were worth more than ordinary books. They fetched more on the market and cost more to produce, or at least involved greater risks, for even in the relative liberty of Swiss towns local authorities, prodded by Calvinist pastors, sometimes impounded editions and imposed fines. Exchanges involving prohibited works therefore required special ratios: two sheets of a "philosophical book" for three of an ordinary pirated edition, or one sheet for two, or three sheets for four, depending on the bargaining power on either side.

The STN got the best terms and the most audacious books from Geneva, where a cluster of small, marginal publishers had grown up in the shadow of the great houses like Cramer and de Tournes. In April 1777 two of the STN's directors received the following reminder from the home office while on a business trip to Geneva: "Until now Geneva has been our main source of philosophical books, which, in accordance with the taste of this century, make up an essential part of our stock. Cailler, G. Grasset, and Gallay have supplied them to us in exchanges at two sheets against three of our own: see what you can arrange with them."[14] The archives do not reveal what happened at that particular bargaining session, but the general nature of the bargaining is clear from the STN's correspondence with two of its most important suppliers in Geneva, Jacques Benjamin Téron and Gabriel Grasset.

Téron scraped together a living by tutoring in mathematics, selling books, running a *cabinet littéraire,* and doing any intellectual odd-job that would fetch a penny. Between bankruptcies in 1773 and 1779, he established a small publishing business. He selected a few forbidden books that seemed to be most in demand and, with some capital advanced by a friend, hired local printers to produce clandestine editions. These he sold under the counter for cash and traded for legal works that could be offered above the board in his bookshop, which was nothing more than a room on the second floor of a house in Geneva's Grand'rue. Sensing a potentially important new source of supply, the STN wrote to Téron in April 1774: "We are also often asked for the kind of books called *philosophical.* Let us know whether you might be in a position to furnish us with them. We would gladly take our supplies from you, and our trade would certainly be worth your while." Téron replied by return of post: "I will give you three sheets of the philosophical books you want for every four that I choose from your stock." Generous terms, but the STN was a valuable customer; and Téron needed to win its good will, because he had failed to pay the bills for some of his earlier speculations. Three weeks later, he sent off its first order: "8 *Histoire critique de Jésus-Christ,* 6 *Lettres de Bolingbroke,* 3 *Traité des trois imposteurs,* 6 *Théologie portative,* 12 *Catéchumène,* 2 *Choses utiles et agréables,* 6 *Saül*"—533 half-sheets in all—or 711 sheets credited to Téron's *compte de change* at the agreed ratio of 3:4. Téron specialized somewhat in Voltaire's works because he tapped the literature that came coursing out of Ferney. But he also carried the odd pornographic volume and some political tracts, notably an edition of the *Journal historique de la révolution opérée dans la constitution de la monarchie française par M. de Maupeou.* In return, the STN sent him the relatively innocent products of its own presses. "I especially need a great many novels, travel books, and historical works," he explained. And so the swapping continued, with ups and downs, for five years, until Téron's business collapsed.[15]

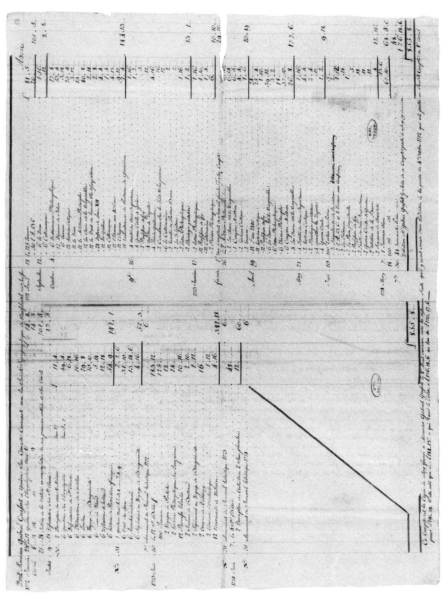

Gabriel Grasset. Account with the Société typographique de Neuchâtel. [August 1775]. Bibliothèque Publi-que et Universitaire de Neuchâtel, Archives de la Société Typographique de Neuchâtel.

The correspondence, accounts, and printed catalogue of the underground printer and bookdealer Grasset reveal how extensive and how sophisticated the illicit book trade had become by the late eighteenth century. Grasset's "List of Philosophical Works," containing both the great works of the Enlightenment and notorious pornographic books, illustrates how "philosophy" had become a euphemism for anything illegal (cat. nos. 53–55).

Gabriel Grasset. Letter to the Société typographique de Neuchâtel. 25 April 1774.

§ (1) §

Note de Livres Philosophiques.

Collection de Piéces pour les Main-mortables, 8;
Commentaire sur les Délits & les Peines, 8.   20 128
De l'origine du Despotisme Oriental, 12.
De l'Esprit par Helvetius, 12. 2 vol.
Déclaration de Mr. de Voltaire sur le procès du comte de Morangiés, 8.   4.
Défense de Louis XIV, 8.   4.
Des Singularités de la Nature, 8.
Dictionnaire Philosophique, 12. 2 vol.
Dieu & les Hommes, 8.
Discours aux Confédérés de Kaminick, 8.
Discours de l'Empereur Julien, 8.   1. 10
Epitre à Horace, 8.
Evangile de la Raison, 8.
Examen critique de Fréret, 8.   1. 10
Examen de milord Bolingbroke, 8.   12
Fragmens d'instruction pour le P. Royal de Prusse, 8.
Histoire critique de la vie de Jesu-Christ ou Analyse raisonnée des Evangiles, 8.   2
  — de Dom B. Portier des Chartreux, 12. fig. 2 vol.
  — du Patriotisme, Français 8. 6 vol.
Homélie du Pasteur Bourn, 8.   2.
Idées sur l'Administration des Villes municipales, 8.   6.
L, A, B, C, Dialogue,   10
La Philosophie de l'Histoire, 8.
La Tolérance, Tragédie, 8.
La Paix perpétuelle, 8.
La Profession de Foi des Théistes, 8.   8.
La Théologie Portative, 8.   2.
La Passion de notre Seigneur, 8.   2
La voix du Curé, 8.
La Fille de joye, 8. fig.
L'an Deux mille quatre cent quarante, 8.
L'Arretin moderne, 12. 2 vol.
Le Parnasse libertin, 8.
Le Point d'Appui ou Hist. Pol. de la dern. guerre entre les Puissances de l'Europe avec les Plans des Siéges & Batailles, 8. 5 vol. fig.
Le Philosophe ignorant, 8.
Lettre de la Montagne, 8.   2.

§ (2) §

L'Epitre aux Romains, 7.   20. 8
Le Cathécuméne, 8.   8
Le Diner du Comte de Boulainvilliers, 8.   8
Le Tocsin des Rois, 8.
Le Christianisme dévoilé, 8.
Le Militaire Philosophe, 8.   2
Le Compere Matthieu, 8. 3 vol.
Le Traité des trois Imposteurs, 8.   1
Les Chôses utiles & agréables, 8. 3 vol.
Les Questions de Zapata, 8.
Les Jésuites en belle hameur, 12.   4
Les Droits des Hommes & les Usurpations &c. 8.   4
Les Colimaçons du Révérend Pére l'Escarbotier, 8.   6
Les trois Epitres, 8.   2
Lettres écrite sur Rabelais, &c. 8.
Lettres Philosophiques, 8.
Lettres sur les Panégyriques, 8.   2
L'Espion Chinois, 8 6 vol.
L'homme aux Quarante Ecus, 8.   12
L'Ingénu ou le Huron, 8.   15
Mémoires de Mad. de Pompadour, 8. 3 part.
Nouveauté de Voltaire, 8.
Poëme sur la Guerre civile de Genéve, 8.   12
Questions sur l'Encyclopedie, 8. 9 vol.
Rélation de la mort du Chevalier de la Barre, 8.   6
  — de l'Expulsion des Jésuites de la Chine, 8.   6
Remontrances du corps des Pasteurs du Gévaudan, 8.   5
Recherche philosophique sur les Egyptiens & les Chinois 12. 2 vol. avec une Carte Géographique.
Recueil de Comedie Gaillardes, 12.
Romans ou Contes Philosophiques, 8. 2 vol.
Saül, Tragédie, 8.
Sermon du Papa Charitesti, 8.
Siècle de Louis XV, 8. 2 vol.
Systême de la Nature, par Mr. Mirabeau, 8. 2 vol.
Systême social, par l'Auteur du Systême de la Nature, 8. 3 vol.   4.
Therese Philosophe, 8. 2 part. fig.
Testament politique de Mr de Voltaire, 8.
Traité sur la Tolerance, 8.
Trois Lettres sur la prétendue Comète, 8.

Grasset
Genève

Gabriel Grasset. "List of Philosophical Works." [1774].

Gabriel Grasset supervised the printing shop of the Cramers for several years before establishing his own printing and bookselling business. Despite some sub rosa patronage by Voltaire, it never amounted to much, because Grasset was more of a printer than a businessman. He ran two presses and handled all the billing and correspondence by himself, scrambling accounts and falling constantly further behind in his payments. Things got so bad by April 1770 that he offered to sell all his material to the STN and to come and work as its foreman. But he kept afloat by printing forbidden books and selling them under the cloak. His exchanges with the STN began in 1772 at the prevailing rate of two sheets to one, for he insisted he would accept nothing less: "As all the other booksellers give me two sheets for every one of the philosophical kind, I propose the same exchange to you." He selected works from the STN's catalogue, and it chose what it wanted from lists he sent of the books he kept in stock.

Soon the STN was trading its edition of the Bible for *La Profession de foy des théistes* and *Traité des trois imposteurs*. It acquired many other clandestine classics—*Thérèse philosophe*, *Le Compère Matthieu*, *L'An 2440*—in this way; and while the books traveled back and forth, it attempted to extract more favorable terms. In April 1774 it tried to get Grasset to accept three instead of four of its sheets for every two of his. But he dug in his heels: "As for your proposition of exchanging three for two sheets, that certainly goes against our old arrangement. Surely you would agree that the costs and risks in the philosophical sector warrant a rate that is greater than two-to-one. In order to continue doing business with you, I will exchange [at the rate of two-to-one] all the philosophical works whose prices have been entered on the enclosed list." Grasset kept up his exchange rate, but he lowered his guard. In January 1780 the Genevan Petit Conseil fined and imprisoned him for printing obscene and irreligious works. When he got out of jail he had to sell off his printing shop, but he hung on to his secret stock of books. He offered to swap 100 *Histoire critique de Jésus-Christ* in August 1780 and seems to have continued his under-the-cloak trade until his death in February 1782.[16]

Grasset's remark about a list enclosed within his letter illustrates another way in which *livres philosophiques* received special treatment. They were listed in separate, clandestine catalogues. Grasset printed his on a small sheet of paper headed "Note de Livres Philosophiques." It included seventy-five titles arranged in alphabetical order with no indication of where they might be procured. Publishers always kept compromising information out of these catalogues, in contrast to the catalogues of their legal list, which carried their names and addresses and circulated openly. For example, when the two Genevan publishers J. L. Chappuis and J. E. Didier merged their businesses in 1780, they announced the event in a printed circular accompanied by two printed catalogues. The first covered the bulk of their stock: 106 titles of books on standard subjects—history, travel, law, religion, belles-lettres, all of them held "in large quantity" and perfectly legal. The second, entitled "Note Séparée," included twenty-five works, all extremely illegal, from *L'Académie des dames* to *Vénus dans le cloître* with plenty of Voltaire, d'Holbach, and political libel in between.[17]

Catalogues of this kind seem to have circulated everywhere in the underground book trade, although they have escaped the attention of modern bibliographers. The STN's papers contain five of them from its suppliers in Genevà and Lausanne and two that it drew up itself: a handwritten list of 110 works headed "Livres philosophiques" (probably from 1775) and a printed list of 16 titles under the heading "Note séparée," dated 1781. The catalogues served two purposes: to publishers and wholesalers, they showed the stock from which exchanges could be selected; to retailers, they indicated what works could be acquired through clandestine channels. But they were dangerous in themselves, so they, too, circulated under the cloak. One of the most incriminating pieces of evidence in the papers seized when the police raided Veuve Stockdorf's bookshop in Strasbourg in March 1773 was a printed "Catalogue de livres françois / à Berne 1772." It included 182 titles and gave the police a splendid view of the stock of a Swiss supplier and his trade with a French customer. Jérémy Wittel, a Swiss publisher on a sales trip to Paris in 1781, was arrested merely for having distributed "a printed catalogue of bad books." When booksellers exchanged such catalogues within France, they employed a certain amount of hugger-mugger: letters written in code, names and addresses expunged, and imprecations such as "Keep mum about my catalogue." The police knew all about these maneuvers. Hoping to ingratiate itself with a key official in the Direction de la librairie, the STN sent one of its biggest customers, Poinçot of Versailles, to argue its case, armed with its legal catalogue. "He was satisfied," Poinçot reported. "But he said to me, 'They have another one for their bad books.'"[18]

Despite the danger, the catalogues were essential for marketing, and the publishers sent them through the regular mail. In August 1776 the STN tried to attract new customers by a circular letter sent to 156 booksellers scattered throughout Europe. While recording their names in the STN's letter-book, a clerk wrote "with phil. books" after some, "without phil. books" after others. The former—reliable veterans like Bouchard in Metz, Babin in Nancy, and Chambeau in Avignon—might be interested in illegal literature and entrusted with the clandestine catalogue. The latter—Molin in Valencia, Bouardel et Simon in Barcelona, Borel in Lisbon, Hermil in Naples—lived in dangerously Catholic countries, where such things were best left out of letters.[19]

French booksellers seemed to have little fear of compromising mail. Despite the occasional use of cryptograms and remarks about seals broken in the secret chambers of the police, they had no inhibitions about asking for philosophical books. When the STN sent him its standard, legal catalogue, Laisney of Beauvais protested. He did not want the standard fare; he wanted "several philosophical works that are not in your catalogue and that I believe nonetheless to be in your warehouse." Prévost of Melun sent in the same complaint: "Your catalogue contains nothing but ordinary books." His customers required "the other sort, philosophical books"; and after the STN sent its clandestine catalogue, they got them. The same message arrived, loud and clear, from Malassis of Nantes: "Send me as quickly as you can—that is, by return mail—a catalogue of all your philosophical books, and I will sell a great many for you." Wherever booksellers dealt in forbidden books, they assumed their suppliers kept a special stock and drew up special catalogues. To set the system in motion, they sent a standard signal: "philosophical books."[20]

The same signal went out from the suppliers, carrying additional messages about marketing and pricing. Sometimes, as mentioned, the STN conducted mail campaigns. But every day it sent letters to its customers, adding strategically placed notes about the newest titles in its stock. Thus, a typical aside in a letter to Bergeret of Bordeaux: "As for philosophical books, we don't print any, but we know where to get them. Here is a short list taken from our catalogue of philosophical books." Bergeret replied with an order full of works like *Thérèse philosophe* and *Théologie portative*. Before embarking on an important clandestine operation, however, the STN thought it wise to send a warning about the prices in this sector:

> Among the works you have ordered we notice that there are a great many from the genre that is called philosophical. We don't keep these in stock, but we can supply them, thanks to our contacts with other houses. We should warn you, however, that these books cost more than others for reasons that are easy to imagine. We cannot supply them at the same price as the others in our catalogue, because we have to buy them ourselves at a higher price. Still, we will try to get them for you on the best possible terms. Books of this kind are now proliferating all around us.[21]

The prices of philosophical books did not behave like those of other books. They began at a higher level, usually twice that of a comparable pirated work, and then dipped and soared erratically, depending on condemnations (always good for business), police raids (a stimulus for demand among readers but a deterrent for customers among booksellers), and the vagaries of supply (the market could be flooded by a half-dozen editions produced secretly and simultaneously by competing houses). In general, the STN fixed the wholesale price of its ordinary books at one sou per sheet and that of its forbidden books at two sous per sheet. It often traded two sheets of a legal work for one of a philosophical book. But, as in its exchanges with Téron and Grasset, the ratio changed whenever someone got the upper hand in the bargaining. And everyone expected the price of a brand-new work to skyrocket if it were sufficiently scandalous and fresh on the market.[22]

The volatility in pricing left its mark on the clandestine catalogues—literally, for the suppliers often added the current prices by hand. Grasset printed his "Note de livres philosophiques" without prices. After agreeing to exchange his works against those of the STN at a rate of two sheets to one, he wrote in prices according to the number of sheets in each book. As the STN charged one sou per sheet, he charged two. He thus set the price of *Théologie portative,* a book of twenty sheets, at two livres (forty sous). But he would exchange only thirty-three of the seventy-five titles on his list at that rate. He expected to get more for the others, which included some classics like *La Fille de joye* and *L'Espion chinois,* and so they appeared without prices. Grasset also insisted on special pricing for his two most recent productions, *Le Taureau blanc* and *Dialogue de Pégase et du vieillard,* just turned out by the "satanic" assembly line in Ferney: "As for the *Taureau blanc* and *Pégase,* which contains six sheets, I sell them for one livre [i.e., twenty sous] in cash to all our Genevan booksellers, because they are both printed on blue tinted paper. But my desire to do business with you has made me resolve to offer you a special price of eighteen sous."[23]

Newness, notoriety, special paper, illustrations, revised and augmented editions—many factors made the prices of forbidden books fluctuate erratically. The same work often appeared in different forms and at different prices in different catalogues. *L'Académie des dames,* a pornographic bestseller that had gone through several metamorphoses since it first appeared on the market in 1680, turned up in three of the clandestine catalogues. In 1772 the Société typographique de Berne listed it without any bibliographical details at a price of twenty-four livres. In 1776 Gabriel Décombaz of Lausanne offered it, "corrected, improved, and enlarged, two volumes octavo with illustrations, 1775, 12 livres." And in 1780 Chappuis et Didier of Geneva proposed two very different editions, "large octavo, a handsome edition from Holland adorned with 37 illustrations, 13 livres" and "2 volumes with illustrations, duodecimo, 3 livres."[24]

At two or three livres a volume, forbidden books fell within the purchasing power of many French people. Skilled workers made as much or more in a day. But the catalogues gave wholesale prices, and the books had to pass through many hands—smugglers, shipping agents, wagoners, retailers—before they reached the readers. The difficulties of distribution magnified the variations in pricing, so a consumer might pay twice or ten times what the producer had charged. Competition produced some leveling out at the retail level, but not in remote areas plied by peddlers who sold philosophical books along with chapbooks for whatever price they could get. Paul Malherbe, who supplied a whole army of peddlers from his secret warehouse in Loudun, noted: "Peddlers are extremely eager to get books of this kind. They make more on them than on others, because they charge whatever they fancy and get whatever a book will fetch, depending on the general desire for it." [25]

The art of marketing was especially hazardous in such an unpredictable marketplace. In order to be informed about sudden changes and to stay in touch with demand, publishers generally relied on their commercial correspondence. But they also sent special agents on sales trips and received detailed reports on the state of the underground trade. In 1776, the STN dispatched its trusted clerk, Jean-François Favarger, on a swing through Switzerland, Savoy, Lyonnais, Burgundy, and Franche-Comté. He loaded his horse with a supply of sample books, title pages, and catalogues—both kinds. Then, town by town and bookseller by bookseller, he reported on his transactions. Thus, after leaving the shop of Brette in Grenoble, he wrote, "Despite his links with the Société typographique de Lausanne, which was a step ahead of me everywhere along my route, he is inclined to order any Swiss editions he may need from us. I gave him a philosophical catalogue. He told me he already had almost everything in it." And after negotiating with Capel in Dijon:

> M. Capel is first rate, or at least his shop is very well stocked. He deals a lot in philosophical books. I gave him a list [of philosophical books] and a catalogue with a prospectus. He will see about placing an order with us. He is the book-trade inspector. All of the crates that we shipped [by smugglers] through Jougne passed through his hands. He isn't scrupulous about that sort of thing.

At every stage in the journey, as at every point in the process of producing, stockpiling, pricing, and marketing, it was clear that philosophical books required special treatment and received it. [26]

The same tendency stood out at the other end of the diffusion process, in the way illegal books were ordered and shipped. Sometimes in writing orders, booksellers scrambled legal, illegal, and quasi-legal works of all

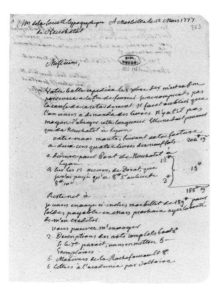

Mossy. Letter to the Société typographique de Neuchâtel. 12 March 1777.

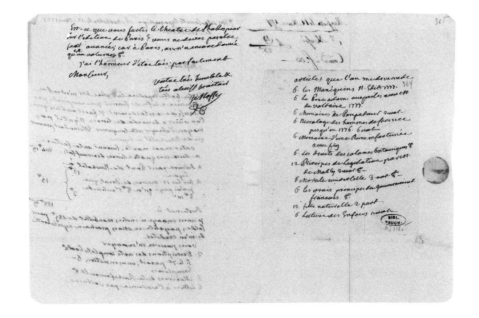

Dealers in illicit books employed various precautions in their correspondence to avoid detection or prosecution by the authorities. Mossy from Marseilles, for example, inserted his request for illicit books on a separate, unsigned scrap of paper simply marked "articles I am asking for." Billault, of Tours, listed the legal works first, then drew a line and listed the illegal ones. Baritel in Lyons marked them with a cross. They also requested special packaging to escape detection if a shipment was inspected. Thus, Bergeret of Bordeaux asked that the printer "marry" or interleave the sheets of illicit books between the sheets of legal ones. Bibliothèque Publique et Universitaire de Neuchâtel, Archives de la Société Typographique de Neuchâtel.

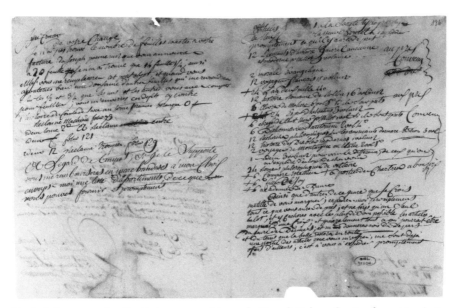

Baritel. Letter to the Société typographique de Neuchâtel. 19 September 1774 (cat. no. 50).

Billault. Letter to the Société typographique de Neuchâtel. 29 September 1776.

Bergeret. Letter to the Société typographique de Neuchâtel. 11 February 1775 (cat. no. 51).

varieties. But when they sensed danger, they took precautions to isolate the philosophical books. They occasionally listed the inoffensive parts of their order in the main body of their letter and then wrote the titles of the forbidden books on a scrap of paper (*papier volant*) that they slipped inside. The scrap did not carry their signature and was to be discarded after the letter arrived, although several of them can still be found in the papers of the STN.[27] More commonly, booksellers used various devices to set off the most dangerous titles in their orders. Manoury of Caen grouped them in one section of his list; Desbordes of La Rochelle placed them at the end; Malassis of Nantes arranged them in separate columns; Baritel of Lyons marked them with a cross; Billault of Tours, Charmet of Besançon, and Sombert of Châlons-sur-Marne listed the legal works first, then drew a line and listed the prohibited ones.[28]

All these techniques served the same purpose: to alert the supplier to books that required special handling in order to escape detection if the crates should be inspected. After listing sixty works that he wanted, Bergeret of Bordeaux marked off eleven, all hard-core philosophical books, with an *X* and explained, "Please marry all the *X* books with the others." To "marry" books meant to stuff the sheets of one into those of the other; booksellers also called this practice "larding." Charmet of Besançon ordered six copies of the obscene and irreligious *La Chandelle d'Arras* along with three copies of the innocent but pirated works of Mme. Riccoboni. "Put another title on the bill of lading and lard this work [*La Chandelle d'Arras*] in the Riccoboni," he instructed. "I show the bills of lading in the intendant's office so that they don't open certain crates. That's why it is crucial to put the philosophical works under other names." The clerks of the STN copied such instructions into its order book, presumably with a straight face, though it is hard to believe that they did not get a few laughs from entries like the following:

Ecole des filles ⎫	
Cruautés religieuses ⎬	in *Liturgie des Protestants*
Parnasse libertin ⎭	*en France*
Fille de joye	in *Nouveau Testament*[29]

They had been instructed to marry Fanny Hill with the Gospel.

In any case, the way the books were ordered bore directly on the way they were packed and shipped. Regnault le jeune wanted everything that he marked with an *X* hidden in the bottom of the crate so he could maneuver it past the inspectors in Lyons. Nubla of Dijon wanted all the illegal books placed in a bundle at the top so that he could remove them surreptitiously before the crate was inspected in his guild house. Jacquenod of

Lyons favored the bottom of the crates along with doctored bills of lading for his philosophical books. And Barrois of Paris wanted his hidden in the packing material (*maculature*). The techniques varied enormously, but all depended on drawing a clear distinction between books that were relatively safe and books that were likely to be confiscated.[30]

If a bookseller wanted to avoid risks altogether, he did not attempt to sneak illegal works through the legal channels of the trade; he hired smugglers, or "insurers" (*assureurs*), as they were known in the business. The shipper often arranged for this service, but the customer paid for it, usually on receipt of the goods. The insurers hired teams of porters who lugged the books along secret trails past customs houses at the borders and inspection stations inside the kingdom. If caught, the porters might be condemned to the galleys, the books would be confiscated, and the insurer would have to refund the loss. The system was cumbersome and expensive (a border crossing near Geneva cost 16 percent of the value of the merchandise in 1773), but it provided what some booksellers wanted most: security. Blouet, a pillar of the book trade in Rennes, ordered prohibited works only when he knew he could sell them safely and at a price that covered his costs, as he explained in a letter to the STN:

> You wrote that you have made an arrangement with insurers to get shipments into the kingdom without passing through guild halls or being subject to any inspection. I think it best for you to use this channel for my philosophical books, which, I believe, will not get through Lyons without being confiscated. As for the other works, you can send them to me through the normal Lyons route. . . . I am quite ready to pay for all costs, but I don't want to run any risk of confiscation.[31]

For a bookseller like Blouet, the distinction between mildly illegal and downright "philosophical" books involved calculations of costs, risks, and routes. For the smugglers, it was virtually a matter of life and death. In April 1773 Guillon l'aîné, an insurer in Franche-Comté, reported that two of his porters had been captured with a load of Mercier's *L'An 2440* and Voltaire's *Questions sur l'Encyclopédie*. They seemed certain to be shipped off to the galleys because the bishop of Saint Claude had taken an interest in the case. Although they were eventually released, the other porters stopped work. To get them back, Guillon tried to persuade the STN to pack its most dangerous books in separate crates so that the men could drop them and run if they came across a flying patrol of the customs. The STN replied that anything shipped through him was bound to be way outside the law, that was the whole point of using the insurance system instead of the packing tricks and sleight of hand that propelled the less-illegal books through the normal channels of the trade.[32]

When things calmed down, the porters resumed work. But a conflict of interest continued to characterize their relations with booksellers, and it ran along the line that divided the truly "bad" from the merely reprehensible books. Men who backpacked eighty-pound crates over tortuous mountain trails could not be expected to have a fine eye for literature. Most of them on the French–Swiss border had picked up their trade by hauling calicoes (*indiennes*) past the customs barriers designed to protect French silks. They were quite ready to strap anything counterfeit on their backs. But they balked at the prospect of carrying anything so illegal that it could result in agonizing death as a galley slave. Thus the advice of another STN agent, who organized "insurance" along the route from Neuchâtel to Pontarlier:

> Your business is particularly tricky, because the porters are afraid that if they get caught they will be held responsible for works that attack religion or that slander certain public figures—a danger that does not exist when they are merely smuggling goods to avoid paying tariffs. If you want to smuggle books that are irreproachable in their contents [i.e., pirated versions of legal works], then the porters will ask you to guarantee that that is the case, and you will find some in our area who will get them to Pontarlier for you for twelve livres a hundredweight.[33]

The practices of smuggling confirm those of stocking, exchanging, pricing, advertising, selling, ordering, packing, shipping, and even talking about forbidden books. At every stage in the production and diffusion process, the men and women who worked in the obscure territory dividing legal from illegal literature knew that a certain class of books had to be handled in a certain way. To do otherwise was to invite catastrophe.

Catastrophe struck the whole system of government in 1789. Was ideological erosion from the "philosophical" sector of the publishing industry a necessary condition for the general collapse? Before we can tackle that question, we need to identify the entire corpus of forbidden books, to examine its contents, and to study its reception. But even at this stage in the investigation, it seems clear that the "philosophy" circulating through the channels of the underground book trade differed considerably from the set of ideas commonly associated with the Enlightenment. In fact, after watching the professionals of the trade go about their business, day in and day out, for twenty years, from 1769 to 1789, one begins to doubt many of the common associations built up in standard histories of the eighteenth century.

The classic question—What was the relation of the Enlightenment to the Revolution?—looks like a *question mal posée*. For if we put the issue that way, we are likely to distort it, first by reifying the Enlightenment as if it were a thing in itself, distinct from everything else in eighteenth-century culture; then by injecting it into an analysis of the Revolution, as if it could be traced through the events of 1789–1800 like a substance being monitored in the bloodstream.

The world of the printed word in eighteenth-century France was too complex to be sorted into categories like "enlightened" and "revolutionary." But the individuals who transmitted literature to the reading public before 1789 devised a very workable category for distinguishing the truly dangerous element in the books they handled. If we take their experience seriously, we must rethink some basic distinctions of literary history—including the notions of danger and of literature itself. We consider the *Social Contract* political theory and *Histoire de Dom B****** pornography, perhaps even as something too crude to be treated as literature. But the bookmen of the eighteenth century lumped them together as "philosophical books." If we try to look at their material in their way, the seemingly self-evident distinction between pornography and philosophy begins to break down. We are ready to perceive a philosophical element in the prurient—from *Thérèse philosophe* to *Philosophie dans le boudoir*—and to reexamine the erotic works of the philosophes: Montesquieu's *Lettres persanes,* Voltaire's *Pucelle d'Orléans,* Diderot's *Bijoux indiscrets.* It no longer seems so puzzling that Mirabeau, the embodiment of the spirit of 1789, should have written the rawest pornography and the boldest political tracts of the previous decade. Liberty and libertinism appear to be linked, and we can find affinities among all the best-sellers in the clandestine catalogues. For once we learn to look for philosophy under the cloak, anything seems possible, even the French Revolution.

MALESHERBES AND THE CALL
FOR A FREE PRESS

RAYMOND BIRN

"BECAUSE THE LAW prohibits books the public cannot do without, the book trade has had to exist outside the law."[1] This authoritative viewpoint was stated in the winter of 1788–89 by Chrétien-Guillaume Lamoignon de Malesherbes. A respected sixty-seven-year-old retired magistrate, Malesherbes was at one time director of the French monarchy's book trade office (1750–63), first president of the tax court known as the Cour des Aides (1750–71, 1774–75), and royal minister (1775–76, 1787–88).[2] From his country property near Paris, Malesherbes considered the circumstances opportune to reiterate and further develop his positions on press freedom, for the exhausted and bankrupt government of Louis XVI had just announced the convening of an Estates General. The king's promulgation provoked an unprecedented flood of unlicensed pamphleteering on the events of the day as well as on proposals concerning the purpose and composition of the representative body.[3]

The mood of the moment invited a new governmental strategy with respect to the printed word. After more than half a century of bitter struggle with the Royal Council over the prerogative to silence writers and punish publishers, the most important administrative court in the kingdom, the Parlement of Paris, now seemed to favor the loosening of the system of preventive and repressive censorship. By requesting commentary on the forthcoming meeting of the Estates General, the king's ministers appeared to be following suit. Nevertheless, as far as toleration of publishing and pamphleteering was concerned, signals remained mixed. Upon orders of the parlement and the Royal Council, some writings still were condemned and publicly lacerated.[4] Only a year earlier the government had removed from search immunity the last safe havens in Paris for book peddlers: the Palais Royal, owned by the duc d'Orléans, and property belonging to the Knights

Templar, Knights of Malta, and members of the royal family.[5] Master printers and booksellers, and their journeymen, apprentices, peddlers, and authors, continued to endure police seizure of their shops, confiscation of their property, and imprisonment.[6] Not only was political commentary suppressed but so were books which, over the past generation, most cultivated French women and men considered to have found an established place in the literary canon. Take, for example, Beaumarchais's edition of Voltaire's collected works, condemned as "a collection of writings which injure religion and morals and tend to destroy the fundamental principles of social order and legitimate authority." According to the timeworn formula expressed in the denunciation of 3 June 1785, printers and booksellers were prohibited from owning or distributing this edition. Those who owned the books were ordered to deposit their copies in the publishers' guildhall nearest their residence. The volumes were to be shredded and burned. Readers caught with them would be fined one thousand livres, sellers and printers driven from their professional communities.[7]

Nevertheless, as Malesherbes noted, matters had been worse a generation earlier. Montesquieu had to work secretly on *De l'Esprit des Lois,* Diderot was thrown into prison for his *Lettre sur les aveugles,* and both Voltaire and Rousseau had to flee the country. The *Encyclopédie* was suppressed; so was *Emile;* and, as director of the book trade office, Malesherbes himself suffered humiliation while trying to protect writers.[8] The arbitrariness of the system was legendary. Although the Koran was approved on the ground that it did not threaten Christian principles, a Paris address directory was condemned. In the 1750s 40 percent of those sentenced to the Bastille were connected with the book trade (136 of 339 prisoners), and in the 1760s this figure was 35 percent (126 of 354).[9] Executive, judicial, and administrative jurisdictions rivaled one another in condemnations and punishments at both national and local levels.

The culmination of arbitrariness was a monstrous *Déclaration du roi* of 1757 sentencing to death anyone convicted of composing, ordering composed, printing, selling, or distributing "writings which tend to attack religion, excite spirits, injure royal authority, and trouble the order and tranquility of the state."[10] Of course, the severity of the declaration assured its unenforceability: Throughout the next three decades authors, printers, booksellers, and peddlers played cat-and-mouse with authorities. Publishers on the frontiers of France made fortunes smuggling books into the country, and readers gained access not only to the classics of the Enlightenment but also to the more vicious political pornography that created an intellectual climate of cynicism and disrespect toward the monarchy and the social structure supporting it.[11]

MÉMOIRES

SUR LA LIBRAIRIE

ET SUR

LA LIBERTÉ DE LA PRESSE,

Par M. DE LAMOIGNON DE MALESHERBES,

MINISTRE D'ÉTAT.

―――――――――

A PARIS,

CHEZ H. AGASSE, IMPRIMEUR-LIBRAIRE,

RUE DES POITEVINS, N°. 6.

―――――――

1809.

C.-G. Lamoignon de Malesherbes. "Memorandums on the Book Trade and on the Freedom of the Press." 1809. Columbia University, Rare Book and Manuscript Library.

  Malesherbes's "Memorandums on the Book Trade," written in 1788–89, represented one of the earliest and most distinguished efforts to introduce greater freedom of expression, legal toleration of conflicting ideas, and an end to the monopoly of the guilds. Nonetheless, this former director of the Royal Administration of the Book Trade cautiously argued for the continuance of royal censorship, at least on a voluntary basis. These views were soon to be eclipsed by less-patient reformers. Though written in 1788–89, Malesherbes's work was not published until 1809 (cat. no. 27).

23

LETTRE DU ROI

POUR LA CONVOCATION

DES ÉTATS-GÉNÉRAUX

A VERSAILLES,

Le 27 Avril 1789,

ET RÈGLEMENT Y ANNEXÉ.

A PARIS,

DE L'IMPRIMERIE ROYALE.

M. DCCLXXXIX.

"Letter from the King for the Convocation of the Estates General at Versailles, 27 April 1789." 1789. The New York Public Library, Rare Books and Manuscripts Division.

When the king announced the convocation of the Estates General in 1788, he called on "all educated persons" to share their views "concerning its convocation." This invitation provoked an unprecedented flood of unlicensed pamphleteering (cat. no. 22).

ARRÊT

DE LA COUR DE PARLEMENT,

RENDU LES CHAMBRES ASSEMBLÉES,

LES PAIRS Y SÉANT,

Qui condamne un Imprimé ayant pour titre : Délibération à prendre par le Tiers-Etat dans toutes
les Municipalités du Royaume de France, *à être*
lacéré & brûlé par l'Exécuteur de la Haute-Justice.

EXTRAIT DES REGISTRES DU PARLEMENT.

Du dix-sept Décembre mil sept cent quatre-vingt-huit.

CE jour, toutes les Chambres assemblées, les **Pairs y**
séant, les Gens du Roi sont entrés : &, M\ Antoine-
Louis Seguier, Avocat dudit Seigneur Roi, portant la parole,
ont dit :

MESSIEURS,

Nous avons pris communication du récit que la **Cour nous**
a fait remettre, & de l'imprimé qui en est l'objet.

A

"Decree of the Court of the Parlement . . . Condemning a Pamphlet Entitled: Delib-
eration to be Taken by the Third Estate . . . to be Lacerated and Burned by the
Executor of High Justice." [1788]. The New York Public Library, Rare Books and
Manuscripts Division, Talleyrand Collection.

Despite the de facto freedom of the press that reigned on the streets in the
months before the meeting of the Estates General, the Parlement of Paris continued
to exercise its authority to shred and burn printed matter that it condemned (cat.
no. 16).

Looking back over thirty years, Malesherbes considered much of the time wasted. A firm believer in the need for a true, popular consensus regarding principles of governance, he was convinced that the only way to attain such a consensus was through a legally tolerated conflict of ideas, such as he had seen in England, where journalism and the book trade provided an arena for conflict. In France political and ideological struggles were far more circumscribed. Ironically enough, it was in the Parlement of Paris, where denunciations of writers had been so loudly proclaimed, that a measure of liberty was doled out. Lawyers pleading before the parlement's magistrates might print their briefs and sell them publicly without prior submission to the censors, just as authors in England could. Cases became objects of public discourse on streetcorners and in cafés and salons. Parlementary lawyers thus submitted their arguments to public judgment and returned to the courtroom armed with the public mood. Desirous of having the Estates General succeed the parlements as buffer between king and people, Malesherbes envisioned national debates on public policy as replacing the private issues argued by the parlementary attorneys. At the moment, however, the transition from a regime of chaotic arbitrariness to one of regulated freedom was far from guaranteed.[12]

This arbitrariness existed within the confines of the book community itself. Based on institutions and procedures established by Louis XIV's minister Jean-Baptiste Colbert in the late seventeenth century, the French book trade consisted, ideally, of rigorous self-regulation that was controlled by an elite of master printers and sellers in Paris, armed with the executive authority of the state. The number of practicing masters was severely limited, apprenticeships were restricted to masters' sons, hired day labor had become the rule, and—most important—a system of publishing privileges dispensed by the royal government guaranteed that the Paris publishing aristocracy would continue to own the most valuable pieces of literary property. In practice the state called the tune, not merely through its control over censorship but also through its granting of economic monopolies and its demand for special tax subsidies from the publishers' guild.[13]

After 1750 the corporate elite that had dominated French publishing for a century came under increased pressure. Readers were now consuming as many as 3,500 editions and 150 different periodicals each year.[14] Salons, public libraries, and reading rooms became social centers of literate culture in urban society, and book lending and renting became commonplace. Subscription purchases, whether for cheap novels or grander *Encyclopédies*, guaranteed an ongoing readership, and the act of reading itself evolved from intensive concentration on a limited number of accessible texts to a passion for accumulating and devouring large quantities of books. Although statistics regarding book ownership and book reading are more elusive than even those for book production, wills and death inventories analyzed by Roger Chartier and Daniel Roche reveal that in the course of the century, for Paris at least, reading had penetrated deeply into society. In 1700, 13 percent of salaried workers and 35 percent of servants possessed at least one book. By 1780 the figures had risen to 30 precent and 40 percent respectively. In the cities of western France on the eve of the Revolution, one-third of the death inventories mention books as property. As early as 1750, 74 percent of royal officers and members of the liberal professions of Lyon left books in their wills, as did 48 percent of the working bourgeoisie, and 44 percent of the nobility. The books were small compared with the luxurious formats of the seventeenth century. Octavos and duo-decimos were now the rule. The books were nearly exclusively in French, rather than in a classical language, and the subjects were laicized.[15]

Constrained by the monopolistic practices of Paris's guild production and by the cultural conservatism of a censorship system that lacked clear-cut ideological boundaries, the mandarins of late-eighteenth-century publishing could not hope to meet the demands of the reading public. A relatively unpoliced enclave like the papal city of Avignon, peripheral towns like Bouillon, Geneva, and Neuchâtel, and foreign publishing centers such as Amsterdam and London contained religious refugees and enterprising businessmen eager to send French readers books that the legal trade was unable to supply.[16] An illicit publishing industry flourished in provincial cities, especially Lyon and Rouen.[17]

Political events in France influenced illegal and tacitly tolerated literature. In the early 1750s the Jansenist religious controversy gave way to the struggles between the clergy and parlements; the attempt in 1757 on the life of Louis XV and its ramifications made big news. In the 1760s the so-called Brittany affair and the subsequent conflict between the parlements and royal ministries found their way into print. In the 1770s publishers seized on the Maupeou coup against the sovereign courts, followed in the next decade by fiscal and constitutional crises. For the generation after 1750 the writings of the Enlightenment counterbalanced the *affaires du temps,* but so did licentious attacks on political figures (Louis XV, Madame de Pompadour, Madame du Barry, Marie Antoinette) or stock social types (grasping clergy, decadent *noblesse*). The royal government responded with waves of condemnations of books and arrests of publishers during flash-point periods. Police dossiers on writers and booksellers were constructed, and more censors were appointed. Tense moments were followed by periods of lassitude and resignation until the next crisis erupted.[18]

All of this infuriated Malesherbes, who thought that genuine political life in France was illusory because it took place in a social vacuum. The Paris publishing monopoly and contradictory government policies conspired to give foreigners large-scale control over the book trade, and illegality was the rule. Public opinion, the only genuine catalyst for political discourse in Malesherbes's view, was reduced to furtive whispers. As director of the book trade from 1750 to 1763, Malesherbes tried to enlarge the boundaries of public discourse by issuing tacit permits (*permissions tacites*) for books that censors might otherwise prohibit. There was a twofold benefit from this policy. First of all, a censor issuing *permissions tacites* could preserve his anonymity and thus escape subsequent prosecution. Second, tacit approval conveyed no privilege rights; thus freed from accusations of producing a counterfeit edition, any publisher might take advantage of a bestseller. Another form of *permissions tacites*, customarily given by a police official with the director's connivance, was orally bestowed (the *simple tolérance*). In this instance, no censor was involved and no registration made of the permission. Such permissions were awarded to undercut sale of a foreign book whose distribution could not be avoided.[19] Malesherbes left himself open to accusations of undermining time-honored policies of monopoly and repression; and, indeed, such was his intention.[20] He had long wished to submit to censorship control only those books dealing with religion, morals, and sovereign authority. For everything else—questions of legislation, politics, military affairs, finances—he preferred simply to have the author identify himself and let the work appear "at his risk, peril, and fortune." Only in this way, thought Malesherbes, would the mindless condemnations, book burnings, and imprisonments cease. Self-censorship by authors would herald a new maturity, he argued, and criminal prosecution could thus be reserved for those who published without permission.[21]

Malesherbes first put his thoughts into writing in 1758 and early 1759, when he submitted five memorandums on the book trade to Louis XV's son, the dauphin. It was a difficult time for the director. The draconian royal declaration of 1757 was in effect, drawn up by a rump group of vengeful *parlementaires*. A scandal of major proportions had just struck Malesherbes's office, with both parlement and pope having condemned Claude-Adrien Helvétius's philosophical treatise *De l'Esprit*, a work duly approved by a royal censor and embellished with a royal privilege. If this weren't a sufficient betrayal of the director's beliefs, on 8 March the *Encyclopédie* was suppressed once and for all, and Malesherbes himself was obliged to draw up the text of the condemnation.[22]

The five memorandums were therefore drafted to serve as a defense of the director's principles. First he addressed the matter of appropriate jurisdiction. The censorship of books, he argued, was an administrative, not a judicial, action. The book trade office alone issued official privileges and permits, and therefore only the book trade office could revoke them. According to Malesherbes, arguments for repression by parlementary or church authorities were constructed on flimsy juridical foundations. Next, Malesherbes called for a new set of regulations governing the trade, based on principles of toleration rather than repression and replacing inconsistent punishments with rationally graded penalties for infractions. Most significant, the director wished to limit the causes of infractions. He therefore considered all-encompassing, obligatory censorship to be philosophically indefensible. In no other sphere of human activity were police auxiliaries called on to exercise specific judgments on the basis of such vaguely articulated orders. Far from being an impartial judge, the director asserted, the censor worked in constant fear of reprisal. This, in turn, forced him to err on the side of severity: "His scruples, timidity, personal affections, and a vague fear of being compromised in matters which really do not concern him," wrote Malesherbes, "force him into frivolous or arbitrary difficulties every step of the way, which discourage authors and extinguish genius."[23] Moreover, he stated, experience proved the condemnations to be unenforceable. Tracking down merchandise in the stocks of masters resulted only in a shift in sources—to clandestine shops or suppliers abroad.

A Rousseau-like conviction that right opinion must ultimately surface guided Malesherbes in his program for free expression of ideas: "Each philosopher, each orator, each man of letters," he wrote in his third memorandum, "should be considered the advocate of what ought to be heard, even when he avows principles believed to be false. Sometimes it takes centuries to plead causes. The public alone can judge them, and in the end, if sufficiently instructed, it always will have judged well."[24] A balance must be struck between the liberty to write and the proper regulation of that liberty. In Malesherbes's view, the necessary first step lay in the reduction, if not elimination, of preventive censorship. He therefore addressed the most controversial (and fashionable) aspects of written discourse: personal satire, licentious and obscene books, political commentary, and religious controversy.

Concerning works directed at individuals, Malesherbes would allow the courts to determine what was libelous. The toleration of "small abuses" and indirect satire would serve to focus attention on what was genuinely condemnable, reducing the activity of clandestine printshops that published all forms of satire indiscriminately. By the same token, the director considered the prohibition and pursuit of sexually risqué literature to be a waste of time. His own personal library containing not only the *contes* of La Fontaine, Jean-Baptiste Rousseau, and Crébillon fils but also *Memoirs of a Woman of Pleasure (Fanny Hill)*, *Priapeia*, and *Les Quinze Joies de mariage*, Malesherbes believed that anyone with common sense could distinguish between erotic books and pornography. In France, the "gentleness of our manners" (*douceur de nos moeurs*) ensured the success of what were euphemistically termed *livres galantes,* and it was preferable to permit native publishers to profit from their sales than to have foreigners amass fortunes by catering to French tastes.

Malesherbes would not permit any challenge to the legitimacy of royal authority. But he proposed toleration of a wide range of political commentary, arguing that by allowing themselves to be criticized in print, government officials at last would energize public opinion and make political movement possible. Nor did he close off public discussion of the origins and course of France's unwritten constitution—a subject of much controversy not only in the chambers of parlement and assemblies of the clergy but also in cafés, salons, and reading clubs. For the moment, however, appropriate magistrates, taking orders from the chancellor, should decide whether a book crossed the boundary separating dispassionate analysis from dangerous criticism.

Finally, with respect to religious controversy, the views of the enlightened skeptic were clear enough. Malesherbes conceded manuscript censorship by clerical experts, adding (not without sarcasm): "Nothing should restrain them, for they have the pleasant task of professing a science where nothing is open to doubt."[25] Because religious censorship was designed to halt clandestinely printed attacks on Christianity, Malesherbes urged toleration of disagreements within the family of the faith. The director, who later in life advocated civil rights for French Protestants, explicitly refused comment on Calvinist books, but urged complete acceptance of Jansenist and Molinist ones. He found an irresistible analogy between these grave works on the one hand and gambling dens and houses of prostitution on the other, considering them "abuses which are tolerated because they cannot be prevented, and which by virtue of toleration are contained and cleared up."[26]

Next in his memorandum, Malesherbes aimed his reformist program at the publishing communities themselves. In place of corporatism, he argued for utility and capitalist expansion as the basic principle of their activity. Opposing the fixed number of printshops for the kingdom (set down in 1686 and modified in 1744), the director proposed that the market should be allowed to determine their evolution. Not only would this encourage French production at the expense of foreign-based industry, but it also would drive poor and incompetent printers—whom he regarded as the source of most illicit production—out of the trade. Malesherbes clearly sympathized less with the producers of books than with the writers of them. In fact, he advocated policing the activities of printers more closely than ever. Remove those in small, isolated communities, he proposed, and relocate them in large towns. He urged that royal intendants and newly appointed *commissaires* be granted police powers heretofore assigned to guild officers. Similarly, journeymen and shopboys should be registered with the police, who would assign them identity cards containing a physical description of the holder. Malesherbes contended that systematic surveillance of workers would provide far more information about illegal production than would sporadic, hit-or-miss police raids based on informants' tips. He also recommended that the shops be as physically uniform as possible—publicly known, bolted wth a standardized lock, rear entrances sealed, presses and equipment duly registered. Quiet presses must be prohibited, and a widow's automatic inheritance of her husband's shop discouraged. The director was certain that poor women were major producers of illicit books:

> The intent of the regulations is only to have safe individuals as printers, financially secure and always restrained by fear of losing their status. However, the succession of widows is absolutely contrary to this principle, because a woman, entirely incapable of directing a printshop on her own, leases her rights to some adventurer or dishonest subject, who runs things with impunity in her name.[27]

Malesherbes proposed that, like sons and sons-in-law of deceased master printers, widows seeking to succeed their spouses in owning a printshop be obliged to apply for formal permission.

As for the sale of books, Malesherbes was convinced that the closed, corporate character of the guilds encouraged corruption and fraud. Because established sellers were not meeting consumer demand, unlicensed peddlers, tolerated by the police, filled the streets of towns, roads of the countryside, fairs, markets, and the great halls of châteaux. "Their trade is so open," wrote the director, "that it is impossible to believe it is unauthorized."[28] Malesherbes considered that the hawking of books by *colporteurs*, with all its attendant abuses, spread enlightenment nevertheless. Therefore, rather than repress their activities, he proposed registering and surveilling the peddlers.

It was the sedentary master booksellers who exasperated the director. He considered their guilds to be decadent. According to Malesherbes, their requirements for admission—six to seven years of journeyman/apprentice status—were too onerous and excluded new blood. Furthermore, sons and sons-in-law were exempt from admission requirements, and since 1730 there had been a freeze on new apprenticeships altogether. Because bookselling was no longer a profession for scholars, Malesherbes considered probationary apprenticeships to be senseless. According to him, master merchants could barely read French, much less the Latin and Greek required by guild regulations. In Paris, as owners of exclusive privileges for most of the works they possess, booksellers' sons "enjoy their masterships without care and without labor, as one enjoys a piece of property that brings in a large revenue. Gone are the active, intelligent subjects who, needing to work to establish their fortune, seek means of making themselves useful to the public."[29] Malesherbes sought to free the trade from the monopoly of these drones by proposing the revocation of the freeze on apprenticeships, accepting married apprentices, and facilitating the entrance of qualified provincial masters into the Paris community. In a dramatic reversal of policy concerning ownership of book privileges, Malesherbes called for a new law recognizing the prerogative of authors to retain their literary property and to sell their own books rather than be forced to pass on their rights to grasping merchants. On book imports, Malesherbes's thinking was consistent with his other positions on the trade: have few regulations, make them consistent, and enforce them rigorously. Public demand will prevail, however much authorities try to suppress a book. He also called for an end to guild self-regulation: Intendants and state inspectors should execute the laws. Finally, Malesherbes spoke to the issue of an important category of books in France, those circulating with *permissions tacites,* which by 1789 would constitute one-half to three-fourths of the total books in circulation. He wished to remove these books from their semiclandestine status and have them registered openly so that publishers throughout the country might take advantage of their popularity and produce them without risk.

Except for accelerating the award of *permissions tacites,* Malesherbes never had the opportunity to put his reforms into practice. Four years after Malesherbes sent his memorandums to the dauphin, Malesherbes's father, the chancellor of France, was disgraced, and Malesherbes had to relinquish his directorship of the book trade office. He held on to his post as first president of the Cour des Aides until 1771, when Maupeou's coup made a shambles of France's venerable sovereign courts. In 1774, during the heady days following Louis XVI's accession, he returned to government, first to the Cour des Aides and then to serve in A.-R.-J. Turgot's reform-minded ministry. Disillusioned over its ineffectiveness, Malesherbes resigned after administering the Maison du Roi for ten months. He settled down on his estate where, for the next twelve years, he led the pleasant life of a country gentleman, fighting for civil rights for Protestants and Jews, working on educational reform programs, attacking slavery, the penal system, and *lettres de cachet,* satisfying his passion for botany and agriculture, and building his library.[30]

His books should interest us. The Newberry Library in Chicago possesses the catalogue of his collection sold at public auction in 1797.[31] There are 7,413 entries, plus entries for oil portraits of René Descartes and Isaac Newton and for a miniature working model of a printing press carved in mahogany, along with a complement of type characters in Cicero font and shop implements. The books themselves are, for the most part, modern editions, most published since the 1720s. As important as what the library contained is what it lacked: diurnals, missals, breviaries, and other aids to religious devotion. Somewhat more strangely for a man who spent most of his adult life as a judge, there were only thirty-six treatises on civil and natural law. Yet it was an up-to-date, humanistic library, with nearly half the books devoted to history and literature. History, overwhelmingly political history, was the most important category, accounting for nearly a third (2,424 entries, or 32.7 percent) of the collection. Half of the history volumes dealt with France. Next came *belles-lettres*, with 1,179 books (15.9 percent) evenly divided between French and non-French authors. Third in importance was the natural history of plants and animals (1,042 entries, 14.4 percent), followed by travel literature (1,008 entries, 13.6 percent). Then came medicine, the physical sciences, and mathematics (747 entries, 9.9 percent); agriculture (2.7 percent); philosophy (2.6 percent); and theology (2.4 percent). Rounding out the collection were books on crafts, trades, industrial production, sports and games, military tactics, economics, and political theory.

In general, this might be considered the typical library of an eighteenth-century gentleman at home in the culture of the French Enlightenment: secular, devoted to the worlds of nature, the imagination, and beyond the seas, yet at the same time grounded solidly in the past.[32] Did Malesherbes practice what he preached? Did his library betray a controversial vision as well as a modern one? Did it contain the books he would fight to protect? A glance seems to confirm this opinion. Towering above all else is the first edition of the *Encyclopédie*. Included as well are Diderot's *Pensées philosophiques* and Helvétius's *De l'Esprit*, both condemned in the book-burning craze of 1758–59. Rousseau's collected works are present in three separate editions, Voltaire in eight, including Beaumarchais's suppressed version, supplemented by a seventy-five-volume collection of memoirs, eulogies, critiques, and defenses of the great man. Mirabeau's works, including his *Histoire secrète de la Cour de Berlin* condemned by the Parlement of Paris in 1789, also rested on the shelves. So did the books and pamphlets of the controversialists S.-N.-H. Linguet and the abbé Mably, the philosophical skepticism of Thomas Hobbes and David Hume, and *Lettres iroquoises, persanes, juives, chinoises, peruviennes, siamoises,* and *turques*—all of which contained criticisms, veiled or otherwise, of eighteenth-century French institutions throughout the course of the century, and which either appeared thanks to the *permissions tacites* perfected by Malesherbes or were produced in the clandestine shops he despised.

Following another brief stint in government in 1787 and 1788, Malesherbes returned home and wrote his *Mémoire sur la liberté de la presse* a few months before the convocation of the Estates General. He knew that the program he had set down a generation earlier had been only partially fulfilled. True, *permissions tacites* and *simples tolérances* were widely used. In 1777 writers gained closer title to ownership of their literary property than had been the case earlier.[33] A significant number of books, whose publication had been monopolized by the rich bookdealers of Paris, were now in the public domain. As Malesherbes was to acknowledge, literacy had increased greatly during the past generation. He noted that no social group, no distant province lacked people able to think for themselves and to express and defend their ideas. "This is the happy consequence of printing," he wrote. Because repressive laws remained on the books, however, only the bold risked their safety by engaging in subterfuge and deception. As a result, Malesherbes's would-be meritocracy of right-thinking, progressive authors and readers still had not emerged to influence politics. Monopolistic publishers continued to bask in their corporate privileges. Worst of all, Malesherbes detected insidious motives in the parlement's advocacy of fewer press restrictions, suspecting that the magistrates were yielding their claims to censorship privilege in order to cow authors appearing before them as defendents in libel cases. In this way the magistrates might frighten off others from assuming antiparlementary political positions. The retired magistrate concluded that a corrupt judiciary was preparing a new terror for writers and publishers alike.

To forestall this threat, Malesherbes offered a temporary safeguard: voluntary preventive censorship for writers fearful of the courts. Authors submitting to such censorship could not be pursued. At the same time, those who insisted on self-censorship alone had to take their chances. Malesherbes put it this way:

> Therefore, the proposed expedient of offering [authors] the choice of submitting to the fantasies of censors or exposing themselves to those of justice seems preferable to me to all the other solutions that can be tried, better than submitting everyone to censorship, better than exposing everyone to the whims of justice, and better than allowing rigorous, unexecuted laws to subsist, because authors do not

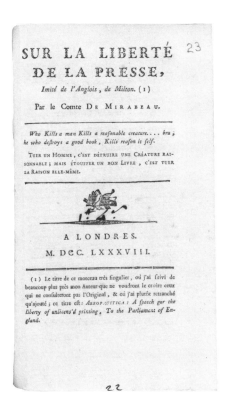

Marie-Joseph de Chénier. "Denunciation of the Inquisitors of Thought." 1789. Archives Nationales, France (cat. no. 6).

Honoré-Gabriel de Riqueti, comte de Mirabeau. "On the Freedom of the Press, after the English, by Milton." 1788. The New York Public Library, Rare Books and Manuscripts Division, Talleyrand Collection (cat. no. 30).

The moderate views of Malesherbes were soon challenged by revolutionaries calling for an end to any regulation of the public exchange of ideas. Mirabeau's *On the Freedom of the Press* and Chénier's *Denunciation of the Inquisitors of Thought* were two of the most militant and widely circulated calls for the freedom of the press after 1789. Here Mirabeau is depicted as the law-giver surrounded by revolutionary books like Rousseau's *Social Contract*.

"Mirabeau Arrives at the Champs-Elysées." N.d. Engraving by Marquelier, after Moreau le jeune. Musée de la Révolution Française, Vizille, France (cat. no. 101).

want to rely upon this tacit tolerance. Those who do so will perhaps be victimized once it pleases Justice to enforce the laws and set an example.[34]

The year 1789 was ill suited for such a reasoned interim proposal. Ironically, the proposal was to prove more useful to A.-A. Barbier, librarian to Napoleon I, who under different circumstances, twenty years later, published the *Mémoire sur la liberté de la presse* to illustrate the contrast between England's wild, untamed ideas of press freedom and Napoleonic France's regulated, restrained version. But Barbier was misusing Malesherbes. While the former director of the book trade saw the need for benevolent censorship as a way of protecting writers from a judiciary that was both politicized and corrupt, the emperor's librarian had returned to the old, coercive purposes. Of course, events rendered Malesherbes's fears obsolete, at least for a time. Writers like Mirabeau and M.-J. Chénier were calling for unrestricted freedom of the press, and the pamphlet barrage early in 1789 made that freedom de facto.[35] Within months the feared parlements were swept away forever. The principle of a free press, stated in Article 11 of the Declaration of the Rights of Man and of the Citizen, was etched into law. It would survive the Restoration, two Napoleons, and the totalitarian regimes of the twentieth century.

PART TWO

REVOLUTION
IN THE PRINTING TRADES

ECONOMIC UPHEAVALS IN PUBLISHING

CARLA HESSE

WHAT DID "freedom of the press" actually mean in practice? Traditional histories of the freedom of the press in France have limited their inquiries to the story of the abolition of royal censorship.[1] As important as this subject is, it does not begin to recapture the meaning or the magnitude of the cultural revolution that occurred as a consequence of the freeing of the press in 1789. The struggle against royal censorship was simply one aspect of a much broader revolutionary assault on the entire literary system of the Old Regime. The destruction of that system would completely transform the legal, institutional, and economic realities of printing and publishing, and, ultimately, the character of France's literary culture.

Consider for a moment a few examples of what the freedom of the press meant to revolutionaries in 1789. The novelist Restif de la Bretonne wrote: "If you want freedom of the press, establish freedom of the professions. Without this, thirty-six privileged printers will become more cruel tyrants of thought than all of the censors!"[2] For Restif it was the corporate monopoly of the thirty-six printers of the Paris Book Guild, rather than royal censorship, that most constrained freedom of expression and of the press. This view was expanded upon by the playwright Marie-Joseph Chénier:

> Let us now recall all the kinds of tyranny . . . the inquisition of the royal censors, the inquisition of the lieutenant-general of the police, . . . of the administration of the book trade, . . . of the keeper of the seals . . . , of the minister of Paris . . . , of the stewards of court entertainments . . . , of the gentlemen of the chamber . . . , of the lawyers . . . , of the Sorbonne . . . , of the issuers of mandates and pastoral letters . . . , of the prosecuting attorneys . . . , of the minister of foreign affairs . . . , of the local governments and royal officials of the

provinces . . . , of the postal system, of the book guilds . . . , of all the valets at Versailles. In all, seventeen inquisitions exercised in France upon the minds of the citizens.[3]

According to Chénier, royal censorship was only the first in a long list of "inquisitions exercised . . . upon the minds of citizens." To Chénier's seventeen inquisitions, an eighteenth was added by Louis-Félix Guyement de Kéralio, a former royal censor, who wrote two pamphlets in 1790 entitled *De la liberté de la presse* and *De la liberté d'énoncer, d'écrire et d'imprimer la pensée.* In these pamphlets Kéralio asserted that: "Printed matter sold to the public belongs to the public."[4] He thus concluded that there should be no private claims to ownership of ideas or texts by authors or publishers. All texts should be freed from particular claims or "privileges" because "public interest is preferable to the mercantile interests of a few booksellers."[5] In the eyes of these men the freeing of the press was to entail the demise of the entire legal and institutional infrastructure of publishing under the Old Regime: the royal patronage of letters; the royal administration of the book trade and its army of censors and inspectors; the system of literary privileges that gave publishers and authors exclusive publication rights to texts; and, finally, the monopoly of the Book Guild over printing, importing, and selling printed matter in France. This ideological revolt was soon translated into legislative action.

On 4 August 1789 the National Assembly abolished all *privilèges,* at least in principle. Then on 24 August it proclaimed in the Declaration of the Rights of Man and of the Citizen that "the free communication of thoughts is one of the most precious rights of man. All citizens can, therefore, speak, write, and print freely."[6] But how were these abstract principles to be enacted? Did this actually mean that censorship was abolished? Did it mean an end to royal regulation and policing of the book trade? Had the abolition of privilege included literary *privilèges* on books and journals? Did the freedom of the press mean that anyone could open a printing shop or sell printed matter?

Between 1789 and 1793 the answers to these questions were not clear even to those whose job it was to interpret and enforce the freedom of the press. Thus, in the summer of 1789 the head of the Paris bureau of the Royal Administration of the Book Trade, Dieudonné Thiebault, wrote to one of his inquiring provincial inspectors: "We must await the future, the laws, the rules or principles established by the Estates-General and sanctioned by the king, but until that time, all I can do is uphold the old regulations."[7] Far from being asked to resign their posts, the censors and inspectors of the Royal Administration of the Book Trade were thus told to enforce the old regulations as well as possible until instructed otherwise.

CODE
DE
L'A LIBRAIRIE
ET
IMPRIMERIE DE PARIS,
O U
CONFÉRENCE
DU RÉGLEMENT
ARRÊTÉ AU CONSEIL D'ÉTAT DU ROY,
LE 28 FEVRIER 1723,

Et rendu commun pour tout le Royaume, par Arrêt du Conseil d'Etat du 24 Mars 1744.

A V E C

LES ANCIENNES ORDONNANCES,
Edits, Déclarations, Arrêts, Réglemens & Juge-
mens rendus au sujet de la Librairie & de l'Imprimerie, depuis l'an 1332, jusqu'à présent.

A PARIS,
AUX DÉPENS DE LA COMMUNAUTÉ.

M. DCC. XLIV.
AVEC APPROBATION ET PRIVILEGE DU ROY.

Communauté des libraires & imprimeurs de Paris. "Code of Bookselling and Printing in Paris or Conference on the Regulations Decreed by the Royal Council,
28 February 1723." 1744. The New York Public Library, General Research Division.

Before the declaration of the freedom of the press in 1789, the bookselling and
printing trades were regulated by an extensive royal code that ensured and en-
forced the monopoly of the book guilds over the printed word (cat. no. 65).

There were signs, however, from early 1789 on that the world of official publishing was beginning to fall apart. Fouquet, the inspector at Caen, requested a leave of absence in January. The Book Guild of Toulouse went into revolt against the central administration. By March the Paris Book Guild was also mobilizing against the royal *règlement* of 1777, which had revoked its hereditary privileges on texts. In April the insubordination of the Toulouse guild became even more strident. By 30 May the inspector in Lyons had ceased to send in his reports, and in June the inspector in Marseille, Marin, resigned his post. Chenu, the inspector at Metz, held fast, but he was forced to concede by early July that he had lost control over the situation. The inspector at St. Malo, Houvin, admitted defeat at the same point. The situation in Nîmes was likewise in total disarray. In La Rochelle the guild began to meet illegally to discuss a pamphlet circulated by the printer Chauvet calling for the abolition of all guilds. The *fermiers généraux* reported the refusal of the printers and publishers of Nantes to abide by royal regulations "on the pretext that the National Assembly has decreed the freedom of the press." Order also broke down in Nancy. By 22 July Thiebault's superior, the director of the book trade, Poitevin de Maissemy, wrote a long letter in his own hand to Villeneuve, the diligent inspector at Toulouse, acknowledging the chaos in Paris and Versailles and his own despair. Within a week, the director himself abandoned ship; then in late July Maissemy's superior, the keeper of the seal, likewise disappeared.[8]

By August of 1789 the entire system of censorship also began to break down. Sélis, professor of eloquence and censor of the *Mercure de France*, wrote on 11 August asking for "clarifications" of his duties. Three weeks after the declaration of the freedom of the press, C.-J. Panckoucke, owner of the *Mercure,* was refusing to pay him. The minister of foreign affairs, however, required Panckoucke to pay the censor's pension, though without submitting to censorship, "until laws concerning the book trade have been definitively enacted." The baron de Dietrich, censor in Strasbourg, was out of work as well. In September the editors of the *Journal Encyclopédique* were refusing to submit to, or to pay, their censor. The report on this affair reveals that censorship of both foreign and domestic journals had broken down completely. The chevalier de Gaigne, censor in Paris, also wrote lamenting the freedom of the press and begging for further employment.

The abbé Gentry, censor of the *Journal d'Orléans,* was told that "under the present circumstances, he could appear to tolerate the conduct of the journalists." Thiebault also began receiving letters from censors renouncing their titles and pensions. The abbé LeRoy, Demeunier, and Béranger asked to be struck from the list of censors in the *Almanach royal* being prepared for the following year. The comte de Kéralio made his views clear in his pamphlets on the freedom of the press. Even the bishop of Boulogne formally renounced his censor's pension before it was suppressed. The censor Bondy, too, rallied to the Revolution. Thus, the publisher Siméon-Prosper Hardy noted cynically in his journal: "He knows how to profit from all the latest events." Conversely, the censor Moreau, "known as a zealous apologist of arbitrary authority and ministerial power," packed his bags and fled Paris.[9]

Thiebault and his assistants held out alone over the course of 1789 and 1790. A new keeper of the seal, Champion de Cicé, was appointed on 5 August. He oversaw the work of Thiebault, who managed to carry on with the aid of a few faithful diehards like Villeneuve in Toulouse, Havras in Rouen, Houvin in St. Malo, Grélier in Nantes, the baron de Dietrich in Strasbourg, and the *fermiers généraux des postes et messageries*. These men continued on through the fall, supervising censors, granting privileges, and policing shipments of printed matter.[10] They were convinced that the "liberté de la presse" could not mean the end to public administration of the book trade, and they awaited the new order, which they expected from the National Assembly as soon as it could attend to the problem of commerce in the world of ideas.

When the National Assembly did finally legislate on the book trade in August 1790, it was to suppress what was by then a mere skeleton.[11] Thiebault's closing report to the keeper of the seal at the end of 1790 states:

> The municipality of Paris reserves for itself all that concerns the book trade in this city, and the other municipalities of the kingdom will doubtless follow this example. It seems likely, moreover, that by a natural extension of the freedom of the press, the nomination of censors will no longer take place. . . . If the municipalities take control of the police for the book trade, they will want to decide for themselves on the number and selection of printers and booksellers. . . . The general administration of the book trade will not continue in all these areas.[12]

The National Administration of the Book Trade had fallen to pieces before his eyes.

The declaration of the freedom of the press and the demise of the office of the book trade, as Thiebault's final report suggests, did not mark an end to public regulation of the printed word. Nor did the Paris Book Guild fall with the Bastille. In fact, its members were quietly holding a meeting to admit a new guild member on 14 July.[13] When the National Assembly

Rôle

de Répartition par Classe de la Capitation du Corps de la Librairie et Imprimerie de Paris, pour l'année 1789, par les Syndic et Adjoints en Charge, et les huit Commissaires ci après dénommés M, en Exécution de l'ordre de M. De Crosne, Lieutenant Général de Police.

Imposants
Messieurs

Syndic — — — Knapen, Imprimeur
Adjoints —
{ Nyon, aîné, Libraire
  Caillau, Imprimeur
  Delalain, aîné, Libraire
  Merigot, jeune, Libraire }

Anciens —
{ M. Didot, jeune, Imprimeur
  Babuty, Libraire
  Sellere (S. franc.) Libraire
  Quillau, Imprimeur }

Modernes —
{ Le Boucher, Libraire
  Stoupe, Imprimeur
  Nyon, Imprimeur
  Delalain, jeune, Libraire }

Première Classe, à 200.

Principal de la capitation	200	
Quatre sols pour livre	40	245
Six deniers pour livre	5	
Deux vingtièmes d'industrie à raison du 9e de la capon	150	165
Quatre sols pour livre du 1er 20e	15	
Milice, à raison du 6e du 9e de la capon	33. 6. 8	

443. 6. 8

M. Panckoucke — — — — 443. 6. 8

Archives de la Chambre syndicale de la librairie et de l'imprimerie de Paris. "Head-Tax Roll for the Paris Book Guild" ("Rôle de repartition par classe de la capitation du corps de la librairie et de l'imprimerie de Paris . . ."). [1789]. Bibliothèque Nationale, Cabinet des Manuscrits.

The Paris Book Guild was in full activity when the Estates General convened in 1789. This register of the tax roll for the guild for 1789 shows the signatures of the guild's officers.

Archives de la Chambre syndicale de la librairie et de l'imprimerie de Paris. Register of the Meetings of the Paris Book Guild. 14 July 1789. Bibliothèque Nationale, Cabinet des Manuscrits.

This entry in the Paris Book Guild's registry of meetings reveals that on 14 July 1789, as the Parisian populace toppled the Bastille, the Paris Book Guild was quietly meeting to admit a new printer into their ranks. The guild continued to meet until 18 March 1791 (cat. no. 60).

abolished all *privilèges* on the night of 4 August, it also acknowledged the need to reform the laws pertaining to the corporations of the *arts et métiers* but then decided to defer the issue. The problem was handed over to the Committee on Public Contributions and would not resurface in the Assembly until February 1791.[14] Thus, despite the declaration of the freedom of the press, the book guilds of France were not formally abolished. The administrative fate of the Paris Book Guild for the next two years had nevertheless been largely determined before the famous proclamation of 4 August.

According to the ultrarevolutionary journal *Révolutions de Paris,* Maissemy, the former director of the book trade, began meeting with the municipal Provisional Committee of the Paris Police in late July 1789 to instruct it "on the most effective means of preventing the circulation of inflammatory pamphlets." The article adds that the meeting "held to the belief that the municipality would be for the conservation of the book guild."[15] In fact, as one of the new representatives of the Commune of Paris during September and October, Maissemy continued to serve both as a consultant to the new keeper of the seal and as a legislator of the new municipal "project to regulate the police."[16]

In early August the suspicions of the *Révolutions de Paris* were vividly confirmed. Sometime during July it was decided that the municipal police would assume the policing and regulation of the printing and publishing industry. On 2 August the Commune decreed that all publications circulating in Paris had to bear the name of the author and printer or bookseller, and had to be registered with the Paris Book Guild, which was to receive a sample copy.[17] This decree, at least formally, allowed the guild to retain its most crucial function—the policing of its monopoly.[18]

The effusive protest of the *Révolutions de Paris* against the decree of 2 August reveals not only the political but also the potential economic ramifications of this decree. The day after the promulgation of the municipal decree, the following statement appeared in the *Révolutions de Paris:* "At the moment in which the freedom of the press has conquered public and personal freedom . . . , the provisional committee has imposed on the book trade an ordinance more encumbering than were all the absurd regulations of the inquisitorial police in force before the Revolution."[19] The journal goes on to argue that this ordinance oppresses: (1) men of letters, because they must have the permission of manufacturers in order to print their works; (2) printers and booksellers, by turning them into censors; and (3) the public, which will be deprived of works that publishers will now hesitate to print.[20] From the journal's perspective, the demise of the book trade office had served only to enhance the power of the Paris Book Guild to control what made its way into print:

Is it possible not to know that the booksellers and the printers are in league against persons of letters, and that this incredible situation compels the latter, at the least, to pay very dearly for printing costs, or to share the proceeds from their works with the booksellers? These are money-making operations, and because the authors need their name, it is quite simple to make them pay to use it.[21]

In effect, in order to have a work approved by the Paris Book Guild it had to bear the name of a printer or bookseller whom the guild was willing to recognize. Thus, in the first battle over the freedom of the press, the Paris Book Guild appears to have emerged victorious. A month after the National Assembly had declared the freedom of the press, the republican *Révolutions de Paris* was calling for: "the retraction of that very strange article of the declaration of the rights of man, where the most blatant ambiguities expose citizens to all kinds of despotic and intolerant harassment."[22]

The officers of the Paris Book Guild saw matters otherwise. They began to protest to the keeper of the seal about the consequences of the press freedoms proclaimed by the National Assembly. On 12 November the guild wrote to solicit "the suppression of printing shops that unqualified individuals have established in Paris."[23] The book trade office counseled them to await legislative action on the part of the National Assembly.[24] When a legislative proposal on the freedom of the press did emerge from the Committee on the Constitution and was presented by Emmanuel Joseph Sieyès to the Assembly on 20 January 1790, it was defeated.[25] Further, the law was silent both on the issue of who had the right to own a printing press and on the status of the Paris Book Guild. This first effort of the National Assembly to set legislative limits for the "freedom of the press" did not bode well for the interests or the future of the Paris Book Guild. Nonetheless, the floundering of the Sieyès proposal brought the guild's members some time to mobilize.

Over the course of 1790 the guild redoubled its efforts to sway the National Assembly. In February the officers paid a visit to the president of the Committee on Agriculture and Commerce. Not finding him in, they left a message and a *mémoire* to plead their case "concerning the multiplying number of printers that set up shop daily in Paris":

We request, sir, that you glance over it and lend all your influence to our demands. From these abuses of the freedom of the press, yet greater abuses have resulted. Countless persons who can barely read have established and maintain shops in every quarter of the capital, hanging over their door their name and the title of Bookseller, which they have no scruple about usurping. We dare to hope, sir, that in light of these details the National Assembly will take the book trade in hand: This corporation has always been excepted from suppressions of guilds, in view of the abuses and thefts as well as the sale of bad books with which France will soon be infected if everyone is free to do business as a bookseller.[26]

The *mémoire* attached to this letter detailed the political dangers and cultural decline that loomed as a potential consequence of the freeing of the press: "It must be realized that those who set up the new printing presses have taken literally those words 'Freedom of the Press,' and that they have taken this to mean freedom of *the presses*. All of France, sirs, is concerned that this freedom of the presses be tempered. You are witnesses to the dangers to which this degenerate liberty in effect today can expose the Nation."[27] The committee registered the *mémoire* and letter in its minutes of 5 March 1790 and then forwarded copies to the Committee on the Constitution.[28]

This appeal did not fall on entirely deaf ears, because the National Assembly was becoming increasingly aware of the range of issues brought to light by the principle of the freedom of the press. The problem could not be reduced to municipal policing of libelous or seditious ephemera, produced locally for local consumption. It was the keeper of the seal who raised the policy problems, writing to the president of the National Assembly's special committee of investigations on 22 June 1790:

> While awaiting, sir, the promulgation of the regulations liable to intervene on printing, I recognize only the former regulations and execute only the dispositions that essentially concern the property rights of authors and printers. It is in accordance with these dispositions that a bundle of books was brought to the book guild and subjected to the inspection of the bookseller-printers. The pamphlet [an attack on the National Assembly included in the bundle] is not in violation, it does not harm anyone's property, and nonetheless the *syndics* have thought it necessary to refer it to me as it is directed against the National Assembly. The packet will not be returned until I have had time to put it in order and I thought I could not take sides without knowing your wishes.[29]

This inquiry raised large questions: How was literary property to be protected? How were the national and international markets in printed matter to be regulated or policed? Who, if anyone, had the right to inspect shipments of printed matter? It also provided evidence of the undeniable fact that the Paris Book Guild performed essential functions by maintaining literary commerce and by protecting the National Assembly from the attacks of its opponents. Over the course of the summer of 1790 the Committee of

..ITALIQUE.

La liberté de la presse et de tout autre moyen de publier ses pensées, ne peut être interdite sus- pendue ni limitée.. Projet de Condorcet.

CARACTERE Sᵗ. AUGUSTIN.

La République Françoise honore la loyauté, le courage, la vieillesse, la piété filiale, le malheur; elle remet le dépôt de sa Constitution à la garde de toutes les vertus...... Tous les hommes naissent et demeurent libres et égaux en droits.

CARĀCT-

PETI.

CANON:

La liberté de la presse et de tout autre moyen de publier ses pensées, ne peut être interdite, suspendue, ni limitée......... *Projet de condorcet.*

"Brochure of Typefaces from the Printing Shop of Guffroy." An IV (1795–96). Archives Nationales, France. The connection between the freedom of the press and the freedom of the *presses* was not lost on the printers of the revolutionary period. Here, a printer celebrates that connection by illustrating his fonts with a quote proclaiming the freedom of the press (cat. no. 3).

Investigations pragmatically solicited the services of the guild to police shipments of books and pamphlets into the capital.[30] The charges in the revolutionary press of a conspiracy among deputies, the municipality, and the guild were very near to the truth.[31]

The committee's response did not resolve the larger questions, but it did inspire new hopes for the guild officers that their services might be rewarded in the anticipated legislation on the book trade. They sent yet another *mémoire* to the National Assembly in September 1790 calling for a full restoration of their privileges.[32] The whole issue finally came to a head in early 1791. Again the keeper of the seal wrote, with even greater eloquence and urgency, to the president of the Committee of Investigations: "I wish to decide only in a constitutional manner and in conformity with the grounds of liberty as the National Assembly meant to establish them. . . . Whose part is it to judge . . . a book, and to order or to have it seized?"[33] He recommended that the committees of Investigation, the Constitution, and Agriculture and Commerce convene to settle the question.[34] The Agriculture and Commerce Committee received the same letter[35] and took the initiative to convene the committee "to propose a law on this matter, which is so important for the book trade and for literature."[36]

The committees finally met in May 1791[37] and proposed shortly thereafter to the National Assembly a formal *projet de loi* "on scientific and literary property."[38] The proposal was not adopted by the Assembly, nor was any law concerning literary property adopted until 1793. There was no mention of the book guild in the *projet* because the Paris Book Guild, along with all other *corporations des arts et métiers,* had in fact been suppressed definitively two months prior to the proposal to give legal definition to literary property and its protection.[39]

Ironically, the law that signed the death warrant of the Paris Book Guild had little to do with guilds or corporations. It was a tax law, sponsored by the Committee on Public Contributions. The law suppressed all corporations and then created a new license tax, *la patente,* which was to be levied on all businesses. The ideology of freedom of commerce was here deployed in the service of state revenues rather than of social, economic, or cultural freedoms: More businesses meant more business taxes.

On 19 July 1793 the National Convention finally passed a decree intended to give a clear legal footing to commercial publishing while endeavoring to prevent the reemergence of publishing monopolies like those enjoyed by the Paris publishers of the Old Regime. This law was drafted for the Convention by none other than the "denouncer of inquisitions" himself, Marie-Joseph Chénier.[40] The "declaration of the rights of genius," as the decree was called in its preamble, guaranteed authors, or those to whom they ceded the work by contract, an exclusive claim upon the publication of

LOI

Portant fuppreffion de tous les droits d'Aides,
fuppreffion de toutes les Maîtrifes & Ju-
randes, & établiffement de Patentes.

Donnée à Paris, le 17 Mars 1791.

LOUIS, par la grâce de Dieu, & par la Loi conftitutionnelle de l'État, ROI DES FRAN-ÇOIS : A tous préfens & à venir ; SALUT.

L'ASSEMBLÉE NATIONALE a décrété, & Nous voulons & ordonnons ce qui fuit :

DECRET DE L'ASSEMBLÉE NATIONA-LE,

du 2 Mars 1791

L'ASSEMBLÉE NATIONALE décréte cé qui fuit:

ARTICLE PREMIER.

A compter du premier avril prochain, les droits connus fous le nom de *droits d'Aides*, perçus par inventaire ou à l'enlèvement, vente ou revente en gros, à la circulation, à la vente en détail fur les boiffons; ceux connus fous le nom d'*impôts & billots & devoirs de Bretagne*, d'*équivalent du Languedoc*, de

"Law [of the National Assembly of 2 March 1791] Suppressing . . . the Guilds and Establishing the Patent Tax." [1791]. The New York Public Library, Rare Books and Manuscripts Division, Talleyrand Collection.

On 2 March 1791 the National Assembly finally abolished the monopoly of the Paris Book Guild, along with the monopolies of all other guilds and corporations (cat. no. 71).

the work for the lifetime of the author plus an additional ten years for heirs and publishers. The decree gave no retroactive protection to former holders of *privilèges en librairie* or *privilèges d'auteur*. With the law of 19 July 1793 the cultural capital of the Old Regime was definitively abolished. All works by authors dead for more than ten years were to enter the public domain.

The law's dispositions regarding claims on new works did not represent a striking break with the Old Regime. Publishers and authors effectively retained the same control they had possessed under the system of royal privileges, except that property rights, unlike privileges, were not renewable or extendable by the king's grace. Although the publishers' hopes for extending their claims were dashed, the heirs of authors saw their previously unlimited claims on the intellectual legacy of the family revoked entirely.[41] The most significant departure in the new legislation was that it contained no stipulations for a centralized administration to regulate or police commercial publishing. The Royal Administration of the Book Trade, which had registered and policed the literary *privilèges* of the Old Regime, was to be replaced merely by a national *dépôt légal* at the Bibliothèque Nationale, where all property claims could be legally registered. Registration of a text, however, was to be a purely *voluntary* means for an individual to establish a legal claim, rather than a requirement enabling the state to regulate or police publications. Consequently, publishers and authors were left to police themselves and one another against pirate editions and to pursue each other retroactively for damages in the courts. No preventive measures existed against pirate editions. Further, the revolutionary government did not revive or replace the system of permissions employed by the Office of the Book Trade to control the number of editions of any given text published at a particular moment. If a work were in the public domain, it could be published freely in any form, at any time, by anyone. Chénier had successfully dismantled all seventeen of his hated "inquisitions."

Between 1789 and 1793 the entire legal and institutional infrastructure of publishing under the Old Regime had collapsed. The challenges to privileges and the declaration of the freedom of the press swept away the monopolies that France's preeminent cultural elites had over the means of producing and disseminating ideas through the printed word, that is, the printing press and bookshops. The members of the old guild also witnessed an irreversible challenge to their exclusive privileges for the publication of the literary inheritance of France. What were the consequences of this collapse of the literary system of the old regime? A descent into the Paris publishing world of the time may offer answers.

The Paris Book Guild registered its last formal meeting on 18 March 1791, for a rectors' procession "in the Church of St. Jacques du Haut Pas."[42]

Thus, the day after the formal suppression of the guild, its members offered their last collective prayers to God. The monumental work of Henri-Jean Martin and others has definitively established the economic "preeminence of the Parisian book trade" in French publishing from the seventeenth through the eighteenth centuries.[43] By royal decree, Parisian printing establishments outnumbered the largest competing provincial establishments in physical plant by more than three to one.[44] Advantageously positioned at the center of national administrative life, police power, and royal patronage, Parisian publishers steadily accumulated monopolies on the most lucrative privileges for the major texts of classical, literary, religious, and legal culture. Paris dominated the field of licit publishing.

Many Parisian establishments were large, specializing in what the French call "grandes éditions"—large, multivolume works.[45] Massive bibliographic studies of the registers of *privilèges* and *permissions* granted by the royal Office of the Book Trade and of officially privileged periodical literature have provided a fairly clear sense of what this system of official publication produced. The picture of literary culture that emerges from the studies of Furet, Estival, and Ehrard and Roger is essentially one of stagnation and steadily consolidated reproduction of the traditional literary inheritance of the seventeenth century.[46]

What was to be the fate of these privileged publishers and printers of Paris after 1789? The major studies of corporations during the revolutionary period, and those pertaining to the Paris Book Guild in particular, have focused primarily on the history of journeymen and on the origins and emergence of working-class associations.[47] How did the old printing and publishing elites of Paris, who specialized in books, respond to the explosion in demand for journals and pamphlets and the opening of a multiplicity of new printing shops between 1789 and 1793? Here is some of their testimony.

The king's printer, Philippe-Denis Pierres, was not a lone voice when he proclaimed in 1790 that his profession was "lost and prostituted." Similar laments echoed both publicly and privately throughout the official Paris publishing world from 1789 through 1793. In August 1789 the printer Jean-Baptiste-Paul Valleyre protested to the Office of the Book Trade that he was being menaced and ruined by a new printer. Louis-François-André Godefroy, a bookseller, wrote to the office as well in September testifying that "our sales are nearly dead." In November Pierre François Gueffier, one of the wealthiest printers of the Paris Book Guild, decried "the decimation of the industry." Debure l'aîné, a publisher from one of the oldest and wealthiest families in the guild testified in December: "I am losing a considerable sum on books." The bookseller Merquignon l'aîné acknowledged "the extreme penury of the business" in the spring of the following year. So, too, the bookseller Jean-Baptiste Gobreau a few months later remarked on "the considerable losses I have taken" and "the current and radical loss of business." Even the richest publisher in Paris, Charles-Joseph Panckoucke, remarked on "the extreme distress in which the book trade finds itself." At the end of 1790 the bookseller Jean-Augustin Grangé presented a collective *mémoire* to the National Assembly on behalf of the printers, publishers, and booksellers of the capital. Here he queried the representatives of the nation: "Shall we today be without means and out of business?"[48]

Laments and testimonies continued over the next several years. The bookseller Langlois fils wrote to the Committee on the Constitution that he had "suffered much in his bookselling business because of losses." In the National Assembly, Deputy Charles de Lameth testified in behalf of a Paris bookseller that, "earning nothing by printing good works," he was being driven to produce incendiary pamphlets. By 1793 Nicolas-Léger Moutard, a printer and the second-wealthiest member of the guild, wrote to a fellow printer and bookseller, Laporte, lamenting "the enormous losses that I have suffered." So, too, Nyon l'aîné, former officer of the Paris Book Guild, testified to the minister of the interior that "our business is totally wiped out." Several months later his brother, Nyon le jeune, was to choose almost identical terms to describe his plight: "From 1789 to this day, my business has been completely demolished."[49]

Were these men and women telling the truth? Or were they merely evoking a picture of financial plight for political and economic purposes, to defend and enhance their monopoly over the printed word? After all, testimony of material duress was almost a required credential of good citizenship during the first years of the Revolution. Further, the statements cited above appeared in somewhat suspect contexts, such as justifications of the modesty of their *contributions patriotiques*,[50] deferrals of payments to creditors,[51] and requests for government subsidies or contracts.[52] That vigilant watchdog of the freedom of the press, *Révolutions de Paris,* was a partisan of this latter interpretation, persistently decrying the Paris Book Guild, its members, and "their scandalous profits."[53] Were the publishing elites of the Old Regime collapsing as a consequence of the freedom of the press? Or were they actually profiting from the explosion in demand for printed matter? The bankruptcy records in the Archives de la Seine (Archives de Paris) offer interesting evidence on this important point.

Between 1789 and 1793 at least twenty-one Paris publishers—that is, booksellers and bookseller-printers—declared themselves in default.[54] At least seventeen of them were members of the Paris Book Guild. More than half of the total number of bankruptcies for this period occurred in 1790. For the Paris Book Guild, 1790 was a year of financial reckoning. As incomplete and as statistically small as these figures are, they nonetheless suggest that publishers declared nearly as many bankruptcies between 1789 and

1793 as there had been for the nineteen-year period from 1770 to 1789.[55] The total liabilities of the twenty-one bankruptcies between 1789 and 1793 ran to more than four million livres.[56] Bankruptcy was not simply a looming possibility within the Paris publishing world. It was a frightening reality (Fig. 1).

The accounts of these bankruptcies reveal that financial interdependence and illiquidity within the publishing world set off a domino-like reaction, transforming a series of discrete crises into collective catastrophe. On 21 January 1789 the publisher Hardy entered the following information in his journal:

> We learn that *Jean Lagrange*, . . . established . . . near the square of the Palais Royal, where he seemed to conduct a thriving business and to have extensive dealings . . . in modern speculations, has just closed up shop and abandoned his establishment . . . to go supposedly to London, leaving in commercial circulation a considerable number of notes all covered with fictional and unreal endorsements, having had the temerity to allow himself to forge the signatures of *four* businessmen . . . , of whom three are his partners: namely Messrs. *Debure-d'Houry*, printer-bookseller, *Durand neveu*, and *Cuchet*, booksellers.[57]

Ironically, this "speculator" in Enlightenment works helped to trigger a crisis within the publishing world of the Old Regime not by conquering markets or reading publics but by abusing his credit and credibility within the old corporate structure.[58]

Within a year Durand and Debure-d'Houry filed for bankruptcy as well.[59] Bankruptcies led to more bankruptcies. The collapse of the maison Debure-d'Houry, the largest creditor of the Paris publishing world, was to have serious consequences. Debure-d'Houry figured in the accounts of nine of the seventeen declarants of bankruptcy within the guild between 1789 and 1793; Durand figured in six. The shock waves reverberated far beyond the fates of those who were forced to file formal declarations: Debure l'aîné lost eight thousand livres in the Durand bankruptcy,[60] and Panckoucke stood to lose thirty thousand livres in just three of these bankruptcies—Debure, Poinçot père, and Savoye.[61] Ninety of the one hundred and sixty-three families of the Paris Book Guild figured in the accounts of the seventeen declarants. And these declarants alone owed at least 800,000 livres to members of the book guild.[62] As the testimony from Toulouse publishers to the Committee on the Constitution suggests, the crisis of 1790 threatened to spread from Paris to the provinces.[63]

Matters would have been even worse had it not been for the intervention of the Crown. In their proceedings for 8 June 1790 the Paris office

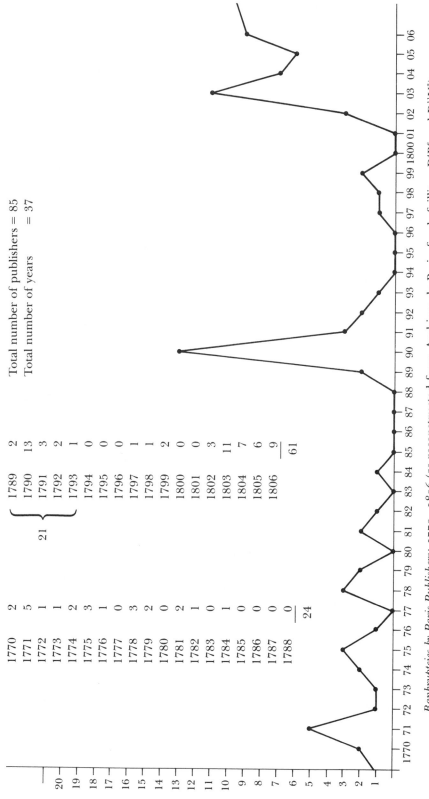

1770	2
1771	5
1772	1
1773	1
1774	2
1775	3
1776	1
1777	0
1778	3
1779	2
1780	0
1781	2
1782	1
1783	0
1784	1
1785	0
1786	0
1787	0
1788	0
	24

1789	2
1790	13
1791	3
1792	2
1793	1
1794	0
1795	0
1796	0
1797	1
1798	1
1799	2
1800	0
1801	0
1802	3
1803	11
1804	7
1805	6
1806	9
	61

21

Total number of publishers = 85
Total number of years   = 37

Bankruptcies by Paris Publishers: 1770–1806 (as reconstructed from Archives de Paris, fonds faillites, D^4B^6 and $D^{11}U^3$)

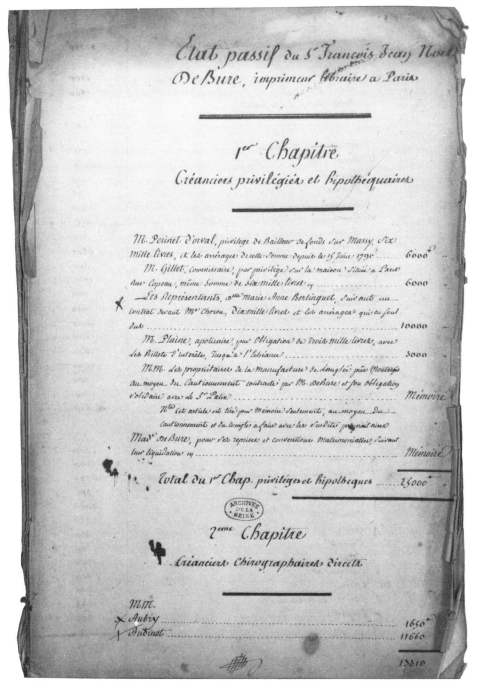

"Declaration of Bankruptcy by Master Debure-d'Houry, Printer-Bookseller in Paris." 26 July 1790. Archives de Paris.

Debure-d'Houry was one of the wealthiest members and creditors of the Paris Book Guild. His bankruptcy in July 1790 would have catastrophic consequences for the publishing elites of the Old Regime. The king himself had to intervene to avert a total financial collapse of the old Paris publishing world (cat. no. 69).

registered receipt of "a memorandum presented by sirs Nyon l'aîné, Didot le jeune, Moutard, Cuchet, Guillot and Huguet, booksellers, printers, engravers, type and paper manufacturers in Paris, containing an exposé on the dangers with which they are threatened by the default of funds in circulation and by the personal bankruptcy of M. Debure-d'Houry, who was the backer for the activity of this business."[64] The office summarized its response in the following manner:

> Considering that the ruin of the six partners would entail that of several thousands of persons, in the capital as well as in the provinces, and that the reaction to this disastrous event could have unheard-of consequences, even for the public weal . . . ; that the shareholders enjoy the most unimpeachable reputations and constitute one of the most important parts of the book trade, . . . [the office] has resolved to send its good officers to procure the access they desire to the National Assembly and the government, in order to acquire an open line of credit for 1,200,000 livres, in bills of exchange endorsed by the six partners. MM. de Joly and de Juissieu have, moreover, been authorized to present themselves to the minister of finance and to do in this matter all that they deem necessary to insure its success.[65]

A series of negotiations ensued over the summer of 1790 among the Paris office, the associated members of the Paris guild, the minister of finance, Jacques Necker, and the king himself.[66] A cache of letters and documents discovered by the revolutionary government after 10 August 1792 in the king's secret *Armoire de fer* revealed that by July the king had decided to subsidize the guild and had made them a personal advance of 150,000 livres.[67] By August the full subsidy of 1,200,000 livres received the stamp of notarial authorization.[68] The king thus succeeded in averting an immediate and total collapse of the old elites of the Paris Book Guild. The monarchy needed their presses and markets. Retaining cultural power was crucial to the fate of the regime. For example, over the rocky course of 1789, it was the head of this partnership, Nyon l'aîné, who faithfully propagated works affirming monarchical authority, such as the *Tableau des droits réels et respectifs du Monarque et de ses sujets.*[69]

The *Révolutions de Paris* was quick to elucidate the broader implications of this royal act of cultural patronage:

> On 4 August, the king stood security for the funds on the civil list for the associated booksellers in the amount of 1,200,000 livres. This act of benevolence is founded on the concern inspired in the king for the fate of these booksellers and the numerous artisans whom they em-

ploy, and who would find themselves without work. . . . The benevolence of his majesty makes a striking contrast with the unjust pursuits of the civil and military leaders of Paris against the press. It is well known that the associated booksellers do not employ a tenth part of the workers who are supported by the enterprises that the freedom of the press has allowed to blossom.[70]

The journal was right. The forces of cultural production were shifting elsewhere, and the Crown, in a desperate effort to maintain control over public opinion and cultural life, was bailing out a dying literary civilization.

Four months after the Crown's subsidy was enacted, the Paris publishing world was still in crisis. In a meeting of 24 December 1790 the Agriculture and Commerce Committee heard a report concerning "a petition from the booksellers of Paris, presented by the municipality, in which they make public how their businesses continue to suffer."[71] The committee responded in much the same fashion as the Crown had. On the same day it decreed the following:

> There shall be entrusted to the municipality of Paris, *assignats* in an amount up to 1,500,000 livres, against the sale of national goods, to be distributed under the direction of the municipal government in various loans to different publishing houses in Paris that demonstrate that, as a consequence of public circumstances, they find themselves unable to meet the terms of their former obligations.[72]

Thus, during the fall of 1790 at least 2,700,000 livres poured from royal and national coffers to the aid of the foundering cultural elites of the Old Regime. But the National Assembly had thrown good money after bad.

The *Révolutions de Paris* correctly linked the crisis within the Paris Book Guild to the declaration of the freedom of the press and the revolutionary mandate to "spread enlightenment." The crisis within the guild was not, in origin, a fiscal crisis. The source of the problem lay in the allegiance of many prominent members of the guild to a system of cultural production and a literary civilization that were both rapidly becoming obsolete. The economic crisis in the guild was a symptom of cultural revolution.

The bookdealers of Paris lamented in their petition to the committee that "the Revolution completely obliterated the value of the major books that they stocked in their shops, of the costliest articles, and of those whose sale formerly was the most assured."[73] Within a few years the Revolution had swept their way of life and the culture it produced into the past. The stock of the most prominent publishers of Paris—spiritual, legal, pedagogical, and historical—lost its commercial value as *nouveautés* and *lumières* flooded the capital. Thus, Debure l'aîné declared in December 1789: "I am losing considerable sums on works of jurisprudence."[74] So, too, Antoine Maugard listed in his declaration of bankruptcy on 26 June 1790: "Works whose sale has been suspended by circumstances: *Code de la Noblesse, Remarques sur la Noblesse, Lettres sur les dangers des abrégés des lois.*"[75] Petit and Despilly, publishers of liturgies, wrote to the National Assembly in January 1791 to protest the ruin of six hundred families that would result from the division of France into departments, the consequent suppression of sixty-two bishoprics, and the proposal to standardize the liturgy of those remaining. They stood to see their privileges on the extant liturgies evaporate into thin air: "twelve to fifteen million in commercial value . . . will be lost."[76] Nyon le jeune protested as well:

> Citizen-legislators, from 1789 until this day, my business has been completely wiped out by the suppression of the religious houses charged with education, by the inactivity of the colleges; elementary books for classes and for religious use which composed almost the whole of my stock are a total loss. . . . I can estimate the nonvalue of my classical books at 60 thousand livres . . . as they are no longer in use.[77]

The classical, legal, and religious culture of the Old Regime had ceased to reproduce itself.

The elites of Old Regime cultural commerce were driven under, together with the culture they produced. Between 1789 and 1793 eighteen members of the guild were forced into bankruptcy. Another twenty-two gave evidence of being on the verge of default. These were not establishments on the margins of Old Regime publishing but those at its very heart: the Debures, Nyons, Moutards, and Merquignons. The king's printer, Philippe-Denis Pierres, sold his printing shop in 1792 and was to die an employee of the postal service in Dijon in 1808.[78] His former rival, the director of the Imprimerie Royale, Etienne-Alexandre-Jacques Anisson-Duperron, saw his monopoly on royal publications eclipsed by the new printer of the National Assembly, François-Jean Baudouin.[79] Anisson-Duperron was to fall under the blade of the guillotine in 1793.[80] By the Year III (1794) Debure l'aîné was working as an employee of the Temporary Commission on the Arts, cataloguing the libraries confiscated from émigrés.[81] Knapen fils, the son of the last *syndic* of the Paris Book Guild, left the publishing business and went to work as a functionary in the Ministry of the Interior.[82] Those who held out would be faced with the task of remaking themselves and their enterprises as the Revolution remade the literary world. What shape was this new world to take?

As the old world of official publishing folded under, the illicit subculture of Enlightenment publishing, which had evolved over the course of the century, surfaced into the light of day from prisons, back alleys, and obscure suburbs and crossed foreign borders to open shop in Paris, its spiritual home. Beaumarchais wrote from Kehl to the office on 16 January 1790 that he intended to "faire transporter à Paris son Imprimerie de Kehl."[83] Thus, Voltaire was to reenter Paris, yet again victorious, this time in spirit only, on printing presses shuttled across the border in carts. The printers of Avignon, too, began to relocate over the borders.[84] Treuttel and Würtz, the Strasbourg dealers in illicit works, announced their intention, because of the "freedom of the press," to set up two printing shops in Strasbourg.[85] Rousseau's *Oeuvres*, produced by the Société typographique de Genève, by 1789 bore the name of Poinçot, and Paris was given as the place of publication on the title page.[86] Panckoucke, too, in the same year brought the whole publishing operation of the *Encyclopédie* back to the city where it had first appeared underground.[87] The publisher Claude Poinçot appealed to the Commune of Paris for the restitution of his editions of the abbé Raynal's *Histoire philosophique* and Rousseau's *Confessions*, which had been released from the Bastille as it fell.[88] Paris, once the crowning jewel of absolutist publishing, was rapidly becoming the center from which to "spread light in every direction."[89]

Furthermore, as the old elites were being driven under, a new generation jumped at the opportunities that emerged from the declaration of the freedom of the press to become the thirty-seventh, thirty-eighth, or thirty-ninth printer of Paris. Such was the case with Pierre LeRoy, bookdealer, who wrote in with his request to the keeper of the seal on 20 October 1789. He was followed by Valade, bookdealer, on 15 November; Jean-Baptiste-Nicolas Crapart, bookdealer, on 12 December; and Jacques-Denis Langlois, bookdealer, on 19 January 1790. They were soon followed by two other minor bookdealers of the Paris Book Guild, Martin Sylvestre Boulard, author and printer of the *Manuel de l'imprimeur* (1791), and Antoine-François Momoro, who was to leave his mark on Parisian revolutionary politics. To these can be added Plassan, Gillé fils, Mérigot l'aîné, Guillaume le jeune, Cussac, Belin, Colas, and DeHansy. Many of the new printers of Paris were booksellers from the lower ranks of the old guild. Printers also came forth— like Dentu, Chambon, and LeNormant—from the ranks of workers in the old printing shops who now, thanks to the abolition of the guild, went into business for themselves.[90] But actually how many presses existed in Paris when the press was freed? We know that 1789 marked a boom in the production of ephemeral and periodical literature.[91] Yet exactly how big an explosion was it? What was its extent, character, and duration? What were the new material dimensions of the printing, publishing, and bookselling world?

Paul Delalain's copiously researched register of printers and booksellers in revolutionary Paris, combined with the statistical data provided by the Napoleonic surveys of Paris printing and publishing establishments in 1810, makes it possible to arrive at a fairly accurate estimate of the number of printers and booksellers/publishers in Paris between 1788 and 1813. These two sources also allow us to date the founding of each new establishment.[92] Over the twenty-six-year period, 1788–1813, approximately 1,224 printing, publishing, and bookselling establishments were active in Paris: 337 printing houses and 887 booksellers/publishers. On the eve of the Revolution, there were approximately 47 printers and 179 booksellers/publishers (totaling 226) in Paris. In 1810, prior to the limiting of the number of printers to 80, there were 157 printing shops and around 588 booksellers/publishers. These figures are significantly more modest than the "four hundred printing shops" frequently invoked in contemporary testimony.[93] Nonetheless, over the course of the Revolution, the number of printers active at any given moment had nearly quadrupled, and the number of booksellers and/or publishers nearly tripled. Even after the Napoleonic decrees limiting the number of printers, the size of the Paris printing world had doubled. These figures, then, as conservative as they are, still disclose an unprecedented expansion and democratization of the productive power and the sites of distribution of the printed word in the capital.

Major changes of regimes (1789–91, 1796, and 1804) ushered in new generations of printing and bookselling establishments. It is not surprising that these political upheavals would be accompanied by spasmodic increases in the production and consumption of printed matter. More interesting, however, is that the new world of printing and publishing was forged during the periods of the constitutional monarchy and the Directory in particular. If we isolate the establishments founded in the boom periods 1789–91 and 1796–98 respectively, it becomes apparent that a significantly higher proportion of the new establishments of the earlier period were printing shops (40 printers, 55 booksellers/publishers: 1789–91), and that the reverse is true for the later period (32 printers, 74 booksellers/publishers: 1796–98). These figures suggest that while the early period was characterized by an expansion of the printing industry, the later period was marked rather by an expansion of publishing. This last point raises an important question. What poured forth from the freed presses?

The expansion of printing shops in the early period corresponds neatly to the dramatic expansion of the periodical press and ephemeral publications. The most distinguishing feature of the printed word in the period between 1789 and 1791 was the explosion in the number of journals. The number of journals produced in Paris skyrocketed from 4 in 1788 to 184 in 1789, and 335 in 1790, settling at 236 in 1791. In contrast, from the Year II

(1793–94) to the Year III (1794–95) the numbers jumped only from 106 to 137, and declined in the Year IV (1795–96) to 105, hovering in the Year V (1796–97) at 190, and declining again in the Year VI (1797–98) to 115.[94] Thus, in comparison with the explosion of 1789–91, the renewed expansion of journal production after Thermidor is but a minor tremor.[95] The production of journals, as Jacques Godechot has observed, required many more presses because they served extensive, rather than intensive, markets.[96] The printing shops emerged to meet this demand.

Even more interesting, the printing shops founded in this early period survived through the course of the Revolution and the Empire. Thus, if we examine the eighty printing shops selected to be retained by the Napoleonic administration on the basis of their scale, wealth, and financial stability, we discover that twenty-one were members of the old guild, thirty-five were founded in the period 1789–93, nine in the period 1795–99, and fifteen between 1800 and 1810. That is, almost *half* of the printing shops of 1811 were founded during the constitutional monarchy.[97] Further, if we break down the eighty richest printers of 1811 by specialization, which is possible for sixty-four of the 80, we emerge with the following picture: journals and periodicals, 19; administration, 12; literature, belles-lettres, *nouveautés,* 11; classical works, 4; theater, 3; religion, 3; foreign languages, 3; sciences, medicine, agriculture, 2; arts, 2; almanacs, 2; ephemera, 2; law, 1.[98] Periodical publications, even more than administrative jobs, were the bread and butter of the new printing world. It was not just Old Regime publishers like Panckoucke, Ballard, Colas, or Demonville who shifted with the winds of revolutionary literary culture toward periodicals and came out on top.[99] The largest group of successful printers were new. They had made their fortunes from the revolutionary periodical press. Thus, the Napoleonic inspector who wrote up the "notes" on the eighty printers of Paris recorded a whole new generation of wealthy printers: Chaignieau l'aîné, "rich from his *Courrier universel*"; Agasse, "Printer of the *Moniteur,* . . . shareholder and editor at 3000 *livres*"; Lenormant, "former worker *parvenu* whom one could always reproach for having printed pamphlets. But the presses of the *Journal de l'Empire* have corrected him of that"; or Prudhomme, "rich, *Révolutions de Paris,* a bad lot."[100] The association of the freedom of the press with both "the presses" and newspapers (*la presse*) is not merely a phonetic coincidence or a clever play on words, it is a historical reality. More important, it suggests that commercial success during the revolutionary period resided in periodical and ephemeral literature rather than in books.

French commercial book publishing, especially the large-scale, multivolume enterprises in which the Paris Book Guild had specialized, floundered as a consequence of the dramatic deregulation of their commerce.

Ironically, in limiting private claims on texts so severely and in abolishing any centralized administration of the book trade, the liberated texts lost their commercial value. The lack of any preventive measures against pirate editions and the exclusive reliance on municipal authorities and civil courts proved wholly inadequate in the face of the cutthroat competition over limited, elite markets.[101] The duration of exclusive claims on texts was so short that the value of works had diminished to the profits from one or possibly two editions. For multivolume works, ten years was totally insufficient for the production and distribution of even a single edition. Finally, the works to which the Convention had been most concerned to ensure public access—that is, the classics of French literary civilization in the public domain—were rendered commercially worthless. Without the insurance of exclusive claims, at least on an edition, the risks and realities of being undercut by a second or even a third competitive edition of the same work drove publishers away from the classics into *nouveautés*, journals, and ephemera such as pamphlets and almanacs.

Despite the "declaration of the rights of genius," massive deregulation combined with the wartime collapse of domestic and international markets to bring book publishing to a near standstill in the Year II (1793–94). The *dépôt légal,* founded to administer the new laws on literary property, registered only seventy-three works in the first five months of operation (21 July–31 December 1793).[102] Many of these works were not even new titles from the year 1793, but rather editions dating back to 1791. Robert Estivals, the most noted bibliographer of the period, considered the entries at the *dépôt* for 1793 statistically so insignificant that he chose not to include them in his table for the revolutionary period.[103] In the entire Year II (22 September 1793–22 September 1794), the *dépôt* recorded receipt of barely three hundred titles. Moreover, very few of the works registered in the first fourteen months of the *dépôt*'s existence were actually book length.[104] They were mostly plays, songs, and pamphlets of an educational or political nature.

Under the Directory, especially after 1796, book publishing begins to show some signs of a revival. The statistics for book publications registered at the *dépôt légal* give evidence of this trend. The number of new titles registered, after a steady decline from 1789, began to turn upward from 240 in 1796 to 345 in 1797, 475 in 1798, and 815 in 1799.[105] Further, Martin, Mylne, and Frautschi show in their extraordinary *Bibliographie du genre romanesque français* that after a dramatic drop in production from 1789 to 1795, the publication of novels in France began to increase in 1796, peaking in 1799.[106] Jean Dhombres's study of scientific publications shows similar trends.[107] The figures thus suggest a new infusion of capital into book publishing during the Directory.

Peace and the reopening of international markets no doubt played a role in this reversal. Moreover, between 1794 and 1796 the government, through the Commission of Public Instruction, injected literally millions of livres in the form of subsidies, prizes, and public credits to "encourage" the publication of books of scientific and educational value.[108] Although a systematic study of the cultural patronage of the Commission of Public Instruction remains to be done, the following contours may be suggested. Smits and Maradan, bookdealers in Paris, were commissioned for fifteen thousand copies of the *Dictionnaire de l'Académie*. The printer Haubout brought out an edition of the *Histoire romaine* with assistance. Stoupe and Servière, printer and publisher in Paris, brought out an edition of Voltaire's *Oeuvres complètes*. The commission investigated newly discovered manuscripts of Rousseau's *Contrat social*. Poinçot fils embarked on an edition of Rousseau's *Confessions*. The commission purchased three thousand copies of Condorcet's *Esquisse d'un tableau historique des progrès de l'esprit humain* from Agasse, bookdealer in Paris, to be distributed "throughout the Republic and in a way that will be most useful for instruction." They purchased collections of laws from the publisher Rondonneau. They especially patronized publishers of scientific works.[109] For example, the important Batillot and Houet editions of Condillac's *Oeuvres* (Year VII [1799–1800]) and *Langue des calculs* (Year VI [1798–99]) would probably never have appeared without government assistance, and even then these editions suffered from continuous financial difficulties.[110]

Yet it was not just classical, scientific, and Enlightenment books that the government encouraged. True to the commission's vision of a mass literary culture, it subsidized numerous educational, scientific, and political journals such as the *Décade philosophique et littéraire*, the *Feuille du cultivateur*, the *Feuille villageoise*, the *Journal des mines*, or the *Républicain français*. It subsidized and distributed educational pamphlets as well. Nor did they overlook efforts to win a popular female reading public over to the Thermidoran regime, like the Citoyenne Bodesère's *Le triomphe de la saine philosophie, ou la vraie politique des femmes*.[111]

A whole new generation of printers and publishers emerged as a consequence of the new climate and patronage of the Directory. Some, like Dugour and Durand, "dealers in works of education, the sciences and arts" (1796), bought out withering old guild establishments like Cuchet's. So, too, Egron bought out Veuve Valade (1798) and Genets l'aîné took over Servière's business (1799). Others went into association with old enterprises, like Ballio with Colas (1796) or Legras and Cordier (1797). Then, there were those who founded new houses, like Bernard, "Printer-bookseller for mathematics, the sciences and arts" (1797); Marchand, "Printer-bookseller for agriculture" (1798); Huzard, "Printer-bookseller for agricultural and veterinary works" (1798); or Duprat, "Bookseller for mathematics" (1797).[112] As

Jean Dhombres demonstrates elsewhere in this volume, scientific works contributed no small part to the revival of the publishing world.

Despite these signs of revival, commercial book publishing continued to flounder. Even with the restoration of peace and significant government subsidies, book publishing remained too deregulated to become financially sound. Without guaranteed subscriptions or subsidies, cutthroat competition, rampant pirating, and, most important, the unregulated competition of different editions of the same work made all but periodical and ephemeral publishing commercially risky if not impossible. Publishers offered eloquent testimony to the Napoleonic authorities of the inadequacies of the law of 1793: "In 1793, the new law regulating us struck at the foundations of literary property. From it resulted the collapse of the major houses, a universal disorder. Immorality succeeded ancient good faith."[113] So, too, the major Lyon publisher Bruysset wrote: "Among the books that became common property, it may come about . . . that four or five editions of the same book are printed at the same time in the same city and enter into an unexpected competition with one another, harmful to each one of the entrepreneurs."[114] As the continued bankruptcies after 1799 suggest (see Fig. 1), evidence and examples could be multiplied. The Revolution had rendered the press *too free* to make commercial book publishing viable. It was not until 1810, with the revival of the National Administration of the Book Trade and its army of inspectors, that book-length classics would again receive the police protection necessary to ensure their commercial success.

To return to our original question, what did the freedom of the press actually mean in practice? Some answers may now be offered. The call for the freedom of the press was more than a plea for an end to censorship; it was an assault on the entire literary system of the Old Regime—the laws, institutions, and practices that regulated writing, printing, and publishing. Between 1789 and 1793 this entire system collapsed or was destroyed by the revolutionary effort to free authors, presses, book publishers, and even the texts themselves from the constraints of the old system. As a consequence, the entire cultural capital of the Old Regime, as embodied in literary *privilèges*, evaporated almost overnight. The preeminent publishing elites of Paris were driven under together with the literary culture they produced. It was not simply that the texts they produced lost their value in face of the revolutionary demand for Enlightenment, but rather that the institutions that had ensured the cultural monopoly of those texts no longer existed.

The most significant, and at least partly unintended, consequence of the destruction of the literary system of the Old Regime was that it precipitated a temporary collapse of the civilization of "the book" itself. The Revolution challenged the cultural dominance of the most treasured literary form of the early modern period: the printed book. In face of the massive de-regulation of the publishing world between 1789 and 1793 book publishing was eclipsed by the production of journals, newspapers, and other forms of ephemeral literature such as almanacs, pamphlets, and songsheets. These new literary forms were to dominate the commerce of the new printing and publishing fortunes of the revolutionary period. The French Revolution was a cultural revolution not only because it liberated Enlightenment thought from the police of the Old Regime but also because it transformed the "Enlightenment" from a body of thought into a new set of cultural practices based on the freest and most extensive possible public exchange of ideas. The periodical and ephemeral press, rather than the book, best served this end. As the revolutionary journalist J. P. Brissot wrote in his memoirs: "It was necessary to enlighten ceaselessly the minds of the people, not through voluminous and well-reasoned works, because people do not read them, but through little works, . . . through a journal which would spread light in every direction." [115]

The freeing of the press and the consequent deregulation of printing and publishing led to an unprecedented democratization of the printed word. The number of printing and publishing establishments in Paris easily tripled during the revolutionary period, allowing much broader social ini-tiative and participation in the production of the printed word and, conse-quently, in the public exchange of ideas. Not surprisingly, the literary forms created by the freed presses were more democratic as well. Ephem-eral publishing was less capital-intensive than book production, and its suc-cess depended upon extensive, rather than intensive, markets. These liter-ary forms were for (and often by) people with little money to spend and little leisure time to read. This is not to suggest that there was no popular literary culture prior to the French Revolution. But with the declaration of the freedom of the press and the collapse of the literary institutions of the Old Regime, the center of gravity in commercial publishing shifted percep-tibly from the elite civilization of "the book" to the democratic culture of the pamphlet and the periodical press.

PRINTERS AND MUNICIPAL POLITICS

PIERRE CASSELLE

ALTHOUGH HE REMAINED a shadowy figure during the Revolution and has now disappeared from its historical accounts, the municipal printer of Paris occupied a strategic position in revolutionary politics. He served as a link between the government and the governed. And because that connection proved to be crucial to the revolutionaries' notion of legitimacy, he operated at the nodal point where governments were made and unmade.

Paris had had its official printers under the Old Regime. The Prévôt des Marchands, lieutenant-general of police, parlement, and intendant all communicated with the 600,000 subjects of the city by printed ordinances and posters. But when the Parisians swept away the old authorities and created a new municipality, they transformed themselves from subjects into citizens. No longer content to be notified of the government's decisions, they now expected to follow its deliberations and to call their representatives to account. In fact, they distrusted the notion of representation itself. But because they could not assemble as a gigantic town meeting, they insisted on more and more information, enough to know of every move made in the Hôtel de Ville and to keep its printer busy—for the only way to maintain the flow of communication was by means of the press. A mountain of printed matter in the archives testifies to the authorities' concern to stay in touch with the citizenry. At the bottom of almost every sheet one can find the name of the municipal printer, the man who made the system work. He remains little more than a name, however, because his activities have been buried under all the documents he produced. By excavating what survives of the record of his career, one can attempt to understand something of the Revolution as a revolution in communications.

Since the beginning of the seventeenth century, the municipal authorities had employed an official printer of the city for the publication of their ordinances.[1] On the eve of the Revolution, that title was shared by two cousins, Augustin-Martin Lottin, known as Lottin l'aîné, and Jean-Roch Lottin, known as Lottin de Saint-Germain. The former was born on 8 August 1726 and was received in the guild as a bookseller in 1746 and in 1752 as a printer. He became printer of the city in 1768. By then he had also become attached to the future Louis XVI, whom he instructed in the art of printing, and served as printer-bookseller from 1760 onward.

Augustin-Martin owed his reputation to his literary and historical writing rather than to his work as a printer. He wrote a great deal, especially on the history of printing, but he neglected his business so badly that on 28 February 1783 he had to declare bankruptcy. His balance sheet showed 320,000 livres in debts against 226,000 livres in assets. But he managed to patch the business together by forming a partnership with his cousin, Jean-Roch, who was born in 1754 and had worked under him as an apprentice. In 1788 the Lottins left their shop in the rue Saint-Jacques and moved to 27, rue Saint-André-des-Arts. They worked there through the Revolution, the names Lottin l'aîné and Lottin de Saint-Germain appearing together on all official publications of the municipality until the summer of 1792. Lottin l'aîné died on 6 June 1793.

The lists compiled by Maurice Tourneux and by André Martin and Gérard Walter[2] permit us to form an idea of the municipal documents published after 1789. Before the opening of the Estates General, the Lottins printed all the documents of the Third Estate, while the printers Claude Simon and Jean-Charles Desaint worked for the clergy and the nobility. On 13 July Lottin printed his first official "revolutionary" document, defining the function of the Permanent Committee of the Hôtel de Ville, which at that time was still under the presidency of the Prévôt des Marchands.[3]

On 7 August the Assembly of the Representatives of the Paris Commune, following the example of the Constituent Assembly, named a committee responsible for the editing of its proceedings and for their printing and publication. The intent to keep the public informed was entirely new, for under the Old Regime the handwritten deliberations of the municipal authorities were never made known to the public. The only texts to appear in print were edicts published as handbills or posters, but they were never collected in book form.[4] The proceedings of the Municipal Assembly's meetings were published from 1789 to 1791 and covered the sessions from 25 July 1789 to 8 October 1790. The Lottins, of course, were commissioned to print these official reports, of which only a few copies remain. In October 1790 they printed a summary, written by Jacques Godard under the title *Report on the Proceedings of the General Assembly of the Representatives* and published at the expense of the representatives themselves, who each paid nine livres. "It sets a good example," the rapporteur wrote, "when civil

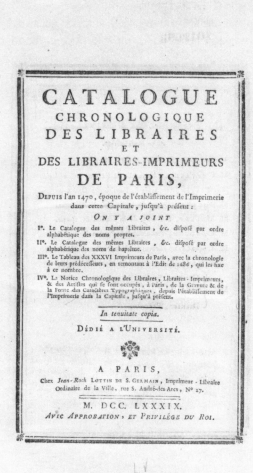

Augustin-Martin Lottin. "Chronological Catalogue of the Booksellers and Book-seller-Printers of Paris." 1789. The New York Public Library, Rare Books and Manuscripts Division.

Lottin's monumental treatise on the history of printing and publishing trades in Paris is one of the most important sources for the study of printing under the Old Regime (cat. no. 76).

servants, not satisfied to let their actions speak for themselves, also record their ideas and principles, so that they may be known to their constituents under any circumstances."[5]

The goodwill of the municipal printer was often sorely tried. In July 1790 Lottin, who was legitimately demanding payment for his printing of the proceedings, received only thanks for the zeal he had shown and was encouraged to speed up his work as much as possible. Sometimes, in order to meet the demands of the municipality, he had to keep his presses running at night.[6] Besides the printing of these important publications and of special documents such as the *Proceedings of the Confederation of the French in Paris,* on 14 July 1790, the Lottins also had to print a great number of notices, decrees, excerpts of proceedings, reports, and so forth, as well as forms and letterheads used by different municipal administrative services.

We do not know the details of the other printing jobs that provided Lottin with a regular income because of the ever-growing needs of the municipal administration that intervened more and more in Parisian life. We have only two figures, which give the total amount of money paid by the city to its printers during the first years of the Revolution:[7] from July 1789 to October 1790—84,000 livres; from July 1789 to January 1791—103,595 livres.

The insurrection of 10 August 1792 brought a temporary end to Lottin's appointment. Although his workmen had made a gift of 120 livres to the war effort on 20 May, Lottin was branded unpatriotic, and the insurgent Commune withdrew his commission on 11 August. The next day, without a dissenting voice, it named Charles-Frobert Patris to replace Lottin, and Patris was authorized to move two of his presses to the Hôtel de Ville.[8]

This nomination was obviously political, because the Commune had chosen a militant revolutionary rather than an experienced printer. Patris, born at Troyes in 1752 or 1753, was a master in a boarding school in 1789. He lived in the Place de l'Estrapade and had taken an active and enthusiastic part in the Revolution from the time of the election to the Estates General. "I loved the Revolution," he said, "I wanted it and predicted it a long time before it happened. Therefore it's not astonishing that I embraced it with fervor and supported it with courage. From the first day of the Revolution I had pledged to overthrow tyranny or to perish rather than witness its triumph."[9] In fact, Patris's revolutionary activities, insofar as one can trace them through the archives, look like a perfect case of sans-culotte careerism.

In April 1789 he was named elector of the Val-de-Grâce district. On 15 July the permanent committee of the Hôtel de Ville chose him and three other electors to bring a resolution to the National Assembly in Versailles. During the month of July 1789 he had also assumed the responsibility of supervising Paris's food supply. As testimony to his patriotism, he claimed that he had paid all his expenses for travel and lodging without reimbursement from the municipality.[10] He also encouraged his students to appear before the National Assembly on 6 February 1790 and to donate the 245 livres they had collected, along with the silver buckles of their shoes, for the good of the country.[11] When the National Guard was created in Paris, Patris was elected commander of the Val-de-Grâce battalion and, as such, took part in the march on Versailles on 5 October 1789, which brought about the return of the royal family to Paris.

He had long been an opponent of General Gilbert de La Fayette. In the name of his battalion, he drafted a letter to protest the general's role in the repression of the mutiny of the Swiss regiment of Chateauvieux at Nancy in August 1790. This document was chosen by L.-M. Prudhomme in his *Révolutions de Paris* as a model for the Parisian battalions. When the royal family fled to Varennes in June 1791, Patris expressed his violent indignation during the meetings of his Observatoire section. He took an active part in the writing and propagation of the petition demanding the deposition of Louis XVI and was among the petitioners fired on at the Champs de Mars massacre of 17 July.[12]

On 20 February 1792 Patris was elected a city official. Having taken up printing by then, he used his position to establish connections with the new members of the municipality who were hostile to the monarchy. Perhaps he was already planning to supplant Lottin as municipal printer.[13] If so, his plans received a setback on 9 May, when he was expelled from the Jacobin Club, of which he had been a member since 1790. An obscure disagreement with Camille Desmoulins about the printing of an issue of the *Tribune des Patriotes* that he had undertaken jointly with A.-F. Momoro resulted, after noisy debates, in his dismissal.[14]

Patris, nevertheless, could not be easily kept away from the political struggle; he was deeply involved in the demonstration of 20 June 1792, when he encouraged the National Guard to let the crowd invade the Tuileries. When at last the mayor of Paris, Jérome Pétion, reached the king, he found him wearing the revolutionary red cap and surrounded by officers of the National Guard, a few representatives, and three municipal officials, one of whom was Patris.[15]

The insurrection that overthrew the monarchy on 10 August gave Patris the opportunity to be rewarded at last for his political zeal. From then on the official publications of the Paris Commune would be labeled "From the press of C.-F. Patris, printer to the Commune, rue du Faubourg Saint-Jacques, aux Dames de Sainte Marie." Married, and the father of a twelve-year-old son, he was given a house on the rue de l'Observatoire by a decree of the Commune, the estimated rent of which was 9,200 livres and in which

"A.F.M. Momoro, First Printer of National Liberty." N.d. Engraved portrait. Musée de la Révolution Française, Vizille, France.

Momoro was one of the most militant new printers in Paris. He was guillotined by the revolutionary government as an agitator in the Year II (1793–94) (cat. no. 59).

he offered a lodging to Pierre-Gaspard Chaumette, the public prosecutor of the Commune.[16]

Patris sold his share in the boarding school in order to devote himself entirely to his new enterprise and made some important investments. Around 1793 he complained in a note found later among Chaumette's papers that his profit fell far short of the expenses he had incurred in support of the Revolution. He was also outraged that Lottin, who had been dismissed for negligence and lack of patriotism, could still compete with him for jobs commissioned by the municipal administration. He claimed that he had fifteen presses in good order and enough type to operate fifty, yet the Commune never gave him enough work to occupy more than four presses, sometimes not more than one or two. Why, he wondered, had the municipal Bureau of Public Property and Finance never employed him, and why had the Bureau of Taxation, one of the industry's most important sources of patronage, given all its work to Lottin?[17]

Patris claimed the monopoly that the municipal printers had enjoyed under the Old Regime. He argued that he had to produce all the forms used by the municipal administration in order to keep his business operating at a profit; one should not forget that since the establishment of the Commune in October 1790 the minutes of the meetings at the Hôtel de Ville had ceased to be printed. Furthermore, Patris had not been commissioned to print the *Affiche de la Commune,* which appeared between June 1793 and February 1794.[18] The municipality clearly did not provide enough work for a printing shop that in the spring of 1794 employed forty or fifty workers. Patris had to find markets elsewhere. On 20 August and 11 September 1792, the National Assembly commissioned him to print *assignats* of twenty-five and ten livres, at fifteen livres per ream. He also won the commission for all the printing for the navy, thanks to the intervention of Jean-Nicolas Pache, the mayor of Paris, with Gaspard Monge, the naval minister.[19]

Municipal printing in the midst of a revolution required that the printer be ready to handle emergency jobs at any time. While the Girondists were under siege in the Convention on 31 May 1793, Patris "had to work until 2 A.M.," he said, "in spite of the fact that I was sick in bed and under medication; and at that point the Secretary of the Commune sent word that I myself had to supervise the prompt delivery of the different decrees voted by the People's Commission jointly with the Commune. The decrees came out so fast, one after the other, that in spite of my illness I had to spend two nights working without sleep."[20]

Patris was twice the victim of police measures taken by the revolutionary government. On 20 September 1793, three days after the promulgation of the draconian law of suspects, he was arrested, following a report by Richard Poiret—a member of the vigilance committee of the Observatoire section

1. "Freedom of the Press." 1797. Color engraving. Bibliothèque Nationale, Cabinet des Estampes.
With the declaration of the freedom of the press, a mania to produce and consume the printed word swept across France (cat. no. 23).

2. "Plan and Exact Representation of Bourbon Hall at the Louvre, Where the Estates General Met in 1614 . . . to Give an Idea of What Should Occur in the Hall at Versailles, Where the Estates General Will Meet in 1789." The New York Public Library, Rare Books and Manuscripts Division, Talleyrand Collection.

Printing, both images and texts, played a key role in mobilizing the various sectors of French society for the convocation of the Estates General in 1789 (cat. no. 35).

3. Stone from the Bastille, executed under the direction of P.-F. Palloy, with a color aquatint of a "Plan of the Bastille," by J.-B. Chapuy after Palloy. 1790. Musée de la Révolution Française, Vizille, France.

The presses were also crucial in transmitting and memorializing the extraordinary events in Paris, especially the fall of the Bastille, through a vast array of printed forms (cat. no. 43).

4. Raymond-Augustin Vieilh de Varennes. "Complete Collection of the Flags of the Parisian National Army." [1790?]. Color engravings. The New York Public Library, Spencer Collection.

Like the storming of the Bastille, the formation of the national revolutionary army was one of the most popular sources for imagery of the heroic people and was a crucial means for inspiring support for the Revolution among ordinary people. Shown here are the flags from the battalions of the sections St-Eustache, Bonne-Nouvelle, St-Louis-en-l'Isle, and Carmes-Déchaussés (cat. no. 44).

5. "A Newspaper Vendor." 1791. Color engraving by Philibert-Louis Debucourt. Bibliothèque Nationale, Cabinet des Estampes.

One of the most immediate and important consequences of the collapse of the institutions that policed the printed word under the Old Regime was the explosion in the production of newspapers. With the declaration of the freedom of the press, "the news," for the first time, became a part of everyday life (cat. no. 57).

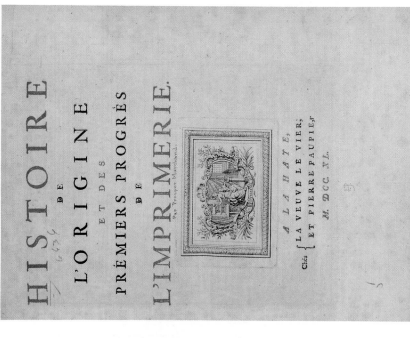

6. Prosper Marchand. "History of the Origin and First Advances of Printing." 1740. The New York Public Library, General Research Division.

Under the Old Regime, the printing press was celebrated as a gift "descending from the heavens," which would spread enlightenment through a benighted world (cat. no. 78).

7. The Isaiah Thomas Printing Press. 1747. American Antiquarian Society, Worcester, Massachusetts.

The Isaiah Thomas printing press is one of the very few remaining examples of a typical eighteenth-century two-strike commercial press (cat. no. 48).

8. Clandestine Press. Eighteenth century. Musée de l'Imprimerie et de la Banque, Lyon, France (photo: Studio Dussouillez, Rutter).

This small eighteenth-century "clandestine press" was designed to be stowed rapidly in a closet to evade detection by the police (cat. no. 110).

who had worked as a pressman for Patris in the printing of the *assignats*. "I had been compelled to dismiss him," Patris explained, "because he was not doing his job properly and because he stirred up trouble in the shop by pitting the workmen against the foremen and the supervisors. I have in my possession some of the letters he wrote to my employees who passed them on to me themselves." Patris was kept confined at the Sainte-Pélagie prison for eleven days. He appealed to E.-G. Panis, a deputy on the Committee of General Security who, like him, had been elected a municipal official in February 1792. This led to his exoneration and a certificate of patriotic behavior, which stressed the role he had played in promoting the Champs de Mars petition in 1791.[21]

More serious was his arrest in March 1794 during the preliminary investigation for the trial of the Hébertists. A warrant for his arrest was issued by the revolutionary committee of his section on 14 March while he was printing the *Maximum* on prices. Patris had been forewarned and managed to escape. For ten days the revolutionaries searched for him without success. On 22 March his foreman, Louis-François Bonnefoy, was interrogated by the committee, presided over by the printer Campenon. They tried in vain to get him to say that Patris could have printed some subversive texts unbeknownst to his workmen. The same day Patris's wife, who had responded evasively and derisively to interrogation, was placed under house arrest. Because work for the Commune could not suffer further delay, it was decided, in accordance with the Convention's decree of 2 September 1793 drafting all printers into public service, that Patris's foreman would replace him and that no worker could take a leave of absence without giving the foreman ten days' notice.

Eventually, on 24 March, Patris turned up at the house of his friend J.-N. Pache. Sent again before the revolutionary committee, he explained he had avoided arrest because, in view of the circumstances, "he was afraid of being jailed at a time when it was said that the discontented among them had planned to have all prisoners executed." When asked where he had slept and eaten during his absence, he replied he had never gone to bed, that he had taken his meals in different cafés and restaurants and had attended the sessions of the Convention during the day. Patris sought to distance himself from the Hébertist extremists being hunted down at the time. He claimed that his dealings with Chaumette, who had just been arrested, were purely professional. The committee sent him to prison in the monastery of the English Benedictines. Under those desperate circumstances he wrote several accounts justifying his revolutionary activities, calling on Georges Danton, Louis Legendre, Jacques Billaud-Varenne, J.-L. Tallien, A.-J. Santerre, and others as witnesses.[22]

We do not know how long Patris remained imprisoned. He was probably released, like many others, after the fall of Robespierre. In July 1795 he was commissioned by the Committee of Public Safety to print bread tickets for the city of Paris. But he had lost his appointment at the Hôtel de Ville, and when the Revolution swung to the right under the Directory, his old rival, Lottin de Saint-Germain, regained his position as official printer of the municipal administration, which had been reorganized under the name of Central Bureau of the Canton of Paris.[23]

Because of his political involvement, Patris remained suspect to the authorities for the rest of his life, even when they entrusted him with printing jobs. Under the Empire he was considered a dangerous Jacobin, although his commission was renewed in 1811. In 1824 he retired and moved to Rambouillet, where he remained under surveillance because of his connection with the liberal party.[24]

Such were the careers of the two most important municipal printers in Paris—a combination of professional rivalry, competition for patronage, and ideological commitment. It is impossible to separate the threads of the story in order to decide which element prevailed. But it is clear that printing at the epicenter of the French Revolution was an arduous business. The *assignats*, posters, and official decrees did not appear by magic. Behind them was a fierce struggle among men who participated in all the key events of the Revolution and at the same time tried to turn it to their profit.

AGITATION IN THE
WORK FORCE

PHILIPPE MINARD

To ATTEMPT A history of the workplace in the eighteenth and nineteenth centuries, the scholar must confront the intersection of many kinds of history. First, in this period leading up to the Industrial Revolution, there is the history of technology. Then there is the history of economic structures, of the material framework of a craftsmanship still practiced in the center-city workshop with its characteristic deployment of technical and practical skills and its equally characteristic work patterns. The third and final historical thread that must be traced before we can write a history of the work force is the changing balance of the forces that link employer to employee. Here we must beware of the myth of a golden age of craft and guild production, in which the workshop is idealized as an extended family and the master is presented as a convivial figure, eager to share his skill and his craftsman's pride with the journeymen working alongside him in an even-tempered and sociable environment.[1] In the real world employer-employee relations had their ups and downs, which parallel to some extent the ups and downs of politics. L. S. Mercier describes prerevolutionary unrest in the workshops of Paris: "The hands are becoming less and less careful; everything is done in haste, and ill done. . . . In our day, the common people have cast aside subordination."[2]

The first impact of the Revolution on industry was to reinforce this general spirit of insubordination. But in the particular case of the printing trades, there was another impact: The market exploded, and demand grew manyfold for political reasons of which we are aware. Hundreds of leaflets, booklets, and pamphlets, as well as nearly two hundred new daily papers, made their appearance in 1789.[3] Although the business of conventional booksellers slumped in comparison to the boom in this ephemera, the revolutionary years nonetheless saw the maturing of a new sensitivity toward the written word. The people wanted to be informed. Freedom of the press was at once the means and the expression of the new democracy.[4]

How did the printing industry of Paris—with its guild of thirty-six master printers, its two hundred presses, its thousand craftsmen—respond to the explosion of demand represented by this proliferation of printed matter? To cope with this question, we must deal with two juxtaposed time-scales: the long one of a three-hundred-year-old industrial framework, and the shorter one of the political changes that provoked a sharp increase in demand, created new needs, and modified attitudes in the social forum of the workshop. Did the Revolution overthrow the established system of production and work process? Did the "typographical old regime," with its guild methods and guild mentality, survive the social and political whirlwind?[5]

The Printing Shop

By studying professional handbooks and treatises on printing, one can form an idea of the long-term norms that prevailed in the trade. The handbooks fall into a recognized category of practical literature—that of dictionaries or descriptions of individual arts and crafts. Their authors, all master printers, wrote with the purpose of glorifying the mystery of their trade and distinguishing printing as the handmaiden of learning. Printers were conscious of their history, forever harking back to the pioneers of their heroic age and thus affirming a notable corporate pride. But these handbooks have a secondary purpose: to teach the rules of the craft. We have been able to study eight treatises, the earliest of which dates from 1723. Written by Fertel, printer at St-Omer, it appears to have served as a model for the others. Three more antedate the Revolution: *L'Art de l'imprimerie dans sa véritable intelligence,* by Castillon (1783); Diderot's *Encyclopédie;* and its successor, the *Encyclopédie méthodique.* But during the Revolution the number of such works (all published in Paris) multiplied; it seems as though there must have been a new market for them. Thus, we have Boulard's *Manuel de l'imprimeur* in 1791, Momoro's *Traité* in 1793, and Bertrand-Quinquet's work of the same name in the Year VII (1799). Couret's *Barême typographique* was announced by Gillé, but never appeared in print.[6] These treatises offer a normative vision of the craft; they claim to expound the best ways of doing the work. But underlying the technical ideal may be discerned a good deal of practical, empirical know-how, worked out over the years on the shop floor. The handbooks combine practical tips with theoretical rules and are in fact very up-to-date.

These texts acquire more meaning when juxtaposed with other evidence. Autobiographies of workers, like those of Benjamin Franklin, Nicolas Restif de la Bretonne, and Nicolas Contat, give us a journeyman's perspective on the eighteenth-century printing shop. In the absence of examples from the revolutionary period, they can contribute (if subjected to critical analysis) to our understanding of workers' rhetoric in the 1790s. Business archives are rare; the Société typographique de Neuchâtel (STN) constitutes a fortunate exception with its rich documentation. Corporate archives, though slender for the years following 1789, do trace some paths which we can usefully follow.[7]

How much, then, can we know about the workshop at the end of the eighteenth century?[8] It is located in an ordinary dwelling-house, ill adapted to the technical imperatives of production: somehow or other the type cases must be installed, along with the presses, a stockroom for paper, a vat for soaking the paper, a cubbyhole for the foreman, possibly a drying room (paper was printed damp), and a store, since most printers were also booksellers. Because the store had to be at street level, the presses were on the floor above. Space was at a premium, and the whole bore little resemblance to the ideal workshop described in the handbooks. It seems that presses and type could be separated; at Nyon's workshop in 1789, the type cases were in what was called "the typesetters' room,"[9] foreshadowing the allocation of special skills to their own areas in the workplace. And what the *Encyclopédie* described as unusual was a matter of course for Bertrand-Quinquet in the Year VII (1799).[10]

The professional writings implicitly expound a whole philosophy of artisanal labor. The implements of the trade and the movements of the craftsmen fall into a pattern and belong to a rationalized, disciplined, aseptic space as illustrated in the *Encyclopédie*—and each of them is to be codified. Just as every tool has its proper place, every motion has its proper rules; physical posture responds to the order imposed by production. When the treatises describe the typographer at work, they leave no single movement to chance: Every finger of each hand is enlisted in the service of production. The same precise recommendations govern the position of the worker at the press; the attitudes of the man who turns the bar are prescribed with the exactness of a handbook on gymnastics. Work is a bodily discipline, and each task requires an appropriate posture. In these texts there is a tendency for professional advice, no doubt already accepted as standard, to slip insensibly into an attempt to discipline the "bad worker," the man who spares himself, who indulges in indifference or frivolity. Their editors rebuke and condemn the instances of economy of effort. So in prescribing norms, the authors and editors of these treatises acknowledge the distance

LE
MANUEL
DE
L'IMPRIMEUR,

OUVRAGE utile à tous ceux qui veulent connoître les détails des uftenfiles, des prix, de la manutention de cet Art intéreffant, & à quiconque veut lever une Imprimerie.

Par M. S. BOULARD, Imprimeur-Libraire, & Électeur de 1790 & 1791.

Prix broché, 2§ *fous.*

A PARIS,

CHEZ BOULARD, Imprimeur-Libraire, rue neuve Saint-Roch, N°. 51.

1791.

Martin-Silvestre Boulard. "The Printers' Manual." 1791. The New York Public Library, General Research Division.

Boulard's manual was a simple, low-cost introduction to the printing trade. It forms a striking contrast to the elegant and copious treatises produced in the eighteenth century by members of the Paris Book Guild (cat. no. 61).

by which daily practice on the shop floor falls short of them: "Take care not to do as I once saw a fellow-worker do," they say.[11] Their store of normative precepts must not be taken too literally; our business is with what falls short of the norm.

To the rational technology of the ideally run workshop, the printers oppose their inventiveness, the tricks of their trade, as a means to reclaim the workplace for themselves. The point at issue is often a minor one. Fertel, for example, warns his readers "not to follow the example of those shirkers who hang their inkballs on the ballracks of the press while their mate turns the bar," rather than rubbing them against each other as they should. "I know of two masters who cut the ballracks off, so that they should have no choice but to hold on to their inkballs." His conclusion is rather touching: "I don't say that a little relaxation may not be taken from time to time, else the work would be too hard; simply, do not make a practice of it."[12] Technical instruction passes into complaint: The hands want "to fall upon the work all at once" and speed up so as to earn more money—but the quality of the printing suffers for it. These workers respect nothing; they dirty everything; they are always prattling. The idlers, the ones who give out on the job, distract the workshop with their incessant talking and telling of stories. They eat on the type cases and the crumbs get into the letters. If they drop a forme, making a "pie" of the type, they try to hide the characters under rubbish instead of distributing them back in their case.[13] Working at the presses, they ink the formes too much or too little. A trick to make the work easier is to slather ink thickly on the forme so that one does not need to bear down so hard on the bar. The trouble is, however, that the excess runs out over the workers' fingers and spots the sheets they are handling. We are familiar with the anecdote, related by Robert Darnton,[14] of the print left by Bonnemain on a sheet of the *Encyclopédie*.

Far from being the ideal space envisioned in the trade treatises or the functional utopia illustrated in the *Encyclopédie*, the printing shop is cramped for space; it is noisy and grimy, like the men who work there. It smells of ink and even of urine, which is sometimes used to soften the leather of the ink balls. The air is damp. In this work space the machine does not impose its cadence on the men; there are five, ten, fifteen, or twenty workers toiling, eating, or joking in their own rhythm.[15]

The organization of the work had scarcely changed in a century. The workshop was laid out in accordance with an elementary division of labor, between type case and press. During his apprenticeship every worker moved according to his ability toward one or another of these specialized tasks. If he could spell, he would become a "monkey"; if he had more brawn than brains, he would be a "bear."[16]

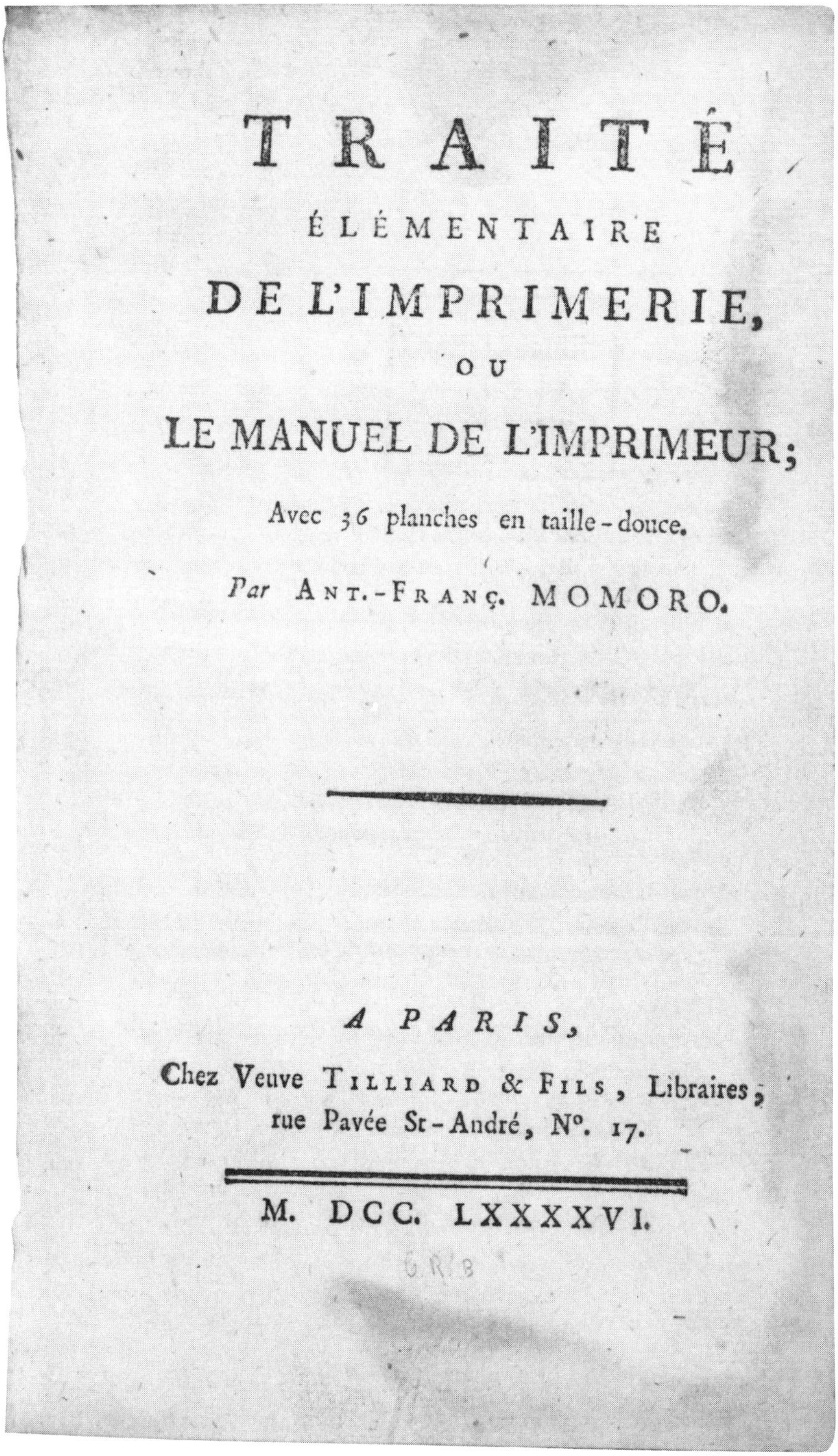

TRAITÉ

ÉLÉMENTAIRE

DE L'IMPRIMERIE,

OU

LE MANUEL DE L'IMPRIMEUR;

Avec 36 planches en taille-douce.

Par ANT.-FRANÇ. MOMORO.

———————

À PARIS,

Chez Veuve TILLIARD & FILS, Libraires,
rue Pavée St-André, N°. 17.

══════════

M. DCC. LXXXXVI.

Jean-François Momoro. "Elementary Treatise on Printing, or the Printers' Manual."
1796. The New York Public Library, General Research Division.
    Momoro was one of the most controversial new printers of the revolutionary pe-
riod. Associated with the Hébertists—radical followers of J.-R. Hébert—he perished under the Terror in 1794. His treatise provides one of the few sources for
printers' slang (cat. no. 79).

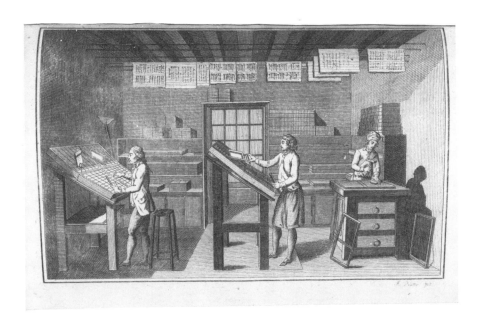

Jean-François Momoro. "Elementary Treatise on Printing, or the Printers' Manual."
These two views of an eighteenth-century printing shop are taken from Momoro's revolutionary treatise but in fact are miniaturized versions of the illustrations of printing in Diderot's *Encyclopédie* (1751–1765).

A compositor could line up 1,000 to 1,200 characters, or almost one octavo page, in an hour. A pressman could pull 1,200 to 1,500 sheets in a day—that is, 2,400 to 3,000 impressions, or 6,000 pulls on the bar, in 8 to 12 hours of "printing" proper, which did not include the time needed to prepare the press. The printer, or his foreman, always confronted the same problem: how to balance the two operations. If you are printing 1,000 copies of an octavo, it takes two compositors to keep one press busy; if your run is 3,000 copies in a larger typeface, one might be enough.[17] In a workshop with several presses (each of the thirty-six master printers in Paris before the Revolution had at least four) it was necessary to print several works concurrently on the same presses, so that nobody should lack work; otherwise the workers would have to be paid for time wasted. Although concurrent production existed since the seventeenth century, it came into general use only gradually. Bertrand-Quinquet, in the Year VII (1799), speaks of it as being universally adopted.[18] Concurrent production is much more efficient than controlling labor costs by hiring or laying off; it allows fine-tuning of the entire work process in all its aspects: payroll, inventory of typefaces, work in progress, layout, printing, and scheduling by priority.

For the pressmen, it scarcely mattered which team was pulling what leaf of what work. For the compositors, however, the handbooks after 1789 hint at an increasing division of labor. It had become common to see two or three typesetters working as a subgroup on a particular job. A system to increase the speed of typesetting was gaining favor. Compositors were divided into teams of *paquetiers,* each of whom would set type for one page and hand it, raw, to a team captain, who would then be in charge of imposition, correction, and lock-up. This "paquet typesetting" was described as current practice during the Revolution.[19] Thus, the division of labor and job specialization had made a little progress and generated a correspondingly small increase in productivity. Was it enough to cope with the increase in demand? At this point it is appropriate to inquire whether the explosion in the early years of the Revolution was made possible by significant technical advances or, on the contrary, brought such advances in its train.

Technical Innovations

This question must be considered against the larger background of modes of innovation and discovery in general—in other words, in terms of the highways leading to, and through, the Industrial Revolution. Without dwelling at length on these, we should at least pause to note certain points: The inventors are the craftsmen themselves, and invention is to some extent the happy chance that attends the tinkerer. In 1785–86 one Boileau, a typesetter with Cellot in Paris, tried to get himself hired at the Imprimerie Royale (Printers to the Crown) by submitting to Anisson his system for saving time on the composition of a forme and for avoiding pied type. Each page was to be composed in a box with hinged rims, which would replace the use of galleys. He also proposed a reformed spelling: "I have the genius of an inventor," he proclaimed—but it does not appear that his inventions came to anything.[20] So, another characteristic of innovation during this period is how slowly it spread and how many attempts had to be made before an invention could establish itself. For the most part, the attempts were the work of master craftsmen trying to increase the productivity of their shops. They involved both typesetting techniques and printing speed. This had to be so, for productivity had to be improved *pari passu* in both phases of the work process, lest an imbalance should cause a bottleneck.[21]

The earliest innovations had to do with composition. Printers wanted to be able to pull new impressions without resetting type. At that time the only way to do this was to keep the original formes, thus immobilizing thousands of expensive characters. Because the procedure was costly, the technique of taking an impression of the finished page to form a matrix was developed. From this matrix the whole page could be recast at any time in a single block of metal, or plate, bearing the text in relief and serving as a substitute for the forme of movable type.[22] Stereotyped printing was introduced in Paris in the 1780s by François-Ignace-Joseph Hoffmann, who after demonstrating his process before the Académie Royale des Sciences was licensed to set up a printing shop and to publish his *Journal polytype des sciences et des arts*. But his political activities and his printing of clandestine pamphlets hostile to the Crown caused his shop to be closed down in November 1787.[23] The benefit of polytyping is that it allows composition to be done with less movable type; once a page has been set, it can be cast, and the type can be reused. If there is no reason to have thousands of characters in stock, the cost of setting up a clandestine printing press is that much lower.[24]

Apart from the "polytyping" of bank notes, bills of the Caisse Patriotique, and later lottery tickets, between 1790 and the Year IV (1796) we find no books printed from plates earlier than the Year III (1794–95). In 1795 Firmin Didot printed Callot's *Table of Logarithms*, and in 1798, with Louis-Etienne Hehran, he published stereotyped editions of literary classics.[25] The process was still controversial. The bookseller Stoupe, in the Year VII (1799), reiterated Lottin's argument of 1789 that the discovery was a step backward because it took printing back three centuries to a point before the invention of movable type. In fact, the stereotyping system was neither perfected nor made economical before 1799.[26]

The printing press itself went through three different kinds of improvement. First, in 1781–83 Laurent Anisson and François-Ambroise Didot

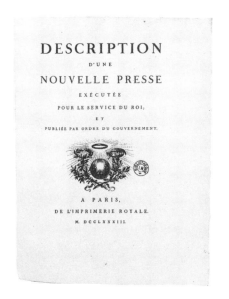

"Description of a New Printing Press" (Diagram of the Anisson-Duperron Press). 1783. Imprimerie Nationale, Paris.

One of the most important technological developments of late-eighteenth-century printing was the one-strike press invented by Laurent Anisson (1781–83). This press required only one pull of the pressman's bar, unlike the traditional two-strike press (cat. no. 132).

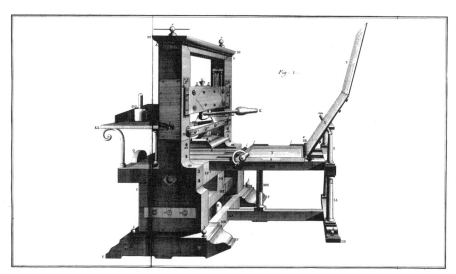

Fig. 1.

both claimed to have invented the one-strike press: By fitting a double screw-thread to a conventional press with two wooden plates, heavier pressure could be applied to the platen (now made of copper, not wood) and distributed across the entire forme; thus, one pull on the bar would be enough.[27] By 1790 the Imprimerie Royale had a press of this kind. In 1793 Momoro credited the invention to Anisson but found many defects in it: "The pull on the bar had too far to travel, and hence was tiring." Moreover, it was expensive. Boulard mentions it as being used in 1791, and Bertrand-Quinquet, in the Year VII (1799), had much to say in its favor—but there seem to have been few in use in Paris.[28]

Second, in 1786, came Philippe-Denis Pierres's invention of the "seesaw" press, but it was never more than a prototype.[29] And the same fate awaited the third development, the metal press built by Haas at Basel in 1772. The prospectus of 1790 shows us a press whose two wooden cheeks have been replaced by a semicircle of metal through which the spindle runs. Here, too, the double screw-thread makes it possible to print a whole forme with a single strike.[30] Stanhope's press of 1795 was a direct successor but was not introduced into France until 1819; the true technical revolution in the printing shop was to arrive in 1812–13 with the rotary press.[31]

In short, though there were many innovations before and during the revolutionary period, they scarcely emerged from the experimental stage. The Revolution did not lend itself to the dissemination of new inventions, and the printing shop under the Revolution remained much like that of Nicolas Contat, Restif de la Bretonne, or the STN. But if there was no qualitative change, it was because the limits of traditional technology had not yet been reached and because the prerequisites of innovation are money, tranquility, and time—none of which the revolutionary printers enjoyed. So their reply to the increase in demand was to push the old system to the structural limits of its technology.

Jacques Rychner and Robert Darnton have demonstrated how irregular the flow of work was in eighteenth-century printing shops.[32] It follows that the shops had unutilized resources and could more nearly approximate true plant capacity by working nights and Sundays, as was commonly done. The nature of their output required them to work fast; books can be delayed, but newspapers and pamphlets must be produced quickly, to keep up with the rapid changes they are meant to record.

The Workshops Multiply

The industry also sought to meet the new public demand for information by expanding its traditional structure. The increase in the flow of printed matter was made possible by an increase in the number of printing shops. The Guild of Printers and Booksellers estimated that 200 printing shops existed in Paris in 1790. Bertrand-Quinquet wrote that "printing shops have sprung up in every corner" of the city.[33] A memorial against the National Presses, signed by 71 printers of Paris in pluviôse, the Year III (February 1795), enumerates 700 presses in use, of which 240 are in the two government workshops.[34] Brival, speaking before the Conseil des Anciens in floréal, the Year V (May 1797) speaks of 300 to 400 workshops, but the *Almanach du Commerce* can find only 224 in the Year VII (1799), and the *Almanach typographique* of the Year VIII (1800) no more than 132.[35]

In the early years of the Revolution the 36 licensed master printers never ceased to rail at the increase in the number of shops: "Men of no quality seek to be printers . . . workers not fit to become masters."[36] True, a new press cost only 450 livres, while for a total of 1,000 to 2,000 livres a small workshop could be assembled.[37] Such small-scale production represented the opposite extreme to the well-appointed shops of the mid-eighteenth century—for example, that of François Emery, with five presses and type weighing 9,600 pounds, which was sold for 11,500 livres in 1743.[38] It is revealing to read the classified advertisements: "Wanted to buy: a good press, with type cases including pica and long primer, each with its italic, and all other stock needed to run a printing business; will pay up to 1,500–1,800 livres."[39] Pamphlet printers worked with no more than a broken-down press and secondhand type bought cheap; that is why Bertrand-Quinquet speaks of newspapers and leaflets "as ill-written as they are ill-printed."[40] According to him and to many other master printers from "the good old days," such as Couret de Villeneuve, the ideal remained rooted in the practices of the Old Regime: "For these ten years [since 1789], it has been easy to set up as a printer and to learn the rudiments of the trade. . . . With a little money and an inexhaustible fund of ignorance, any man could put together a workshop and call it a printing establishment." The trade has been debased, he remarks, by the many who seek to enter it "as a speculative venture."[41]

True, the Revolution gave birth to a few great workshops like C.-J. Panckoucke's, which in the Year II (1793–94) boasted twenty-seven presses and a hundred workers, or the Imprimeries Nationales, which employed as many as four hundred workers;[42] but, above all, it increased the number of traditional, small shops such as those later described by Michelet and Balzac,[43] which indeed came into being because of the favorable conjunction of events and later, when the flood of political pamphlets had subsided, capitalized (especially in the provinces) on the great increase in official printed matter. These lay quite outside the scope of technical improvement.

Thus, under the Revolution, the "typographical old regime" survived. The traditional technology was at once improved and disseminated, but not radically changed. What did change was the interplay of social forces in the workplace. Of course, the printing shop had never been the agreeable scene of mutual understanding depicted in the mythology of the craft. It is beyond dispute that there had been tensions and questionable work practices on the shop floor before 1789 (which were sometimes too strong for the masters to resist), but the Revolution strengthened the employees' bargaining power and so increased those tensions.

Organizing the Labor Force

Ever-rising pressruns from a growing number of printing shops created a temporary sellers' market for labor in the industry, as all contemporary comment attests. On 8 February 1790 Panckoucke writes: "Twenty new printing shops set up in Paris have stolen the typesetters and pressmen from the old ones." In the *Mercure de France* he exhorts the master printers: "Your workers are being corrupted on every hand; they are being offered wages with which you cannot compete. . . . High-paid night work . . . has tempted them away from everything else."[44] In the same year a spokesman for the old guild reports that "johnny-come-lately printers are tempting away our workmen by offering them double pay." It is concluded that the workforce must be replenished by increasing the number of apprentices. "Workers are being made," reports Momoro, "of all who come to the door, and although there is a multitude of printers, hands are still needed."[45]

In such conditions, it can be readily understood that workers obtained worthwhile raises. In 1770 a printer earned around three livres, or three livres ten sous, for a working day that began at 6:00 A.M., ended at about 8:00 P.M., and involved twelve hours actually on the job. Typographers' wages, though more erratic, were of the same general order. By 1791 all these rates had doubled, involving an improvement in real purchasing power. Moreover, the "normal" workday was reduced by two hours: Overtime became payable for work beyond the 8:00 A.M.–8:00 P.M. day at a rate of three livres for nights and two livres for Sundays.[46]

Only the exceptional circumstances of the Revolution could account for such a situation. The workers were participating in the general political agitation, and we see them playing their part in political demonstrations. Several times in 1790 the newspapers report contingents of printers marching under a banner which proclaims "Freedom of the Press!" or "The Press, Liberty's Torch."[47] Although these are political pronouncements, they have obvious social overtones: A free press means a sufficiency of work for working printers.

Workers were organizing institutionally as well. On 27 June 1790 they set up a mutual-aid association whose statutes have come down to us under the title "General Regulations for the Typographers, Drawn up by the Committee of the General Assembly of the Representatives of the Letterpress Printers of Paris."[48] The typographers met every Sunday and set up a committee as well as a system of relief for the sick, who received fifteen livres a week for the first three months, and seven livres ten sous for the next three months. There was an entrance fee of twelve livres for those joining the association, as well as weekly dues. Every printing establishment designated a delegate (or two, if it had more than twenty members) to the weekly meetings. The association, which seems to have had about 1,100 members, also boasted a weekly newsletter, the *Club typographique et philanthropique,* with a pressrun of 550 copies and 400 subscribers; its 31 issues appeared between 1 November 1790 and 31 May 1791.[49] This publication offers indispensable contemporary evidence of the thrust of the discussions among workers' groups. Their roots can be traced back to the clandestine workers' organizations of the Old Regime; thus, one of the signatories of the General Regulations, Duval, is a worker in the printing shop of the Royal Lottery who had been dismissed on 20 August 1788 for being absent without written permission.[50] In other words, the mutual-aid association was a direct outgrowth of the fraternal organization of workers which, before 1789, used to meet at the Church of St. John Lateran in the Latin Quarter.[51] The employers who fulminated against a conspiracy of labor were not mistaken. In May 1790 there was supposed to be an arbitration under the auspices of J. S. Bailly, the mayor of Paris, at the offices of the syndics—but the workers stayed away.[52] In January 1791 a mysterious "Encyclopedic Assembly" sitting at the Grands-Augustins addressed a petition to the mayor that opened with a ringing paean to liberty and went on to denounce the activities of the typographical association, which stood accused of preventing the master printers from taking on new apprentices and of conspiring to maintain high wages. The same charges were presented before a captain of police in April 1791.[53]

For the workers, the apprenticeship system was the central question; the employers had made a practice of using apprentices and underqualified laborers (*alloués*) as a low-cost way of expanding the work force, thus reducing the general level of wages. It was on this matter that emotions rose highest. The workers of Didot le jeune published in 1790 a *Plan de règlement concernant les apprentis imprimeurs,* which proposed nothing less than complete oversight by the workers of the hiring of apprentices—after an initial two-year moratorium on such hiring—to protect the interests of the exist-

Nᵒ. I.

CLUB TYPOGRAPHIQUE
ET
PHILANTROPIQUE.

(La Publicité eſt la ſauve-garde du Peuple. BAILLY.)

FEUILLE HEBDOMADAIRE,
DÉDIÉE
A MM. LES CONTRIBUABLES.

FRATERNITÉ, UNION POUR LA PATRIE.

TABLEAU DE BIENFAISANCE.

RECETTE.	DÉPENSE.	BONI.	EXTR.
450 liv.	315 liv.	1617 liv.	liv.

L'AN II. DE LA LIBERTÉ FRANÇOISE.
Du Lundi, 1 Novembre.

UNION, FRATERNITÉ, BIENFAISANCE, AMOUR DE LA PATRIE : voilà la tâche honorable à laquelle nous oſons nous livrer, & conſacrer tout le tems de notre vie. S'abandonne qui voudra au délire de la penſée (1) ; arrache des douleurs & des

---

(1) On nous a fort mal compris : dans tout ce que nous avons imprimé, nous n'avons ſoutenu que la cauſe commune.

A

"Typographical and Philanthropic Club Newsletter." No. 1, 1 November 1790. Bibliothèque Nationale, Département des Imprimés.

The political climate of the Revolution led to the formation of a mutual-aid association for printing-shop workers, which could boast of its own weekly newsletter from 1790 to 1791 (cat. no. 64).

ing work force. Apprenticeship was to be fixed at a standard four-year period and subjected to strict quotas. The underlying intention was made very clear:

> Gentlemen, the abundance of printing shops, especially in the metropolis, has given rise to an even more marked increase in the number of apprentices, above and beyond the facilities which can be made available to them by the master printers or skilled workers, so that the apprenticeship required of them is a matter of months only. This situation brings in its train abuses which tend toward nothing less than the overturning of our livelihood; we have therefore thought it only prudent to invite you to join us, and lend us your aid in a project which is of capital importance for the whole work force.[54]

If the workers now felt free to organize openly in defense of their interests, however, it was not only because the situation in the workplace was propitious but also, above all, because they now felt that such action was wholly legitimate. In practice, the guild of master printers—until then the only group representing the profession—had ceased to function after June 1790. From then on the craft had no recognized corporate representation, and all internal regulation of the printing trades had disappeared, because the guild had been the principal regulator. Therefore, the workers' association could claim authority over the entire profession. The craftsmen were now the true, the only, champions of their craft. Their paper set itself the goal of striving "against the decay of the typographer's art"; they remarked on a lowering in the quality of printing, and declared that they intended to set it right. As long as they were engaged in a defense of the principles of the craft against incompetent masters, against the new breed of master printers who were no better than low speculators—they felt they were on firm ground. This is why they took the slogans of the old master printers and applied them to their own cause, even against the masters old and new. Confronted with masters who knew nothing of the business, they, the workers, presented themselves as the only true trustees of the art and mystery of the trade: "We are once again the owners of our craft."[55] Following the d'Allarde law of 2 March 1791, which confirmed the demise of the guild, the workers appropriated for their own purposes the old guild pride in workmanship and craft tradition. From then on they, and they alone, *were* the guild. Their newssheet invited even masters, those who loved their craft, to join the workers' association![56] They looked on themselves as a "constituent body"; their representatives were discharging a "public trust";[57] they were a little nation which, like the French nation, existed by virtue of the awareness and the voluntary adherence of its members, held together by love of their craft and veneration of their great predecessors, such as the much-admired Benjamin Franklin.

Then came the bourgeois backlash, the Le Chapelier law of May–June 1791. What sort of wound did it inflict? The *Club* ceased publication; the association withdrew into the shadows. We do not know what became of it. Contemporary sources fall silent, except on the struggle of the workers at the Imprimeries Nationales. Here we are dealing with large workshops employing several dozen men *en conscience*—that is, paid by the day rather than on piece rates—in a work environment where specialization had been pushed to uncommon lengths. Here, compositors and pressmen had organized separately and were making separate demands. Disputes here revolved around wages, stripped of the illusory overtones of "art and mystery" from the days of the guild. The d'Allarde and Le Chapelier laws signaled the end of the artisanal mentality of the Old Regime. The workers wanted better pay and opposed some dismissals, particularly of those who had gone on strike, as at the printing shop of the National Assembly in November 1791. They were wage earners, and did not conceive of themselves as possible future masters.[58]

The old mentality was manifest in little more than pride openly displayed and a conviction in the dignity of the craft. Even as they dissociated themselves from the guild, these workers retained the concept of association: The unity of wage earners was their strength and confirmed their sense of identity.

It may, then, be confidently asserted that if the French Revolution did not fundamentally disturb the structure and the work patterns of the industry (except perhaps for its general impact on night work in the early years), it changed the workers' attitude to their work. The atmosphere of the workplace was transformed, and that, in its way, was as important as anything that technology might have wrought.

A PROVINCIAL PERSPECTIVE

MICHEL VERNUS

DURING THE THREE decades preceding the Revolution the circulation of books in Franche-Comté increased substantially—among poor peasants as well as the cultural elite. The types of publications and the extent of their diffusion, of course, varied in relation to the different literary needs of the social classes and depended on where the readers lived. Franche-Comté was sparsely populated: Only 20 percent of its inhabitants lived in cities. During the Revolution the diffusion of all manner of printed material accelerated, as Franche-Comté, and indeed the entire country, entered a new stage of literary culture. Villagers in particular received a great many posters, pamphlets, and tracts, and at the same time discovered the newspaper.

Book Distribution before 1789

The publishing situation in Franche-Comté was unique in several respects. In spite of a tradition of independence, this frontier area was not restricted by a backward provincial mentality. Located at crossroads leading to the important publishing centers of Paris, Lyons, and Switzerland, Franche-Comté had an intense circulation of books. The region also served to link Switzerland with Lorraine and Burgundy as well as with provinces deep inside France. Alongside the open, authorized commerce in books, there existed an illicit traffic in printed matter using clandestine channels.

The inhabitants of Franche-Comté were within easy reach of well-known publishing centers, where they made a good part of their purchases. Individuals bought books when they traveled, although they did so more often through catalogues and subscriptions. Booksellers in the province—twenty-five major vendors worked in Franche-Comté—placed their orders with these publishers because the local production of books far from satisfied the needs and interests of their readers, especially the better-educated ones.[1] The eight local publishers printed mainly religious booklets, primers, and traditional chapbooks. Occasionally, works of theology, local or regional history, or texts of law and medicine were published, but local production still could not satisfy the province's demands.

Franche-Comté's cultural elite was relatively small. In 1789 educated citizens who read regularly constituted barely 10,000 out of a total population of almost 800,000 inhabitants. The group broke down as follows: clergy, about 3,500; nobility (among whom the level of education varied considerably), 2,000; and another 2,000 middle-class professionals, mainly lawyers and notaries, along with a good many doctors and a few engineers and tradesmen. There were about fifteen schools in different cities and towns with no more than 3000 students.[2] Under these circumstances the market for a book, especially an expensive one, remained restricted—typically somewhere between 400 and 700 potential buyers. Thus, *Almanach historique de Besançon et de Franche-Comté*, intended for an educated public, was printed in an edition of 500 copies. A historical work in-quarto such as *Sires de Salins* by the abbé Guillaume was printed in an edition of 700 copies and sold by subscription.[3] We also know that the quarto edition of the *Encyclopédie* in 1777 obtained 392 subscribers.[4] A weekly publication, *Les Affiches de Franche-Comté*, published for the first time in 1766 and intended for this same public, had great difficulty surviving, which explains the many interruptions in its publication.

However limited in size, this cultural elite was receptive to the ideas and tendencies of the modern era. Such, at least, is the impression one gets from their libraries, which usually contained several hundred volumes, and quite often a thousand or more. Recent works lined the shelves, along with ancient tomes passed down from one generation to another.[5]

The elite's initial response to the *Encyclopédie* was enthusiastic. Indeed, the success of the Neuchâtel edition (1777) was so impressive it astonished the province's booksellers. Other signs also indicated a frenzy for encyclopedism. In 1772–73 Jean-François Lepin, a bookseller in Salins, had to battle customs to obtain crateloads of the *Encyclopédie* entering the province through Morez. He appealed repeatedly to the royal subdelegate, Faton, a friend of his, who wrote several times to the intendant on his behalf. "I appeal to you again, my dear Griois," he wrote on 8 December 1773, "to obtain passage for two crates of the *Encyclopédie* in a Genevan edition, which are now at Les Rousses and belong to the bookseller Lepin in Salins. Only the Yverdon edition is banned. . . . I beg you to send the customs authorization tomorrow, because Lepin is in great distress."[6] *Les Affiches de Franche-Comté*, in addition, printed about ten advertisements offering individual copies of the *Encyclopédie* for sale, which reveals the existence of an active secondhand market for this work.

The *noblesse de la robe* followed the tendency of the times. President de Vezet was steeped in the reading of the philosophes, even though he remained circumspect about the new ideas. Voltaire, who lived nearby at Ferney, was also well-known in Franche-Comté, and was much read in legal circles. But the influence of Rousseau was even greater. The library of François Ferdinand Joseph Brenez—who lived at Lons-le-Saunier and died in 1788, just before the Revolution—is a striking example of the private collections established by influential lawyers. He had been one of the subscribers of the Jura region to the in-quarto Neuchâtel edition of the *Encyclopédie*. In addition to the thirty-six volumes of the *Encyclopédie*, he owned the complete works of Rousseau, Montesquieu, and Voltaire, the *Histoire philosophique* by the abbé Raynal, and the *Histoire naturelle* by Buffon. He also possessed works by Diderot and Helvétius. Among the works of fiction in his library were the *Tableau de Paris* and *L'An 2440* by Sébastian Mercier. Altogether, there were more than a thousand volumes in his collection. Brenez came from a family of notaries connected to the local nobility of lesser rank; he was a member of the Company of Arquebusiers and of the Masonic lodge of his town.[7]

Besides the famous books of the Enlightenment, the cultural elite bought a great variety of other works. According to a recent study of the legal world of Besançon, "the percentage of religious works in the libraries was declining."[8] On library shelves, works of science and the arts were to be found along with a few books of local history—which expressed pride in their province—and a great number of novels. A real passion for fiction took possession of the elite; members of the local nobility subscribed to *La Bibliothèque universelle des romans.*[9]

Les Affiches de Franche-Comté propagated the taste of the day, and the advertisements of Besançon booksellers revealed the direction of this taste. Of 377 advertised works (1766–73), 8.4 percent concerned theology, 7.6 percent law, 21.4 percent history, 28.6 percent *belles-lettres*, and 33.6 percent arts and sciences. The list suggests that Besançon booksellers served as middlemen in forming the reading habits of the province.

A new social life developed with this reading and exchanging of books within small groups. Three cities—Besançon, Saint-Claude, and Vesoul—had public libraries. Readers' clubs and societies were formed. In the small town of Saint-Amour "several influential persons" asked the authorities in 1771 for permission "to rent a room where they could meet, read gazettes and newspapers and indulge in games of chance, as has been done for a long time in different towns of the province."[10] In Besançon the booksellers Pierre-Etienne Fantet (a friend of Voltaire) and Dominique Lepagnez opened reading rooms. A certain canon of Salins admitted to having borrowed several volumes of the *Encyclopédie* from a lawyer. The influence of books thus extended far beyond the limited circle of their owners.

What was the diffusion of books in the countryside? One should first remember that Franche-Comté is located in northeastern France, where literacy was relatively high.[11] The villagers had been exposed to books mainly through the efforts of a particularly active clergy. The Counter-Reformation provided a framework for encouraging literacy in the province; clergy used books, together with religious images and objects, to spread Catholicism among families and to win souls. The clergy was helped in the distribution of religious booklets by a well-developed commercial network of master booksellers and *colporteurs*—newsmongers and peddlers of small wares who, although they owned shops, did not mind hawking their merchandise through the mountains.

The clergy of Franche-Comté promoted the distribution of religious publications in many ways. For instance, the bishop of Saint-Claude, Meallet de Farges, distributed pious booklets in his diocese free of charge.[12] The missionaries of Beaupré,[13] who had in the course of the century been very active in different parishes, visited houses in the company of booksellers approved by the authorities, both to search for bad books and to distribute religious works. The missionaries became publishers themselves, and on 20 July 1780 they obtained permission to publish *Les Pensées sur les plus importantes vérités du christianisme* (in-12), written by one of them, in an edition of ten thousand copies.[14] Many families owned collections of religious songs used in church services as well as in readings at home. In a pastoral manual entitled *Méthode pour la direction des âmes* (1782–83), the necessity for Christian families to own pious works was clearly explained. The author, Joseph Pochard, a former priest and director of the Besançon seminary, mentioned four times that "a good priest will be distressed to realize that certain families have no crucifix, no pious images, and no devotional books." He also advised that the evening around the hearth end with a reading that encouraged meditation, citing for this purpose a number of suitable books, among which were the above-mentioned *Pensées sur les plus importantes vérités*, along with *Pensez-y bien*, *L'Introduction à la vie dévote*, and *Le Pédagogue chrétien*.[15]

What effect did this activity have on the population? Surveys show that only 6 percent of the country people (farmers, day laborers, vine growers) possessed books, and that 80 percent of these were religious works. The number of religious books thus far exceeded that of popular chapbooks and almanacs.[16]

In the years preceding the Revolution, books had spread to every level of Franche-Comté society. Books differed greatly, and so did the reasons for their diffusion. In some cases, intellectual curiosity and modern tastes determined reading habits; in others, as we have seen, the propagation of religion played a role. The books that ended up in the hands of the peasants were far different from the works of the Enlightenment, which, as a matter of fact, were not always present in the large libraries of the elite. Nevertheless, the presence of pious books in the province demonstrates a real capacity for reading on the part of at least a segment of the country population. The peasantry may well have been primed for the transition to secular literature when the opportunity arose after 1789.

The Rising Flood of Political Publications

The Revolution introduced a new stage in the distribution of printed material in Franche-Comté. Propaganda and proselytism provided powerful stimuli for printing, especially because of two strongly opposed factions: on one side, the patriotic militants who wanted to push back "fanaticism"; on the other, those resisting the Revolution, who were far from passive. In this great ideological battle, the weapon on both sides was the printed word. Two distribution networks were established, one using the official channels of the revolutionary authorities, the other employing clandestine routes. The goal was control of the countryside, and pamphlets, booklets, posters, and newspapers were widely distributed toward this end and dealt directly with current events.

Can we measure the extent of this rising flood of printed material? A complete list of the printed works of this period has not yet been compiled, although some classifications according to the printer and the date of publication have been established. These give us some idea of the activity of the printing shops. Between January and May 1789, when the electoral campaign for the Estates General was in full swing, 220 titles (booklets and pamphlets) were printed in Franche-Comté. With an average printing of 1,000 copies of each title, the total number of publications would have been 220,000. A few months later the debate over the Civil Constitution of the clergy produced another 30 tracts. All the printing shops were kept busy, and new ones were established at Arbois, Poligny, and Saint-Claude.

The division of France into departments split the province but still favored the official printer of each of these new governing units. In Besançon Antoine-Joseph Simard, who had been in business since 1784,[17] received large payments from the department, but he was unable to execute all the orders, and the authorities had to appeal to other printers (Jacques-François Couché, Jean-François Daclin). From November 1790 to the summer of 1794, the department of Doubs spent fifty thousand francs for vari-

LOI

Portant suppreſſion de tous les droits d'Aides ; suppreſſion de toutes les Maîtriſes & Jurandes, & établiſſement de Patentes.

L OUIS, par la grâce de Dieu, & par la Loi conſtitutionnelle de l'Étar, ROI DES FRANÇOIS : A tous préſens & à venir ; SALUT.

1770	2			1789	2
1771	5			1790	13
1772	1			1791	3
1773	1	21		1792	2
1774	2			1793	1
1775	3			1794	0
1776	1			1795	0
1777	0			1796	0
1778	3			1797	1
1779	2			1798	1
1780	0			1799	2
1781	2			1800	0
1782	1			1801	0
1783	0			1802	3
1784	1			1803	11
1785	0			1804	7
1786	0			1805	6
1787	0			1806	9
1788	0				—
	—				61
	24				

État passif du S. François Jean Noël
De Bure, imprimeur libraire a Paris

Créanciers privilégiés et hipothéquaires

M. Perinet d'orval, privilege de Bailleur de fonds sur Massy, Six
mille livres, et les arrérages de cette Somme depuis le 15 Juin 1790 6000

M. Gillet, commissaire, par privilege sur la maison Située a Paris
rue Copeau, même Somme de Six mille livres cy 6000

Les Représentants, d.lle Marie Anne Berlinguet, Suivant un
contrat devant M.e Choron, Dix mille livres et les arrérages qui en sont
dûs 10000

M. Plaine, apoticaire, par Obligation de Trois mille livres, avec
des Billets d'interets, Jusqu'a l'échéance 3000

MM. Les propriétaires de la manufacture de douglés près Montargis
au moyen du Cautionnement contracté par M. DeBure et Son obligation
Solidaire avec le S.r Palix .... Mémoire

N.ta Cet article est tiré pour Mémoire Seulement, au moyen du
Cautionnement et du temps a faire avec les Susdits propriétaires

Mad.e DeBure, pour Ses reprises et conventions Matrimoniales, Suivant
leur liquidation cy .... Mémoire

Total du 1er Chap. privileges et hipotheques 25000

Créanciers Chirographaires directs

M.M.
Aubry 1650
Audinot 11660

N°. de Paris. MOTIONS DU PALAIS ROYAL LE 12 S. 1789. N°. Pages.

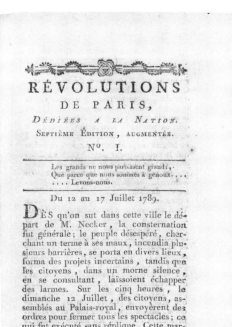

RÉVOLUTIONS
DE PARIS,
DÉDIÉES A LA NATION.
SEPTIÈME ÉDITION, AUGMENTÉE.
N°. I.

Les grands ne nous paroissent grands,
Que parce que nous sommes à genoux. . . .
. . . . . Levons-nous.

DÈS qu'on sut dans cette ville le départ de M. Necker, la consternation fut générale ; le peuple désespéré, cherchant un terme à ses maux, incendia plusieurs barrières, se porta en divers lieux, forma des projets incertains, tandis que les citoyens, dans un morne silence, en se consultant, laissoient échapper des larmes. Sur les cinq heures, le dimanche 12 Juillet, des citoyens, assemblés au Palais-royal, envoyèrent des ordres pour fermer tous les spectacles ; ce qui fut exécuté sans réplique. Cette marque d'honneur, décernée à un grand homme, fit connoître, avec certitude, quel étoit le dégré de l'affliction publique.

L'on fut ensuite au cabinet du sieur Curtius, pour prier cet artiste de se dé-

A sept heures du soir arrive la nouvelle des hostilités des troupes à la Place de Louis XV. Des Orateurs, au Palais Royal, montent sur des chaises et dénoncent les ennemis de la Patrie. Aux armes, à la liberté, voilà le cri général. On fait fermer les spectacles, on suit le torent, la fermentation s'augmente et le Peuple veille toute la nuit.

Bureau des Révolutions de Paris, rue Jacob, F. S. G. N°. 28.
Et au Mont de Mars, rue des Marais, Faub. S. G. N°. 20.

Révolutions de Paris retained the traditional small format of eighteenth-century journals. It was originally conceived of not as a periodical but rather as a news pamphlet that could be collected and bound into volumes. The illustrations were printed separately and sent to subscribers to be bound with their collections (cat. no. 111).

quired no special equipment. They were the natural choice for the first issues of enterprises, such as Louis Prudhomme's *Révolutions de Paris*, which were not originally conceived of as continuing periodicals but rather as news pamphlets describing the extraordinary events surrounding the storming of the Bastille (Rolf Reichardt discusses these pamphlets in detail elsewhere in this book).[19] Easy to bind in volumes if readers decided to preserve their papers, the octavo format was, as one publisher put it, "the most convenient both for the reader and for libraries."[20]

The octavo-format papers did eventually adopt some regular features of organization: They employed rubrics such as "Assemblée nationale" to distinguish articles and frequently had a short summary of their contents on the first page, which could be cried aloud by street vendors. Indeed, publishers recognized that readers quickly became accustomed to a particular sequence of materials and needed to be reassured whenever changes were made. When the *Journal de Perlet* experimented with placing its account of the Convention's daily debates at the end of each issue rather than at the beginning, the printer promised: "This will not mean that it will be less complete, or less extensive. This change [is] purely typographical, and . . . will not result in any change in editorial policy."[21] But the octavo format and the adherence to a rigid sequence of news rubrics deprived many revolutionary journalists of the fundamental resource of modern newspaper design—the placement of an item on the page so as to underline its importance relative to the other items in the paper.

In the course of the 1790s the somewhat larger quarto format gradually won out over the octavo. Although the octavo size had initially been used by newspapers of all genres, it was particularly associated with agitational pamphlet papers like Marat's *Ami du peuple* and with newssheets designed for a rural or lower-class audience, like the *Journal de Perlet*. From the start of the Revolution the quarto format, with copy distributed in two columns on each page, marked papers that stressed their function as reporters of news more than their ideological bias, and that sought a more educated audience. The quarto format recalled the sober, respectable news press of the Old Regime rather than its polemical pamphlets. Readers could find the rubrics that interested them more easily in a four-page quarto paper than in an eight- or sixteen-page octavo booklet. But the publishers who used the quarto format remained conservative about layout. Unlike their London contemporaries, they stayed away from such shocking innovations as headlines and illustrations, and their two-column formats resembled books printed before 1789, such as the *Encyclopédie*. However radical their contents, the French papers of the revolutionary period remained resolutely conservative in appearance and demanded no revolution in reading habits from their readers.

N°. LXXXI.

L'AMI DU PEUPLE

O U

LE PUBLICISTE PARISIEN,

JOURNAL POLITIQUE ET IMPARTIAL,

Par M. MARAT, auteur de l'Offrande à la Patrie, du Moniteur, et du Plan de Constitution, etc.

Vitam impendere vero.

Du mardi 29 décembre 1789.

Concussions de plusieurs intendans et de leurs sub-délégués, dénoncées. Conspiration contre la Patrie et le Roi. Arrestation du marquis de Favras, chef des conjurés. Comparution de Monsieur, frère du Roi, à l'hôtel-de-ville. Observations de l'auteur. Assassinat commis, rue des Quatre-Fils, par un conjuré sur un soldat citoyen.

ASSEMBLÉE NATIONALE.

Séance du lundi 28 décembre.

La pièce délivrée par le comité des rapports, dans l'affaire de l'intendant d'Alençon et de son subdélégué à Bellesme, a été rapportée sur le bureau, et remise à M. le président. Ce n'est, dit-on, qu'un simple arrêté du comité, et la signature de

---

Jean-Paul Marat, ed. *L'Ami du peuple*. [1789]. The New York Public Library, Rare Books and Manuscripts Division, Talleyrand Collection.

Jean-Paul Marat's *Ami du peuple* became the model for agitational pamphlet-papers addressed to popular audiences (cat. no. 85).

Revolutionary journalists continued to follow long-standing typographical traditions, but they had to innovate in selecting and printing the news. Not that they were forced to undertake a task completely without precedent: In reporting the sessions of the National Assembly and its successors, they could draw on traditions of parliamentary news coverage established by the English press and the well-known French-language international gazettes such as the *Courrier de l'Europe.* Many revolutionary journalists adapted rhetorical techniques used in pre-1789 political pamphlets, or drew inspiration from the phenomenally successful *Annales politiques,* published by the eccentric social theorist Simon-Nicolas-Henri Linguet from 1777 to 1788, whose highly personalized approach to politics foreshadowed the tone of many of the revolutionary pamphlet-journals.[22] But the journalists of the revolutionary decade were writing in a fundamentally new situation, and they had few guidelines to help them decide which of the available approaches would work best.

A good way to examine the variety of journalistic methods employed during the Revolution is to compare the different ways that journalists resolved the crucial problem of reporting on France's new legislative bodies, the National Assembly and its successors. Together with the press itself, the assemblies were the focus of the competing political discourses at the center of revolutionary politics, and the question of how the words spoken in them would be communicated to the nation at large was critical not only for the press but also for the entire revolutionary experiment. The first newspapers founded in the early weeks of the Revolution, such as the *Point du jour,* published by the future Jacobin Bertrand Barère, were devoted almost exclusively to coverage of the Estates General's public sessions. Within a few months, however, it became clear that there were many different approaches to the reporting of parliamentary proceedings, with very different implications for the political role of the press and the nature of the political process.

At one extreme were newspapers that eschewed any independent role for themselves and claimed to be no more than the passive transcription of politicians' words. Lehodey de Saultchevreuil's *Journal des Etats-Généraux* and its continuation, the *Journal logographique,* were among the most important of these journals. Lehodey's philosophy, scrupulously carried out in his paper, was to report "literally, with the most complete fidelity, everything said in our Representatives' Assembly. . . . Nothing, absolutely nothing, will be omitted." Carrying out this promise required nothing less than the invention of a primitive method of stenography. Other journalists, less scientific in their pretensions, subsequently admitted (like Charles Lacretelle, a minor journalist whose autobiography is the most extensive depiction of a newsman's life during the 1790s) that "imagination sometimes had to come to the aid of memory" in reconstructing their versions of the debates.[23] But such methods distorted the communication between the deputies and the nation and prevented achievement of the goal Lehodey set for his paper: to ensure that "the inhabitants of regions furthest from this capital . . . will virtually be present at the sessions of this august Senate, as if they were attending in person." The *Journal logographique* was to be a completely neutral medium, exercising no influence whatsoever over its readers' reactions to the Assembly's proceedings. It condemned rival papers, which "interpret in their own sense or that of the party they want to favor what is said there," and lazy readers "who, incapable of thinking and reflecting, want someone else to spare them the trouble."[24] The result of the logographic process was a portrait of the nation's legislature as a scene of long-winded confusion and chaos. Speakers, identified by name or sometimes not at all (but never by any party label or any other clue as to their position on major issues), competed with the faithfully recorded murmurs and applause of the galleries for space in the newspaper's columns. Indispensable to historians, the newspaper of record was less effective in communicating to the French nation a sense that it was being wisely led. By swinging to the opposite extreme from the Old Regime's laconic official press, which gave no background information at all on the governmental decision-making process, the *Journal logographique* underlined the transformation the Revolution had wrought in French politics, but at the cost of making that process nearly as unintelligible as it had been before 1789.

Although papers like Lehodey's made a definite niche for themselves as repositories of record, they never became the dominant journals of the Revolution. Most readers subscribed to journals that edited and summarized the Assembly debates and reported their outcome as soon as it was clear, but there were many ways to accomplish that task. One could simply copy the formula of the prerevolutionary *Gazette de France* and give only the final results of the Assembly debates, as the *Journal des décrets de l'Assemblée nationale, pour les habitans des campagnes* started out to do—although the editor soon had to admit that "it would be more attractive and useful if one provided a summary of the principal arguments raised in the preceding discussions."[25] But what he provided bore little resemblance to parliamentary reporting: Speakers' names were omitted, and the arguments for and against each measure were reduced to a few sentences in each case, reorganized into simple lists of pros and cons. This formula turned the Assembly into a rationalized law-making machine, devoid of passions—and completely different from the depiction of the same body in the *Journal logographique*.

Between these two extremes of objective parliamentary reporting were many other journalistic formulas. Most differed from those employed by the two newspapers of record just described because they involved both more active and visible intervention on the part of the journalist and the juxtaposition of news about the Assembly with other reports. In the *Feuille villageoise,* a highly successful weekly aimed at a rural audience, the emphasis was on explaining the significance of the issues raised in the debates, rather than on transcribing them. Unlike the *Journal logographique,* this paper assumed that if the average Frenchman could listen to his representatives debating, he would be utterly bewildered, and its political articles were thus conceived in the same spirit as its propaganda for agricultural improvement. The weekly summary of the Assembly's sessions made up only a small part of the paper, considerably less than the space devoted to didactic articles aimed at clarifying the issues. The *Feuille villageoise* habitually analyzed arguments rather than summarizing debates, and rarely identified the deputies who had spoken—although it contributed to a sense of the Assembly as the battleground of opposing forces of good and evil by referring to *aristocrates* and *patriotes,* while struggling to preserve the image of the latter as a unified group. Although hesitant to emphasize such party labels, it was not reticent in identifying the central issues at stake. Typical of the paper's presentation of controversies was an article on royal authority from 1791, beginning: "If the least-educated villager took it into his head for a minute to reflect on the word 'king,' the first idea he would come up with is that a king is a man like himself, simply entrusted with a very important function."[26] When the paper did break with its normal practice of giving only very short summaries of parliamentary sessions in order to provide fuller coverage of Louis XVI's appearance before the Convention during his trial, it still did not leave readers on their own but told them that this report would show them "the solemn dignity of the representatives of a great people, the humiliation of the former king, his denials, his subterfuges."[27]

The success of the *Feuille villageoise*—it had perhaps 15,000 subscribers in 1791[28]—proves that this condescending attitude did not offend potential subscribers. Journalists interpreting the revolutionary assemblies' debates for a more sophisticated audience had to take a different tack, however, particularly if they intended to be part of the political fracas as well as to report on it. Brissot was among the early masters at expressing the essence of the National Assembly's debates from a partisan point of view, and his *Patriote françois* was justifiably considered one of the best prorevolutionary newspapers. Unlike the authors of the *Feuille villageoise,* he addressed his comments on the Assembly's work not only to the public but also to the deputies themselves, chiding and directing them in line with his "patriotic" outlook. Brissot understood his role as one of teaching: "The point is to spread the enlightenment which prepares a Nation to receive a free Constitution, by instructing the People about the National Assembly's operations,"

LA
FEUILLE VILLAGEOISE,

ADRESSÉE, CHAQUE SEMAINE,

A TOUS LES VILLAGES DE LA FRANCE,

POUR LES INSTRUIRE

Des Loix, des Événemens, des Découvertes
qui intéressent tout Citoyen;

PROPOSÉE PAR SOUSCRIPTION

Aux Propriétaires, Fermiers, Pasteurs, Habitans
& Amis des Campagnes,

A 7 liv. 4 sols par an, Franc de Port:

PROSPECTUS

PUBLIÉ PAR M. CÉRUTTI.

*Si un Peuple Esclave a besoin du joug de l'ignorance, un
Peuple Libre a besoin du frein de l'instruction.*

A PARIS,

Chez DESENNE, Libraire, au Palais-Royal, N°. 1 & 2.

1790.

Joseph-Antoine-Joachim Cérutti, ed. *La Feuille villageoise . . :* ("The Village Leaflet"). 1790. The New York Public Library, General Research Division.

    La Feuille villageoise was an extremely successful paper aimed specifically at rural
audiences. It was highly pedagogical in spirit and tone (cat. no. 176).

LE PATRIOTE FRANÇOIS,

OU

JOURNAL LIBRE,

IMPARTIAL ET NATIONAL;

PAR UNE *Société de Citoyens.*

Une Gazette libre est une sentinelle qui veille sans cesse pour le peuple. D. JEBB.

CE seroit insulter à la Nation Françoise que de lui démontrer longuement l'utilité & la nécessité de ce Journal dans les circonstances actuelles. Elle touche au moment d'obtenir une constitution qui doit à jamais assurer sa liberté ; cette constitution ne peut être que le fruit de l'harmonie entre tous les membres de l'Etat, & cette harmonie ne peut exister que par l'instruction universelle.

La foule de brochures qui ont paru depuis la naissance de cette révolution a commencé cette

A

he stated in his first issue. But the paper was not merely an adjunct of the Assembly nor merely a reflection of the public mood. "It will devote itself above all both to defending the rights of the People . . . and to keeping the People from being led into continual fermentation, which would perpetuate disorder and postpone the Constitution."[29] The paper's Assembly reports, only one part of its larger news coverage, were designed to guide the deputies in their work and to forestall external obstruction to it by either an unenlightened populace or by the forces of aristocratic reaction.

Brissot immediately demonstrated his willingness to teach both the Assembly and the people. "One does not *create* the rights on which any free constitution is based, one can only state them," he thundered in a preface to his report on an early debate about the constitution in 1789, denouncing hesitant deputies who feared giving the people too many freedoms.[30] The *Patriote*'s treatment of the famous confrontation over the royal veto later in 1789 gives a good example of its method of presentation. Rather than leaving matters in the hands of the speakers, the *Patriote* began by framing the question itself: "The celebrated matter of the *veto* is beginning to become clear." The terms being employed in the debate, such as "suspensive veto," were "rather abstract," but "that is the case with many new words." The paper was pleased to see that the members of the Assembly had now succeeded in grasping the concept. "Our readers will also succeed in understanding it well, by following the different explanations of the greater or lesser power accorded to the king," it continued, and then proceeded to give a masterful summary of the points made by the principal opponents of an absolute veto for the king.[31] The paper's clear, confident tone, and its assurances to readers that their deputies also needed enlightenment from the press on constitutional matters, constituted an effective approach to promoting particular ideas without insulting the public. The presentation of the Assembly debates as confrontations between right-thinking patriotic deputies and their aristocratic enemies provided a sense of clarity and drama. This selective coverage of the Assembly from a consistent partisan point of view was probably the most common method of representation in the Paris press throughout the Revolution. It naturally outraged deputies who disagreed with a particular paper; parliamentary complaints that the press distorted the debates for partisan purposes echoed and reechoed throughout the decade. But such journalism served the purposes of all those groups, from the moderate constitutional monarchists on the right to the mainstream of the Jacobins on the left, who saw an elected legislative assembly as the proper focus of France's new political life.

Whatever their private feelings about Brissot's style of journalism, which was typical of many revolutionary newspapers, the deputies had much stronger reactions to the extremist press of left and right, which mentioned the legislative debates only to deny the political legitimacy of the entire legislative enterprise. The most celebrated radical paper of the Revolution, Marat's *Ami du peuple*, brilliantly epitomized this style. From the moment his paper began to appear, in September 1789, Marat's commentary on the Assembly was clearly more important than the sketchy and exceedingly biased summary he gave of its proceedings. He justified his outspoken criticism of the Assembly on the ground that no other course was open to a friend of the people but "to enlighten the Nation, to settle its ideas, and to give public opinion a way of showing itself."[32]

A typical early issue of Marat's *Ami du peuple*—a small-format pamphlet-journal—began with a highly compressed summary of the latest Assembly debates. Then, as if he could restrain himself no longer, Marat would break in with his expostulations against the deputies, denouncing those he disliked in the strongest possible terms. He lambasted the views of one supporter of the royal veto as "more than suspect; they are the ideas of aristocracy covered with the veil of love for order and the public good," expressing astonishment that any deputy could defend a bicameral legislature or the veto, while reminding readers somberly that the enemies of the people would never have made any concessions "without the bloody scenes that followed the storming of the Bastille."[33] Condemnations of the Assembly were mixed with overt attempts to mobilize the force of the people against "the criminal faction" in the Assembly, and when he looked back on the first revolutionary Assembly from the ripe perspective of the spring of 1792, it was only to conclude that "cruel experience has taught the whole nation that its deputies to the Estates General sold out its imprescriptible rights and its most vital interests to the monarch, and only seven or eight came out pure."[34] For Marat, the purpose of describing the Assembly's sessions was neither to provide an impartial transcript nor to guide the thinking of the patriotic members of that body and of the public toward a common goal, but rather to expose and unmask the deputies' treasonous intentions and to mobilize the people against them, in imitation of his own highly emotional reactions expressed in his journal.

The royalist press, which flourished almost as extensively as the prorevolutionary papers in the first years of the Revolution, shared Marat's indignant rejection of the National Assembly and all its works, but not, of course, for the same reasons. Some royalist papers, like the abbé Royou's *Ami du roi*, depicted the Assembly in terms not very different from Marat's, as a criminal conspiracy against the people, "a colossus already grown to an immeasurable height" and oppressing both people and king.[35] Others, like the satirical *Actes des apôtres*, assessed the Assembly's problem as madness rather than criminality. It enjoyed imagining the wildest possible consequences of the principles enunciated by the *patriotes*, as when it predicted—

LES ACTES
DES APOTRES.
INTRODUCTION.

LE TABLEAU DE FAMILLE.

Fragment de l'histoire de France.

Tableau de la position de la France pendant la jeunesse de Charles V , dit *le Sage.*

LE roi Jean régnoit, et l'aîné de ses fils étoit Charles V , dit le *sage* , que l'histoire appella , dans ces temps de trouble , tantôt le duc de Normandie , tantôt le dauphin , puis le régent.

Charles *le mauvais* , roi de Navarre , étoit beau-frere de Charles V.

Les états-généraux du royaume furent convoqués le 2 Décembre 1355 , à Ruel.

L'archevêque de Rheims y présida le clergé.

Gauthier de Brienne , la noblesse.

Marcel , maire de Paris , le tiers-état.

La guerre désoloit la France , et il falloit pourvoir aux subsides.

Des loix assez sages pour le temps furent promulguées.

On y décrêta l'égalité des impositions.

On y supprima les servitudes personnelles , les corvées , les évocations , les capitaineries et garennes , et les épices des juges.

On y vota une armée de trente mille hommes ; et pour que

A

Antoine-Joseph, comte de Barruel-Beauvert, ed. *Les Actes des apôtres* ("The Acts of the Apostles"). [1796]. The New York Public Library, Rare Books and Manuscripts Division.

This version of the *Actes des apôtres,* from 1796, continued a tradition of right-wing political satire developed in the original journal in 1789–91 (cat. no. 84).

no doubt without believing such a thing would actually come to pass only four years later—that French ambassadors would soon be sent abroad with instructions "to spread the great ideas of liberty which have given France the happy constitution she has," and to overturn the institutions of their host countries.[36]

Brissot's prerevolutionary vision of the newspaper press as the invention that would restore to modern democracy the immediacy and participatory quality of politics in ancient Greece and Rome thus failed to anticipate the actual effects of the intervention of journalists and their words between the legislators and the people. Whereas the monarchy had displayed itself in Versailles's Hall of Mirrors and had contrived to control its own reflection, the revolutionary assemblies found themselves being depicted by the distorting mirrors of a carnival funhouse. Although the deputies had their own printer publish decrees depicting themselves as united and working together for the nation's interests, the press interposed itself between the citizens and their representatives, offering its alternative representations of the legislature as disorderly, split by bitter partisan strife, conspiring against the people, or simply insane. Small wonder that the staunchly prorevolutionary deputy J.-B. Louvet, himself a journalist, was driven to denounce "this eternal domination of writers over . . . the magistrates, the people's representatives, the leading public officials" and to warn that "the press . . . this perpetual fomenter of revolution," would destabilize even a government based on popular consent if it was not controlled.[37] The French revolutionaries were among the first to confront the paradox inherent in freedom of the press under a representative system of government: The people may choose their representatives, but they do not necessarily prefer the latter's image of themselves over images created by the press. In the revolutionary era, it was Napoleon who resolved the deadlock between politicians and journalists by bringing both under his firm control. But the problem posed by the press of the French Revolution has reappeared in all representative political systems ever since. For that reason, the old-fashioned newspapers of the French Revolution are not merely historical artifacts; they exemplify a central problem of the press in the modern world.

PAMPHLETS:
LIBEL AND
POLITICAL MYTHOLOGY

ANTOINE DE BAECQUE

FROM 1787 ONWARD the political pamphlet assumed increasing importance in France. Indeed, the process began almost officially: Once the king invited his subjects to proffer views and advice on the meeting of the Estates General, printing presses enabled a general debate about the reorganization of finances and the reform of abuses. Thereafter, as a matter of course, the ever-agile pen of the pamphleteer kept pace with the accelerating course of events. Tracts about the best way to convene the Estates General, the agitation in the parlements, and the relative merits of the nobility, the clergy, and the Third Estate poured out. This ephemeral literature provided a running commentary on nearly everything, and it often did so by concentrating on spectacular episodes or prominent public figures. From 1789 to 1799, the *Catalogue de l'histoire de France* in the Bibliothèque Nationale lists more than 12,000 pamphlets—a number that, while certainly falling short of the truth, is nonetheless much larger than that of any preceding period (for example, the 5,000 diatribes against Cardinal Mazarin in the mid-seventeenth century which engaged the interest of Christian Jouhaud).[1] The *Catalogue*'s listing of pamphlets produced yearly shows the greatest concentration of activity in the period 1789–92:

Year	No. of Pamphlets	
1774–1786	312	
1787	217	
1788	819	
1789	3,305	
1790	3,121	9,635
1791	1,923	
1792	1,286	

165

Year	No. of Pamphlets
1793	663
1794	601
1795	569
1796	182
1797	245
1798	154
1799	211
TOTAL	13,608

The reader will at once be struck by the diversity of this rich literature. Treatises on finance, proposals for new systems of government organization, and scholarly reflections all figure prominently; but so do such less respectable varieties as pornographic pamphlets, political denunciations, eulogies, or "Les Cris de Paris" ("The Cries of Paris")[2]—bespeaking the pamphleteers' attempt to adapt traditional forms to the evolving realities of revolutionary politics. Several categories of literature are evident in these pamphlets, each with its own style, imagery, rhetorical technique, and purpose.

The first such category—reflections on government and institutions—arose from the educated classes, which had been attempting, with more and more success since the mid-eighteenth century, to contribute to political theory. This category is confined to propositions, sometimes controversial but always courteously offered. These pamphlets are a gold mine for the historian of ideas, who will find famous men side by side with impoverished scribblers, in a literary attitude that is undeniably constructive but painfully earnest and, at times, tediously repetitive.

A second category, the political essay, includes well-known figures like Sieyès, Mirabeau, and Target alongside an abundance of second-rate or unknown thinkers. The sheer size of this category of works makes it interesting: Behind all the essays on constitution-making, the declarations of rights, and appeals for unity among the three estates can be sensed the continuous intellectual ferment that accompanied the rapid march of events in the early years of the Revolution.

The third major group of pamphlets, those commenting on current affairs, is even larger, owing to the reading public's enormous appetite for news. Such pamphlets contain innumerable descriptions, following more or less the same pattern, of such events as the Royal Session of the Estates General, the Tennis Court Oath, and the taking of the Bastille. Here, commentary provided a point of departure for tribute to some hero or some brave act—as in the pamphleteering of the Old Regime—but topics became increasingly explosive after 1788.

Finally, although closer analysis would allow us to distinguish yet more subcategories, there was political polemic—perhaps the most purposeful genre. It was stimulated during the ten years of the Revolution by constant strife between factions behind whose leaders the pamphleteers, with real or feigned enthusiasm, fell in. One work would appear, another come out in reply, a third would rebut the rebuttal, and so on in a "paper conflict," to quote a contemporary.[3] Such a conflict, involving perhaps dozens of pamphlets with their various positions and objectives, is a veritable barbed-wire entanglement for the student. One must be mindful of the pamphleteers' rhetorical devices, from intellectual debate and the narration of events to violent criticism (or exaggerated praise). Such pamphleteering turns on the apposition of praise and denunciation. Through metaphors of rebirth and degeneracy, the genre seeks to determine the nature of the New Man and the heroes of his mythology, whether as individuals (Louis XVI, Lafayette, Necker, Mirabeau) or types (the reborn Frenchman, the conqueror of the Bastille, the sans-culotte). The image can also be that of the enemy, either, again, as an individual (Lambesc, Maury, the younger Mirabeau, Louis XVI in flight from his people) or as a type (the nobleman, the aristocrat, the émigré). A constant play on words, with lavish use of metaphor to exalt or demean, seeks to engage the reader's interest with new revelations and denunciations; it sets the scene for political controversy where the imaginary looms as large as the real, spinning a whole web of political mythology out of its rhetoric.[4]

As we have suggested, this ephemeral literature is best approached only in sections involving limited and relatively homogeneous material. In this chapter I discuss the political pornographic pamphlet from 1789 to 1792. This subcategory, ribald and anonymous, nonetheless conceals beneath its scurrilous surface a certain subtlety in its delineation of political figures. This self-contained body of writing helps us begin to understand the methodology of the revolutionary pamphlet across its entire range.

The "Enfer" (reserve) of the Bibliothèque Nationale houses a large collection of these strident pamphlets, which came out in ever-increasing numbers in the last years of the monarchy; even more were produced after 1789. The Bibliothèque Nationale's collection bears witness to this trend. The number of titles in the collection rose each year from 1774–75 until 1788. The early years of the Revolution witnessed an even sharper increase. The seventy titles surviving from 1789 to 1792 are not only more tendentious, more politically committed, and more defamatory than their predecessors, they also far outpace the previous output of the eighteenth century. The prerevolutionary literature had prepared the way for the short, sharp burst of ephemeral literature at the beginning of the Revolution, particularly 1789–90. These little works have a specific form; booklets rather than books, they are octavo pamphlets of eight, sixteen, or thirty-two pages. They are linked to other pamphlet literature by other indicators. For instance, almost all are anonymous; only one of our group is signed (by "Mlle Théroigne," the licentious muse of the young Revolution). The dates are sometimes imaginary—"Second Year of the Copulatory Revolution," for example (no doubt 1790). Finally, the places of publication are very fanciful: some "at Amsterdam," many "at Cythera," others more overtly outrageous, "at Bawdopolis," "at Heliocopulopolis," "at Democratis." Second-rate literature, which can fairly be compared to the caricature of the same period, it makes use not only of a framework of obscenity and a pornographic vocabulary but also of certain rhetorical devices that are effective in a political context, such as insult or tongue-in-cheek denunciation.

Few literary graces are evident here beyond the dubious pun, and the corpus is in no way comparable to the glorious libertine literature of the second half of the eighteenth century. It consists of more than sixty obscene texts, in their special way a fair sample of the ephemeral writing that flared up at the beginning of the Revolution, commenting on the news of the hour from both the streets and the new deliberative assemblies of the state. Characteristic of the pamphlet form of literature, too long overlooked and even scorned, they offer us a commentary on the Revolution: virulent enunciation of the degeneracy imputed to the symbolic Aristocrat, a skeptical but often-penetrating eye turned on the stage of politics and its actors, and a tendentious use of every literary device to contrast the sick, impotent, and decadent old order with the regenerated new society. Herein resides the fascinating value of these little books, playing their part in the creation of a new political mythology, stamped by a strange, frenetic Manichaeanism that contrasts the degenerate aristocrat of the dark with the new revolutionary man of the light. We are forced to ask ourselves how inflammatory language and mythologizing can offer a legitimate exegesis on the politics of the day.

Declaiming the decadence of the aristocracy in scandalous books was not a novel strategy in 1789. In the eighteenth century alone, ecclesiastics were often subjected to ribald ridicule; "Dom Pederast," so often encountered during the Revolution, epitomizes these pornographic attacks on the supposed homosexuality of the clergy. The Crown itself was not spared; the relations of the young Louis XV with the comte de Clermont, to give but one example, were much written about. Although court life could lend credence to such sharp and salacious attacks, the genre never reached the height of intensity, especially political intensity, until just before the Revolution. Rob-

ert Darnton has discussed the excesses of the fringe literature of the day—
what Voltaire referred to as "the *canaille* of literature"—in the direction
of sexual sensationalism about the royal circle.[5] Beginning with certain
pamphlets, of which the best-known is probably Théveneau de Morande's
Gazetier cuirassé (*Armor-plated Journalist*), there was a systematic campaign of
destruction and accelerated profanation conducted by "Rousseaus of the
gutter." A whole series of lewd "Private Lives" dealt with figures at the royal
court, a tradition recapitulated during the Revolution when similar "Private
Lives" dealt with such political leaders as Lafayette, Brissot, the Mirabeau
brothers, Pétion, and Robespierre. The love affairs of Louis XV, the alleged
impotence of Louis XVI, and the "sexual ardors" of Marie Antoinette were
all the targets of such lewd and violent pamphlets as *La Naissance du Dauphin
dévoilée* (*The Dauphin's Birth Disclosed*), *La Gazette noire* (*The Black Gazette*), or
Les Amours de Charlot et Toinette (*The Loves of Charlot and Toinette*).

After 1789, with leaflets falling like rain across the country, this trend
accelerated. Pornographic attacks on great personages proliferated apace
with the developing situation. *L'Autrichienne en goguette, ou l'orgie royale* (*The
Austrian Woman on the Loose, or the Royal Orgy*), *Les Entretiens secrets entre la
reine et le cardinal de Rohan après son entrée aux Etats-Généraux* (*The Secret Relations of the Queen with the Cardinal de Rohan After His Appearance at the Estates
General*), *Dom Bougre aux Etats-Généraux* (*Dom Pederast at the Estates General*),
Les Enfers de Sodome à l'assemblée nationale (*The Fires of Sodom in the National
Assembly*), *L'abbé Maury chez les filles* (*The Abbé Maury among the Girls*) all keep
a sharp, albeit lewd, eye on political developments. The Parisian public was
more and more openly being offered a new literature, explicitly sexual in
its terminology, and using sexual sensationalism above all in a tireless effort
to prove that the old ruling classes were unfit to survive into the new age.
Impotent, riddled with veneral disease, wholly given over to distempered,
narcissistic pleasures, the aristocrat was depicted as irrevocably destined for
the dustbin of history.

The literary "invention" or the degenerate aristocrat was a masterpiece
of propagandistic moral destabilization; he became the symbol of a society
the pamphlets presented as worn out. In contrast are the "patriotic sexual
practices" trumpeted by the pamphlets—less clearly drawn because irony
lends itself less readily to eulogy. More controlled, hygienic, and virile, the
sexual practices of the republicans were presented as the antithesis of the
orgies imputed to the old order. This "political" Manichaeanism is a paramount device in the pamphleteering of the period. The lewdness of political pornography (it puts things very bluntly) offers us an interesting approach to the study of this duality in the politics of the day.

In the bawdy literature of the Revolution, a place is found for the traditional forms: erotic banter, new editions of the classics of salacious litera-

ture, "practical guides," and lists and descriptions of Parisian prostitutes and houses of entertainment. Erotic banter and verse were scarcely affected by the Revolution, apart from the intermittent and contrived inclusion of "patriotic" terms, which disappeared just as quickly as they were introduced. The classics of erotic literature, from Aretino to Mirabeau or Voltaire and on to Sade, continued to appear regularly in new editions. The "practical guides" to amatory positions and behavior also came through the Revolution untouched. Two best-sellers were *Les Tableaux des moeurs du temps aux différents âges de la vie* (*Pictures of Moral Habits at Different Times of Life*),[6] and *La Science pratique des filles du monde* (*The Practical Science of Women of the World*);[7] the latter presents the "forty amorous positions" without the least reference to the "patriotic position" as described in other lewd manuals of the period. The last category, the listings of prostitutes and brothels, was less immune to revolutionary vagaries (witness all the pseudo-histories of the "Republic of Whoredom" that appeared toward the end of the eighteenth century), but they appeared regularly for the rest of the decade, often without any political coloration at all.

By contrast, political pornography was aimed directly at the most visible figures in Paris. Works of this kind, which account for almost half the bawdy literature of the early years of the Revolution, used two themes to deride the aristocracy: impotence and homosexuality. These are not new themes; many of the hygienists among the writers of the Enlightenment had developed them earlier in the century. But during the Revolution the idea of decadence passes into that of decay, of organic breakdown. The aristocracy thus becomes, for the purposes of such writing, a dying race; moral corruption and physical debauchery become intimately linked.

In all the lewd satire, the technique of denunciation is identical: Degeneration of the body goes hand in hand with moral turpitude and political duplicity. The pamphlets thus characterized the sexual practices of the aristocracy as vicious or effeminate. Accusations are leveled against opponents of the Revolution, always dwelling on sickness, want of vigor, awkwardness—nebulous qualities, no doubt, but certainly the converse of the coveted "patriotic energy." The flaccid indolence thus imputed to the leaders of the old order was imputed even to the Crown: *Les Amours de Charlot et Toinette*,[8] which appeared in several editions between 1789 and 1791, speaks of

> a young and amorous Queen
> Whose august Husband was no use in bed.

The lewd fantasy of the day depicts Marie Antoinette as a sexual bombshell who wore out poor Louis as well as the comte d'Artois before turning to Mme. de Polignac as a last resort. To the accusation of royal impotence was thus added the charge of the queen's "unnatural lust"—her lesbian-ism—so that in the end the decadence is complete.

Another ancient terror, one addressed in many eighteenth-century treatises, was venereal disease. The polemics of pornography transformed it into a political and personal liability. Tendentious pathological descriptions are piled one on top of another in a caricature of the decadent aristocracy—a caricature the pamphlets can then bring to market as needed. One pamphlet has Loménie de Brienne confess he had contracted "thirty venereal maladies," placing these diagnostic words into his mouth: "My body was poxed all over; my cock glistened as though covered in pearls; my legs, rotting outward from the bone, would no longer bear me; I could scarce open my cankered mouth for pain; my body oozed a poxy suppuration; my breath was a charnel-house."[9] The mordant irony of these pamphlets is that the aristocracy takes a narcissistic pleasure in its own decay.

The self-love of the privileged under the old order was exemplified in their lofty disdain, often directed to the Bohemian scribblers; they themselves are now the object of their autoerotic contemplation and held up to derision thereby. Such mockery was in the usual vein of the pamphleteers. They write of the Last Judgment awaiting the debauched, the final extinction when all the aristocrats' material being is consumed: "to die on a bed of terror, to be gnawed to the bone, to feel your limbs rot and fall away one after another," such is the death of the aristocrat in the work dated "in the Second Year of Copulatory Regeneration."[10] Around this decrepit figure—an emblem of the old society that looms so large in the pamphleteers' fantastical political landscape—there grew up the myth of the "revolutionary rebirth." This was a whole structure of thought, distinctly millenarian, conveying the idea (vividly illustrated with parodies of the Last Judgment or descriptions of the end of the world) that the outbreak of revolution had overthrown the vestiges of a decadent society. To the image of the sick, impotent, degenerate aristocrat is contrasted that of the healthy, virile patriot who necessarily personifies the evocative, and oft-invoked, concept of new birth.

Moral degeneration, of course, accompanies the physical in this literature; the homosexuality imputed to the old, privileged orders was the second favorite theme of polemic pornography. Suspicion of the clergy's homosexuality, reflecting a long tradition of satire, quickly made churchmen the first target. "We'll be perverts, that's the game!" chorus the prelates of France, conceived as meeting in a ribald apostolic conclave.[11] "May it please Your Holiness," they implore the pope, "to remit to us the needful Brief, sanctioning our pious resolve to love one another as we desire." Dissolute in soul, in body, and in his pleasures, the churchman is wholly degenerate.

We can see the same methods at work stripping any aura of reverence from the nobility. Pornographic pamphlets present vice and self-indulgence as the two principal attributes of the aristocrat. Naturally, this contemptible figure feels more comfortable outside France; Koblenz is therefore often mentioned in the pamphlets of 1791. Indeed, the émigré is central to the political mythology of the pamphleteers and cartoonists.[12] Koblenz is repeatedly described as the center of depravity; nobles befoul all that they touch, and the city is the scene of a continuous orgy. A pamphlet entitled *Les Délices de Coblentz* (*The Delights of Koblenz*)[13] writes ironically of the "brilliant festivities given by the Prince de Condé to the illustrious French émigrés before their departure for Paris." Here, the only thing to be feared is boredom, so every care has been taken to facilitate carnal perversion, down to special mattresses whose "elastic springs are so attuned to pleasure, that when they receive the impress of its movements they redouble its enjoyment."[14] The pleasures here presented are so unbridled that they almost seem to confirm the other, and superficially contrasting, accusation of impotence. The political objective is to call into question the aristocrat's place in society by dwelling on his sexual escapades. He is made to appear a pervert, not a soldier. The aristocrats are shown as dreaming of more orgies in a reconquered Paris:

> As one, they swore to come to Paris at the head of their army and renew their sport. . . . "Yes!" cried Condé, clasping his mistress to him, "I swear that you shall have the same festivities in Paris, in the teeth of the Parisians. . . . How better could we take our revenge on that vile rabble, and all the rascals who now presume to call themselves legislators, than by enjoying our mistresses under their noses?" "Indeed," added the Cardinal de Rohan, "and let us not forget to invite to our amorous contests the most beautiful of the deputies' wives, and take our pleasure with them before their husbands' very eyes."[15]

Cuckolding the enemy is here a sweeter revenge for the nobleman than fighting him; his vocation as a soldier is trivialized. Sexual decadence is shown as the corruption of what used to be the nobleman's finest quality: his manly strength in battle.

The ribald literature has something to say about "patriots," too, but it remains true to its own rules. Commentary is always ironic, and though there are some positive figures—the democratic brother-in-arms, the democratic bawd—they are not invariably treated with respect. The pamphlets cannot be taken at their word; they use imagery to manipulate the reader, always striving to be up-to-date and intellectually modish. Thus they are quick to present distorted likenesses, owing more to political mythology (that is, catering to the tastes of the times) than to verisimilitude. This is not to say that the pamphlets, busily spinning their pornographic fantasies, failed to employ a new, albeit superficial, tone reflecting the new values. "My cock is no fop's cock"[16] might serve as a light-hearted epitome of this approach. The lovemaking of aristocrats is slow and awkward; that of patriots is brisk and certain, voluntarily conforming to an ideal of virility. The comparison between the robust good looks of the free man and the decadent refinement of the aristocrat would be the starting point of a lewd treatise.

The other great theme has to do with health; its purpose is to contrast the healthy patriotic body and the diseased aristocratic body. It gave rise to an explanation and justification of the "political and moral rebirth" of the Revolution—a rebirth that would purify the sexual act and bring it under the purview of the new government.[17] This was another fantasy, needless to say, for no revolutionary government could burden itself with organizing the whores and brothels of Paris.

The pamphlets that deal with prostitution (the most famous, which went into many editions, being the *Catéchisme libertin* [*Libertine's Catechism*], attributed to "mademoiselle Théroigne") take up where Restif de la Bretonne's *Pornographe* left off, proposing that a new patriotic organization should enforce strict rules of morality and hygiene in the new houses of pleasure. "A girl who is sick should not work. . . . A prostitute should earn as much as she can, but by honest conduct with no trickery." "Retirement" age is set at forty, but "thirty-five for blondes, who fade more quickly than brunettes." Even interior decoration is provided for: "Now that everything is patriotic, a tricolor ribbon should suffice to render sex patriotic, too."[18] Indeed, this is a guide to patriotic sexual practice, pornographic to be sure, but colored throughout by political allusions. It explicitly condemns the elderly libertines of the old order, men who seek commercial sex while diseased, or for the satisfaction of perverted tastes. The conditions of entry to the new establishments are set out: "You must be able to display sound, healthy sexual parts; you must also prove that you are a good patriot and bitter foe of the aristocrats."[19] Such, in the fevered imagination of the pornographers, were the laws needed to codify the patriotic sexual rebirth.

From this rebirth, homosexuality was to be excluded. To put an end to "the acts of idle pederasts" was the object of *Requêtes contre les bougres* (*Appeal against the Perverts*), an imaginary address to the Estates General, which implores "the gentlemen of the Estates, for most good and sufficient cause shown, [to decree that] all such persons be required to wear an especial plume, whereby they may be distinguished"[20]—a good instance of the bawdy parody of the proceedings of the Estates General, which was a specialty of the pamphlets. The old pleasures are to be displaced by the "sexual rebirth," so that we are offered "The Story of the Revolution" in a

CATÉCHISME
LIBERTIN

A L'USAGE DES FILLES DE JOIE ET DES JEUNES DEMOISELLES
QUI SE DÉCIDENT A EMBRASSER CETTE PROFESSION

PAR Mᴸˡᵉ THÉROIGNE

THÉROIGNE au district, aussi bien qu'au bordel,
De ses talents divers a fait l'expérience;
Par sa langue et son cœur précieux à la France,
Son nom va devenir à jamais immortel.

Sur la copie imprimée
A PARIS
—
1792

AUX DÉPENS DE LA VEUVE GOURDAN

Mlle Théroigne [pseud.]. "Libertine's Catechism for the Use of Girls of Pleasure and Young Women Who Decide to Take up the Profession" (*Catéchisme libertin à l'usage des filles de joie et des jeunes demoiselles qui se décident à embrasser cette profession*). Paris, 1792. Bibliothèque Nationale, Département des Imprimés.

BORDEL NATIONAL,
SOUS LES AUSPICES
DE LA REINE,

A l'ufage des Confédérés Provinciaux;

DÉDIÉ ET PRÉSENTÉ

A Mlle. THÉROIGNE,

Préfidente du Diftrict des Cordeliers,
& du Club des Jacobins;

Auteur de cet Etablissement patriotique.

Lancea carnalis vulnera nulla facit.
OVID.
La flèche de l'Amour ne fait point de
blessures.

A CYTHERE,
Et dans tous les Bordels de Paris.

1790.

Club des Jacobins. "National Brothel . . . for the Use of the Provincial Confederates." 1790. Bibliothèque Nationale, Département des Imprimés (cat. no. 91).

One of the purposes of revolutionary pornography was to celebrate political and moral rebirth by contrasting the healthy patriotic body with the diseased aristocratic body.

pornographic sensationalism prized by this ephemeral literature. The story has several components. It begins with expressions of patriotic ardor: "This collection will be followed by others, if our public should condescend to accept it as patriotic—for we disdain the tribute paid to the semblance of aristocracy," says the dedication of the *Echo foutromane* (*Erotomaniacal Echo*),[21] for example. Another indispensable component was the "licentious Muse," an imaginary lady who is always very clever and ardently patriotic—an acknowledged member of the revolutionary pantheon. The most famous of them was Théroigne de Méricourt, called "Lambertine" and later known as "Mlle Théroigne." She was the patriotic counterpart (said to be a Girondin) of the omnipresent, obscene figure of Marie Antoinette. The story also has its hero, as must every fable: the national comrade-in-arms who figures in much revolutionary pornography as the type of simple, healthy virility. The ideal he represents is underlined by the longing attributed to "the greatest bawd in Paris. . . . To be possessed at the same time by four vigorous comrades-in-arms, so that I may be filled with the national seed."[22] If the "patriotic rebirth" idealizes the revolutionary it is because he, being politically correct, is entitled to the trappings of a classical demigod. The political stage imagined in the pamphlets is peopled with such vigorous beings, symbolizing the irresistible will of the New Society. The rebirth thus becomes tinged with irony, as witness this short passage from a lewd "anecdote":

Mrs. Lickerish was married in the flower of her age, beautiful and a virgin; what joy there was on her wedding-night! . . . That was the night of the grand climacteric day of the French Revolution: July 14, 1789. In that she chose that day to unite herself to a Frenchman, it might be presumed that she was espousing a hero, and on her wedding night, by the same reasoning, she should have tested the mettle of a victorious Hercules. . . . At least, such was the titillating idea she conceived of the man who was to come to her bed from the storming of the Bastille, and to take possession of her after overthrowing a tyranny—for it is certain that a regenerated man is a demi-god coiled to spring. The young and ardent husband had made the rounds of the Bastille's eight towers, and had set himself to defeat despotism before confronting a maidenhead; as a straightforward patriot, he sought to weave some sprigs of laurel into the garland of myrtle.[23]

Some disreputable writers found in polemic pornography a means, at once very direct and very allusive, of holding up the former establishment to ridicule. It seems to have worked, because this Manichaeanism (whereby a degenerate aristocracy is, as it were, hoist with its own petard) may be

encountered not only in early revolutionary caricature, where the aristocrat cuts the same ludicrous and distorted figure, but in political controversy as well. Again and again, when the subject is the counterrevolutionary, we are confronted with coprophilia, whether from Marat, or Hébert,
or other patriotic commentators. These images, constituting a vivid metaphor for the radical break between the old order and the new, became an
indispensable part of the mythology of the Revolution. The pornographic
pamphlet, with its sensational treatment of current events, illustrates this
clearly. It takes us on a voyage through the fantasy world of the contemporary pamphleteer, but it never relinquishes its hold on reality, and its characters reappear again and again. Although only very partial treatment has
been possible here, a discussion of these pamphlets emphasizes the overwhelming importance, in the new political mythology of the Revolution, of
certain intellectual trends that are the reverse of aristocratic.

BOOKS: RESHAPING SCIENCE

JEAN DHOMBRES

TWO ANECDOTES WILL serve as a summary introduction to the climate of an age. We are in pluviôse of the Year II (February 1794) at one of those high-strung, heated, and productive meetings of the Committee of Public Safety, which guided France through the Revolution and the Terror. A flunky leaves the room to bring not refreshments, not news from the front, not the names of new victims of the guillotine, but a bundle of new books on mechanics and chemistry.[1] Science has insinuated itself into politics via the most natural of media: the book.

We now move a decade hence and a few hundred yards away to the somewhat stilted court of the Emperor Napoleon at the Tuileries, where the writer Bernardin de Saint-Pierre, a member of the moral and political sciences section of the Institut de France, is complaining peevishly of the indifference, nay, the contempt, with which he is viewed by his scientific colleagues. Asks Napoleon: "Monsieur Bernardin, do you know the differential calculus?" "No," replies the writer. "Then go home and learn it," commands the emperor, "Your question will answer itself!"[2]

How many Bernardins, seeking to be in fashion, and to pass for educated men, were thus constrained to lay siege to mathematics and to the exact sciences in general? To learn, they needed books, so scientific books were once again the rage. Many and various such books were written, published, and—no doubt—read.

The new infatuation served to quicken, in its own way, a long, slow trend that had emerged at the turn of the eighteenth century. We may well be astonished at the evanescence of this phenomenon, because with the restoration of the Bourbons in 1815 the figures reveal a sharp drop in scientific books as a percentage of all books published in France. The following figures on scientific books (as a percentage of all titles published for selected years) should serve as something of a benchmark: 1798, 14.4 percent; 1799, 14.6 percent; 1800, 14.1 percent; 1801, 14.3 percent; 1802, 14.0 percent; 1803, 17.7 percent; 1804, 23.2 percent; 1805, 23.3 percent; 1812, 25.1 percent; 1816, 14.5 percent.[3] True, the total number of books published continued to grow, but gone was the steady gain of the sciences at the expense of other aspects of culture. Historians agree that the early years of the nineteenth century were an era of science. Bearing Socrates' profound observation in mind that contrary opinions provoke intellectual inquiry, we intend to offer some paths along which the reader may choose to reflect.

For a review of the output of scientific books, the last decade of the eighteenth century—the very decade of the Revolution—might, a priori, appear a surprising choice. This cultural sector, after all, is thought to be relatively unresponsive to the accidents of history—so much so that the sciences tend to be relegated forever to Fernand Braudel's "long term." The choice is nonetheless justified by its results.

What, then, was the place of the scientific book in the culture of the revolutionary epoch? Which of the sciences were best served, and which most neglected, by these books? For what readers were they intended? We shall attempt to supply plausible answers to these questions by using quantitative analysis. These answers may also cast light on the more general study of printing during the French Revolution; it is not often that the historian of this period dons the spectacles of science!

Many Books, Many Scientific Books

In the later years of the Revolution the number of titles published in all fields increased so sharply that it was not until 1825 that the record production in 1798 of 1,500 titles was equaled (at least if we follow the indications of the *Journal général de la littérature de France, ou répertoire méthodique*, which will be our guide).[4] In 1785 only about 900 books were published in France, and a similarly low level is recorded for 1804.[5] The figure for 1785, however, is taken from a different source (depository-library list for the king's library). Detailed studies are lacking, and we cannot detect a clear pattern—such as a surge and then a slump in intellectual production around 1789—until the late 1790s.

Whereas overall book production crosses a watershed with one side much steeper than the other, the scientific sector shows more consistent growth. Figures are still lacking for the years 1790–97, but scientific titles as a percentage of all titles published constituted about 12 percent if we average the years around 1785[6] and had risen to about 15 percent by around 1798; in 1803 the figure was 19 percent and even reached 20 percent around 1812.[7] By "scientific books" we mean to include only those works that are strictly scientific. Not included are technical books, those on agriculture, texts on "arts and manufactures" that we would now consider industrial, nor works on the arts of war, architecture, and civil engineering. These self-imposed limitations will permit us to distinguish the impact of pure science from that of the applied sciences, which often operated interdependently with economic and technological considerations. Later we shall consider those specific applications of science of which the Revolution made much, and which have (wrongly, in my opinion) been taken for the entire scientific output of the period.

In summary, publication of scientific books in France steadily gained ground through the abundant output of the second part of the revolutionary decade; the overall decline under the Empire did not affect this steady growth as a proportion of all titles published. But under the Restoration this growth was stopped in its tracks, and the relative importance of scientific titles reverted to conditions under the Directory. Such is the story the figures tell. But before trying to interpret them, let us consider specifically what they are. As we have already seen, between 1789 and 1799 some 1,500 scientific titles were published, or republished, in France. So great a number may be hard to contemplate, so let us prudently confine ourselves to the Year VII (1798–1799), the last of the Revolution.

Scientific Books in 1799

Between 1 nivôse, Year VII, (December 21, 1798) and 30 brumaire, Year VIII (November 20, 1799) 1,377 titles were published; new works and new editions of old works are included (Table 1).[8] If literature occupied the largest portion of the production pattern—the novel alone, 177 titles, accounted for 13 percent of all the books published in this year—the sciences did well enough for themselves. The titles in geography, in technical fields, and in the pure sciences amount to more than a quarter of all production— a much larger share than that held by politics, although we have included under the latter rubric law and other aspects of government. Philosophy, which in 1785 had claimed 6 percent of all titles, now stood at only 2 percent. The age of the philosophers was over.

Scientific titles published in 1799 can be broken down by category (Table 2).[9] Table 3 deals with technical books, which were actually less nu-

TABLE 1

Books Published in 1799, by Category

	Number of Books	Percentage of Total
Science	205	15
Technical	65	5
Geography	91	7
History	93	7
Literature	541	39
Politics	119	9
Education	88	6
Arts	101	7
Other	74	5
Total	1,377	100%

TABLE 2

Scientific Titles Published in 1799, by Category

(in percentages)

Natural history	16.0
Botany	8.0
Physics	4.5
Chemistry, pharmacology, mineralogy	6.0
Medicine	28.0
Surgery	5.0
Veterinary medicine	2.5
Weights and measures	13.0
Mathematical sciences and astronomy	17.0

TABLE 3

Technical Titles Published in 1799, by Category

	Number	Percentage
Architecture	14	22
Military arts	14	22
Commerce & industry	20	31
Agriculture	17	25
Total	65	100

merous than strictly scientific works. Although these statistics cover only one year, we can be confident that they are not misleading. The three tables would not be much different had they been for 1798 or 1800.

The medical sciences accounted for the largest proportion of all scientific books published, a trend that accelerated to the point where, by 1818, one out of every two scientific titles published could be classed as a medical text. Society was improving, to the profit, it was hoped, of human health. Even if the art of healing had achieved no major breakthroughs, it was expected to benefit through a sort of percolation of general progress. Consider *Advice to Parents on Inoculation* (*Avis aux pères et mères sur l'inoculation*), by D. Laroche, published in the Year VII (1798–1799) by Fuchs in Paris. It was forty-eight pages long and cost a modest 75 centimes. Its avowed purpose was "to place inoculation within the reach of all classes of society."[10] Consider also *A Physician for the Gouty* (*Le Médecin des Goutteux*), by L. Bodin, published in Paris by Croullebois and priced at 1.50 francs. Perhaps because the practice of medicine had been open to everyone since March 1791, a spate of texts was published attacking the methods of "charlatans." For example, J. Mignard wrote on the "imaginary benefits of the Antisyphilitic Syrup," setting out to confound, in fifty-four pages, the proposals of Citizen Laflecteur for the prevention of venereal disease.[11]

The remedies of Mesmer were still in vogue in 1799, and his publisher made no bones about it: "For the dubious principles, which until now have served as rules for the practice of medicine, he has substituted an approach as simple as it is natural."[12] All of this notwithstanding, the quality of some of the medical writing is even more remarkable, as is the manifest intention of providing the public well-wrought treatises dealing not only with the current revolution in medical studies but also with the new theories developed by practitioners. Chaussier, a regular instructor at the Ecole de Santé as well as a visiting instructor at the Ecole Polytechnique, published a book on anatomy courses.[13] Desault, a well-known surgeon and the teacher of Xavier Bichat, collaborated with Bichat in writing the 330-page *Treatise on Maladies of the Urinary Tract* (*Traité des maladies des voies urinaires*), published by Deroi and priced at 4.50 francs. In the interest of enlightenment, C. Brewer brought out his *German Medical-Surgical Library* (*Bibliothèque germanique médico-chirurgicale*). The spirit that prevailed in Year VII (1798–1799) is exemplified in the title of a textbook by N. P. Gilbert: *Modern Medical Theories Compared with Each Other, and Conformed to the Results of Clinical Observation* (*Les Théories médicales modernes, comparées entre elles et rapprochées de la médecine d'observation*).[14] Indeed, as Michel Foucault has so authoritatively shown, it was a clinical method, and a statistically oriented one at that, which was evolving here.[15] The concern with analytical taxonomy is clearly shown in *Philosophical Nosography, or an Analytical*

Method Applied to Medicine (*Nosographie philosophique ou méthode de l'analyse appliquée à la médecine*), written by Pinel and first published in Paris in the Year VII (1798–99).

In the output of books for this Year VII, natural history and botany took second place after medicine, in traditional eighteenth-century fashion. In February, Plassan began publication of a new edition of Buffon's *Natural History* (*Histoire naturelle*)—fifty-two volumes in duodecimo—as well as of a *Natural History of Monkeys, Classified in Their Families, According to the System of Linnaeus* (*Histoire naturelle des singes, divisée par familles, suivant le système de Linné*), by J. Audebert. But a new bias toward school textbooks was emerging, apparent in the number of handbooks, such as *Elementary Handbook of the Natural History of Animals* (*Abrégé élémentaire de l'histoire naturelle des animaux*), published at Lille for the Ecole Centrale of the Département du Nord; a coherent course of instruction at 140 pages, it was sold by Jacquez for 3 francs. Successful textbooks were republished, as, for example, the *History of Insects Whether Annoying or Useful to Man, to Animals, to Agriculture, to Gardening and to the Arts* (*Histoire des insectes nuisibles et utiles à l'homme, aux animaux, à l'agriculture, au jardinage et aux arts*), published by Courcier and offered for 6.50 francs. Botanical dictionaries flourished, following in the train of the second edition of Jean-Baptiste Lamarck's *France's Flora* (*Flore françoise*)[16] published in the Year III (1794–1795), in three volumes, and of the same author's lengthy *Dictionary of Botany* (*Dictionnaire de botanique*), which appeared in the *Methodical Encyclopedia* (*L'Encyclopédie méthodique*) published by C. J. Panckoucke and his successors from 1782 to 1832.[17] That year, Treuttel and Wurtz offered a translation from the German of A. J. Batsch's *Botany for Women and for Amateurs of Plants* (*Botanique pour les femmes et les amateurs des plantes*). The publisher's synopsis noted that "the obscurity and dryness of the original have been so refreshed as to make this little book accessible to the fair sex." A more serious work was *The Table of the Vegetable Kingdom According to the System of Jussieu* (*Le Tableau du règne végétal selon la méthode de Jussieu*).[18]

This zeal for analysis and classification, at work since the mid-eighteenth century, occasioned a few marginal and hazardous ventures such as the *Meteorological Annual for the Year VIII* (*Annuaire météorologique pour l'an VIII*) in 116 pages, which Lamarck unwisely published in the Year VII (1798–1799). The work contained predictions inferred from "unvarying causes," and "probabilities established by a long series of observations of the state of the heavens." This worthy aim was only a dream in 1799, and indeed still is. The scientific community was not impressed.

Holding a brilliant third place in book production were the mathematical sciences, which had not figured in the encyclopedists' tradition. Conspicuous in the Year VII (1798–1799) was Pierre-Simon Laplace's two-

HISTOIRE NATURELLE,

GENERALE ET PARTICULIERE,

PAR LECLERC DE BUFFON;

NOUVELLE EDITION, accompagnée de Notes, et dans laquelle les Supplémens sont insérés dans le premier texte, à la place qui leur convient. L'on y a ajouté l'histoire naturelle des Quadrupèdes et des Oiseaux découverts depuis la mort de Buffon ; celle des Reptiles, des Poissons, des Insectes et des Vers ; enfin, l'histoire des Plantes dont ce grand Naturaliste n'a pas eu le tems de s'occuper.

OUVRAGE formant un Cours complet d'Histoire Naturelle;

REDIGE PAR C. S. SONNINI,

MEMBRE DE PLUSIEURS SOCIÉTÉS SAVANTES.

TOME PREMIER.

A PARIS,
DE L'IMPRIMERIE DE F. DUFART.
AN VIII.

Le Genie de la Nature dans la Contemplation de l'Univers

Georges Louis LeClerc, comte de Buffon. "Natural History, General and Particular." An VIII (1799–1800). The New York Public Library, General Research Division.

After medicine, natural history was the most popular scientific subject of the revolutionary period. This 1799 edition of Buffon's "Natural History" exemplifies the revolutionary cult of nature (cat. no. 62).

volume *Treatise on Celestial Mechanics* (*Traité de mécanique céleste*), published by Duprat and printed by Crapelet. It was priced at 30 francs for the standard edition; the deluxe edition in satin-finished vellum cost 96 francs. The publisher's newsletter was lyrical: "The production of this work is a model of its kind. The eye is delighted alike by the symmetrical presentation of the formulae, the elegance of the layout, the beauty of the letterpress and the sharpness of the printing."[19] Below is a mathematical formula as it appeared in a textbook by Laplace published in the Year III (1794–1795):[20]

$$(a+b)^n = a^n + n. a^{n-1}. b + \frac{n. \overline{n-1}. a^{n-2}. b^2}{1 . 2} + \frac{n. \overline{n-1}. \overline{n-2}.}{1 . 2 . 3}$$

$$a^{n-3}. b^3 + , \text{etc.}$$

Compare the typography of the Year VII (1798–1799) applied to a formula by the same author,[21] and the extent of the improvement is clear:

$$T = \pi . \sqrt{\frac{r}{g}} . \sqrt{\frac{2r.(a+b)}{(a+b)^2 + r^2 - b^2}} . \left\{ 1 + \left(\frac{1}{2}\right)^2 . \gamma^2 + \left(\frac{1.3}{2.4}\right)^2 . \gamma^4 + \left(\frac{1.3.5}{2.4.6}\right)^2 . \gamma^6 + \&c. \right\}$$

The higher quality of the mathematical symbols is not merely an extrinsic beauty, delighting the eye alone. It also expresses a mathematical way of reasoning which had been fashioned by Condillac, whose works[22] were reappearing in a flood of new editions, including such writings as the *Language of Calculation* (*Langue des calculs*).[23] According to Condillac, a well-chosen symbol is a furtherance to thought, because "algebra is a well-constructed language, and moreover the only such." It permits the manipulation of abstractions: "Whether words or algebraic signs be used for the solution of a mathematical problem, the method employed is the same. If it is mechanical in the one case, why not in the other? And why not mechanical still, if the problem at hand be one of metaphysics?"[24]

The conjunction of astronomy and mathematics must already have been held in high esteem when such a textbook could be so highly praised in a publisher's leaflet intended to describe, and thus to market, new works of all sorts and kinds. As the writer added, by way of dotting his *i*'s: "It is only fitting that the *Celestial Mechanics* of France's own Newton should appear in a dress worthy of the immortality that awaits it."[25]

In 1799 Laplace was ready to erect, on the strong foundation of his reports to the Académie, the crowning structure of his life's work—this after

OEUVRES

DE CONDILLAC,

Revues, corrigées par l'Auteur, imprimées sur
ses manuscrits autographes, et augmentées
de LA LANGUE DES CALCULS,
ouvrage posthume.

ESSAI

SUR L'ORIGINE

DES

CONNOISSANCES HUMAINES.

A PARIS,

DE L'IMPRIMERIE DE CH. HOUEL.

AN VI. — 1798. (E. vulg.)

Etienne Bonnot de Condillac. "Works of Condillac." An VI (1798). The New York Public Library, General Research Division.

The new edition of Condillac's "Works," amended by the "Language of Calculation" (1798), expressed the rise of mathematical reasoning and celebrated the visual beauty of mathematical expression (cat. no. 66).

years of unremitting toil on all aspects of theoretical astronomy, mathematics, and probability. His point of departure was Newton's law of universal gravitation and a set of mechanical axioms, to which he applied both integral and differential calculus. By theoretical reasoning alone, Laplace contrived to account with absolute precision for all the known and apparent motions of the planets around the sun and of the moon around the earth—as well as those of the Medici satellites around Jupiter. Here and there may be found traces of direct observation, as opposed to pure analytical calculation. Laplace fully explained such aberrant anomalies of certain planetary motions as that of Saturn (which the inexhaustible patience of earlier astronomers had been content simply to note) as perturbations caused by the mass of other planets. The cumulative effect of these perturbations, he declared, would not lead to the annihilation of the solar system; on the contrary, they confirmed its durability. These anomalies were repetitive and periodic and had their place in the ordered harmony of the universe. At the end of Laplace's long skein of finely spun equations lay the stability of the solar system: Did this not tear away part of the inviolable robe of eternity in which God had shrouded himself?

The work attained considerable fame, completing as it did the Newtonian system, which was itself the crowning glory of the analytic method. It was a theme that exercised the ingenuity of the best French versifiers, such as Gudin de la Brenellerie, who in Year IX wrote:

> Il faut chercher, il faut oser marquer la place,
> Que chaque être divers occupe dans l'espace,
> Etre exact à tel point, que de leur mouvement
> Je me trouve informé, malgré l'éloignement.
> Voilà ce que je veux, voilà ce que je tente,
> Leur multiplicité remplira mon attente.

> We must search, we must dare to mark the place
> Appointed in the void for each different body.
> We must be so precise that their movements
> Are known to me, be they ever so remote.
> That is my goal, that is my endeavor,
> And my hope shall be rewarded by manifold truths.[26]

As significant a work as *Celestial Mechanics* (*Mécanique Céleste*) was, it was also an inaccessible one to any reader who approached it without a sturdy groundwork of mathematics—as becomes clear in the first few pages.[27] The best English translation, in particular, abounded in additional footnotes and expository passages.[28] Fortunately, Laplace had prepared the way with an introductory text, *Explanation of the Universal System* (*Exposition du système du monde*),[29] of which the second edition appeared in the Year VII (1798–1799). It was bare of mathematical equations and technical academic terms. In straightforward, natural language—albeit emphasized here and there for effect—it marshaled all the riches of scientific learning into a coherent explanation of planetary motion. It even called on probability theory to provide a hypothesis for the origins of the solar system. One of the strongest impressions left on the reader by Laplace's exposition is that, although there are many and various branches of science, there is but one scientific method that transcends them all. "Such analogies are among the greatest delights attending on mathematical speculation. When observation takes note of phenomena, and transforms their mathematical outcome into natural laws; when these laws, embracing the entire universe, disclose to our eyes what it was in time past, and what it shall be in time to come, the sublime panorama confers on us the noblest pleasure of which human nature is capable."[30] Whether Laplace, in *Universal System* (*Système du monde*), had truly succeeded in creating a popular astronomy is a question we will return to at greater length.

In this same year there appeared a short work by Lazare Carnot, the Terror's "Organizer of Victory." A recent victim of the coup of fructidor (4 September 1797), he was able to recover his notes, which he had compiled before the Revolution. From his exile in Germany, Carnot came out with *Reflections on the Metaphysic of the Infinitesimal Calculus* (*Réflexion sur la métaphysique du calcul infinitésimal*). He hit his mark, for the mathematics of differential calculus were in a sorry state, having suffered since 1734, when Bishop Berkeley leveled an acid philosophical accusation that it lacked rigor. According to Berkeley, the mathematical imagination, thus freed from restraint, might come to sport as wantonly as did speculative theology.[31] No one could question the utility or the accuracy of this calculus, but was it really necessary, wondered contemporaries, to manipulate "infinitesimal" or "vanishing quantities" lying at the fringe of reason and therefore close to the snares of the infinite? It was all very well for D'Alembert to point along the path of spirituality: "Go forth, and faith will come to you";[32] but he did not convince everyone.

Carnot, making a syncretic comparison of the different methods available, set himself the task of "determining wherein resides the true nature of infinitesimal analysis."[33] This kind of analysis had been brought to some degree of public attention by J. Labey's 1797 translation of Euler's *Introduction to the Analysis of Infinitesimals* (*Introductio in analysin infinitorum*),[34] but Lagrange in the Year V (1796–1797) played for higher stakes by recapitulating a collection of learned papers published in Berlin in 1772. In his *Theory of Analytic Functions* (*Théorie des fonctions analytiques*), published in Paris in one quarto volume by Bernard, Lagrange set out to uncover "the principles of differential calculus, independent of all consideration of infinitesimal quantities, limits and fluxions, and reduced to the algebraic analysis of finite quanta."[35] Persuasive though his approach was, it was never adopted in practice by mathematicians and was superseded in 1821 when A. L. Cauchy introduced the presentation still in use today.[36] Lagrange's work represented a kind of peak of mathematical abstraction, but around the Year VII (1798–1799) treatises and manuals appeared at every imaginable level of the subject. This point will be taken up below, because it is an important one for the study of scientific books during the Revolution, at least in the years after 1795.

The physical and chemical sciences were not neglected. They occasioned fewer books, but more treatises. Here the schoolmaster's influence was paramount. In the Year VII (1798–1799) Baudouin published the course taught by F. Barruel at the Ecole Polytechnique, under the title *Physics Explained in Reasoned Tables* (*La Physique réduite en tableaux raisonnés*), while M. J. Brisson brought out his *Reasoned Dictionary of Physics* (*Dictionnaire raisonné de physique*) under the imprint of Magimel.[37] Brisson's pretensions were too high, but his texts were nevertheless adopted by regional high schools. The two-volume *Manual for a Chemistry Course* (*Manuel d'un cours de chimie*), by Bouillon-Lagrange, was also adopted by the high schools. Chief demonstrator in chemistry at the Ecole Polytechnique, Bouillon-Lagrange published his work with Bernard. An original feature of this book, reflecting its close ties to L'Ecole Polytechnique, was a "series of experiments to be made during each lesson." Fuchs published a 530-page translation by Jadelot of Humboldt's *Experiments in Galvanism* (*Expériences sur le galvanisme*).

We should not leave Year VII (1798–1799) without leafing through the "forthcoming titles" announced during a typical ten-day period, beginning on 20 fructidor (September 6). Fiction aside, there were fourteen titles, five of them scientific, including particularly the *Celestial Mechanics*, but also B. Peyrilhe's *Methodical Table for a Course in Natural History* (*Un Tableau méthodique d'un cours d'histoire naturelle*). The fiction included a new, fourth edition of *The Greek Journey of the Young Anacharsis* (*Voyage du jeune Anacharsis en Grèce*); two novels—one of them, *Praxiles* (*Praxile*), imitated from the Greek and published in Paris by Desenne; and *The Troubadour's New-Year's Token: A Book of Lyrical and Drinking Songs for the Year VIII* (*Etrennes des troubadours, chansonnier lyrique et anacréontique pour l'an VIII*) published by Caillet. The ninth and final volume of the *Compilation of the Laws of the French Republic* (*Recueil des lois de la République française*) was also announced, as was Aubry's *Conversion Handbook, or Decimal Equivalencies for Traditional Measures* (*Manuel du transformateur ou tables centimales pour la transformation des anciennes mesures*). All in all, a truly "revolutionary" selection.

Republican Weights and Measures

As a direct result of the Revolution and its decrees, works on metrology came to occupy a notable place, which is understandable, given the need to explain the decimal principle and the metric system—the new system of measurement based on the standard meter. The system was inaugurated by the decree of 18 germinal, the Year III (April 7, 1795) and confirmed by the law of 19 frimaire, the Year VIII (December 9, 1799) after platinum standards for measurement and weight had been deposited in the Archives Nationales (22 June 1799). Between these two dates, the system was administered by a whole liturgy of official directives. The printed book, the schoolroom, and the law were three of the many methods adopted for introducing and disseminating the new system, which was adopted in all the textbooks mentioned above.[38]

The scientific community was unremittingly vigilant while this system that it devised was instituted. The government had been persuaded to measure the meridian of latitude between Dunkirk and Barcelona; the dimension of the meter, after all, must derive from some feature of the earth common to all nations. In the Year VII (1798–1799) J. B. J. Delambre, assisted by A. M. Legendre in the calculus of spherical triangulation, published *Analytic Methods Employed to Determine the Definitive Length of the Meter* (*Méthodes analytiques employées dans la détermination de la longueur définitive du mètre*), a single quarto volume. This comprehensive treatise on the science of metrology cost 7.50 francs. The cost to the surveyors, who had worked without a break since 1792, was somewhat greater.

Other learned men undertook much more prosaic tasks. Their publications demonstrate with equal clarity both their zeal and the weakness of their teaching skills. In the Year II (1793–94), for example, the priest and mineralogist René Just Haüy edited the *Book of Instruction Concerning the Mensurations Deduced from the Earth's Circumference, Now Uniformly Applied Throughout the Republic, and on the Method of Dividing Them into Decimal Parts* (*Instruction sur les mesures déduites de la grandeur de la terre, uniformes pour toute la République, et sur les calculs relatifs à leur division décimale*). The handbook, distributed on 1 April 1794 and aimed at the widest possible readership, contained an overwhelming 224 pages! Clearly an abridged *Instruction* was needed. Completed and published only ten days later, the abridged version was still 147 pages long. Further stages of popularization obviously had to be undertaken. Schoolteachers took on the task, producing a plentiful supply of handbooks.

Prieur (de la Côte d'Or), an engineering officer who had entered the Royal Engineering School at Mézières in 1781 and was a member of the Committee of Public Safety from August 1793 to October 1794, also played

RAPPORT

*Sur les moyens préparés pour établir l'uniformité
des Poids et Mesures dans la République,*

Et pour substituer prochainement le *mètre*
à l'aune, dans le département de Paris ;

*Sur le mode à déterminer pour le remplacement
successif des anciennes mesures dans toute la
France ;*

Enfin, sur les réglemens à promulguer à ce sujet;

SUIVI

D'UN PROJET DE DÉCRET:

Lus à la séance du 25 fructidor, an 3e. républicain,

Par C.-A. PRIEUR (de la Côte-d'Or),

AU NOM DU COMITÉ D'INSTRUCTION PUBLIQUE.

IMPRIMÉS PAR ORDRE DE LA CONVENTION NATIONALE.

A PARIS,
DE L'IMPRIMERIE NATIONALE,
FRUCTIDOR, L'AN III.

Claude-Antoine Prieur. "Report on the Methods Planned for the Establishment of Uniform Weights and Measures in the Republic" (*Rapport sur les moyens préparés pour établir l'uniformité des poids et mesures dans la République . . .*). Paris: Imp. Nationale, an III (1794–95). The New York Public Library, General Research Division.

The republican government imposed the metric system on France in the spring of 1795. Consequently, a huge number of works appeared to explain how the new system functioned.

a role in scientific publishing. In ventôse, the Year III (February–March 1795), by order of the National Convention, Prieur directed the publication of a report on the methods adopted for introducing the new weights and measures throughout the Republic. The state assumed the cost of the textbooks, and 2,400 copies of a new manual by Prieur were printed. One such work followed another. An author like Aubry, whose *Decimal Arithmetic* (*Arithmétique décimale*) had a pressrun of 1,000 during the Terror, was still present in the literary marketplace in the Year VII (1798–99), not only with *Universal Metrology* (*Métrologie Universelle*) but also with *Decimal Ready-Reckoner, or How to Calculate* (*Barème décimal ou les comptes faits*). That same year, the publisher Caillot came out with Buron's 125-page *Methods and Principles of Decimal Calculation* (*Méthode des principes du calcul décimal*), "for use by citizens of either sex and of any age." Blavier published his *Decimal Mathematics* (*Mathématique décimale*), and so on. Posters were everywhere, and double-decimeter measures were distributed as well.

If the Revolution thus offered the world a new and logical metrology, if it took pride in its scientific achievements, it did not rely solely on its own resources. Translations abounded, and scientific novelties from outside France were eagerly sought after,[39] particularly in chemistry, where learned men in France and England raced against time, and each other, to identify new substances. In general, the outlook of scientists was still international, and the French were surprised when the metric system was not internationally adopted. We all know how long the English-speaking world has taken to accept it. Without a doubt, for all Laplace's precautions, the meter came into the world with a sans-culotte pedigree that was not universally acceptable. In their haste, learned men had allowed their science to assume the flavor of politics. A few years later they knew better and spoke philosophically of "awaiting the happy day when the men of learning and the friends of humanity may see their hopes fulfilled."[40]

Some politicized books of science existed, such as Decremps's *Sans-culotte Astronomy* (*Astronomie sans-culottisée*), but they were rare. It is true, though, that a man like Fourcroy, at once a famous chemist and a committed politician, assumed a tone in his lectures that combined science and politics. Such attitudes left almost no trace in the printed book; no such outward signs occurred, as they did during the Cultural Revolution in China. Yet, it would be wrong to postulate a scientific world that was ideologically inert and exempt from political responsibility. Some scientists committed themselves to the Revolution: consider Guyton de Morveau and Fourcroy, who sat on the Committee of Public Safety; Monge, who was Georges-Jacques Danton's minister of the navy; and above all Carnot, who was in effect minister of war during the Terror and for a long time afterward. But this is not

La distance de la Lune à la Terre, trouvée par le simple usage de la règle et du compas.

L'Amiral Anson dit, dans la relation de son voyage autour du monde, que l'incertitude d'un point d'Astronomie, causa la mort de 80 hommes de son équipage. Je m'estimerai heureux, si, contribuant à faciliter cette science aux sans-culottes de la Marine française, je peux sauver la vie à quelques-uns de mes frères.

LA SCIENCE SANCULOTISÉE.

PREMIER ESSAI sur les moyens de FACILITER l'étude de l'Astronomie, tant aux amateurs et aux gens de lettres , qu'aux MARINS de la République française, et d'opérer une

REVOLUTION
DANS L'ENSEIGNEMENT.

Ouvrage où l'on développe succinctement , 1° l'utilité de l'Astronomie ; 2° les défauts des Auteurs qui ont écrit sur cette science ; 3° le moyen de remédier à ces défauts ; 4° des exemples d'explications SIMPLIFIÉES , pour mettre tout homme de bon sens en état de prouver, 1° que la Terre est ronde; 2° qu'elle tourne sur son axe ; 3° qu'elle a neuf mille lieues de contour ; 4° que la Lune est éloignée de la terre de 90 mille lieues ; 5° que cette planète secondaire n'a que 818 lieues de diamètre; 6° qu'il y a dans la Lune des montagnes qui ont trois lieues de hauteur ; 7° qu'un pilote peut aisément trouver la route pour aller joindre, en pleine mer, une flotte qu'il ne voit point, etc. etc. (13 fig.) avec les remarques satyriques de Zoïle et d'Aristarque.

Par le Citoyen DECREMPS ,

Auteur de la Magie blanche dévoilée et de plusieurs autres ouvrages.

A PARIS,

Chez l'Auteur, rue des Droits de l'Homme, N° 5.

L'an deuxième de la République.

Henri Decremps. "Sans-culotte Science: . . . The Study of Astronomy." An II (1793–94). The New York Public Library, Science and Technology Research Center.

The Revolution witnessed efforts to politicize and popularize the sciences, like this astronomy for the "sans-culottes" (cat. no. 67).

ESQUISSE

D'UN

TABLEAU HISTORIQUE

DES PROGRÈS DE L'ESPRIT HUMAIN.

, Marie Jean Antoine Nicolas Caritat

Ouvrage posthume de CONDORCET. *, Marquis de*

SECONDE ÉDITION.

A PARIS,

Chez AGASSE, rue des Poitevins , N°. 18.

L'AN III DE LA RÉPUBLIQUE, UNE ET INDIVISIBLE.

AWVb

[1795]

Marie Jean Antoine Nicolas Caritat, marquis de Condorcet. "Outline . . . of the Progress of the Human Spirit" (*Esquisse . . . des progrès de l'esprit humain*). Paris: Agasse, an III (1794–95). The New York Public Library, General Research Division.

Condorcet's "Outline" exemplifies how science became the model and hope for all progress in human understanding in a world that had outlawed religion.

the place to dwell on the political role of the scientist;[41] our historical quest here is the book, on which our discussion may properly be focused.

The printed book allows us to consider a less emphatic mode in which the scientists of the day played their part. Their goals for science were so high that it is reasonable to speak about the birth and development of the scientific community sustained by a progressive ideology, by a concern for the interconnection of different branches of learning, and by faith in the precision of the analytic method. A single book illustrates all these aspirations. It came from the pen of Condorcet, the former secretary of the Académie des Sciences, at the beginning of 1794 (he committed suicide in March). Accused of Girondin sympathies in June, he had gone underground in Paris, a hunted man. Condorcet's *Outline of the Progress of the Human Mind* (*L'Esquisse d'un tableau historique des progrès de l'esprit humain*) was published after his death by his widow and Daunou. It assigns to science no less significant a function than giving humankind the means to control its own destiny. With religion outlawed, another kind of hope was now offered, more in tune with the progressive secularization of society.

Reshaping Science

Although it is true that not all scientists shared Condorcet's vision, their writings during the Revolution did not, on the one hand, restrict science to the refining of specific points for the benefit of a closed circle of specialists. On the other hand, they easily transcended simple popularizations of technical discoveries. Widespread attempts were being made to design a common armature for the different branches of scientific knowledge, old and new. The "analytical" spirit informed the "metaphysic" of the sciences, making them—or so it was believed—accessible to most people and useful to all. In this sense, the sciences became effectively part of the political discourse as they were aimed at modifying social life, bringing a warrant for progress.

One book served as an archetype for this intellectual movement: Lavoisier's two-volume *Elementary Treatise on Chemistry* (*Traité élémentaire de chimie*), presented in a new form, appropriately enough, in 1789. Its language was a kind of algebra of chemistry, inflecting the names of the elements that constitute matter so that the composition of any substance could be immediately recognized from its linguistic terminations.[42] The new names for common chemical substances were more rational: The former "dephlogisticated muriatic acid" became "chlorine," which in turn took its logical place as a component of "hydrochloric acid." All of a sudden, the as-yet-uncharted territories of science became less daunting; the future had been tamed. We should note that Lavoisier's adjective *elementary* was originally an allusion to Euclid's *Elements* (*Eléments*) and referred, rather, to the mathematical rigor of the new chemistry's reasoning than to its accessibility.

A feeling nevertheless persisted that if a science could only be presented "analytically," it would be made easy. In the spirit of the times, Horace Say tried to persuade the readers of the *Philosophical Weekly* (*Décade Philosophique*)—which is to say just about every intellectual alive in 1797—to read the 530 pages of the first volume of Lacroix's *Treatise on Differential and Integral Calculus* (*Traité de calcul différentiel et de calcul intégral*) published by Duprat. The third and final volume, itself a long dissertation, *Treatise on Differences and Series* (*Traité des différences et des séries*), appeared on 30 prairial, the Year VIII (June 18, 1800). Say told his readers: "It is easier to learn differential calculus today than it was to learn algebra a century ago; algebra today is a simpler study than arithmetic was then."[43] The "perfecting of symbols" and the discovery of the "most direct paths to Truth" were the two phases of a new and easier expository method now available to the sciences.

The learned men of the Revolution tried hard to render a public account of even their most difficult scientific works, waiting only until these could be properly positioned within an overall framework of intellectual discovery. They did not leave it to popular writers to disseminate their work, as Voltaire had done in his original fashion for Newton's optics. Speaking as a teacher of mathematics but even more as an observer of the trend we are here engaged in reconstructing, Lacroix said in 1805:

> Learned men thought to add luster to their achievements, by cultivating a style of writing which could disseminate their ideas beyond the circle of specialists to which they were originally addressed. Approached by way of related disciplines, their principal subject-matter could be made to stand out more clearly. Relieved of its burden of abstractions, their work could speak to the concerns of society in general, from which until then they had been excessively isolated.[44]

Laplace's *Explanation of the Universal System* (*Exposition du système du monde*), published in 1796, was the most splendid instance of this popular dissemination, but we should not overlook Haüy's admirable *Treatise on Mineralogy* (*Traité de minéralogie*), published in 1801 in four volumes with an atlas. Its beautiful drawings explained the geometry of crystals in terms of six fundamental shapes, developing the thesis he propounded in his work of 1793, *Abridged Explanation of the Structure of Crystals* (*Exposition abrégée de la structure des cristaux*). But such a textbook served also to mark the boundaries of even the most skillful popularization. The uninitiated—Condillac and his imitators notwithstanding—found themselves at once rebuffed, and were never able to seize the thread that would lead them through the argument. Haüy set out a descriptive geometry lying at the heart of matter and described certain laws (purely theoretical and having nothing to do with the way crystals are actually formed in the earth) of crystallography. In doing so he excluded the merely curious reader, uninstructed in solid geometry. Hélène Metzger, a historian of crystallography, noted early in the twentieth century that since Haüy's texts, "the science of crystals is no longer accessible to amateurs; only those with the necessary grounding, almost at a professional level, can hope to understand it." [45] This perceptive comment applies well beyond the bounds of crystallography. As the analytic method uncovered a series of universal truths beneath the bewildering multitude of appearances, it brought about specialization. After a fashion, mathematics and mechanics had been specialized before 1789, but it was during the revolutionary period that specialization overtook many other sciences in France, owing to the trend toward simplification that was originally considered just a concession to the general reader. This is perhaps the clearest historical lesson we learn from reading the scientific books of the Revolution—one not fully appreciated at the time because of Condillac's pervasive (and persuasive) myth of "science made easy."

Even the fine, sinewy prose of the learned men of the day could not conceal so profound a disagreement. Laplace tried hardest, in his *Explanation of the Universal System*, eliminating all mathematical equations (but not omitting to say that, if included, they would confirm his argument). It was against Laplace and his system that Mercier was railing when he wrote, in 1803:

> Quand l'univers est simple, et se montre au bon sens
> Qui donc a pu créer ce chaos algébrique?
> Système ruineux, symbole despotique,
> Dans des signes abstraits qu'a-t-il imaginé?

> Since the universe is simple, seen by the light of common sense,
> Who, then, saw fit to create this chaos of algebra?
> A ruinous system, a despotism of symbols—
> What did he think to find amid these abstract signs? [46]

Filtering reality through the analytic method, and thus putting it quite out of the layperson's reach, science "took the enchantment out of nature." [47]

This striking expression, coined by Chateaubriand in 1802, quickly became all the rage among politicians and supporters of the clerical reaction.

The great scientific texts that are the glory of the period all tend in the same direction: toward specialization through the rigorous (and sometimes mathematical) organization of reasoning. Certainly one of them is *Treatise on the Solution of All Kinds of Numerical Equations* (*Traité de la résolution des équations numériques de tous les degrés*), with notes on several aspects of the theory of algebraic equations, published by Duprat and written by Lagrange. Another was *Elementary Conspectus of the Natural History of Animals* (*Tableau élémentaire de l'histoire naturelle des animaux*), by Georges Cuvier in the Year VI (1797–1798); yet another, clearly, was Monge's *Descriptive Geometry* (*Géométrie descriptive*), published in 1799 at Paris, and taken directly from his course taught at the Ecole Normale, though enriched with some fine illustrations. True, Lacépède's natural history of fish, which came out between 1798 and 1803, could be used by a layperson—but not Legendre's 1798 *Essay on the Theory of Numbers* (*Essai sur la théorie des nombres*), nor the second edition of Montucla's *History of Mathematics* (*Histoire des mathématiques*; Paris, 1799–1802), nor even the *Philosophical Nosography* (*Nosographie philosophique*) of Pinel mentioned above. These dazzling volumes were often awarded as prizes both at *écoles centrales* and at *lycées;* perhaps they nurtured vocations, but only for those students willing to "go into science." But, as school prizes, they lead us naturally to a study of the world of education and the books that served it.

A Profusion of Textbooks

Perhaps because the learned were not aware of the widening gulf between themselves and the public, the process of scientific popularization was scarcely begun during the revolutionary period.

By contrast, a horde of authors set eagerly to work on the production of school texts, creating in the process a line of least resistance for the dissemination of scientific knowledge, in addition to a new form of writing. Impetus for this movement was given in 1795, when the government erected its educational system on the ruins of the various and sundry *collèges* of the Old Regime. The *écoles centrales,* which began operation in the autumn of 1795, fostered a demand for texts by organizing classes by subject, and even more by encouraging teachers to work out a structured curriculum. The *Ecole polytechnique,* at the summit of the system, diffused its course materials far and wide, urging its professors to take thought for all the curricula of France:

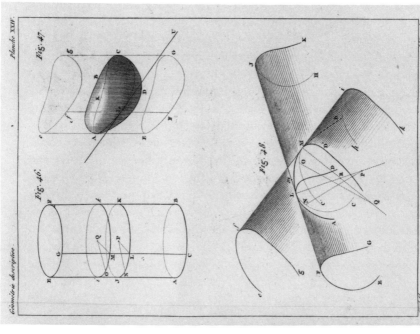

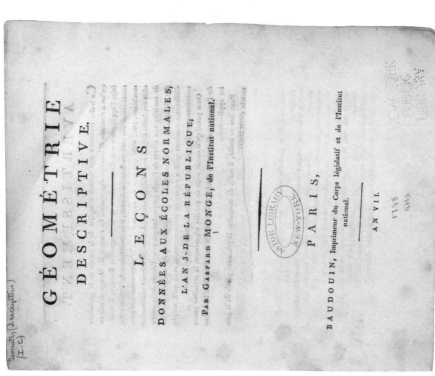

Gaspard Monge, comte de Péluse. "Descriptive Geometry." An VII (1798–99). The New York Public Library, Science and Technology Research Center.

The new educational system erected by the revolutionary government gave impetus to scientific publishing by encouraging teachers like Monge to work out structured curricula (cat. no. 80).

The council has not seldom had occasion to reflect how it would re-
dound to the benefit of the pupils, and to the renown of the School
itself, if the programs for all these different courses could be set out
in textbooks edited for this especial purpose by the members of the
faculty. Such books would treat their subjects with the exactness of
the classical authors, but also in such depth as may be required to
keep the level of instruction in step with the advance of knowledge.[48]

The school thus enshrines a goal pursued throughout the Revolution:
Books must be written about the latest discoveries. Popularization was held
to coincide with organization and also with modernization. All branches of
scientific knowledge, and the very ways such knowledge was disseminated,
were being restructured. Soon a race was afoot among schoolteachers to
become authors of mathematical textbooks; they were urged on by publishers seeking to offer the best-rounded lists adorned by the best-known
names. Duprat, succeeded by Courcier and then by Veuve Courcier, was
one of the most active publishers of the day. He was close to Lacroix, the
most prolific of the authors, who came near to monopolizing the market.
Of course, when textbooks were made obligatory, Lacroix was a member of
the commission that selected them.

Lacroix's treatise on mathematics[49] appeared in seven volumes, *Arithmetic* (*Arithmétique*) went into its thirteenth edition in 1813, and *Geometry*
(*Géométrie*) into a tenth in 1818. Even so, Legendre's *Elements of Geometry*
(*Eléments de géométrie*) gave Lacroix's *Geometry* a run for its money, owing to
its clear style and, even more, its much-appreciated reversion to the Euclid-
ean presentation abandoned under the influence of Port-Royal. This 335-
page book, first published in 1794 by F. Didot in Paris, was reissued in October 1799 with new notes; nine editions followed until 1812. It sold for
5 francs, compared to 4 francs for Lacroix's similar work. The real competition, however, turned out to be a book by a man who had been dead
since 1783, the mathematician Etienne Bézout; the Revolution knew how
to make use of good things from an earlier day. "The Bézout," as the book
was commonly called, was not highly regarded in the early years of the
Ecole polytechnique because it lacked a well-grounded approach to integral
and differential calculus, a systematized algebraic usage, and structured
examples of analytic method. Nevertheless, the editions of its different
sections always sold well. Other teachers—Garnier, Reynaud, Peyrard,
and more—pieced together Bézout's mathematical textbooks in order
to adapt their mathematics courses to different specialties: the artillery
(first published in 1770) and the Naval and Color Guard (first published
1764–69).[50]

Technical Knowledge for Everyone

The statistics fail to show a considerable increase, from 1789 to 1799, in the production of "useful" books devoted to explaining particular skills. The figures are untrustworthy on this point because they take no account of the size of the edition. Public men never tired of praising the useful sciences. In 1794 it was generally recognized that science had indeed furnished the means to the Republic's victories. Fourcroy, among many others, spoke eloquently to the Convention on 7 vendémiaire, the Year III (28 September 1794): "It is these lights [of learning] that began the French Revolution; these same lights have led the French people from triumph to triumph; their duty is to overcome every obstacle, to lay the foundation of every success, to support the French Republic on the pinnacle which it has attained."[51] It was the power of science that fed these "lights."

It should be noted that these eulogies are accorded to the applied sciences only in a military context. War, "which is just," Fourcroy said, "only when a people is fighting to recover its rights and its freedom," had become, for the French Republic, "a welcome opportunity to develop all the strength of the [useful] arts, to challenge the inventive genius of artists and learned men, and to find ingenious methods of storing and applying their usefulness."[52] The most noteworthy sciences—forming a kind of refrain in all writings about the Revolution—were the "manufacture of weapons, of saltpeter and of powder." Such technology left its traces in books, because they were intended to diffuse knowledge and to produce practical results at a time of supreme crisis. When France decreed a military mobilization in the Year II (1793–1794), learned men also mobilized to teach according to the "revolutionary system." Three factors were expected to ensure its success: technical originality, an exposition of the steps of the procedure simplified by the same scientific analysis that had led to the original discovery, and revolutionary enthusiasm to speed everything up.

The gage thus thrown down was taken up with triumph; most French writers write lyrically of the efforts during the Revolution to produce gunpowder.[53] In 1803 a physician, recently graduated from the *Ecole polytechnique,* concluded that "the learned men who had wrought such great wonders enjoyed a boundless credit."[54] Technical writing was more decked out in revolutionary phraseology than works of science; a collection of eight lessons on the manufacture of saltpeter was entitled "Death to Tyrants: A Program of Revolutionary Lessons in the Manufacture of Saltpeter, Explosives and Cannons" ("Mort aux tyrans, programme des cours révolutionnaires sur la fabrication des salpêtres, des poudres et des canons"). Vitality was imparted to these instruction courses by Guyton de Morveau, Fourcroy, Dufourny, Berthollet, Carny, Monge, Pluvinet, Hassenfratz, and Per-

GALATÉE,

ROMAN PASTORAL;

IMITÉ

DE CERVANTES,

PAR M. DE FLORIAN,

DE L'ACADÉMIE FRANÇOISE, &c.

ÉDITION ornée de Figures en couleur, d'après les
Dessins de M. MONSIAU.

A PARIS,

Chez DEFER DE MAISONNEUVE, rue du Foin S. Jacques.

1793.

9. Jean-Pierre Claris de Florian. "Galatée, Pastoral Romance; After Cervantes." 1793. The New York Public Library, Spencer Collection.

This edition of the popular romance by Florian offers color illustrations designed by M. Monsiau and executed by the newly developed printing technique known as *à la poupée*. Instead of overlaying colors by printing each color with a separate plate, the printer would color different sections of a single plate with a "rag doll" to produce the multicolored illustrations in a single strike (cat. no. 70).

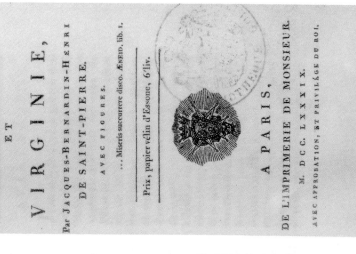

10. Jacques Henri Bernardin de St-Pierre. *Paul et Virginie.* 1789. The New York Public Library, Spencer Collection.

This beautiful edition of *Paul et Virginie* with color illustrations is one of four or five copies printed by Didot le jeune on vellum bearing the arms of Louis XVI as the title vignette (cat. no. 82).

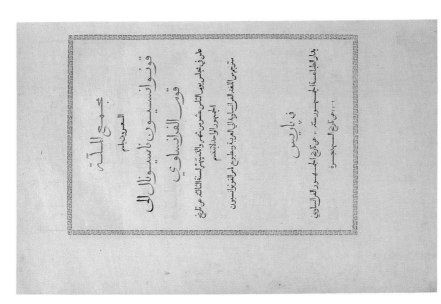

11. "Address from the National Convention to the French People . . . The Year III of the French Republic, One and Indivisible, Translated into Arabic by P. Ruffin." An III (1794–95). The New York Public Library, Oriental Division.

The National Printing Shop had type characters for nearly every known language, modern or ancient. They were used by the revolutionary government to spread republican principles throughout the world. Arabic type characters were first introduced into France by the king's printer in 1632 (cat. no. 206).

VIVE LA RÉPUBLIQUE.

LA GUERRE EST DÉCLARÉE

AUX OPPRESSEURS DU MONDE.

SI dans la République il se trouvoit un Traître,
Qui regretât LOUIS et qui voulût un Maître :
Que le Perfide meurt au milieu des tourmens :
Que sa Cendre coupable abandonnée aux Vents,
Ne laisse ici qu'un Nom plus odieux encore,
Que le Nom du Tyran qu'en ces Murs on abhorre!

---

12. "Long Live the Republic. War Is Declared Against the Oppressors of the World." 1793. Broadside. The New York Public Library, Rare Books and Manuscripts Division.

The use of broadsides made it possible to spread revolutionary principles to the widest possible audience and even integrated the printed word into the lives of people without the means to purchase printed matter (cat. no. 45).

13. Revolutionary Playing Cards. Designed by the Comte de St-Simon; manufactured by V. Jaume and J.-D. Dugourc, an II (1793–94). Albert Field Collection of Playing Cards, Astoria, New York.

The revolutionaries found ways to encode symbolic meanings in printed matter for the most casual leisure activities. Thus, the Kings, Queens, and Jacks on playing cards were replaced by Geniuses, Liberties, and Rights (cat. no. 188).

14. "Liberty, Patroness of the French." 1789–90. Fan, with color engraving. Musée de la Révolution Française, Vizille, France.

The most common objects of everyday life, like the lady's hand fan, could be transformed into agents of revolution if they contained a printed element (cat. no. 187).

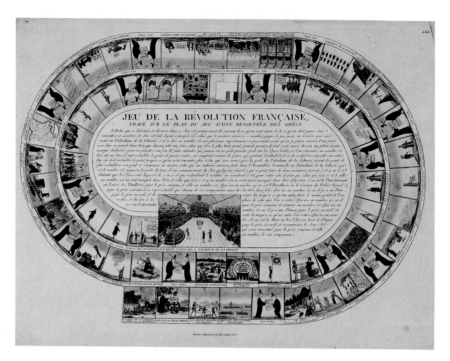

15. Board Game of the French Revolution. Paris, n.d. Color engraving. Bibliothèque Nationale, Cabinet des Estampes, Collection Histoire de France.

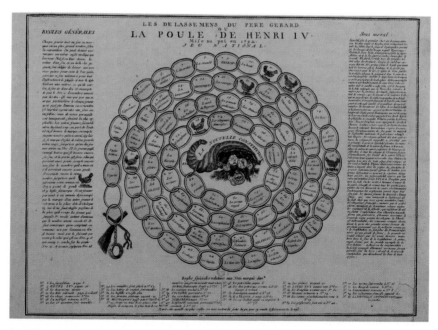

16. "The Pastimes of Père Gérard." [1792]. Engraving. Color proof. Bibliothèque Nationale, Cabinet des Estampes.

Games, too, were used to communicate the meaning of the Revolution to the masses, especially to children. After 1789 the ancient "goose game" was adapted to revolutionary ends: Players progressed by squares from the storming of the Bastille through the major events of the Revolution to the National Assembly (cat. no. 180).

17. *Assignats*: (*a*) 50 sous, January 1792; (*b*) Commune d'Avignon, 1 sou, bon pour 12 deniers, n.d.; (*c*) 10 sous, May 1793; (*d*) Département de Côte d'Or, 5 sous, 1793; (*e*) Commune de Montpellier, 6 deniers, n.d.; (*f*) Nîmes, Billet d'un sou, n.d.; (*g*) Commune d'Avignon, 1 sou, 6 deniers, n.d. Bibliothèque Municipale de Lyon, France.

With the introduction of paper money, the printing press became crucial in transforming not only leisure activities but the essentials of everyday existence as well (cat. nos. 162–66).

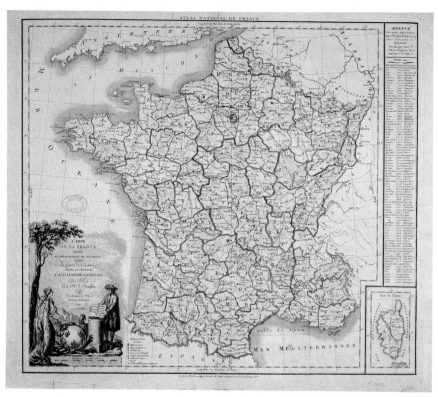

18. "Map of France, Divided into Departments and Districts Verified with the Committee on the Constitution." 1790. Color engraving. The New York Public Library, Map Division (cat. no. 174).

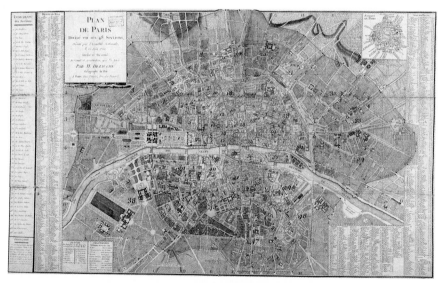

19. M. Dezauche. "Map of Paris Divided into Its 48 Sections." 1790. Color engraving. The New York Public Library, Map Division.

As the committees of the National Assembly redefined notions of space and time according to more rational and unified principles, the printing presses were marshaled to spread these new dimensions of everyday life to all corners of the nation (cat. no. 181).

rier. We should mention, among many other technical works, the thirty-two-page book by Trusson and Vauquelin, entitled *Instructions on the Burning of Vegetable Matter, on the Manufacture of Salts, of Granulated Charcoal, and on the Making of Saturated Solutions of Saltpeter* (*Instruction sur la combustion des végétaux, la fabrication du salin, de la cendre gravelée, et sur la manière de saturer les eaux salpêtrées*), published in the provinces.[55] On weapons, there was the highly instructive *Advice to Blacksmiths on the Making of Steel* (*Avis aux ouvriers en fer sur la fabrication de l'acier*), in thirty-four quarto pages with five plates; published in the Year II (1793–1794) by order of the Committee of Public Safety, it was the fruit of a collaboration of two mathematicians, Vandermonde and Monge, and a chemist, Berthollet. We should not overlook either the stationary balloons—whose presence at Fleurus enriched the Revolution's iconography in addition to providing intelligence on enemy positions—or Chappe's semaphore.

The war obscured another tendency in books, and even more in periodicals: the dissemination of techniques for more comfortable living, which arose naturally from progress. The quality of life and the advance of scientific learning were closely tied. The *Village Leaflet* (*Feuille villageoise*), which boasted eleven hundred country subscribers in 1792 and which Ginguené kept alive until 1795, proclaimed in its first issue: "Persuaded as we are that light kindles light, and that the mind of man is enlightened in proportion as light is thrown upon it, we shall lay before you all those useful discoveries which may improve your lot, enrich your leisure and lighten your labors; we shall instruct you in those arts and crafts which can open to you new sources of prosperity."

The poets chose to sing of the sciences and of pure learning instead—such, in those days, was the glory of science. There were even odes to astronomy! One of France's finest masters of language, André Chénier, intended to devote a lengthy poem, entitled *Hermes* (*Hermès*) to that very glory, but the scaffold cut the project short in the Year II (1793–94). There remain only a few beautiful fragments:

> La science
> Porte son austère compas
> La balance à la main, le doute suit ses pas.
> L'expérience alors de siècles entourée
> S'avance lentement[56]

> Science
> Carries her stern compass,
> Scales in her hand
> And uncertainty dogging her steps.

> Thus through the surrounding centuries
> Experiment moves slowly forward.

Chénier's calm view of the hesitant advance of science was tempered by disquiet, arising from a wisdom vouchsafed to few. The learning of the day saw no grounds for such disquiet; it took a poet's prevision:

> La raison à nos yeux
> Montrant la vérité, mais comme dans un songe,
> Nous réveille asservis sous les nœuds du mensonge.

> To our eyes Reason
> Displays the truth but, as if in a dream,
> Awakens us entrapped in the bonds of falsehood.[57]

A Brushfire

It was hoped that, sooner or later, all educated people could avail themselves of treatises to gain access to the mysteries of the sciences. Although this process antedated the Revolution, the Revolution lay at its heart and hastened the process by the publication of notable works. But from now on each science was to be approached separately, was to have its own methods, its own language, and even its own goals. This specialization—made increasingly plain by the flow of printed books—summarily ended the dreams of the encyclopedists and sounded the knell of a humanism that could gather in its hands all the manifold threads of learning. The scientific book was now addressed only to the faithful (whose numbers, to be sure, were growing impressively); its pages were no longer of interest to the layperson. Two new kinds of writing arose to fill the gap. The first was the scientific popularization, carried to great heights in the nineteenth century. But despite the attempts of many revolutionary writers, it was never able to impose itself on scholarly scientific writing. The second was the production of textbooks up to university entrance level. The flowering of this new literature dates, for the sciences, from 1795 and is contemporary with the development of a body of trained schoolteachers. The development, under the Revolution and Empire, of a scientific literature addressed to the scholar and layperson alike was no more than a brushfire, though admittedly a splendid one.

ALMANACS: REVOLUTIONIZING A TRADITIONAL GENRE

LISE ANDRIES

MANY DIFFERENT KINDS of almanacs were published during the Revolution: Some were publications distributed by door-to-door salesmen, others were local directories, and still others were literary collections. But all of them belonged to a special genre that was part of a tradition going back to the medieval Book of Hours and to astrological predictions. Practical manuals that people carried around during the entire year, almanacs always included a calendar and were often given as New Year's gifts. Already by the eighteenth century the postmen, who were called at the time "postal-box officials," used to offer, at the end of the year, a calendar accompanied by these verses:

> Recevez ce petit présent,
> C'est L'Etrenne du sentiment
> Et n'oubliez pas le commis
> De la p'tit' Poste de Paris[1]

> Accept this pretty present,
> Which is given from the heart;
> And remember the Paris postman
> Who gave the gift its start.

This tradition explains why the almanacs differed from the other publications during the Revolution. Because they were published only once a year, they could not compete with daily or weekly newspapers.

The word *almanac* comes from an Arabic term meaning "book of the weather." From the beginning, therefore, the almanac fits into what Fernand Braudel calls *la longue durée* (the long term). Consequently, the very

203

44 *Tauolette e Libri per li Putti*

"The Trades of Bologna: Seller of Books and Pictures for Children." N.d. Engraving by Simon Guillaume, after Carraccio. Musée de l'Imprimerie et de la Banque, Lyon, France (photo: Studio Dussouillez, Rutter).

Door-to-door salesmen were crucial for the dissemination of popular literature in both city and countryside (cat. no. 58).

meaning of the word *almanac* sets it apart from two basic aspects of the news—daily events and politics. Although the almanac's essential aim is to foretell seasons, wars, and diseases for the coming year—a process that implies a sort of renewal—it is based on the idea of cyclical time, expressed not only in the presence of a calendar but also in the very choice and conception of information. This traditional genre adapted itself, however, to the untraditional conditions of the Revolution. In fact, the almanac's ability to adapt and be innovative under new conditions is of great interest and will be discussed below.

There are about four hundred extant copies of almanacs published during the revolutionary period.[2] Most of them are versions of pre-1789 almanacs and perpetuate themes developed under the Old Regime. The popular almanacs sold by peddlers, such as the *Almanach des Bergers*, the *Dieu soit béni*, or the *Mathieu Laensberg*, presented advice on health and gardening along with weather forecasts for the coming year, as they had in the past—imitating in this respect the *Grand Calendrier et compost des bergers*, the first known edition of which appeared in 1488. These almanacs had enormous printings (150,000 copies of the *Mathieu Laensberg* were apparently in circulation every year),[3] and they underwent very few changes during the Revolution. Their readers were mainly lower class and rural, and as one contemporary put it, "they are now read only by the riff-raff." Peasants always dreamed of knowing the weather a year in advance, and the almanacs sold by the peddlers undertook to fulfill this dream. Almanacs could also cast horoscopes or give dietary advice according to one's age, sex, or astrological sign. This astrological and medical knowledge drew on precepts known since antiquity and had nothing in common, of course, with science as it had advanced in the eighteenth century.

The revolutionaries, who claimed to follow the rationalist principles of the Enlightenment, often attacked the popular almanacs, by both parody and political pressure. In 1794 the *Dieu soit béni* published for the first time the republican calendar and cited certain deeds of patriotic valor. The following year, however, everything returned to normal. On a larger scale, the editors of the almanacs were asked to raise themselves

> finally this year to the level of the Revolution. It is important that our institutors in this area [the almanacs] pride themselves on not sullying them with old prejudices and with the nonsense of the Old Regime. . . . The people—and I am one of them—will be grateful to you to strike from your annual publication meteorological foolishness and the other lies that you still include from sheer habit. . . . One should never lie to the people. That is more important than you real-

ize. Most people consult their almanacs all year, and if they find only nonsense in it, they risk becoming fools themselves, which is the last thing we patriots wish.[4]

All these fine declarations were in vain. The almanacs, printed in Troyes and Liège, were peddled without difficulty throughout the Revolution. The same thing may be said for numerous local and regional yearbooks such as the *Almanach de la ville de Sens,* the *Almanach général du département des Hautes-Alpes,* and others. These extremely useful volumes, which each year listed the principal authorities and leading citizens, underwent some changes during the Revolution. They became departmental instead of regional, noting changes in the various administrations, and after 1793 they often called attention to the reform of weights and measures. Yet what is most striking is their inertia: From 1789 to 1799 they continued unperturbed, as they had before the Revolution, to give the dates of fairs and markets and the hours of departure and arrival of stagecoaches and passenger barges.

After studying these two categories of almanac, which appealed to a very wide audience and in fact constituted a form of popular communication, one has the impression that the Revolution did not fundamentally alter the rhythm of daily life. For those uninvolved in the political struggle, change probably took place much more slowly during the entire nineteenth century. This is the public to which the traditional almanacs were directed and to which, in their way, they bear witness.

Another kind of almanac scarcely touched by the Revolution was the *almanach galant,* which included love poetry, and the literary almanac, which combined a selection of poems with a calendar and was very much in fashion on the eve of the Revolution. But we mention these works only in passing. Actually a separate category (only a few of them continued to appear during the Revolution), these almanacs were carefully printed and rather expensive; *Almanach des Muses,* for example, cost thirty-six sous, while the popular almanacs sold for an average of two sous. Such almanacs were intended for an aristocratic or wealthy clientele, no doubt predominantly female. For our purpose, their chief interest lies in their having influenced, in both appearance and content, a certain number of republican almanacs.

Having spoken of the inertia of this genre, we should at the same time call attention to the almanac's capacity for innovation. The Revolution marked a point of rupture and radical transformation for this medium. Not that the content of traditional books was modified (as the enlightened would have wished); instead, a wholly new sort of almanac—the *political* almanac—made its appearance. This new genre was not designed, at first, to combat the influence of the other almanacs; it simply reflected a new spirit, the signs of which were in evidence before 1789. For instance, Sylvain Maréchal's *Almanach des honnêtes gens,* for "the first year of reason," was published in 1788 and substitutes a calendar of "great men" for the traditional calendar of saints. It caused a scandal: The work was condemned and Maréchal was imprisoned. This book was the first of a series of almanacs that proposed, each in its own way, different modifications of the calendar, until the reform of Fabre d'Eglantine brought an end to these flights of fancy. In one republican calendar, Gutenberg, Solon, Barra, Homer, and Washington were featured together, and in another the name of Jesus Christ was evoked: "Let us pardon the charlatanism of his life and remember his death, which was rather beautiful. Condemned to the gallows by the aristocrats for having attempted a holy insurrection with the help of the sans-culottes of Jerusalem."[5]

From 1789 on, "historical" almanacs also appeared—attempting to draw up a balance sheet of the preceding year. This new genre, which was quite successful throughout the Revolution, most effectively reconciled annual publication with the changing complexion of events. As in the case of the *Almanach historique de la Révolution* for 1792 by Rabaut Saint-Etienne, the best-known example of the genre, the authors undertook to present less a chronology than an analytical selection of events. In this way, they show how people were conscious of living through a crucial period of history: The fall of the Bastille, the night of 4 August, and the Celebration of the Federation (14 July 1790) stand out in them as red-letter days, marking off a new vision of history in the making. These booklets were thus linked to the schoolbooks of the nineteenth and twentieth centuries, which for generations of young French students forged the collective memory of the Revolution.

Some political almanacs, more frivolous in appearance, took the form of songbooks—*La Lyre républicaine, La Muse républicaine,* or the *Chansonnier de la Montagne.* Although their tone was determinedly patriotic, they resembled the *almanachs galants* of the Old Regime—even in the engravings that illustrated them. After the customary calendar, they offered a sort of anthology of poems and songs of the year. For the most part, these were reprintings of hymns sung on patriotic occasions or martial songs or poems glorifying personified abstractions such as liberty. But erotic inspiration sometimes colored political outbursts, as in the poem by Claude-Joseph Dorat-Cubières entitled "Ma Maitresse nouvelle" ("My New Mistress Was the Law") or in this dubious verse: "L'amour a cent fois plus d'appas . . . quand il est sans-culottes" ("Love has a hundred more allurements . . . when it is sans-culotte").

The republican almanacs are, to my mind, the most interesting because they were the most innovative. It is true that the almanac had already been used as an instrument of propaganda: *Mathieu Laensberg,* for example, had

Nicolas-Edmé Restif de la Bretonne. "National Women's Calendar." 1794. Musée de la Révolution Française, Vizille, France.

Historical almanacs were a new genre developed to cope with the problem of reconciling annual publication with the changing complexion of events: "history in the making." This one was addressed specifically to women (cat. no. 192).

ALMANACH
RÉPUBLICAIN
CHANTANT,

POUR L'AN 2e.

DE LA RÉPUBLIQUE FRANÇAISE,

Commençant le 22 septembre 1793, et
finissant le 21 septembre 1794;

*Avec la Déclaration des Droits de
l'Homme, et le Maximum.*

Par le citoyen B***.

A PARIS,

Chez LALLEMAND, libraire, sur le
Pont-neuf, n°. 19.

A AMIENS, au Bloc, chez MARIELLE,

"Republican Almanac, in Song, for the Year II of the French Republic." [1793]. The New York Public Library, Rare Books and Manuscripts Division.

"Singing almanacs" offered collections of poems and songs as well as the customary calendar. This one from the Year II also offers an image of the Republic as Hercules conquering the aristocratic hydra (cat. no. 160).

sometimes served to denounce the destitution of the people. Moreover, every major crisis before the Revolution—the League, the Fronde, the Jansenist quarrels—had given rise to a war of scurrilous satire carried forward by newsmongers. Sometimes the almanacs were also politicized. This was the case with an almanac of Troyes, which was transformed into a lampoon during the Fronde.[6]

But it was during the Revolution that the almanac was used for the first time as propaganda—systematically and on a large scale. Although, as noted earlier, the traditional almanac prevailed throughout the revolutionary period as a whole, political almanacs constituted 73 percent of the production of the genre during the Terror, from 1793 to 1795.[7] The Jacobins were the first to understand the advantage they could draw from this form of the press, which already resembled our modern mass media. They got off to an early start in September 1791 when the Jacobin Society of Friends of the Constitution launched a contest to reward the almanac that could best instruct the people about the political changes that were taking place. This "manual for country people," which would form "their entire library," must include (the rules of the contest stated) a calendar of lunations and eclipses together with some notions of agriculture, in addition to "1. The history of our Revolution; 2. The change in the condition of a Frenchman; 3. The sense of himself, of his rights, his duties, and his hopes." J.-M. Collot d'Herbois won the contest with the *Almanach du Père Gérard*, which was quite successful.

But for all that, can these almanacs be said to belong to popular literature? It is clear that for the Society of Friends of the Constitution and for the different popular associations with Jacobin leanings, the main thing was to create "a publication expressly for the people, one that would be read in the villages."[8] The editors chose the almanac rather than the newspaper with the express idea of being able to reach not only a large public but also a rural one. Rouy l'aîné thus declared in his preface: "Since I thought that these works would be proper for the instruction of the people, I decided that it would be best to assemble them in almanac form so that they might be more widely circulated." In addition to the *Almanach du Père Gérard*, other works appearing between 1793 and 1795 were the *Almanach des campagnes*, the *Annuaire du cultivateur* of Gilbert Romme, which was sent to all the municipalities and schools of the Republic, and even an *Almanach des bergers pour la seconde année républicaine*, which, by twisting it a bit, used the title of one of the traditional almanacs.

The fact that these almanacs were aimed especially at country people is all the more significant because the rest of the press had so little interest in them. Except for *La Feuille villageoise* of J. A. J. Cérutti and a few others, the newspapers were intended mainly for readers in the cities. It may be pre-

ALMANACH

DU

PÈRE GÉRARD,

POUR L'ANNÉE 1792,

La troisième de l'ère de la LIBERTÉ;

Ouvrage qui a remporté le prix proposé par la SOCIÉTÉ DES AMIS DE LA CONSTITU- TION, *séante aux* JACOBINS, *à Paris;*

PAR J. M. COLLOT-D'HERBOIS,
Membre de la Société.

SE VEND A PARIS,

Au Secrétariat de la SOCIÉTÉ DES AMIS DE LA CONSTITU- TION, rue Saint-Honoré;

Au Bureau du PATRIOTE FRANÇOIS, Place du Théâtre Italien, rue Favart, n°. 3.

Chez BUISSON, libraire, rue Haute-Feuille.

1792.

J.-M. Collot d'Herbois, ed. "Père Gérard's Almanac for the Year 1792." 1792. Bibliothèque de l'Arsenal, Paris (photo: Bibliothèque Nationale).

Revolutionaries began to see the pedagogical importance of the almanac, often the only book a family owned. In 1791 the Jacobin Club thus sponsored a contest for the best pedagogical almanac. Collot d'Herbois's "Père Gérard's Almanac" was the winner (cat. no. 159).

sumed, therefore, that political almanacs—the most militant of them in any case—filled a particular gap in the dissemination of propaganda, especially among the peasant masses. Furthermore, the readers of traditional almanacs had been drawn from this milieu: They were thus offered works in a new style that at the same time kept the familiar appearance so dear to them. For the same reasons, the successful titles of traditional chapbooks had reappeared in bookstores. The blue cover was the same, but the contents had been transformed into "patriotic Christmases" or "republican catechisms." In their effort to educate the people and to popularize the information available to them, the Jacobins quite naturally had recourse to the traditional, indeed, even archaic, models of the popular press and of literature—broadsheets, almanacs, catechisms, and chapbooks. In this respect the Jacobins were both the propagators of political ideas and the inheritors of the Enlightenment: In these works propaganda was almost always coupled with moral, patriotic, and economic teachings. But, then, had not one of the great pedagogical dreams of the eighteenth century been to have knowledge shared by everyone?

The political almanacs were not, however, completely identified with popular literature. The latter, whether almanacs or chapbooks, had under the Old Regime a network of specialized publishers, a catalogue of titles, and a standardized appearance (based on techniques of cheap serial production), all of which were its trademark and which, in the eyes of the public of the time, allowed them to be considered specific productions destined for the people. During the Revolution there was nothing of the sort. Although they borrowed a certain number of titles from chapbooks, the revolutionary almanacs were distinguished more by the complexity of their contents, the relative care taken in their production, and their high prices. It seems, therefore, more correct to say they belonged more to the printed material of wide circulation than to popular literature as such.

Furthermore, the revolutionary almanacs were closer to the revolutionary press than they were to traditional literature—at least to the press created "with the intention of informing this interesting segment of the people which fashionable men of letters have always disdained and for which they have never written," as J. R. Hébert says of his journal, *Le Père Duchesne*.[9] The parallel drawn between the newspapers and almanacs of the time will perhaps seem astonishing today. But it should be remembered that because of censorship the French press under the Old Regime was still at a rather primitive stage of development: News circulated primarily in the form of gazettes and newspapers published abroad. As for French periodicals, they followed events from a certain distance by reason of the long intervals between their appearance. In this muzzled world, almanacs and broadsheets still made a good impression despite their antiquated nature. By giving news once a year and by concentrating not on politics but rather on strange and unusual events (records of longevity and monstrous births appeared time after time), they also provided information much as the tabloid press does today.

At the same time, certain of the revolutionary almanacs, especially the political ones, were transformed in ways that allowed them to acquire the political and historical dimension their predecessors lacked. By recording the events of the past year, by quoting extracts of speeches and the texts of laws and by commenting upon them, they approximated the functions of the modern political press. Moreover, the editors were drawn from the same milieu as the journalists. We have mentioned Collot d'Herbois; we should add the names of Sylvain Maréchal and Galard de Montjoie (the latter presumed to be the author of several royalist almanacs), J. F. N. Dusaulchoy and Jean-Paul Rabaut Saint-Etienne, all men of letters, politicians, and publicists. The links between newspapers and almanacs were all the closer because of the extremely rapid recycling of texts during the Revolution. It was not rare for a speech or a hymn published in a newspaper, or a quatrain accompanying an engraving, to be reprinted a little later in an almanac. The Revolution brought about such an explosive and anarchic liberation of the written word that the newspapers and the other print media sometimes simultaneously gave the same information. Despite ideological conflicts, wasted energy, and the haphazard nature of the information it printed, the revolutionary press acquired a level of critical analysis that distanced it definitively from the Old Regime and opened the way for modern journalism. The republican almanacs, which were ideological popularizers, contributed their share to this evolution.

But was the circulation of political almanacs as great as had been hoped? Did they play a real role as popularizers? The answer is not easy. First of all, we should note that in 1793–94, when the greatest number of almanacs appeared, laws and decrees were promulgated to protect the authorized press to the exclusion of any other. Even before the September 1793 law against certain writers,[10] a decree in March of that year stated: "The peddlers, sellers, and distributors of prohibited writings will be punished by three months of detention if they reveal the authors of such writings, and two years in irons if they do not." Furthermore, street inspections were instituted, and areas were partitioned off for the purpose of searches, especially in Paris. Section by section, Paris entered a regime of intense surveillance by both the sectional inspectors and the political clubs. During the Year II of the new calendar (1793–94), games of chance were forbidden in the cafés and dances on street corners prohibited. Any unlawful assembly was suspect. People brought before the Revolutionary Tribunal risked being sentenced to death for a few seditious remarks uttered in a tavern (drunkenness was not an extenuating circumstance) or while queuing up at a bakery.[11] It is true that these were hard times: War raged on the border and in the interior of the country, and the economic crisis was worsening. It is difficult to imagine that the trade in books and newspapers could stray in such a climate from official channels or escape the control of those in power.

Life in the streets of Paris in the Year II (1793–94) had lost the full, noisy character that it had under the Old Regime. The news vendors, the peddlers of almanacs, and the charlatans—that is, the soothsayers, astrologers, and forecasters of every sort—were particularly threatened. Peddling in itself became suspect, irrespective of the works sold: Thus the case of a Parisian peddler whose pack, seized during a search, contained serious literature—the works of Racine, *Les Liaisons dangereuses, Tom Jones*—as well as a few almanacs and songbooks.[12] Political almanacs like the *Almanach du peuple* by C. Thiébaut—himself an official in the department of La Meurthe—for their part, benefited from the use of official channels. Sold by licensed peddlers, they were sent to the communes and to diverse administrative authorities. Some were distributed in the political clubs and the schools. One should remember furthermore that the success of an almanac in the Year II (1793–94) depended to a large extent on its presentation to the Convention. A number of almanacs were actually dedicated to the Convention, before which the authors themselves came to champion their works.

But it would be a mistake to believe that the system controlling the circulation of texts functioned with perfect efficacy. In Paris and in the provinces, police records show the arrest of peddlers selling forbidden almanacs, even at the height of the Terror. Publishers were much more severely punished than peddlers or simple tradesmen, who often pleaded ignorance. The owner of a bookstall in Montmartre was arrested in the Year II (1793–94) for having displayed several erotic works, among which was the *Catéchisme libertin.* He declared he could neither read nor write and had displayed these books "without any evil purpose and that in the future he would not display any others."[13] Counterrevolutionary almanacs, too, were sometimes seized: In May 1794 Pierre Chanteloup, a tailor, and Louis Philippe, an innkeeper, appeared before the Revolutionary Tribunal for having peddled and distributed a counterrevolutionary almanac, the *République en vaudevilles,* a collection of songs ridiculing the Revolution that had been openly sold in Epernay and Châlons. They were acquitted, but the bookseller, Bouillart, whom they had denounced, was condemned to death.[14] Finally, there is the case of Thomas Rousseau, the publisher of several patriotic almanacs who complained in 1793 that "20,000 copies of the vile, abominable *Constitution en vaudevilles* had been sold while his *Chants du patriotisme* had sold barely 500 [copies]."[15]

ALMANACH DU PEUPLE

Pour l'année 1792.

Par JOSEPH F. N. DUSAULCHOY.

Pour qu'il soit juste, humain, éclairez son esprit.

Le prix est de 12 sous pour Paris, et de 16 s. franc de port, par la poste, pour les Départemens.

A PARIS,

Au Bureau des *Révolutions de France et de Brabant*, rue Guénégaud, n°. 24.

Et chez les Marchands de Nouveautés.

Joseph-François-Nicolas Du Saulchoy de Bergemont. "The People's Almanac for the Year 1792[–93]." N.d. Bibliothèque Nationale, Département des Imprimés.

Many almanacs advertising themselves as "popular" and "of the people" were in fact officially sponsored and sanctioned by the government. The author of "The People's Almanac," for example, was actually an official in the department of La Meurthe (cat. no. 182).

LA CONSTITUTION
DE L'AN VIII
EN VAUDEVILLES.

TITRE PREMIER.
De l'exercice du droit de Cité.

ARTICLES 1, 2 et 3.

Air : O *ma tendre Musette.*

POUR l'avenir assise
Comme par le passé,
La France se divise
Comme par le passé ;
L'étranger qui s'en pique
Comme par le passé,
Obtient le droit civique
Comme par le passé.

ART. 4 et 5.

Air : *Des Trembleurs.*

Toute personne interdite,
L'accusé qui prend la fuite,
Le débiteur en faillite,

"The Constitution of the Year VIII in Vaudeville" (*La Constitution de l'an VIII en vaudevilles*). Paris: Gauthier, [1800?]. The New York Public Library, General Research Division.

The official appropriation of traditional genres such as almanacs and songsheets was countered by antirevolutionary satirical appropriations of the same genres. Vaudeville, or the popular song, was a favorite cultural form among government satirists.

These different cases bear witness to the fact that the most careful police control and the heaviest legal sanctions were unable to close down the unauthorized press or to end the circulation of counterrevolutionary almanacs during the Year II (1793–94). But such works were relatively rare compared with the republican almanacs then being published. One may also wonder whether the court records slightly misrepresented the facts by inevitably stressing utterly marginal derelictions. The "good patriots" never appeared on the police blotter except by the merest chance. Thus, in the Year II (1793–94) the home of some wealthy intellectuals was searched. They possessed, as was the fashion, a private natural history collection and a handsome library; discovered in the apartment of the mistress of the house were some catechisms and other patriotic instructions "for the training of her young family" as well as "engravings and patriotic works of the Revolution."[16]

Furthermore, police records concern, as one would have expected, an urban rather than rural population. Many political almanacs were intended especially for country people, about whom we have little information. Shall we take literally the testimony of Collot d'Herbois that "the *Almanach du Père Gérard* made the love [of public education] ripen in all the countryside and in every cottage"? Perhaps, because this almanac—frequently revised and quickly translated into several other languages—was a real best-seller at the time. The same was apparently not true for many other almanacs which, following the example of Romme's *Annuaire du cultivateur*, tried to propagate new farming techniques, along with the republican calendar and principles of good citizenship. These almanacs, often rather didactic and difficult, seem to have been intended more for the leading citizens of the village than for the masses of the countryside; these teachers and minor officials were cultural intermediaries. They replaced the priest, who had been the traditional intermediary, and represented the spirit of the Enlightenment, acting as secular agents for the diffusion of revolutionary principles. The old distribution channels were no longer appropriate for this form of the propagation of ideas. Peddling was replaced by distribution through the new administrative bodies and through mailings and subscriptions. The rural municipalities and political clubs (where they existed) wrote to the capitals of their district or to Paris to ask that specific patriotic works, newspapers, and almanacs be sent to them.

That does not mean, however, that the peddling of almanacs disappeared altogether. Two parallel forms of distribution developed, one of which was quasi-official and virtually institutionalized. Deputies often functioned as middlemen between Paris and the countryside. The editors of the *Almanach général du département des Hautes-Alpes* recommended sending packages and petitions to the departmental deputies and even gave their

Parisian addresses. Sometimes a simple citizen, a member of his commune's revolutionary committee, would write to his political representative, asking for newspapers and other printed material: "We are without any newspapers. I beg you, in the name of the association, to subscribe for six months to a paper entitled the *Père Duchesne;* it is entirely suitable since it is written unaffectedly in a style accessible to everyone." He also requested "copies of speeches, addresses, hymns, and patriotic songs," in addition to plays, caricatures, and so forth.[17]

Given our knowledge that, in the Year II (1793–94), the tiniest communes organized political clubs (sociétés populaires) to prove their patriotic zeal, we cannot doubt the efficacy of this distribution system. Even in the depths of the countryside, the zeal of administrations, to which after the end of 1792 civil commissioners were dispatched, is evident. Less certain is the response of the public. The people seem to have rejected the official patriotic almanacs that condemned the traditional ones and sought to replace them; they probably continued to purchase almanacs from peddlers.[18] In all likelihood they applied the republican calendars sparingly, preferring to treat Sunday as their day of rest rather than the *decadi* or tenth day of the week (*décade*) in the revolutionary calendar. For in the countryside, and even in the city, the almanac was often the only book people possessed, their seasonal companion, the agenda of their daily lives. Radical changes, imposed from above, would not have been accepted lightly. That is why the commissioner of the government of Landes still complained in the Year VII (1798–99) that despite the efforts to promote revolutionary works, the old almanacs were still popular with the public and widely distributed throughout the countryside. He wrote to the minister of the interior:

> I believe it is my duty to speak out against the almanacs that once circulated during the Old Regime with the names of all the saints and the holidays included. . . . There is no better way to foster fanaticism; everybody rushes to get hold of these almanacs and turns up his nose at those that speak only of the new era. People want to celebrate the old holidays; they repudiate those of the new calendar. . . . The most forceful speeches would not do as much harm as this poison that makes the rounds of the people all the more quickly and all the more effectively by reason of its accessibility and its kinship with their inherent prejudices.[19]

This protestation probably remained a dead letter, no more effective than all the past or future incitements or threats.

Let us, in conclusion, examine the contents of the revolutionary almanacs. Rather than undertake a tedious textual analysis, let us call attention to certain broad, general characteristics. First and foremost, fundamental to this type of work is the change in the calendar. This reform, adopted by the Convention to take effect on 22 September 1793 (and used in most of the almanacs that published the old calendar so as to establish concordance tables) attempted, as with the reform of weights and measures, to set up a new world order. The legislators really had the unbounded ambition to impose a new organization of time and space on everyone.[20] In a sense, they wanted to build a utopia, sweeping away the remnants of the Old Regime. And, in fact, the notion of regeneration was central to revolutionary symbolism: Not only had the revolutionaries built a new world on the ruins of the past, but they also imagined springing forth from those ruins a race of people with new blood, a people straight and strong like the poplar of liberty from which all the dead branches had been cut—a recurrent image in the almanacs. As the *Tableau historique des événements révolutionnaires* for the Year III (1794–95) put it, "The Republic resembles a garden. Cut back its dead, useless branches."

The almanac, which from its beginnings had emphasized everyday tasks, seemed to the legislators the most appropriate way to educate the French about this new symbolism. Gilbert Romme's report before the Convention is explicit in this regard, and reveals the extent to which he understood, ahead of his time, the role of the almanac in mass culture. After this grand statement: "Our time has opened a new book of history, and in its forward movement, as majestic and simple as equality, it must engrave with its new and vigorous burin the annals of a regenerated France," he added: "Our almanacs will no longer be filled with dominical letters, nor with golden numbers. We have sought out what was most suitable for the farmer, whose calendar ought to be as simple as the nature from which he is never separated."[21] In reality, the success of the revolutionary calendar depended on the almanac, for the Jacobins sought to adhere as closely to nature as possible (with all the implications the term represented in eighteenth-century philosophical thought), perhaps less through idealism than through a carefully calculated policy. What better mode of indoctrination for the peasant than a calendar, every month of which would recall by its name the rhythm of nature, in which each day would be dedicated to a plant ready to be sowed or to an agricultural tool ready to be used at precisely that moment? No need even to be able to read: The calendar of the almanac should be memorized to summon forth a series of images carefully arranged in time, in keeping with the rhythm of agricultural work, as the stained-glass windows and the sculpture of the great cathedrals reflected in images the different moments of religious life.

This conception of time, however, ran counter to that of the traditional almanacs. Not only did it substitute secular time for that of the religious holidays (the dates of which were calculated according to dominical letters and golden numbers), and thereby shifted the sense of the sacred to a new cult of labor, but it also initiated from the "Year I of the Republic" a new world in place of what had been the changeless order, which the traditional almanacs mirrored. These almanacs were, in fact, backward-looking in that the new year was calculated in relation to the years that separated it from the creation of the world (about 5,797 years for the year 1792) and from the flood, the birth of Jesus Christ, Charlemagne, and so forth.

The introduction of the new rationality did not go smoothly, even though reformers like Romme and Fabre d'Eglantine went so far as to invoke astrology in an attempt to rescue their enterprise. Arguing that 22 September, the date of the beginning of the new calendar and the first meeting of the Convention, corresponded in the signs of the zodiac to Libra, Romme declared:

> The French Revolution offers such a striking harmony, perhaps unique in the annals of history, between heavenly movement, the seasons, the ancient traditions and the course of events that the entire nation should rally around the new order that we present to you. Thus the equality of day with night was marked in the heavens at the very moment when civil and moral equality was proclaimed by the representatives of the French people as the sacred base of its new government.[22]

Perhaps the leaders of the Revolution, and Romme in particular, were profoundly convinced that the Revolution was written in the stars. Was not Libra, the emblem of justice which presided over the first moments of the Convention, a sign from the heavens? Besides, the Enlightenment had always had its obscure side, from the time of Mesmer to Cagliostro.

I should like to stress another quite striking quality of the republican almanacs; namely, the way in which they were written. Although they sought to reach the greatest number of readers, they paradoxically resorted to abstract language. Abstraction in a generally allegorical form was, in fact, omnipresent, particularly in the poems and songs that obviously lent themselves to this type of treatment. Revolutionary engravings also celebrated great feminine figures who had sprung fully armed from the imagination, figures such as Liberty, Justice, Equality, Law . . . or France. Around these central figures there developed a series of emblems, red caps, scales, pikes, cockades. Even in the almanacs written in dialogue form, such as the *Almanach du Père Gérard,* instruction depended more on abstract notions (a definition of the Constitution, for instance) than on practical examples. Propaganda was thus blended into a systematizing of ideas, which probably caused the propaganda to lose some of its effectiveness.

This systematizing and fascination with the power of words, and the profoundly bookish and intellectual nature of the Jacobin culture, sometimes resulted in a serious lack of connection between language and reality. It is strange that so many political almanacs, in contrast to historic ones, gave so little attention to the great events taking place while insisting on these transformations of rural culture. This taste for abstraction is all the more astonishing because it was combined with the constantly recurring desire to speak the language of the heart. These effusions of sentimentality had not merely been a literary mode since Diderot and Rousseau: They had been adopted by the militants of the Year II as a principle of behavior. The almanacs echoed them. What counted for the authors was the sensibility of their writing, the mark of authenticity. "I do not know how to trace the outline of a work coldly and methodically; when pressed by my heart, I let it pour out," Dusaulchoy declared in the *Almanach du peuple* of 1793.

Perhaps one of the great dualities of the Revolution is that it had forged a political ideal with abstraction, violence, and sentimentality. Political violence—the outcries of hatred for all it rejected, past and present—was always accompanied by ethereal professions of faith. Within the most ferocious patriot was hidden an admirer of Rousseau. The revolutionary had to be a good soldier, a good citizen, a good husband, and a good father. This linkage of morality and politics, already set forth in *Emile* ("those who would deal separately with politics and morality will never understand anything about either one") was taken up in most of the republican almanacs. They were not simply vehicles of information, they were pedagogical instruments designed to spread a patriotic morality. Their message, directly inspired by *Emile* and the *Contrat social,* appeared in a vulgarized and simplified form.

Bathed in sentimentality, the republican almanac celebrated purity of conscience in the public sphere (a tendency that threatened to erase the distinction between private and public worlds and thus to undermine individual liberty) while stressing the value of the social order and glorifying work and the family. The nation appeared as one large family—the fatherland—while the call to work, especially to work in the fields, resounded in all the almanacs of the Year II (1793–94). To these virtues was added a respect for thrift and modest living. In this respect, it should be remembered that Benjamin Franklin's *Poor Richard's Almanac,* which propagated the same values, was very influential in its French translation, which circulated widely with the chapbooks sold by peddlers before the Revolution. It should also be remembered that the Jacobins, following Voltaire, had great admiration for the Quakers, to whom they intended to dedicate one of their holidays. Mixed with the praise of frugal domestic life was the ideal of the ancient Roman Republic, the myth of a revival of a Golden Age, and the Rousseauistic ideal of a return to nature, as expressed in the emblem of the Mountain.

This pedagogical and political vision of France, produced for the edification of country people, was in reality a dream of towndwellers and intellectuals. It is not certain that the people saw themselves in this dream, except for those readers whom the Revolution had already acquired, such as the innumerable officials who staffed the administration of the new regime and who were the real propagators of the Jacobin spirit.

The reform of the calendar, although not lasting, was significant. For it was the Revolution that invented the notion of the Old Regime. From then on there was a time before and a time after, divided by the Revolution. A break, more than merely a change of the calendar, had been made in human memory. But one must also stress the ambiguity of this mad ambition to restructure time through the medium of the almanac. Was it a question of establishing the Revolution on a permanent basis or of stopping the course of history by celebrating Year I of utopia?

In this study I have paid more attention to the republican almanacs than to the traditional or royalist ones, and I have favored the years 1793–94 and the Jacobin ideology that inspired them. The reason is simple: They are truly more innovative and richer symbolically, whatever one may think of their message. By the force of their conviction and their appeal to the political conscience of a mass readership, these almanacs belong to the press of the modern era.

PRINTS:
IMAGES OF THE BASTILLE

ROLF REICHARDT

POLITICAL ENGRAVINGS, usually in the form of broadsides, represent a significant proportion of the multifarious material printed during the French Revolution. At the end of the Old Regime, so far as we know, copperplate engravers had limited themselves to portraits of lofty personages, idealized representations of nature, family and genre scenes, and devotional images. The censors regarded political images, at least satirical cartoons, with suspicion. These had therefore become the province of a few outsiders or of engravers working in neighboring countries, particularly the Netherlands. With the Revolution and the advent of greater press freedom, however, this changed. The production of illustrated political broadsides boomed, and for a few years they dominated the field of engraving, making wealthy men of engraver-publishers like André Basset. These broadsides are so numerous and so scattered that they have never been comprehensively and systematically catalogued. The catalogue of the Collection de Vinck in the print department of the Bibliothèque Nationale alone encompasses more than six thousand items from the revolutionary period.[1]

The Significance of Revolutionary Prints

With different kinds of publication, imagery, and execution, these prints addressed different social groups. For example, only well-heeled subscribers could afford the *Tableaux historiques de la Révolution française,* finely detailed but detached from the events. Charles Monnet, Jean Antoine Duclos, Joseph Duplessi-Bertaux, and Isidor Stanislas Helman conceived them as a long-term collection in memory of the Revolution, and they were published in folio from 1793 to 1798.[2] The *Gravures historiques*, in contrast, were more current, less expensive, and aimed at a wider audience. The engraver François Janinet published his "patchwork" of fifty-six narrative aquatint etchings together with eight-page reports on the spectacular events of the Revolution from 1789 until March 1791.[3]

The engravings printed in many newspapers (often not until after the appearance of the relevant story) fulfilled another function by contributing to the creation of public opinion, whether from a conservative (*Actes des apôtres, Accusateur public*) or a radical standpoint (*Révolutions de Paris, Révolutions de France et de Brabant*).[4] The great majority of revolutionary engravings, however, consist of anonymous broadsides directly interpreting the news of the day. Their technical simplicity and rudimentary coloring testify to hasty production and large print runs, and their obvious imagery was calculated to make them immediately comprehensible to ordinary sansculottes. Most of these broadsides were produced in the rue St. Jacques, between the Sorbonne and the Ile de la Cité in central Paris. Hawked in the streets by *colporteurs,* they were also sold in the Palais Royal, where the bookseller Desenne had opened a sort of club where the politicized public could catch up on the latest news.[5]

Like other revolutionary printed matter, illustrated broadsides were produced in vast quantities. Their emphasis on pictorial representation renders them fundamentally significant for the Revolution because they helped mobilize a broad social base that made the Revolution's political process, and its radicalization, possible in the first place. If we take into account that one-half to two-thirds of the population of the time could not or could only barely read, and that they lived in a traditional world of oral communication, it becomes clear that illustrated broadsides fulfilled a more than supplementary function. Together with the nonwritten media of public speeches and songs, they approached the man and woman in the street in the terms of their own oral or semioral culture. They not only rendered the revolutionary message accessible but also drew ordinary people into the communication and opinion-making process of a widening public sphere, with its tendency toward democratization. These prints were at once a means of political education and testimony to popular ideas. Many of them belong to an oral culture that, after having been suppressed by absolutism and the Enlightenment, was revived by the Revolution[6] and shared in its ascendency.

Contemporaries were quite aware of this. For example, when the Parisian Jacobin Club debated on 27 November 1791 whether the *Almanach du Père Gérard* (probably the most successful popular almanac of the Revolution, which the club had awarded a prize) should be illustrated with engravings, J.-M. Lequinio won over the assembly by arguing: "You are aware of all the ills that fanaticism has caused by the dissemination of pictures in the provinces. I propose that the Society enlist artists to work in the opposite direction, by creating images analogous to the Revolution."[7] Conservatives, for their part, lamented the mobilizing effect of revolutionary prints: "We have seen that in all revolutions caricature has been used to spur the people to action, and we cannot deny that this abuse is as insidious as its effects are prompt and terrible. Caricatures are the thermometer which indicates the temperature of public opinion."[8] A moralistic observer and journalist, who had become a conservative under the Terror, grumbled in 1798 that revolutionary engravings were still highly visible, despite increased newspaper censorship: "Caricature seeks to continue its encroachment, and to constitute an addition to the unbounded license of the press. Crowds of passersby are stopping before the showcases of the print shops."[9]

The Committee of Public Safety formed a special fund for propaganda broadsides, out of which it commissioned at least a dozen works between September 1793 and October 1794. These ranged from two caricatures by Jacques-Louis David to Roo's *La Chute en masse*, each with a print run of 1,000 (half in color). The artists received fees of 1,000 to 3,000 livres.[10] Thus, an architect and member of the Assembly, speaking before the Council of Five Hundred on 5 April 1799, expressed the revolutionary politicians' common experience with political engravings when he asserted: "The utility [of engraving] rivals that of the printing press. By its means one can multiply, at little expense, patriotic and moral pictures which must influence public opinion more than we know."[11] Until recently, scholars have scarcely recognized the true significance of revolutionary illustrated journalism, and have therefore not studied it systematically. Art historians have seldom descended from the aesthetic peaks of great painting to study political prints for the masses, and historians of the Revolution have been content to illustrate their accounts with a few engravings of events, with an occasional "curious" caricature thrown in for good measure.[12] We have only recently begun to recognize that the genuine and unique value of revolutionary prints as historical sources lies not in their depictions of individuals or events but in their symbolic, metaphorical, and allegorical interpretation of collective ideas and the questions of the day. They can show us the ways that contemporaries processed and interpreted their experiences—ways that remain hidden in the written sources.[13] The following observations are an attempt to elucidate this assertion, taking as an example a subject ubiquitous in the illustrated journalism, particularly of the first years of the Revolution.[14]

The Bastille as Revolutionary Symbol

Even from the purely quantitative standpoint, the Bastille plays an important role in the symbolic repertoire of the Revolution; in fact, of the more than 150 broadsides taking the Bastille as a theme, we can discuss only a few. The fortress-prison also holds a significant place in the semiotic system of the Revolution, as one can see from the various editions and reprints of the 1791 *Jeu de l'oie* (The Goose Game).[15] Miniatures taken from popular illustrated broadsides, along with the concepts associated with them, cover the board. Through the rules of the game, the different fields on the board create a complex of meaning that renders visible the experience of the revolutionary caesura. The Bastille, as a symbol of the transition from Old Regime "despotism" to the new era of "Liberty," functions as a semantic turntable.[16] Let us look at some of the major social aspects of this revolutionary symbol, which appear to be typical of much illustrated journalism of the French Revolution.

INVOKING THE FUTURE

The symbolic power of the Bastille does not emerge out of nowhere in 1789. From 1715, at the latest, the Bastille was increasingly attacked as a concrete embodiment of "ministerial despotism," visible to all, and as a stain on the Enlightenment. The vehicle for such accusations was anti-absolutist underground literature, particularly the grim tales of suffering told by former inmates, which became more vehement even as actual prison conditions improved.[17] The creation of a Bastille myth reached its prerevolutionary zenith in a pamphlet by the eloquent journalist Nicolas-Simon-Henri Linguet, who had spent two years imprisoned there. The pamphlet was printed in six editions and reprinted in Linguet's journal *Annales politiques et littéraires*. It not only carries the vocabulary associated with the concept "Bastille" and its attendant fear and horror to new heights of radicalism[18] but it also concretizes underlying concerns in an attention-getting frontispiece (see illustration opposite). This engraving both summarizes past events and looks into the future. It translates the text's accusations into an appeal to the king (who is being deceived by his ministers) to end the despotism of the Bastille. It holds out the prospect of a monument in Louis XVI's honor, if he finally frees the Bastille's unjustly imprisoned victims. The latter, recognizable from their clothing as members of the upper classes, are portrayed as thankfully and humbly stretching up their arms to the king. The king's words of clemency, "May you be free and live!" (which give the print its lapidary title), repeat a phrase, by then proverbial, from Voltaire's 1736 drama *Alzire* (act II, scene 2). Although Louis XVI dis-

SOYEZ LIBRES: VIVEZ.

MÉMOIRES

SUR

LA BASTILLE,

ET

SUR LA DÉTENTION

DE M. LINGUET,

ÉCRITS PAR LUI-MÊME.

Surrexit è mortuis.

A LONDRES,

De l'Imprimerie de T. SPILSBURY, Snowhill.

M. DCC. LXXXIII.

Simon-Nicolas-Henri Linguet. "Memories of the Bastille." 1783. The New York Public Library, General Research Division.

The creation of a myth of the Bastille as the embodiment of despotism reached its prerevolutionary zenith in a pamphlet by the eloquent journalist Linguet. Its frontispiece depicts the king, Louis XVI, freeing unjustly imprisoned victims above the caption: "May you be free and live!" (cat. no. 24).

CONVOI DE TRES HAUT ET TRES PUISSANT SEIGNEUR DES ABUS

Mort sous le Règne de LOUIS XVI.

Sergent Marceau. "The Funeral Procession of His High and Mighty Lordship Abuse Dead under the Reign of Louis XVI, 27 April 1789" ("Convoi de très haut et très puissant seigneur des Abus Mort sous le règne de Louis XVI le 27 avril 1789"). Paris, 1789. Aquatint. Bibliothèque Nationale, Cabinet des Estampes, Collection de Vinck.

This print portrays a funeral cortege, which has become a pageant of political disgrace, with the "Third Estate" carrying the "gigantic corpse" of abuses to its grave.

plays the attributes of royal power in this engraving, the prisoners' release is not left to his pleasure. Rather, it is demanded as a right, reminding the king of his own call for moderation of the penal code in the reform edict of 30 August 1780: "These unimaginable sufferings and gloomy punishments," wrote the king, "are useless to our system of justice, if their publicity and example do not contribute to the maintenance of order." That such "needless cruelty" indeed characterized the Bastille is suggested by the relief that adorned the clock in the prison courtyard, depicting two chained prisoners. Linguet denounces its humiliating effect in his memoirs. The ruins of the Bastille frame the scene, six years before the fortress was actually razed. The lightning bolt, which flashes out of dark clouds to blast the prison walls and the clock, appears to come from an unnamed higher power (the press?). It will, the picture suggests, destroy the Bastille; Louis XVI is appointed as its executor.

The wide dissemination of this visual invocation of the future was not the least of the factors leading to a whole series of *cahiers de doléances* calling for the Bastille's abolition in the spring of 1789. A new expression of the general hopes for reform went beyond Linguet's expectations and attacked the general state of affairs under the Old Regime, embodied by the "très haut et très puissant seigneur des Abus" (see illustration opposite). The print portrays a funeral cortege that, in an inversion of the triumphal processions of the clerical and princely tradition, has become a pageant of political disgrace, with the Third Estate carrying the "gigantic corpse" of abuses to its grave. Crozier, miter, sword, moneybag, judge's cap, and iron crown indict clergy, nobility, and magistracy for the tyrannical state of affairs. Led by J.-J. Rousseau, the "miserable victims of the abuses," victims of justice from Joan of Arc to Jean Calas, step to the head of the procession. Among them is the self-styled Bastille martyr Maseis de Latude (his real name was Henri Dahry), whose spectacular escape and successful memoirs had made him a popular figure. Before the sarcophagus, we see a Fury and the vices dedicated to "seigneur des Abus"—Avarice, Folie, and Orgueil—taking their last desperate steps, followed by the virtues Egalité, Prudence, Force, and Justice who, in quite another mood, prance into a new era. The jester capering about them reinforces the pageant's carnivalesque element.

The second half of the cortege, led by the Chief Minister Jacques Necker, finds it less amusing. Here aristocrats, the previous beneficiaries of the "*abus*," mourn their losses. Leaving the ruins of the edifice of abuses (half palace, half temple), past rotted tree stumps and discarded implements of torture from the Bastille (ball-and-chain in the right foreground), the procession of jubilation and mourning moves toward the regeneration of France. In the foreground, genii announce the approaching national renewal by reading aloud to the Estates General from reform writings. Visible in outline in an unfinished painting—with a spyglass representing the promise of the future—the imminent rejuvenation is symbolized, finally, by an oak tree in the full vigor of life. Although men of the Third Estate are already playing an active role as pallbearers, the vignette accompanying the caption exhorts Louis XVI to act so that he may enter the book of history as a *roi citoyen:* Chronos and Fama have yet to engrave the death date for *"abus."* This broadside, too, met with an enthusiastic response. Although forbidden immediately after its publication in May, it was successfully displayed and sold in at least six copies and imitations on the quais along the Seine and in the Tuileries.[19]

POPULAR REPORTAGE AND THE CULT OF HEROES

The storming of the Bastille by the Parisian populace on 14 July 1789 unleashed not only a flood of newspaper and pamphlet accounts but also a number of engravings. These satisfied the need, particularly of the simple people in the streets, to relive, in pictorial and oral as well as written form, the act that had liberated them from an existence of fear and had given them the sense of being a patriotically united force. Of all the depictions of events, two popular broadsides were particularly successful in this regard. Both were *canards,* a genre of traditional popular gazettes that appeared irregularly to report the sensational events of the day.[20] The *canards* combined picture, sound, and writing to reach the people through all of their senses. Hawked and performed by *colporteurs,* they lent themselves to communal singing in the streets and thus belong to the semioral culture mentioned earlier. Previously devoted, as a rule, to the executions of famous criminals, the *canards* were converted into a means of revolutionary mass education. Our two crude broadsides informed the public with greater commitment than other, less impassioned but more technically sophisticated, prints.

One of the prints (see illustration opposite) was produced by the engraver Jean-Baptiste Gautier of the rue St. Jacques using the new, much quicker procedure of etching rather than the usual laborious copperplate engraving. Thus, it was being sold on 28 July 1789, just two weeks after the storming of the Bastille. This naïve and clumsy etching depicts the victors of the Bastille before the fortress they have just captured. On its battlements, the first conquerors are taking the governor prisoner. What makes this picture special is not its portrayal of a specific event but rather the context of meaning it creates with the surrounding texts. Etched beneath the picture is a report of the "heureuse révolution," linking this broadside with the genre of radical revolutionary pamphlets. Indeed, it repeats almost verbatim key sentences from a pamphlet printed in central

"The Siege of the Bastille, Captured by the Bourgeoisie" ("Le Siège de la Bastille prise par la bourgeoisie"). Paris: Gautier, 1789. Color etching. Bibliothèque Nationale, Cabinet des Estampes, Collection Hennin.

Previously devoted, as a rule, to depicting the executions of famous criminals, crude broadsides were now used for revolutionary mass communication. This etching of the storming of the Bastille was ready to be peddled in Paris on 28 July 1789, a mere two weeks after the event.

Paris immediately after the storming of the Bastille.[21] To judge from the minor changes, misunderstandings, and variations in spelling between the two versions, it seems doubtless that the text was dictated to an incompletely literate engraver, thus lending it a semioral character. But it conveys the message undiluted: the obvious "necessity to storm the Bastille."

The text provides additional justification for the attack on the Bastille because of the "abominable treason" on the part of the governor, whose just execution by the people on the Place de Grève, together with the heroic deeds of the Bastille conquerors Jean-Baptiste Humbert and Joseph Arné, forms the heart of the polemic. The texts framing the etching are unmistakably directed at oral folk culture; songs celebrating the events of 14 July have been set to well-known melodies, dispensing with musical notation and easing the memorization of new texts. The triumphal song on the left-hand side adopts a dance tune written around 1750 by the chansonnier Pierre Laujon. Traditionally in honor of Henri IV, the melody now assists the plebeian text in evoking the old despotism of the Bastille and in threatening traitors of the people with decapitation. Following the opening essay in the brochure entitled *La France régénérée et les traîtres punis* (Paris, n.d.) the second song, on the right-hand side, extols the virtues of the French Guards.

This politicized Parisian *canard* served, in turn, as a model for a provincial woodcut (see illustration opposite) published by Jean-Baptiste Letourmi of Orléans, who successfully sold his pictorial broadsheets via some hundred outlets throughout France.[22] His representation of the storming of the Bastille depicts even more schematically than Gautier's the Guards charging the fortress with muskets and cannon, capturing Bernard René Jordan, marquis de Launay, and unfurling the victory flag on the battlements. It is precisely this emblematic reduction (which also characterizes the title page of the first volume of Prudhomme's *Révolutions de Paris*) that gives the woodcut the effect of an icon, a political devotional image.

The "Récit mémorable" printed underneath adopts Gautier's text literally, but politicizes and radicalizes it in three ways: First, the caption glorifies the Fourteenth of July as the beginning of the "first year of Liberty"; second, the report reinforces the uprising's popular character ("a great number of patriotic citizens"); and third, it clarifies the popular justice exercised at the time with the addition, "the head of the governor was carried in triumph throughout the city and was exposed for several days." This particular aspect of the traitor's just punishment was the focus of other illustrated broadsides as well.[23] The "double portrait" of Launay, who seems to have deserved his death simply by virtue of being the Bastille's governor, is an example. Finally, Letourmi's pictorial broadsheet is also framed by songs in

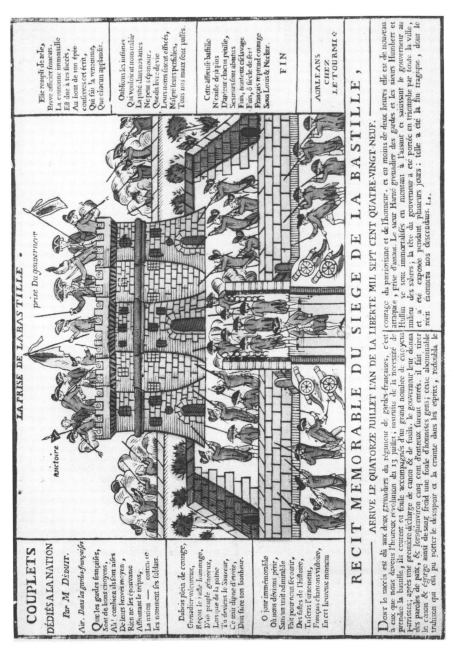

"The Taking of the Bastille" ("La Prise de la Bastille"). Orléans: Letourmi, 1789. Color woodcut. Bibliothèque Nationale, Cabinet des Estampes, Collection de Vinck.

The Parisian-etched broadside, in turn, served as a model for a provincial woodcut published in Orléans and distributed via some hundred outlets throughout France.

which the author, the petit bourgeois Parisian chansonnier Déduit, politicizes a melody traditionally associated with a soldier's love by using it to celebrate the insurgents' deeds, the end of despotism, and the dawning of a new Golden Age:

> Cette affreuse bastille
> N'existe déjà plus.
> D'ardeur chacun pétille
> Ses murs sont abattus.
>
> Fuis, honteux esclavage,
> Fuis, ô siècle de fer!
> Français reprend courage
> Sous Louis & Necker.
>
> This horrible fortress
> Exists no more;
> All scintillate with ardor;
> Its walls are razed.
>
> Away, shameful slavery,
> Away, age of iron!
> People of France, take courage
> Under Louis and Necker.

It is no accident that such popular broadsides were more likely than other prints to combine accounts of the events of 14 July with songs of praise for the heroes. In 1789 the victors of the Bastille—simple men rooted in a traditional, semioral culture—suddenly emerged from political inarticulateness onto the public stage to portray themselves as the nation's heroes.[24] Their new self-confidence, as well as the public admiration they received (for example, in the numerous thanksgiving masses), found expression in a series of "victor portraits." For the first time the heroic portrait, heretofore the exclusive province of princes and noble officers, celebrated rebellious freedom fighters from the ranks of the people. Another woodcut accompanied by songs and citations from an earlier interpretation of the Fourteenth of July depicts the two most popular victors of the Bastille. The Grenadier Arné, who had gone over to the people's side, and the watchmaker and author of an eyewitness account, Humbert, are shown with the attributes of glory, at once in self-confident conqueror's pose and patriotic harmony (see illustration opposite). Their heroism remained both inspiration and legacy, a model for revolutionary activists. In Year II (1793–94) the cult of the martyrs of the Revolution still invoked the battle

"Portrait of Du Harnée, Drawn from Life" ("Portrait d'après nature de Du Harnée . . ."). Paris, 1789. Woodcut. Bibliothèque Nationale, Cabinet des Estampes, Collection de Vinck.

Popular broadsides were more likely than other prints to combine images of the heroes along with accounts of the events and songs praising them. With these broadsides, for the first time the "heroic portrait" celebrated fighters from the ranks of the people.

"Martyrs of Liberty" ("Martirs de la liberté"). 1793. Etching. Bibliothèque Nationale, Cabinet des Estampes, Collection de Vinck.

The heroism of the stormers of the Bastille remained a model for revolutionary activists. In the Year II (1793–94) the cult of the martyrs of the Revolution still invoked the battle for liberty on the Fourteenth of July, making it the yardstick against which candidates for national fame in the Panthéon were to be measured.

for liberty on the Fourteenth of July, making it the yardstick against which candidates for national fame in the Panthéon were to be measured (see illustration opposite).

HISTORICAL JUSTIFICATION

However sensational the Fourteenth of July may have been, it owes its true significance, and its permanent status as the founding event of modern France, to a symbolic interpretation that went far beyond the insurgents' military achievements and the actual conditions in the Bastille. A series of etchings popularized this interpretation, an interpretation that met the revolutionaries' need for greatness and legitimacy.

We may recall the famous broadside *Réveil du Tiers Etat* from July 1789, which depicts the Third Estate awakening from centuries of oppression, bursting its chains, reaching for its weapons, and rising up to conquer the Bastille (seen in the background) while a horrified nobleman and a priest look on.[25] Less well-known are the etchings that carry this interpretation further. A first sequel to the aforementioned, for example, shows the Third Estate's growth in stature since the storming of the Bastille. No longer prone on the ground, the Third Estate now towers over both the nobility and the clergy. With the lion that follows him, the Third Estate is all-powerful. He has reduced the two higher estates to marionettes, making them dance to his pipes before the crumbling walls of the Bastille, like one of the itinerant puppeteers who entertained the Parisian populace.

A second sequel makes it clear that the Third Estate has gained his new stature not only through his victory as such, but also through his services to Liberty (see illustration next page). The figure of the Third Estate dominates the picture, fighting under the flag of Liberty (see Phrygian cap and banderole), and strikes a last blow at the six-headed Hydra of despotism while nobility and clergy flee. The accompanying text names Hydra's henchmen as the Bastille's governor and his alleged coconspirator, the head of the merchants' guild Jacques de Flesselles, who were executed on 14 July by the people as a just punishment for lèse-majesté against their new sovereign, the Nation. This "victory over the enemies of Liberty" clears the way for the destruction of the symbol of their former subjection, the Bastille. Onlookers of all ages and estates, both men and women, watch the demolition, cheering every tumbling stone with applause and a cry of "*liberté!*"[26]— a scene portrayed often enough on its own.

The pictures mentioned above only hint at the connection between the vanquished enemies of liberty and the despotism of the Bastille. Another broadside, reprinted at least four times, goes into more detail (see illustration next page). Here, too, rebellious citizens, now shown in great

Destruction de la Bastille après la Victoire remporté sur les Enemis de la Liberté le 14 Juill. 1789.

"Destruction of the Bastille after the Victory over the Enemies of Liberty" ("Destruction de la Bastille après la victoire remportée sur les ennemis de la liberté . . ."). 1789. Color etching. Bibliothèque Nationale, Cabinet des Estampes, Collection de Vinck.

A series of etchings popularized the Third Estate's awakening from centuries of oppression and its rising up to conquer the Bastille. No longer prone on the ground, the Third Estate now towers over both the nobility and clergy. In front of the walls of the crumbling Bastille, the Third Estate has gained its new stature not only through victory as such but also through its services to Liberty.

"The Aristocratic Hydra" ("L'Hydre aristocratique"). 1789. Color etching. Bibliothèque Nationale, Cabinet des Estampes, Collection de Vinck.

Dragged from its hiding place in the Bastille, the Hydra embodied both the collective fear of "aristocratic conspiracy" that preceded the storming of the Bastille and the people's joy at having foiled the plot.

numbers armed with the weapons of 14 July, destroy the Bastille twice: in the background concretely, and in the center allegorically, in the form of a many-headed, dragonlike monster. Its predatory claws resemble those of the man- and beast-eating harpy, familiar from the caricatures of Marie Antoinette of 1784–88.[27] The print's title identifies the creature as *aristocratie*, a catchword of the day used to denounce enemies of change—especially the privileged nobles, but also enemies of the Revolution in general. The detailed accompanying text characterizes the "Hydre Aristocratique" as an insatiable "Monstre . . . féroce, Barbare, Sanguinaire." Having gorged itself on the blood and marrow of the miserable populace until it could hide no longer, it was discovered on 12 July on the road from Versailles to Paris, and it sought refuge in the Bastille.

The description obviously refers to Necker's dismissal as a result of a reactionary cabal at court, to the threatening concentration of royal troops around the National Assembly, and to rumors that the Bastille was to figure in a planned destruction of Paris.[28] Dragged from its hiding place in the Bastille, and then surrounded and already partially decapitated by the crowd, Hydra embodies "Despotisme terrassé."[29] It also symbolizes the collective fear of "artistocratic conspiracy" that preceded the storming of the Bastille as well as the people's joy at having foiled the plot. In the foreground, the regeneration of the long-unconscious *Francia* is portrayed as the fruit of victory, while Louis XVI is mentioned only in the conclusion of the accompanying text (as the nation's hope for the *roi citoyen*).

For the revolutionaries, the Bastille was despotic not only because it was perceived to be involved in an aristocratic plot; the "barbaric" conditions prevailing there until 14 July were an equally essential factor. The crueler and more numerous the horrors committed there in the king's name, the more justified and glorious was the Bastille's conquest and destruction at the people's hands. The presses worked in feverish haste, drawing material from the newly discovered Bastille archives, from oral testimony, and from finds made during demolition to provide ever more support for Linguet's old claim that the Bastille's sole purpose was to imprison men of the Enlightenment and other innocent victims arbitrarily and without trial in order to murder them in secret. None of the seven prisoners liberated on 14 July fits this image, however; ideal Bastille martyrs therefore had to be created. Among the many depictions of idealized or fictional prisoners, a *canard* once again proves particularly rich. It consists of two equally fictional scenes, both set in the Bastille dungeons (*cachots*) in July 1789 (see illustration opposite).

On the left, the "Nation" arrives to liberate the "comte de Lorges," who according to the text was arrested under Louis XV in connection with an

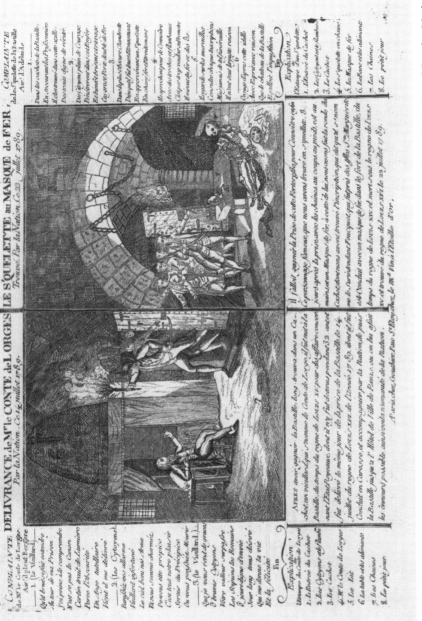

"The Liberation of the Count of Lorges by the Nation . . . The Skeleton with the Iron Mask found by the Nation" ("Délivrance de M. le Comte de Lorges par la Nation . . . Le S'quelette au masque de fer trouvé par la nation . . ."). Paris: Gouthier, 1789. Etching. Bibliothèque Nationale, Cabinet des Estampes, Collection de Vinck.

Among the many depictions of idealized or fictional scenes, both set in the Bastille dungeons in July 1789. On the left, the "Nation" liberates the long-imprisoned "comte de Lorges" to lead him in triumph through Paris. On the right, the victors of the Bastille finally bring to light the mysterious "Man in the Iron Mask" (the mask can be seen next to the skeleton), reputed to have died incognito under Louis XIV.

"affaire concernant l'Etat Royal," and to lead him in triumph through Paris. The count is now free of his chains, but thirty-two years of arbitrary imprisonment have left him a bearded, nearly blind old man. The *complainte* beside the picture laments his fate not as that of a criminal (as under the Old Regime) but as the fate of a victim of the now-vanquished despotism itself. The life-sized, fictional "comte de Lorges"—exhibited in Curtius's wax museum complete with chains, *cachot,* and all[30]—and the written dissemination of his tale both in a separate brochure[31] and in the radical press mark him as a key figure in collective obsessions after 14 July: "We did not ourselves see, but many have assured us that they saw, an old man leaving that place of horror [the Bastille], with a full gray beard more than a foot in length; if the reports are to be believed, he had suffered in its dungeons for more than thirty years."[32]

On the right of the etching, we see the victors of the Bastille bringing to light the mysterious "Man in the Iron Mask" (the mask can be seen next to the skeleton), who was reputed to have died incognito under Louis XIV and was the subject of much speculation since the mid-eighteenth century. The gloom of the barred vault, the long-decayed straw pallet, and the still-chained skeleton of the unknown man who had been intentionally tormented to death illustrate the words of the accompanying ballad:

On juge d'après cette idille
Avec Esprit, avec raison
Que le château de la Bastille
Egalloit l'inquisition.

One can see from this scene
With one's wit and reason
That the fortress of the Bastille
Equaled the Inquisition.

COMMEMORATIVE CELEBRATIONS AND MONUMENTS

As revolutionary events, the capture and destruction of the Bastille—longed for, prophesied, passionately related, celebrated, idealized, and interpreted in many images—were ideally suited to found a new symbolism of national identity; more so, in any case, than the later key events of the Revolution, which were politically more controversial. This symbolic function of the Bastille, which found expression from 1790 on in public festivals, was embodied before that in various plans for monuments. The fol-

242

lowing newspaper report, which concluded one of the most successful accounts of the capture of the Bastille, could count on the unanimous agreement of the popular classes and the revolutionaries: "This horrible lair of hellish tyranny, which so many times through so many centuries caused outraged humanity to tremble and swallowed so many innocent victims, shall be totally torn down, and in its place will be erected a monument to Liberty the Glorious!"[33]

A picture was soon to follow (see illustration next page). An anonymous etching, transforming Linguet's suppliant image (see above, p. 227) into a symbol of achievement, leaves the king on the pedestal of his monument of 1783 but dispenses with the Bastille ruins seen in the earlier engraving. The Bastille has ceased to exist, as the Hydra of despotism expiring under the royal foot and the engraving of the events of 14 July (on the ground to the right) make clear. Louis XVI can claim to be the patron of the monument to Liberty because he sanctioned the storming of the Bastille with his visit to Paris on 17 July (the subject of the second engraving on the ground). The National Assembly therefore declared him "Restaurateur de la Liberté Française," reflected in the monument's dedicatory inscription. Another inscription, on the pedestal's side, exhorts him to follow the principle: "Je ne veux faire qu'un avec mon peuple" ("I don't want anything other than to be one with my people"). Nevertheless, he resembles a marionette, watching the novel behavior of the estates that have grown over his head. The print suggests that, with the Fourteenth of July, the previous struggles among the estates have given way to national harmony, and that the two higher estates have been transformed from the oppressors of the Third Estate into its allies. In the guise of future militiamen nursed by *Francia*, the Third Estate (which the caption equates with the "Nation") finally receives its due: from the clergy its livings and misused tithes, from the nobility the feudal rights lost in the night of 4–5 August. Thus the picture depicts a "royalist" victory celebration and an invocation of national unity.

Translated into a concrete design for a monument (a competition was announced immediately after 14 July), this allegory yielded designs of Pierre-François Palloy, Jean-Louis Prieur, and others, including one drawn by the architect Davy de Chavigny in the summer of 1789 but not engraved by Jean-Gustav Taraval until 1790. Louis XVI, to whom the monument is dedicated as "Restorer of French Liberty," stands in a ruler's pose atop a colossal Liberty column. At its base are sculptures representing the four new guiding principles ("France," "Liberté," "Concorde," and "Loi") and the various provinces and estates, which are all equal as sources of taxes for the Nation.

LOUIS XVI.
Restaurateur
de la Liberté
Française

A P.

1789

NOUVELLE PLACE DE LA BASTILLE.

"The New 'Place de la Bastille'" ("Nouvelle Place de la Bastille"). 1789. Color etching. Bibliothèque Nationale, Cabinet des Estampes, Collection de Vinck.

The capture and destruction of the Bastille were better symbols for building a new national identity than were the more politically controversial events later in the Revolution. Plans for monuments attempted to rely on Bastille symbolism for their inspirational content.

Such projects for monuments commemorating events related to the Bastille, which included king and estates as a sort of appeal, are a phenomenon of the years 1789–90. As Louis XVI distanced himself more clearly from the Revolution, and as the social tensions, which had initially been smoothed over, began to erupt, other designs emerged. In the revolutionary column he designed in 1790 for the Place de la Bastille, Nicolas-Marie Gatteaux, "Graveur des Medailles de sa Majesté," has already replaced Louis XVI with the figure of "Liberté" complete with lance and Phrygian cap. On 16 June 1792 the Convention decided to name the square left empty by the razing of the Bastille "Place de la Liberté," and to erect a Liberty column in the middle, whose foundation stone was festively laid a month later on 17 July. The building contractor Pierre-François Palloy, a self-styled *architecte* and *démolisseur de la Bastille,* celebrated these decisions with plans of his own for a monument larger than Trajan's column and built entirely of stones from the demolished fortress (see illustration p. 246). In the end, then, designs for a monument to the Bastille focused exclusively on "Liberté."

Although these monuments remained mere paper dreams, numerous broadsides commemorating revolutionary public festivals demonstrate the importance of Bastille symbolism for the concrete mise-en-scène of the Revolution. When the politicized Parisian populace responded to the official Confederation festivities held in July 1790 on the Champ de Mars with a spontaneous countercelebration on the rubble of the Bastille, several broadsides captured the gesture (see illustration p. 247). Taking as its motto "Ici l'on danse," the populace has converted the site of the old stronghold of terror into a fairground.[34] Arbors created by Palloy and his workers from freshly cut trees sketch the former outlines of the Bastille and form a dance floor. Above the nocturnal festival's strings of lights, the Liberty cap floats. Next door, however, the guests could view a re-creation of a *cachot,* a chamber of horrors with instruments of torture and other terrifying artifacts from the Bastille. Their guide must have used words much like those employed a year later by the chairman of a revolutionary club when the festival was repeated:

> Citizens, brothers and friends! . . . Here the Bastille once stood. With what joy we trample its stones underfoot, which so long imprisoned the man of genius, the man who had the courage to enlighten his fellow citizens. . . . Here in these dungeons, the remains of which are before us, were incarcerated those famous writers who prepared and hastened our Revolution. To the fall of this cherished monument of despotism we owe the success of our Revolution: henceforth, we will

"Perspective View of the Monument to be Erected on the Ruins of the Bastille" ("Vue en perspective du monument à ériger sur les ruines de la Bastille"). Paris, 1792. Etching. Reprinted from Alain Weil, *Histoire numismatique du patriote Palloy démolisseur de la Bastille* (Paris, 1976), Plate XIV.

Projects for monuments commemorating the events around the Bastille that included images of the king and the estates are a phenomenon of the years 1789–90. In the end, designs for a monument to the Bastille focused exclusively on "Liberté."

VUE

de la Décoration et Illumination faite sur le Terrein de la Bastille

pour le Jour de la Fête de la Confédération Française le 14 Juillet 1790.

"View of the Decoration and Illumination of the Site of the Bastille for the Day of Celebration of the French Confederation on 14 July 1790" ("Vue de la décoration et illumination faite sur le terrain de la Bastille pour le jour de la fête de la Confédération française le 14 juillet 1790"). Paris, 1790. Etching. Bibliothèque Nationale, Cabinet des Estampes, Collection de Vinck.

While monuments remained mere paper dreams, numerous broadsides commemorating revolutionary public festivals demonstrate the importance of Bastille symbolism for the concrete *mise-en-scène* of the Revolution. When the politicized Parisian populace responded to the official Confederation festivities held in July 1790 on the Champ de Mars with a spontaneous countercelebration on the rubble of the Bastille, several broadsides such as this one captured the symbolic gesture.

date our political era from this time. July 14th shall be a date remembered through the centuries.[35]

If the Bastille functions here, above all, as a symbol of the victory of the Faubourg St. Antoine's petite bourgeoisie, it later gained universal acceptance—beyond the yearly Fourteenth of July commemorations[36]—as an identifying symbol of the French Revolution itself. It became a must at all revolutionary festivals, which began almost obligatorily at the former site of the Bastille.[37] And so it was when Voltaire was admitted to the Panthéon on 11 July 1791. The night before, the sarcophagus of the philosophe was displayed on the ruins of the prison where he had twice been confined, bearing the inscription: "Reçois dans ce lieu où le despotisme t'enchaîna, Voltaire, les honneurs que te rend la Patrie" ("Receive in this place where despotism kept you in chains, Voltaire, the honors that the fatherland pays to you").[38]

Basset of the rue St. Jacques captured the procession itself in an etching (see illustration opposite). In the background, representatives of the most important political forces, including the revolutionary clubs and the "Forts de la Halle" (nos. 2 and 6), among them the victors of the Bastille, escort the remains of the Bastille martyr Voltaire in monarchical splendor to the newly opened temple of fame. Most of the "trophées de la liberté" held aloft in the middle section of the procession refer to the Bastille. A flag depicts the events of 14 July on one side, referring to them on the other as "La dernière raison du Peuple."[39] Next comes the "Cortège du quatre vingt troisième modèle de la Bastille" (no. 10); that is, the last of the models that Palloy's workers built in 1790–91 for distribution as patriotic *ex voto de la liberté* in all departments.[40] The citizens of the Faubourg St. Antoine follow. Surrounded by banners bearing the likenesses of the fathers of the Revolution—Rousseau, Franklin, Desille, and Mirabeau—they carry atop a stone from the Bastille the *Procès-verbal . . . de l'Assemblée générale des Electeurs de Paris,* Jean-Sylvain Bailly and Honoré Marie Nicolas Duveyrier's official 1790 account of the events of 14 July.

The same image recurs in subsequent Parisian revolutionary festivities and in the engravings recording them. One example is the procession to honor the soldiers of Châteauvieux on 15 April 1792, at which Palloy's workers and the "vainqueurs de la Bastille" carried a model Bastille and four ashlars from the building inscribed, respectively, "Constitution," "Liberté," "Bravoure," and "Dévouement." Another is the constitutional celebration of 10 August 1793, planned and organized by David, which began at the former site of the Bastille, where a fountain in the form of an Egyptian nature goddess now stood. Water flowed from her breasts and was distrib-

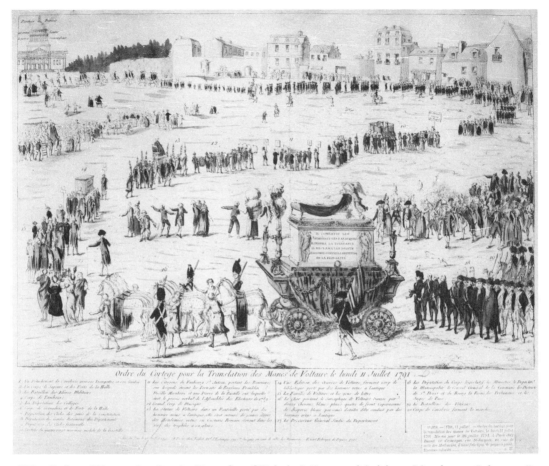

"The Order of Procession for the Transfer of Voltaire's Departed Spirit on Monday, 11 July 1791." Color etching. Bibliothèque Nationale, Cabinet des Estampes.

The Bastille gained universal acceptance as an identifying symbol of the French Revolution itself. It was a requisite symbol at all revolutionary festivals, which were almost obliged to begin at the former site of the Bastille. And so it was when Voltaire was admitted to the Panthéon on 11 July 1791 (cat. no. 108).

DÉDIÉ
AUX
VAINQUEURS DE LA BASTILLE

14 JUILLET
1789

14 JUILLET
1880

LIBERTÉ

ÉGALITÉ

FRATERNITÉ

PRIX : **10** CENTIMES

Se vend chez tous les Libraires, Marchands de Journaux, dans tous les Kiosques

ET CHEZ L'ÉDITEUR, RUE VISCONTI, 12.

"14 July 1789–14 July 1880" ("14 juillet 1789–14 juillet 1880"). Paris, 1880. Etching.
Bibliothèque Nationale, Cabinet des Estampes, Collection Histoire de France.

On the first official celebration of the Fourteenth of July, in 1880, cheap illustrated pamphlets evoked the Bastille's symbolic traditions.

uted to representatives of the departments, who, in drinking it, acted out a scene of national rebirth or political baptism. Even on the first official national holiday, held on 14 July 1880, cheap illustrated pamphlets conjured up the Bastille's symbolic traditions. The victory of the inspired "Republic," which finally sweeps aside the old aristocracy and the upper bourgeoisie, attains its full significance only against the background of the despotism, conquest, and destruction of the Bastille.[41]

SONGS:
MIXING MEDIA

LAURA MASON

IN YEAR II of the Revolution (1793–94) the vaudevillian Antoine Piis, remarkable both for his seemingly limitless capacity to produce songs and for his unerring instinct about the directions in which the political winds blew, wrote a hymn to the printing press:

> C'est par toi que chaque pensée
> se change en signes de métal;
> C'est par tes yeux qu'elle est classée,
> A son tour, dans un ordre égal;
> C'est par tes bras qu'elle est pressée
> Pour doubler de force et de prix;
> C'est par tes mains qu'elle est lancée
> Pour atteindre tous les esprits.[1]

Here was a most felicitous partnership between song and print in the service of the Revolution, a partnership to which was added still another dimension by the inclusion—on the printed page—of the time and place of the song's first performance. This neat confluence was characteristic of only a single phase of the Revolution, however, and "Hymn to the Printing Press" represented only one aspect of the multifaceted relationship between revolutionary song and printed page.

Songs differed from other types of print culture during the French Revolution in two ways. In the first place, they followed a very different publication trajectory from that of revolutionary newspapers. Whereas newspaper publication rose dramatically in the period 1789–90 and declined steadily to reach a nadir during the Terror,[2] the printing of songs

252

gained momentum with the progress of the Revolution, reaching a zenith at the same moment that journals seemed about to disappear.[3]

Second, because of their essentially oral nature, songs had a unique relationship with the printed page: Songs were written to be sung aloud or performed for others, and this oral transmission made their circulation among the illiterate possible. During the Old Regime songs facilitated the dissemination of critical lyrics otherwise likely to attract the attention of the police. In addition, public performances facilitated the exploitation of a song's suggestive possibilities. The interaction of these oral traditions with the medium of print created the dynamic of revolutionary-song culture. Once fixed in print, the texts and performances of songs stretched beyond their listening public to reach a reading public as well, adding yet another dimension to the shifting relationship between songs and revolutionary politics.

During the Revolution, printing presses continued to fill the traditional function of preserving song texts, but a new relationship grew up between song and printed page as performances also began to be preserved. The explosion in newspaper publishing that accompanied the start of the Revolution created new possibilities for the representation of objects and activities to the public eye: Letters to editors and anecdotal columns captured some of the otherwise ephemeral occurrences in the street, merging newspaper with street and theater as forums in which unofficial ideas about revolutionary culture could be elaborated and publicly debated. Songs and singing, part of this street experience, were among the topics treated in the newspapers.

Newspapers that carried descriptions of the singing of particular songs—which happened with varying frequency and detail over the course of the Revolution—extended a song's suggestive possibilities to a wider audience, beyond the listeners on the street. But describing a song performance, like printing a song text, was not a neutral act; it was a way to express opinions about the nature, course, and goals of the Revolution. Nor was this means of expression static: Like the nature of song performances and the content of song texts, the conditions of reporting performances and publishing texts underwent several changes during the Revolution.

Despite its profound impact on political relations, the taking of the Bastille in 1789 did not herald the beginning of revolutionary song. Between July 1789 and July 1790, popular practices of singing were very much those of the Old Regime—only the subject matter of the songs had changed. Popular songs written in 1789—"composed" by setting new verses to an already well-known tune—celebrated noteworthy events and then lost popularity as the event receded into the past.[4] A few older songs, deemed

HYMNE A L'IMPRIMERIE,

PAR LE CITOYEN PIIS,

Chanté à la section des Tuileries, le décadi 30 Pluviôse.

Air du Vaudeville de l'Officier de Fortune.

C'EST sur l'autel de la Patrie
Que des Français reconnoissans,
En l'honneur de L'IMPRIMERIE,
Viennent brûler un grain d'encens.
Quel Citoyen mettroit en doute
Les bienfaits de cet Art divin ?
Il a dû commencer sans doute ;
Mais il n'aura jamais de fin. } *Bis.*

O des inventions humaines
La plus sublime invention !
On s'épuise en recherches vaines
Pour fixer ta création ;
Mais d'être auteur de ta naissance
Si plus d'un savant s'est vanté,
A tous, toi, par reconnoissance, } *Bis.*
Tu donnes l'immortalité.

Pierre-Antoine-Augustin de Piis. "Hymn to the Printing Press." [1793–94]. Bibliothèque Nationale, Département des Imprimés.

Piis's "Hymn to the Printing Press" is a vivid illustration of the felicitous partnership between song and print media in the service of revolution (cat. no. 81).

relevant to current events, were also revived and played, or sung, at various celebrations and popular gatherings.[5] Songs appeared in print irregularly—in a few newspapers or in the cheap half-sheets and six- or twelve-page booklets that had been common to songsellers throughout the eighteenth century—and only a few newspapers described incidences of popular singing, usually in the context of reporting a particular event. Although almost all of the songs written in 1789 celebrated the Revolution, the few journalists and politicians who paid any attention to them considered popular singing a generally suspect activity. The abbé Fauchet claimed that "while the partisans of the old order and the old ways amuse themselves with songs, epigrams, and slander, the friends of the Constitution and of the habits that are appropriate to a newly liberated people produce writings that are serious, austere, and just."[6] Camille Desmoulins, less rigid about the ideal character of the revolutionary and occasionally enjoying the streetsingers himself, was also distrustful. He warned his readers that the muse of song, "who so loves champagne," was the one most easily corrupted by the aristocracy.[7] Singing in the streets, of course, continued unabated. Then, in the middle of 1790, one aspect of popular singing underwent a profound transformation. It was reflected in print.

During the first two weeks of July 1790 Parisians volunteered by the thousands to help prepare the Champ de Mars for the first fête of the Federation. As they worked, they sang, and all reports agreed that the favored song was "a new song that's called the *Carillon national.* Everyone sings at the same time, *ça ira, ça ira, ça ira.*"[8]

"Ça ira" was an extremely simple song, which needed to retain only its melody and the refrain, "Ah! ça ira, ça ira, ça ira," to remain the "ça ira."[9] The verses could be, and were, altered with great frequency. The printed versions of the song sung in 1790 were hopeful about the future of the Revolution and sought conciliation between social orders.

> Ah! ça ira, ça ira, ça ira
> Réjouissons nous le bon temps viendra
> Les gens des Halles jadis *a quia*
> Peuvent chanter *alléluia.*[10]

There were other versions of the song, however, which were not printed; nor were they so conciliatory. The *Chronique de Paris,* in describing the work at the Champ de Mars, added, "We can't repeat all the songs that were being sung . . . ; it's enough to say that the aristocrats were not spared."[11] The *Mercure de France,* less discreet, stated flatly: "The chorus of most of the songs was *ça ira, hang the aristocrats, kill the aristocrats!*"[12]

CHANSON
SUR
LA PRISE DES INVALIDES
ET DE LA BASTILLE.

A MON PARENT
M. MOREAU DE SAINT-MERRY,
Préſident des 300 Electeurs de Paris.

Air : *Dans ma Cabane obſcure*, &c.

LIBERTÉ qui m'ès chere,
Cent fois plus que le jour ;
Toi que mon cœur préfere
Au bonheur de l'amour :

Ma Muſe t'offre un Temple,
Où ton œil radieux
Et careſſe & contemple
Tes François glorieux.

Pierre-Jean-Georges de Callières de l'Estang. "Song for the Taking of the Invalides and the Bastille." [1789]. The New York Public Library, Rare Books and
Manuscripts Division, Talleyrand Collection.
    The revolutionaries carried on the popular tradition of composing new
verses for well-known tunes in order to celebrate noteworthy events (cat. no. 4).

"National Festival, 14 July 1790." [1790]. Broadside. Bibliothèque Nationale, Département des Imprimés. "Ça ira" was the first revolutionary song to transcend the ephemeral popularity of songs celebrating particular events. It became a means of displaying allegiance to the Revolution and the new regime (cat. no. 12).

For the next two years "ça ira" was the emblematic song of the various parties of the Revolution, distinct from the traditional songs and singing practices that continued to hold their place in revolutionary culture. The adoption and sustained popularity of the "ça ira" marked a departure from tradition in two important ways. By not fading away within a few weeks after the National Festival, 14 July 1790, "ça ira" transcended the ephemeral popularity characteristic of most popular songs. And, although it had arisen in the context of preparing for the festival, it was not sung to celebrate a particular event but to display political positions and attitudes toward the Revolution.

Revolutionaries saw the singing of the "ça ira" as a sign of faith in the progress of the "Revolution, and of hostility toward a recalcitrant clergy and aristocracy: "A man . . . was singing the song ça ira, ça ira, ça ira in his shop when another man, a former noble, passed by the door, took it as an insult, and so made a formal complaint to the municipality."[13] Royalists, on the other hand, interpreted it as a sign of a popular, blind commitment to demagogues: "ÇA IRA: trivial refrain with which the fanatics of a misguided liberty have deafened an ignorant people, who repeat it mechanically."[14] And both parties saw it as a gauge of the advance, or retreat, of the Revolution.

What is of special importance in this context is that the lyrics of "ça ira" remained almost radically an element of oral culture. Revolutionaries and royalists alike accorded the song a place of singular importance—as was clear from the ways they discussed and reported its performances. The lyrics were rarely printed, however, and almost never appeared in collections of revolutionary songs. This predominantly oral transmission of "ça ira" gave the song a topical and ideological flexibility that was central to its continuing popularity during the early years of the Revolution. The absence, from print, of a definitive lyric version made the song more adaptable to the radically fluctuating circumstances under which it was being sung.[15]

Most newspapers, revolutionary and royalist alike, that reported on the "ça ira" were interested simply in the fact that it was being sung. The anecdote sections of some revolutionary journals related the singing of the "ça ira" at a particular gathering, how many times it had been sung, and the reaction of the audience. Royalist journals complained of the song's repeated performances, or swore no one sang it anymore, and printed angry parodies. And those newspapers (in the majority) that did not want to concern themselves with detailing the career of a popular song, acknowledged the importance of "ça ira" by using it as shorthand for a complex of revolutionary opinions—deemed either noble or ridiculous depending on the political position of the journal.

Newspaper stories about its performances reflected prevailing attitudes toward popular song and a particular vision of the Revolution. Only a handful of newspapers described performances of "ça ira," because few of them were particularly interested in popular songs. Although some publishers acknowledged the importance of the "ça ira" by occasionally describing its performances, the acknowledgment was only implicit. The descriptions themselves suggest a binary vision of the Revolution: One either supported or opposed it, one either sang "ça ira" or one did not. Although the "ça ira" of oral tradition encompassed varying conceptions of the Revolution, print culture tended to simplify the conflicts. Even in their scarcity and simplicity, however, newspaper reports did accelerate and broaden the dissemination of this new kind of singing via their celebration of popular and local practices. It was not only Parisians who sang "ça ira" but also the inhabitants of outlying villages, of Lyon, and even of London. Popular song was an aspect of revolutionary culture that had been given a public voice, even if that voice was still muted.

With the advent of a new revolutionary song in 1792 (the "Marseillaise") and the urgency of fighting a war and creating a republican citizenry, an explicit change in opinion about popular song took place. This change was accompanied by a shift in the way songs were treated, as emphasis moved from performance to text, and in the relation of songs to print culture, as the number of revolutionary songs being published began to shoot upward.

As France prepared for the sustained crisis of foreign war in the spring of 1792, one of the issues raised was the question of what songs were an appropriate accompaniment for the armies of the Revolution. In Paris, both the *Chronique de Paris* and Gorsas's *Courrier* began discussing the issue even before the formal declaration of war.[16] When the declaration of war reached Strasbourg at the end of April, Mayor Dietrich raised the same question: He believed popular songs such as "ça ira" and "Carmagnole" were far beneath the task of bearing French soldiers to victory. Having listened to the urging of the mayor, Rouget de Lisle went home that night and wrote the "Marseillaise."[17]

The "Marseillaise" was and is a uniquely powerful song. During the first years of the Republic both its text and its performances were considered equally important. Initially, however, the text alone had excited little enthusiasm in Paris. Printed in two different newspapers, the song had been performed at a banquet before the end of July without raising much comment.[18] But when the troops from Marseilles arrived in Paris on 30 July 1792, they brought both a striking performance and hundreds of men who knew the song and were willing to teach it. By the end of August the *Chronique de Paris* reported, "In all the theaters one hears requests for: Allons en fants de la Patrie. The words are by Monsieur Rougez [*sic*]. . . . [The tune] has a character that is at once touching and warlike. The volunteers from Marseilles brought the song with them. . . . They sing it to great effect, and the moment when, shaking their hats and their swords, they shout all at once: Aux armes, Citoyens! sends chills down one's spine." [19] By the middle of October the same paper reported that the "air fédéral et révolutionnaire *ça ira*" had given way completely to the "Marseillaise." [20]

The singing of the "Marseillaise," like that of the "ça ira," became a sign of unity and attachment to the Revolution. But the new song was held in much higher esteem by learned revolutionaries: The thought of it accompanying the armies of France as they went to war evoked images of the Greeks and the ancient Gauls charging forth into battle, songs upon their lips. [21]

The "Marseillaise" also commanded greater respect because it was, quite clearly, a more formal song. Whereas reports of the singing of "ça ira" always left some question as to what exactly had been sung, the lyrics of the "Marseillaise" were firmly established; at least sixty different editions of the "Marseillaise" were printed between 1792 and 1794, as opposed to about twelve editions of the "ça ira." [22] Although parodies were written and new verses occasionally added, six (later seven) verses indisputably made up the "Marseillaise." Such formality reduced the possibilities for invention, [23] but it also created a unity through song that stretched throughout the nation: Parisians knew they sang the same words that French soldiers had taken to the front.

Songs were drafted to another task during this same period—that of creating a republican citizenry. In this context songs were turned to a variety of ends: disseminating republican principles and morals, commemorating the "martyrs of the Revolution"—such as Jean-Paul Marat, Michel Lepelletier, and Joseph Barra—and celebrating the *décade* and the existence of the Supreme Being. The use of songs to mold a republican citizenry was actively discussed at a national level. A provincial mayor wrote to the National Convention to point out that Lepelletier's plan for national education had neglected the teaching of music, through which the Republic might hope to break the hold of priests and superstitious habits. [24] The Jacobin songwriter Thomas Rousseau urged the Convention to invest in sixteen thousand copies of one of his songs because "the people sing more than they read." [25] The Convention acted as well, calling on the public to write songs in celebration of the adolescent martyrs of the Revolution, Barra and Viala, and underwriting the efforts of the National Institute of Music to produce song- and hymnbooks. [26]

Given the greater interest being taken in the possible uses of songs and their newfound respectability, it is hardly surprising that more and more

LA CONSTITUTION

FRANÇAISE,

ET LES DROITS DE L'HOMME,

CHANSON PATRIOTIQUE.

AIR : Vive Henri IV.

RENDONS hommage
A nos Représentans ,
  A leur courage ,
Ainsi qu'à leurs talens :
  Leur grand ouvrage
Vivra dans tous les tems.

L'homme est né libre ;
Tous sont égaux en droits ;
  Tous peuvent suivre
Leurs penchans & leurs choix ,
  Mais doivent vivre
Sous l'empire des lois.

"The French Constitution and the Rights of Man—a Patriotic Song." [1791?].
The New York Public Library, Rare Books and Manuscripts Division, Talleyrand Collection.

Songs like this rendering of the Constitution and the Declaration of the
Rights of Man were used to transmit republican ideals and principles of citizenship to the widest possible audience (cat. no. 125).

songs were being written. From about 199 revolutionary songs written in 1791,[27] numbers rose to about 305 in 1792, 504 in 1793, and 701 in 1794. But, although the number of song texts was increasing, other aspects of song culture were in decline.

At the same time that newspapers were becoming more likely to print the texts of songs, they became less and less likely to print accounts of singing. Reports of performances did not entirely disappear from print (almost all printed songs included a note about where and when they had first been sung), but they became noticeably less detailed. Performances also became more structured. Singing in theaters continued unabated, but printed accounts tended to emphasize singing in sectional assemblies. Performances at festivals or popular celebrations were emphasized over spontaneous singing in the streets.[28] These accounts of more structured performances were paralleled by efforts to raise the status of the song. Printed songs were now as likely to be called the more formal "hymn" or "ode" as they were to be called songs, even though most remained simple compositions created by setting new verses to popular tunes.

While reports of public singing had become more formalized, oppositional songs and singing were—like oppositional journals—driven from public view. Royalist and anti-Jacobin songs, previously abundant, were now to be found only in the dossiers compiled for the Revolutionary Tribunal and the Committee of General Security. And yet, during this same period, French men and women were producing songs at a rate unknown at any other point of the Revolution.

This proliferation of songs resulted largely from the creation during the first two years of the Republic of a range of new possibilities for preserving and publicizing songs—many of them part of efforts to prosecute the war and to create a coherent and uniform citizenry. Republican songwriters were no longer restricted to the traditional channels of booksellers and commercial printers, whose primary consideration in deciding to print a song was profit. The printing presses at the service of several sectional assemblies and of the committees of the National Convention were now available as well. Songs that were not printed could still be preserved in the *procès-verbaux* of the sections and of the National Convention, as well as in the files of the Committee of Public Instruction. Periodic calls for songs issued by the Convention encouraged French citizens to present their compositions; the printing of (or according of honorable mention to) such songs suggested that other criteria than those of commercial success were being applied. The popular belief in such criteria, which emphasized patriotism over talent, was attested to by numerous letters received by the Convention and by the Committee of Public Instruction. Christophe fils sent a note along with his verses ("music to be composed") that explained: "I make an

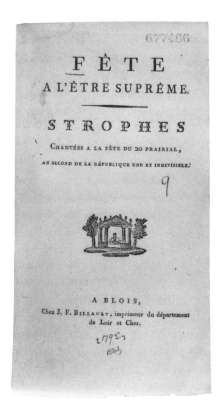
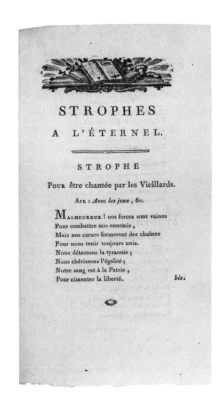

"Festival for the Supreme Being." [1794]. The New York Public Library, General Research Division (cat. no. 183).

Ignace Pleyel. "Hymn to Liberty." 1792. The New York Public Library, Music Division (cat. no. 190).

As the revolutionary government became aware of the pedagogical value of songs, it gave increasingly formal structure to the lyrics and music as well as to the contexts in which they were performed. Songs were now given the more formal titles of "hymn" or "ode" and were written for official occasions such as the festivals for the Supreme Being.

homage to the National Convention of my poor essay on the dedication of our brothers at arms who perished defending the ship *le Vengeur*. I have only said what I felt and patriotism here replaces talent; that's enough to earn the indulgent esteem of just men, who know how to distinguish intention from the useless blossoms of history."[29]

This proliferation of song texts and the narrowing possibilities for printed descriptions of song performances arose from a changed conception of popular song and from the dominant concerns of the French nation during the first two and a half years of the Republic. The quality and success of the "Marseillaise" helped to improve the image of the popular song. But the republican project to create national unity, prosecute the war, and sweep away the habits and beliefs of the Old Regime is what inspired the praise showered on songs during this period. This project, and the consequent recognition of the pedagogic value of songs, raised their status and encouraged the increased attention and improved resources that favored their publication.

The other face of this success story was the narrowing of possibilities for song performances in print. In part, newspaper descriptions of performances gave way to printed song texts because of the pedagogic importance of the texts. But the absence of pluralism and the paranoia of the Terror played important parts as well. Many of the earlier stories of performances of "ça ira" had involved the actual or the implied presence of royalists. During the Terror the use of song (now the "Marseillaise") against the enemy was moved outward to the frontier where it accompanied bayonets and assaults; in Paris suspected royalists were not serenaded, they were arrested.[30] And, in more general terms, the Republic in crisis simply had no room for the celebration of the spontaneity and diversity implied by reports of the "ça ira."

High rates of song publication and less-detailed descriptions of song performances did not vanish the morning after the fall of Robespierre and the Committee of Public Safety on 9 thermidor, Year II (27 July 1794). Change was sporadic and uneven: Singing in the Paris sections had already begun to decline before Thermidor, but the presentation of songs to the Convention continued, albeit at a slackening pace, for some time afterward. Newspapers continued to print revolutionary songs, with little or no detail of their performances; revolutionary-song collections also continued to be published. But fewer new songs were being written: Constant Pierre's catalogue records an astounding drop from the 701 songs written in 1794 to only 137 songs in 1795 (nivôse, Year III–brumaire, Year IV).

This sharp decline, however, did not signal the disappearance of songs from the revolutionary stage. For the next two years the attention of newspapers, public, and government returned with particular intensity to the performance of songs, as an extended public battle took place over the meaning of the singing of the "Marseillaise" and of a new anti-Jacobin song, "Réveil du peuple." This battle stretched over much of years III and IV (1795–96), crystallizing and intensifying each time the government involved itself, and marking still another shift in the relationship between the printed page and song performance.

"Réveil du peuple" was first performed publicly at a celebration of the decade in the section William Tell, on 30 nivôse, Year III (19 January 1795). It was sung by the actor Pierre Gaveaux, who had composed the music. The song began by asking:

> Peuple français, peuple de frères
> Peux-tu voir sans frémir d'horreur
> Le crime arborer les bannières
> Du carnage et de la Terreur?[31]

The four verses that followed passionately conjured up images of bloodthirsty tyrants, slaughtered innocents, and the desire for vengeance.

> Quoi! cette horde anthropophage
> Que l'enfer vomit de son flanc
> Prêche le meurtre et le carnage!
> Elle est couverte de ton sang![32]

The final verse, calming considerably, praised the remaining members of the National Convention and assured them of the immortality of their reputations.[33]

For the next several months "Réveil" reigned supreme. At times it seemed it was only the song of a particular party whose opposition had been silenced, as in early pluviôse (February 1795), when the *jeunesse d'orée*[34] terrorized several actors accused of Jacobinism by calling for them to sing the "Réveil" and then shouting them down as unworthy of the song.[35] At other moments, it seemed more widely popular because it expressed a prevailing anti-Jacobin mood. In germinal (March 1795), Mercier's *Annales patriotiques*, in no way a mouthpiece of the *jeunesse d'orée*, reported: "Parisians cannot watch without unease the slow and encumbered progress of the proceedings against the *décemvirs* [Robespierre's former colleagues]; in all the theaters, as soon as they hear that alarm of the people ["Réveil du peuple"], all the spectators express their sentiments by means of the most prolonged applause."[36]

What was certain was that the "Marseillaise" was no longer in public favor. The last reports of its singing had been during the final, violent days of the Jacobin club.[37] Soldiers returning from the front might defend the song—it had accompanied them into battle—but in Paris the "Marseillaise" had been tarnished by its intimate association with the Terror.

The first battle between the "Marseillaise" and "Réveil du peuple" arose after the National Convention's decree that, in honor of the anniversary of the taking of the Bastille, the text of the "Marseillaise" would be inserted in their *Bulletin* and the song would be played at the mounting of the guard on the following day.[38] The next morning, a crowd of angry youths appeared to prevent the playing of the "Marseillaise." "This hymn, they said, was dishonored by its adoption by Jacobins and cannibals; why wasn't the singing of the 'Réveil du peuple' decreed instead? Is there a desire to resurrect the Terror?"[39] The commander of the guard, uncertain in the face of this opposition, sent a messenger to the Convention, who returned with word that the order had been rescinded.

The incident nevertheless became the opening shot of a battle that raged through the streets, theaters, and newspapers of Paris for the next two weeks. In various theaters, efforts to sing the "Marseillaise" were shouted down and actors forced to sing the "Réveil" instead. The *Chronique de Paris* reported that a soldier in the *parterre* at the opera had shouted that the "Marseillaise" had been sung while soldiers' families had been murdered when they were away fighting the war.[40] For days newspapers carried details of the events, which varied in tone according to the political position of the paper and added reflections or suggestions as to how the conflict might be ended. The committees of Public Safety and General Security passed a decree that no songs were to be sung independently of the pieces being performed, but audience members ignored it and sang "Réveil du peuple" themselves.[41]

On the last day of messidor (18 July 1795), posters seeking to end the disputes began to appear; they were reprinted in various newspapers. They ranged in tone from violent attacks on the singers of the "Réveil" as royalists and new terrorists,[42] to more conciliatory reminders to the same group— as the "defenders of prairial"—of their commitment to upholding the Convention.[43] Boissy d'Anglas struck a note between these two positions in his speech on 1 thermidor (19 July 1795) (printed in the *Courrier de Paris* on 4 thermidor). He acknowledged that "Réveil du peuple" celebrated 9 thermidor. "But [these verses] are also the seeds of dissension among good citizens; more than once, in Lyon and in the South, they have been the signal for massacres. . . . Under any other circumstances such singing would not be reprehensible; but when malevolence abuses it, you must abstain."

Not surprisingly, none of these devices worked. An act of the Convention having begun the disputes, it took another act of the Convention to mark their closure. On 9 thermidor, over the "violent muttering" of "the remainder of what was the Mountain," "Réveil du peuple" was played before the Convention, along with the "Marseillaise" and "ça ira."[44]

This dispute is striking because it marked such an extensive departure from the textual focus so characteristic of the early years of the Republic and a return to an emphasis on song performances. Although both songs were parodied, the important issue was not what either song said—which text was more representative of the ideals of the Revolution—but the circumstances under which each had been sung. The "Marseillaise" was attacked because it had been sung while the guillotines of the Terror worked furiously; it was defended as the song that had driven the armies of the Republic to victory. "Réveil du peuple" was alternately the song of the Convention reasserting itself against tyranny or the tune of a blood-spattered southern reaction.

Just as both songs drew differing meanings from the differing conditions under which they had been performed, their battles for supremacy were also organized around performances; and these performances were magnified and altered by newspaper accounts. Newspapers that reported on the conflicts not only described them, but they also commented on and sought to extend or circumscribe them. The *Annales patriotiques* and the *Courrier de Paris*, both moderate journals, were perplexed by the Convention's endorsement of the "Marseillaise" but, in reporting each development, counseled Parisian youth to behave judiciously. The *Messager du soir*, a notoriously reactionary journal that often exceeded even the reactions of the streets, favored emotionally heightened terms and shrill denunciations of the defenders of the "Marseillaise." Yet, whether they counseled judiciousness or fury, journals bestowed a certain legitimacy on the battles and helped to generalize the issue from songs to politics simply by reporting and commenting on them. This was undoubtedly part of the reason the remaining papers of the left maintained an almost total silence on the subject.

Although revolutionary newspapers were once more reporting song performances (now of the "Marseillaise" and "Réveil du peuple"), they had not simply returned to the practices of the first years of the Revolution. In the first place, these new reports were far more numerous and more detailed than any of the pre-1792 articles on the "ça ira." The image of the popular song had also improved during the intervening years, owing both to the success of the "Marseillaise" and to the recognition of its pedagogic value. Thus, having acquired a definable place within revolutionary culture, singing—and particularly disputed singing—was more likely to appear in newspapers.

The oppositions characteristic of the earlier period no longer applied either: The dispute between those who sang the "Marseillaise" and those who sang "Réveil du peuple" was not between supporters and opponents of the Revolution but between two differing conceptions of what the meaning and goals of that Revolution should be. The "ça ira" had been able to encompass orally, if not in print, differing conceptions of the Revolution. But, in a society that had experienced the violence of both Terror and Reaction, the explicit intertwining of songs and politics and the complex of hopes and fears about the implications of political positions had made peaceful coexistence impossible at either level.

There was a sequel to the dispute in the Year IV. In nivôse (January 1796) the Directory issued a decree forbidding performances of "Réveil du peuple" in theaters, ordering that the "Marseillaise" and three other republican songs be sung before each performance. Once more, theaters became a site of cultural debate; Parisian journals argued the issue, but the Directory would not budge. The conflict dragged on for two months until theater audiences became bored with it, and a police spy could report: "Everyone in the theaters has become quite cool toward the patriotic hymns. Two verses, hurriedly sung, seems sufficient for the actors. These hymns are heard peacefully enough by the different parties."[45] The Directory reiterated the decree, and then four months later, when all interest in what was being sung seemed to have died, it retracted the decree and let the matter drop.

After this incident, revolutionary song culture began to fragment. Individuals continued to sing, but public discussion of the meaning of songs and their relationship to the Revolution became increasingly rare. There was also a bifurcation of text and performance that corresponded to the widening gap between the official and the popular, between the elites and the working classes. While the Directory concerned itself almost solely with the production of hymns, and newspapers reviewed avowedly apolitical songbooks, popular singing continued in the streets and cafés of the working-class neighborhoods. But these performances were no longer reported in newspapers; they were in police reports which stressed that the singing was only the accompaniment to an evening's drinking.

The shifting and multifaceted relationship between songs and printed texts corresponded to the period of the Revolution's greatest cultural experimentation and invention. As popular songs gained revolutionary respectability, and as their relationship to political ideologies became clearer, they were more and more likely to find their way into print. Larger political circumstances determined whether newspapers focused on the performances or the texts of songs. Performance dominated during periods of uncertainty and debate about the Revolution's direction. For singers of "ça ira" before 1792, as well as for singers of the "Marseillaise" and "Réveil du peuple" in 1795 and 1796, popular cultural invention and popular violence became ways of establishing symbolic models and thus of laying claim to the meaning of the Revolution. During the first years of the Republic (1792–95), uncertainty and debate were silenced, and cultural production was channeled in very specific directions. But the intensity of the efforts to propagate republicanism and prosecute the war created new means of cultural growth and preservation, and revolutionary-song texts flourished. Both roads, of performance and text, were closed by the Year V: The Directory had silenced debate by decreeing the official songs of the Revolution, and noncommercial publishers of songs had long since disappeared.

As had been the case during the early years of the Revolution, cultural change was lagging behind political change. The widening political gap, which had been growing between the Parisian populace and the national government since the middle of the Terror, found its cultural reflection in the "Marseillaise" / "Réveil du peuple" disputes and the silence that followed. Parisians would have to wait until the nineteenth century to find those voices again.

EPHEMERA: CIVIC EDUCATION THROUGH IMAGES

JAMES LEITH

IN HIS *Gutenberg Galaxy* the guru of the mass media, Marshall McLuhan, argued that, as the earliest example of mass production, the printing press produced a flood of identical copies of a text that vastly surpassed anything scribes could produce by hand.[1] McLuhan was right to emphasize the impact of the printed word on modern culture, but his analysis failed to emphasize that the printing press also made possible a proliferation of images through engravings on a scale unprecedented in human history. We can consider the outpouring in France of engraved images from the great collections that were established as a result of the law issued under Louis XIV requiring that two copies of every engraving be deposited in the Bibliothèque royale, now the Bibliothèque Nationale. The vast collections of engravings from the Old Regime and the Revolution attest to the flood of images as well as words that issued from the printing press.

The decade of the Revolution itself produced thousands of printed images. In addition to larger engravings such as allegorical compositions, political caricatures, scenes of contemporary events, portraits of leaders, and even wallpaper, smaller images proliferated everywhere—on certificates given to the conquerors of the Bastille, on paper money, on official letterheads, on legal headings and stamps, on membership cards of political clubs or sectional committees, on copies of the Rights of Man, on the new calendar, on lists of republican adages, on children's games, playing cards, ladies' fans, tops for little boxes, and frontispieces and vignettes in civic manuals. These images, especially those on a small scale, are sometimes called "ephemera," but this underrates their importance. Because they were sometimes produced in tens of thousands of copies, these images reached large numbers of people who might not have been reached by newspapers, pamphlets, or books. In any case, as heirs to the sensationalist psychology of the Enlightenment, the revolutionaries had great faith in the power of images to make a lasting impression on the minds of the citizenry. Above all, they believed images could arouse emotions in a way printed words could not.

Early in the Revolution the certificates given to the conquerors of the Bastille and to members of the new National Guard were decorated with emblems of the new order. In June 1790 the National Assembly decided to accord special recognition to citizens who had distinguished themselves in the attack on the old prison-fortress. At the top of the certificate, in an oval formed by oak branches, appear the names of a trinity representative of this phase of the Revolution—the National Assembly, the Law, and the King. As we shall see, the Revolution produced a succession of trinities, mostly short-lived. On one copy of this certificate in the Bibliothèque Nationale, someone has stroked out the word "King."[2] On the left, atop a column, is a figure of Hercules, the demigod who was already becoming associated with popular power. On the right, atop an identical column, is Mercury, bearing a copy of the new constitution. In a cartouche underneath is a scene of the attack on the Bastille, surmounted by a French cock and surrounded by cannon. Broken chains lie on the ground. Later, Hercules appears again on the certificate of membership in the new National Guard, once again associated with the capture of the Bastille, along with the slogan "Live free or die."[3] On the other side is a figure of Justice with the inscription "Men are equal under the law."

The new paper money became a major medium for diffusing revolutionary slogans, allegorical figures, and symbols.[4] Originally the *assignats*, as they were called, were bonds backed by confiscated church property, but they quickly developed into the basic currency of the country. At first they bore the likeness of Louis XVI as he had appeared on coins before the Revolution, but revolutionary symbols were soon added and eventually took his place. Most interesting was the use of the equilateral triangle on the *assignat* of ten sous issued in 1792. The equilateral triangle had been used in the past as a symbol of the Trinity for Christians or of the Supreme Being for Masons. The Masonic version appears on the back of U.S. one-dollar bills. From early in the Revolution this triangle was used to consecrate various ideals—the so-called three good kings: Louis XII, Henry IV, and Louis XVI; the union of the three Estates, now all equal; or the three-fold ideals of the constitutional monarchy—the Nation, the Law, and the King,[5] as it appears on this *assignat*. Like the others, this trinity did not survive for long and was soon replaced by another threesome: Liberty, Equality, and Security.

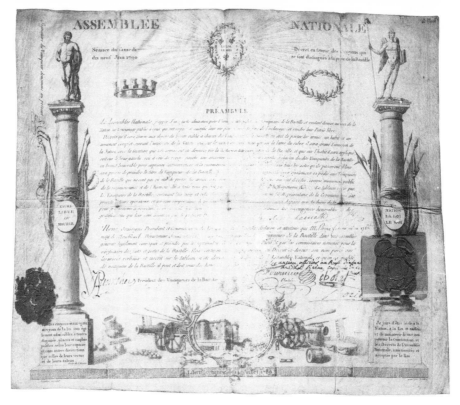

"Certificate of a Conqueror of the Bastille" ("Brevet de vainqueur de la Bastille . . ."). N.d. Engraving. Bibliothèque Nationale, Cabinet des Estampes, Collection de Vinck.

"Certificate of the National Guard." [1793]. Engraving. Bibliothèque Nationale, Cabinet des Estampes (cat. no. 2).

Early in the Revolution the certificates given to the conquerors of the Bastille and the members of the new National Guard were decorated with emblems of the new order.

Soon after 10 August 1792 the figure of Liberty replaced the image of the king. An ancient allegorical figure going back to classical antiquity, Liberty is usually attired in a flowing gown, holding a rod capped with a bonnet. The rod reminded the viewer of the one a Roman magistrate had used to touch and thereby emanicipate a slave; the bonnet stood for those worn by former slaves as a sign of freedom. Sometimes Liberty is accompanied by a broken yoke, and occasionally by a cat, another age-old symbol of freedom. The image of Liberty had become more prominent in France at the time of the American War of Independence. There had been engravings showing Franklin leading her to America or being crowned by her atop a globe with the rebel colonies in the center. With the outbreak of the Revolution in France, Liberty became an increasingly familiar figure, at first in the company of the King, then frequently standing by herself. At the time of the overthrow of the monarchy she was ready to move over to become the central symbol of the Republic. Already she dominates the *assignat* of fifty livres issued in December 1792, where she appears holding the rudder of state in one hand, a civic crown in the other. A French cock stands at her side atop a pedestal, which in turn is decorated with a fasces and a Liberty bonnet.

At the peak of the Revolution, Liberty also dominated the letterheads of the multitude of government bodies—various ministries, committees, commissions, and units of the army.[6] Her characterizations depended on the function of the particular government bodies. In the vignettes on stationery for generals, Liberty (or the Republic) was usually accompanied by weapons, whereas on that of the Committee of Public Instruction she appears reading a book. Especially interesting is the letterhead of the Committee of Public Safety, where Liberty appears holding a pike surmounted by a Liberty bonnet in one hand, and in the other fasces—symbol of national unity and state authority. In the background are other symbols of power: a club, lightning bolts, a warship, a cannon, a sword, the scales of Justice, and a volcanic mountain. The latter was an obvious allusion to the radicals who sat on the high benches of the Convention, earning them the nickname *la Montagne,* and who dominated the revolutionary government during the Terror. Overhead was an All-Seeing Eye, no longer so much a symbol of the Supreme Being as of the ubiquitous surveillance of the committee and its agents. This version of Liberty was altogether too militant, too closely associated with the dreaded committee to survive the end of the Terror.

The headings of laws were probably seen by more people than the letterheads on official stationery. In December 1793 the Convention decided to publish a bulletin in order to disseminate laws in a readily available form

273

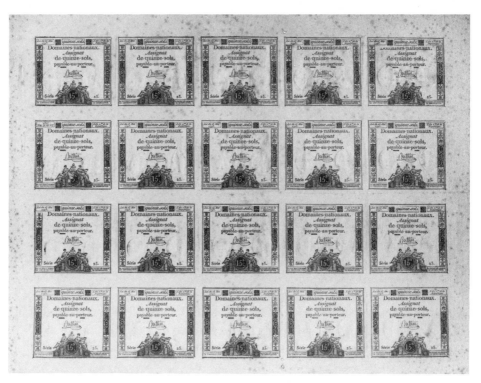

Sheet of *Assignats:* 15 sous. Eighteenth century. Musée de l'Imprimerie et de la Banque, Lyon, France (photo: Studio Dussouillez, Rutter).

Sheet of *Assignats:* 50 sous. Eighteenth century. Musée de l'Imprimerie et de la Banque, Lyon, France (photo: Studio Dussouillez, Rutter).

The new paper money became a major medium for diffusing revolutionary slogans, allegorical figures, and symbols. The *assignats,* as they were called, first bore the likeness of Louis XVI as he had appeared on coins before the Revolution, but revolutionary symbols were soon added and eventually took his place.

Assignats of 1792: 50 livres, série 4127. Musée de l'Imprimerie et de la Banque, Lyon, France (photo: Studio Dussouillez, Rutter).

Assignats of 1792: 400 livres, série 1213. Musée de l'Imprimerie et de la Banque, Lyon, France (photo: Studio Dussouillez, Rutter) (cat. no. 161).

Soon after 10 August 1792, the figure of Liberty replaced the image of the King. An allegorical figure going back to classical antiquity, Liberty is usually attired in a flowing gown and holding a rod capped with a bonnet. The rod recalled the one used by Roman magistrates to emancipate a slave; former slaves wore the bonnet as a sign of freedom. By December 1792 Liberty dominated the *assignats* of 50 livres.

(*a*), Identity Card, Commissioner to the Central Bureau.

At the peak of the Revolution, the figure of Liberty also dominated identity cards and letterheads of the multitude of government bodies—ministries, committees, commissions, and army units. How she was characterized depended on the function of the particular division. Liberty often appeared holding a pike surmounted by a Liberty bonnet in one hand; the fasces was another common symbol of national unity and state authority (cat. no. 193).

Identity Card, Friends of Wisdom. Bordeaux: (*b*), obverse: "General Security—No Admission to the Assembly without This Card"; (*c*), reverse: Municipality of Bordeaux. Section of the Friends of Wisdom.

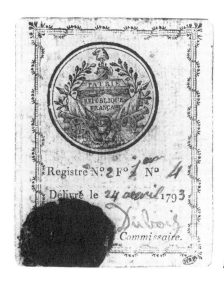

Deputy's Badge to the National Assembly. Department of Sarthe: (*d*), obverse; (*e*), reverse.

Identity Card, Franklin Section. Bordeaux: (*f*), obverse; (*g*), reverse. All from Musée de la Révolution Française, Vizille, France.

BULLETIN DES LOIS

DE LA RÉPUBLIQUE FRANÇAISE.

(N.º 10.)

"Law Bulletin of the French Republic" (*Bulletin des lois de la République française . . .*).
[Paris]: Imp. Nationale des Lois, 11 messidor, an II (29 June 1794). The New York
Public Library, General Research Division.

The headings of laws were probably seen by more people than identity cards or
the letterheads on official stationery. In December 1793 the Convention decided to
publish a *Bulletin des lois* to disseminate laws in a readily available form throughout
the Republic. In the center of the rectangle that formed the heading was Liberty,
sitting enthroned like the kings of the Old Regime and holding a fasces.

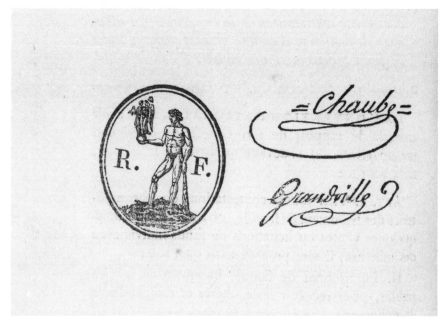

"Law Bulletin of the French Republic" (*Bulletin des lois de la République française . . .*).
[Paris]: Imp. Nationale des Lois, [1794]. The New York Public Library, General Research Division.

At the end of each *Bulletin* was a stamp, a sort of printed seal, portraying the
French people as Hercules trampling on broken monarchical symbols.

throughout the Republic. Called the *Bulletin des lois,* the first number did not appear until the following May. In the center of the parallelogram that formed the heading was Liberty, sitting enthroned like the kings of the Old Regime and holding a fasces in her right hand. Later an axe was added to the center of the fasces, suggesting even greater power (in ancient Rome it meant a magistrate could impose the death sentence), and an equilateral triangle was placed in her left hand.[7] Two other equilateral triangles balanced each other at the ends of the heading, one resembling the old symbol of the Divinity with an All-Seeing Eye in the center, and the other in the form of a carpenter's level, the usual symbol for equality. There were thus three mystical triangles altogether. At the end of each *Bulletin* was a stamp, a sort of printed seal, portraying the French People in the guise of Hercules trampling on broken monarchical symbols. In his right hand he supports Liberty and Equality with their usual emblems, suggesting that with the support of the people the ideals they represent would triumph over the world.

The original heading and stamp on the *Bulletin des lois* survived longer than one would expect. Following the overthrow of Robespierre and his colleagues and the subsequent reaction against the excesses of the Terror, the Convention approved a more conservative constitution than the one proclaimed in 1793 but never implemented. The Constitution of Year III (1795), which established the Directory, was accompanied by a declaration that emphasized duties as well as rights. In 1797 the heading and the stamp were finally revised to reflect the more conservative Republic.[8] In the center of the heading, instead of Liberty enthroned, appeared an octagon enclosing the number of the publication. In place of the triangles at either end were figures of Law and Justice. The radical Level of Equality was still there, but shrunken in size and almost lost among the other symbols. Even more significant was the change in the stamp at the end. The People–Hercules gave way to tablets of the law, radiating light and resting on a winged thunderbolt, symbol of swift execution. All this was encircled by a serpent biting its tail, a traditional sign for eternity. The message was clear: The rule of law was to replace the awesome power of the people.

Just as printed laws were indispensable for informing citizens of new legislation, so printed versions of the Declaration of the Rights of Man were essential for acquainting them with the underlying principles of the new regime. Because each phase of the Revolution produced a new version of the Declaration—1789, 1793, and 1795—there were three waves of publication of their texts. Usually these were handsomely decorated so that they could be mounted on citizens' walls. A fine example is a version of the Declaration of 1789 dedicated to the free French and their friends by a Helvetian.[9] The Feudal Monster has been toppled from his pedestal, leaving only

AU NOM DE LA RÉPUBLIQUE FRANÇAISE.

(N.º 1225.) *ARRÊTÉ du Directoire exécutif, contenant rectification d'erreurs dans le texte d'une édition originale de la Constitution française.*

Du 14 Prairial, an V de la République une et indivisible.

LE DIRECTOIRE EXÉCUTIF, vu , 1.º une édition originale de l'acte constitutionnel imprimé à l'imprimerie de la République , portant , article 216 :

« Tous les cinq ans , on procède à l'élection de tous
» les *membres* du tribunal.

« Les juges peuvent toujours être réélus. »

2.º Une autre édition également originale de la Constitution imprimée à l'imprimerie nationale , où cette disposition de l'article 216 est ainsi transcrite :

« Tous les cinq ans , on procède à l'élection de tous
» les *juges* du tribunal.

« Ils peuvent toujours être réélus. »

3.º Les extraits délivrés , collationnés et certifiés conformes par le citoyen *Camus* , garde des archives de la République , tant de la minute originale authentique de l'acte constitutionnel , déposée aux archives de la République , que de celle du procès-verbal de la Convention nationale , du 5 fructidor an III ; desquels il résulte que le véritable texte de l'article 216 de l'acte constitutionnel

3.   A

"Law Bulletin of the French Republic" (*Bulletin des lois de la République française . . .*). [Paris]: Imp. Nationale des Lois, 14 prairial, an V (12 June 1797). The New York Public Library, General Research Division.

The constitution of Year III (1795), which established the Directory, was accompanied by a declaration that emphasized duties as well as rights. In 1797 the heading and the stamp were revised to reflect the more conservative Republic. In the center of the heading, instead of Liberty enthroned, an octagon enclosing the number of the publication appeared.

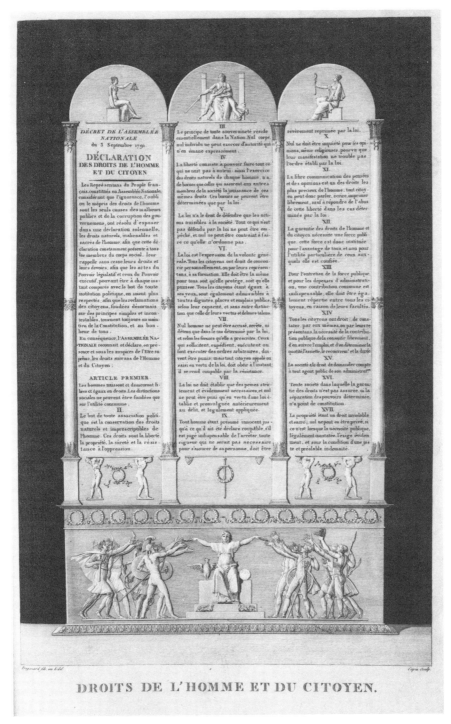

DROITS DE L'HOMME ET DU CITOYEN.

"Rights of Man and of the Citizen," in *Collection complète des tableaux historiques de la Révolution française,* vol. 3. An VI (1797–98). The New York Public Library, The Miriam and Ira D. Wallach Division of Art, Prints and Photographs.

Just as printed laws were indispensable for informing citizens of new legislation, so printed versions of the Declaration of the Rights of Man were essential for acquainting them with the underlying principles of the new regime. Because each phase of the Revolution produced a new version of the Declaration—1789, 1793, and 1795—there were three waves of publication of its text (cat. no. 133).

his boots in place. Little *putti* celebrate his downfall around a musket, capped with the Liberty bonnet, which rises from where the Monster had once stood. On one side a pelican feeds her young with her own flesh and blood, an ancient symbol of self-sacrifice, while on the other side lightning and an eagle emerge from clouds. The seventeen clauses of the Declaration are engraved on tablets leaning against the pedestal, probably evoking the tablets of Moses. To the left Hercules tramples on a hydra on whose various heads are visible a tiara, a cardinal's hat, a bishop's mitre labeled "inconstitutionnel," and the mortarboard of a *parlementaire*. Little details are eloquent: a dog urinates on the fallen Monster while children play among the debris; in the background on the upper-left, peasants chase a deer, exercising their new freedom to hunt; and in the sky, Renown trumpets, "Ah, ça ira, ça ira," the popular refrain of the period. Later on, copies of the republican Declaration of 1793 were decorated with fasces, Mountains, and busts of republican martyrs.

In order to spread revolutionary principles and create a new civic morality, leaders encouraged publication of numerous manuals and catechisms, many of them designed for the rising generation. Some of these were richly illustrated, for example *L'Ami des jeunes patriotes, ou catéchisme révolutionnaire*, by Chemin fils, a little handbook approved by the Commune of Paris and accepted by the Convention.[10] The frontispiece depicted the martyrdom of Bara (which it spelled "Barra"), a thirteen-year-old boy who had attached himself to the republican army fighting counterrevolutionaries in the Vendée. When captured, he was killed, the story goes, when he refused to cry "Vive le Roi," and cried out instead "Vive la République!" Underneath were pictures of two other young heroes, Richer and Pajot. Other plates were interspersed among the text. Some dealt with writing letters, but one depicted the attack on the Tuileries Palace on 10 August 1792, and others portrayed the principal allegorical figures of the Revolution—Equality holding a level and a fasces, Liberty holding a cannonball and a club, and the Sovereign People in the guise of Hercules. Other plates illustrated the need for public security and respect for private property. Besides some lessons in reading, writing, and arithmetic, the text recounted the story of young Bara and explained the Declaration of Rights and the Constitution of 1793.

Another medium for inculcating the new civic ideals consisted of lists of adages and maxims that could be mounted on walls. These, too, were sometimes richly decorated; for example, the list entitled *Maximes du jeune républicain* embellished by the well-known engraver François-Marie Quéverdo.[11] In the center of the heading is a medallion featuring the Republic, who is wearing the luminous eye of Reason as a pendant and is holding the Book of Destinies. In the background is a Temple of Immortality atop a mountain. Over her head is the equilateral triangle denoting the Divinity, along with the injunction "Adore the Eternal." On either side of the medallion stand infant *genii,* one holding doves, the other holding a club like Hercules. The latter, along with a French cock, stands on a defeated hydra. The medallion on the left shows Equality, accompanied by Nature with two rows of breasts to suggest bountifulness. The medallion on the right frames Liberty, holding an orb in one hand and a fasces in the other. The thirty-eight republican maxims appear below in two columns divided by a pike entwined with branches, a tricolor banner, and images of four republican martyrs—Lepelletier, Marat, Chalier, and Bara—the models of ultimate self-sacrifice, with a ring of stars over their heads suggesting immortality. On the banner is the inscription from the facade of the Panthéon, "To Great Men, the Grateful Fatherland." At the bottom is a beehive, a symbol of community, and, once again, the pelican feeding her young with her own flesh and blood.

The republican calendar adopted by the Convention in September 1793 strikes many people today as very odd, but in fact it embodied a new view of history. The Convention had chosen to number years from the declaration of the Republic on 22 September 1792 instead of from the birth of Christ, implying a new start in history. Because the beginning of the Republic coincided with the autumnal equinox, the revolutionaries interpreted this to signify that the heavens were in favor of equality.[12] The fact that the sun also moves from dominating one hemisphere to dominating the other was taken to augur the course of the Revolution around the world. The new names of the months not only jettisoned the names of ancient gods and a couple of Roman emperors but also were supposedly based on nature and on the changing seasons (ignoring the fact that they described the climate only in the north of France). Moreover, the new ten-day week, like the projected ten-hour day, represented the drive to metricize everything. At the same time it purposely made it difficult to keep track of Sundays, saints' days, and other Christian holy days. Like the new laws and the Declaration of Rights, this new calendar had to be impressed on the minds of the citizenry. Publishers responded to this challenge with lavishly decorated versions suitable for hanging in homes, usually in two parts, one covering fall through winter, the other spring through summer.[13] Once again, these calendars were laden with symbolic Mountains, figures of Liberty and Equality, and images of republican martyrs.

Games, too, were used to communicate the meaning of the Revolution to the masses, especially to children. "How then can one move hearts and arouse love of the fatherland and its laws?" Rousseau had asked before the

Institutrice républicaine.
A Paris chez l'Epicier
Rue des Marmousds N°1.

"Republican Schoolteacher." [1793]. Engraving. Bibliothèque Nationale, Cabinet des Estampes (cat. no. 149).

To spread revolutionary principles and create a new civic morality, leaders encouraged the publication of numerous manuals and catechisms, many of them designed for the younger generation.

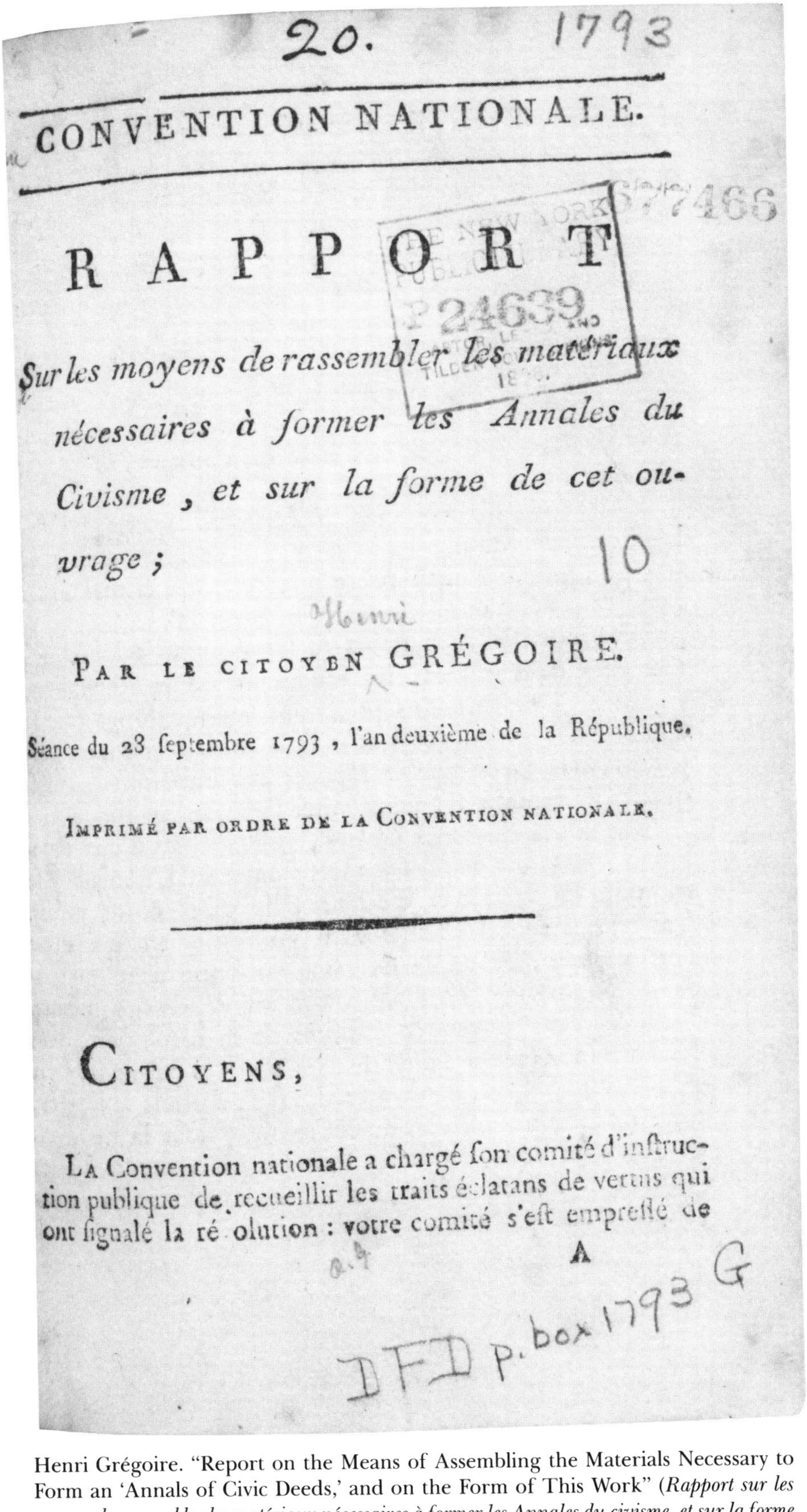

CONVENTION NATIONALE.

RAPPORT

Sur les moyens de rassembler les matériaux nécessaires à former les Annales du Civisme, et sur la forme de cet ouvrage ;

PAR LE CITOYEN GRÉGOIRE.

Séance du 23 septembre 1793, l'an deuxième de la République.

IMPRIMÉ PAR ORDRE DE LA CONVENTION NATIONALE.

CITOYENS,

LA Convention nationale a chargé son comité d'instruction publique de recueillir les traits éclatans de vertus qui ont signalé la révolution : votre comité s'est empressé de

A

Henri Grégoire. "Report on the Means of Assembling the Materials Necessary to Form an 'Annals of Civic Deeds,' and on the Form of This Work" (*Rapport sur les moyens de rassembler les matériaux nécessaires à former les Annales du civisme, et sur la forme de cet ouvrage*). Paris: Imp. Nationale, [1793]. The New York Public Library, General Research Division.

J.-B. Chemin-Dupontès fils. "Friend of Young Patriots, or the Revolutionary Catechism." An II (1793–94). Bibliothèque Nationale, Département des Imprimés.

Some of these civic manuals were richly illustrated, such as "Friend of Young Patriots, or the Revolutionary Catechism," by Chemin fils, a little handbook approved by the Commune of Paris and accepted by the Convention. Plates were interspersed throughout the text depicting events of the Revolution, like the attack on the Tuileries Palace on 10 August 1792 and portrayals of key allegorical figures, such as Equality holding a level and a fasces (cat. no. 177).

CATHÉCHISME
FRANÇAIS, RÉPUBLICAIN.

DES SOCIÉTÉS EN GÉNÉRAL.

De chez BESIAN, Imprimeur de la Municipalité, près la place Calas, N°. 285.

"French Republican Catechism." [1792?]. Broadside. The New York Public Library, Rare Books and Manuscripts Division.

Another medium for inculcating the new civic spirit consisted of lists of adages and maxims, which could be mounted on walls (cat. no. 175).

Revolution. "Dare I say it? By children's games."[14] After 1789 the ancient *jeu de l'oie*, the goose game, was adapted to revolutionary ends. In the game players toss dice to determine how far they advance along squares toward the goal. In the seventeenth century the goal had been to move from squares showing Roman emperors through those with early French monarchs to those depicting the reign of Louis XIV.[15] Early in the Revolution updated versions of the goose game appeared in which players progress from the storming of the Bastille through major events of the Revolution to the National Assembly, "The Palladium of Liberty."[16] The squares, each depicting an important event or achievement in miniature, provided children an illustrated history of the Revolution. The unlucky squares, bearing images of geese, each represented one of the old parlements, now discredited as strongholds of reaction. The player landing on a square depicting bridled geese was forced to retreat. Some versions of this game presented an even longer view of history, beginning before civilization, in the "state of nature," tracing the growth of abuses, and moving finally through the Enlightenment to the Revolution.[17]

The effort to mobilize all the available media to convey the revolutionary message reached its peak in Year II of the Republic (1793–94). "Actually everything ought to have a moral purpose among a republican people," argued one of the reports of the Popular and Republican Art Association; "they ought to meet with lessons even in their diversions."[18] In line with this objective, even playing cards were brought into conformity. The old symbols on cards and their names were no longer tolerable because they recalled despotism and inequality: *Lois* (Aces), *Rois* (Kings), *Dames* (Queens), and *Valets* (Jacks); "Valet" especially suggested social subordination. One pair of publishers had the idea of printing new cards that would constitute a civic manual on the Revolution by confronting the player only with images of Liberty and Equality.[19] For Kings they substituted Genii of War, Peace, Arts, and Commerce; for Queens they substituted Liberties of Religion, Marriage, the Press, and the Professions; and for Jacks they substituted Equalities of Duties, Rights, Ranks, and Colors. With their new cards they published a little brochure explaining the new images. Other printers produced packs of cards bearing images of philosophes, republican soldiers, and sans-culottes.

These are only some of the ways in which printed revolutionary images were conveyed to the French people. Space does not allow us to deal with all the other places where printed images appeared, but we have enough examples to see that the revolutionaries came close to realizing an ideal of some of the thinkers of the Enlightenment. When Helvétius had declared, "Education can do everything,"[20] he did not mean that instruction in school alone could shape individuals; he meant that if all the influences that impinge on individuals from birth onward could be coordinated, then one could mold any kind of citizenry one desired. This was what the revolutionaries sought to do. They believed that, combined with republican schooling, printed words in various formats, revolutionary music, didactic plays, civic festivals, and public monuments, the flood of images could contribute to an educational environment which could create a *nouvel homme* for the new society.

EXHIBITION CHECKLIST

THIS CHECKLIST INCLUDES books, pamphlets, prints, and other materials included in the exhibition "Revolution in Print: France, 1789," presented at The New York Public Library, D. Samuel and Jeane H. Gottesman Exhibition Hall, 18 February–29 April 1989. Items are books or pamphlets unless otherwise indicated. Dimensions are given in inches, with centimeters in parentheses; height precedes width precedes depth. For eighteenth-century books and pamphlets, formats are indicated as 4°, 8°, etc. Spelling, capitalization, and use of diacriticals in French titles have been modernized. In citations, place names have been anglicized and publishers' names have been standardized. Dates, places of publication, and publishers' names supplied in brackets represent information that has been established but which does not appear on the work. Where information represents a scholarly estimate, the bracketed information is followed by a question mark. Parenthetical numbers following checklist entries refer to pages on which illustrations of the items appear.

Introduction: The Explosion of 1789

1. *Adresse des Gardes nationales de la campagne, sous les ordres de M. le duc de Duras, à l'Assemblée nationale.* Bordeaux: Imp. de l'Armée Patriotique Bordelaise, n.d. 8°. The New York Public Library, General Research Division.

2. "Brevet de Garde nationale." [1793]. Engraving. 10 × 13 (26 × 33). Bibliothèque Nationale, Paris, Cabinet des Estampes, Collection Hennin. *(272)*

3. *Brochure de l'Imprimerie Guffroy.* Paris: Imp. Guffroy, an IV (1795–96). 4°. Archives Nationales, France. *(79)*

4. Callières de L'Estang, Pierre-Jean-Georges de. *Chanson sur la prise des Invalides et de la Bastille, les lundi 13 et mardi 14 juillet 1789.* [Paris: Nyon le jeune, 1789]. 8°. The New York Public Library, Rare Books and Manuscripts Division, Talleyrand Collection. *(256)*

5. *Chanson des dames de la place Maubert.* N.p., [1789]. 8°. The New York Public Library, Rare Books and Manuscripts Division, Talleyrand Collection.

6. Chénier, Marie-Joseph de. *Dénonciation des inquisiteurs de la pensée.* Paris: Lagrange, 1789. 8°. Archives Nationales, France. *(64)*

7. Desmoulins, Camille. *La France libre.* 2d ed. N.p., 1789. 8°. The New York Public Library, Rare Books and Manuscripts Division, Talleyrand Collection.

8. *Discours du roi, à l'ouverture des Etats-généraux, fait à Versailles le 5 mai 1789.* Bordeaux: Michel Racle, 1789. 8°. The New York Public Library, General Research Division.

9. Duchesne, le père [pseud.]. *Catéchisme de la liberté.* [Paris]: Imp. des Patriotes, 1790. 8°. The New York Public Library, Rare Books and Manuscripts Division, Talleyrand Collection.

10. *Etat, par ordre alphabétique, des bailliages royaux & des sénéchaussées royales des pays d'élections, qui députeront directement ou indirectement aux Etats-généraux, avec le nombre de leurs députations; chaque députation composée d'un député du clergé, d'un de la noblesse & de deux du Tiers-état.* Paris: Imp. Royale, 1789. 8°. The New York Public Library, General Research Division.

11. *Etats-généraux.* Ed. Honoré-Gabriel de Riqueti, comte de Mirabeau. [Paris: Le Jay fils, 1789]. 8°. The New York Public Library, Rare Books and Manuscripts Division, Talleyrand Collection.

12. *Fête nationale, 14 juillet 1790.* Paris: Bonvalet, [1790]. Broadside. 8¼ × 10½ (21 × 26). Bibliothèque Nationale, Paris, Département des Imprimés. *(257)*

13. France. Assemblée nationale constituante. *Constitution française, présentée au roi par l'Assemblée nationale, le 3 septembre 1791.* Dijon: Imp. de P. Causse, 1791. 8°. The New York Public Library, General Research Division.

14. France. Assemblée nationale constituante. *Procès-verbal de l'Assemblée nationale, contenant les articles qu'elle a adoptés de la Déclaration des droits de l'homme & du citoyen, & ceux pour la Constitution & l'organisation du pouvoir législatif.* [20–26 août 1789]. Paris: au bureau général du Journal général de la cour & de la ville [Imp. de la Veuve Hérissant], 1789. 8°. The

New York Public Library, Rare Books and Manuscripts Division, Talleyrand Collection.

15. France. Convention nationale. *Acte constitutionnel précédé de la Déclaration des droits de l'homme et du citoyen.* Paris: Imp. Nationale, 1793. 8°. The New York Public Library, General Research Division.

16. France. Parlement (Paris). *Arrêt . . . qui condamne un imprimé ayant pour titre: Délibération à prendre par le Tiers-état dans toutes les municipalités du royaume de France, à être lacéré & brûlé par l'Exécuteur de la Haute-justice. Du 17 décembre 1788.* [Paris: N. H. Nyon, 1788]. 4°. The New York Public Library, Rare Books and Manuscripts Division, Talleyrand Collection. *(54)*

17. France. Parlement (Paris). *Remontrances . . . sur l'usage des Lettres de cachet.* [11 mars 1788]. N.p., [1788]. 8°. The New York Public Library, Rare Books and Manuscripts Division, Talleyrand Collection.

18. *L'Ermite sans souci ou Le Capuchon à tous les diables, dédié à l'abbé Maury.* Goa: Dans le Palais de l'Inquisition, 1790. 8°. The New York Public Library, General Research Division.

19. Joseph-François-Nicolas. *Bouquet des braves sans-culottes à Louis XVI, ci-devant Roi des Français, à présent premier Bourgeois du Temple.* [Paris]: Imp. de Tremblay, 1792. 8°. The New York Public Library, General Research Division.

20. *Journal de l'autre monde, ou Conversation vraiment fraternelle du diable avec St. Pierre, sur des objets de grande importance. Nouvelles Recrues arrivant en Enfer. Réjouissances à ce sujet. Intrigues de Robespierre en l'autre monde. Ses liaisons scandaleuses avec Proserpine. Sédition aux Enfers. Châtiment des conspirateurs. Rapport de l'Avocat-général près du Tribunal de Pluton.* Paris: Toubon et Lefevre, an III (1794–95). 8°. The New York Public Library, General Research Division.

21. *Lettre à un censeur royal sur la liberté de la presse.* [Paris: Volland, 1789?]. 8°. The New York Public Library, General Research Division.

22. *Lettre du roi pour la convocation des Etats-généraux à Versailles, le 27 avril 1789, et règlement y annexé, pour le Languedoc.* Paris: Imp. Royale, 1789. 8°. The New York Public Library, Rare Books and Manuscripts Division, Talleyrand Collection. *(53)*

23. "Liberté de la presse." 1797. Color engraving. 11 × 13⅛ (28 × 34). Bibliothèque Nationale, Paris, Cabinet des Estampes, Collection Histoire de France. *(Pl. 1)*

24. Linguet, Simon-Nicolas-Henri. *Mémoires sur la Bastille, et sur la déten-*

tion de l'auteur dans ce château-royal, depuis le 27 septembre 1780, jusqu'au 19 mai 1782. London: T. Spilsbury, 1783. 8°. The New York Public Library, General Research Division. *(227)*

25. *Litanies du Tiers-état.* N.p., n.d. 8°. The New York Public Library, General Research Division.

26. Lombard, Vincent de Langres. *Le Dix-huit Brumaire ou tableau des événements qui ont amené cette journée. . . .* Paris: Garnéry, an VIII (1799–1800). 8°. The New York Public Library, General Research Division.

27. Malesherbes, C.-G. Lamoignon de. *Mémoires sur la librairie et sur la liberté de la presse.* Paris: H. Agasse, 1809. 8°. Columbia University, Rare Book and Manuscript Library. *(52)*

28. Marat, Jean-Paul. *C'en est fait de nous.* [26 juillet 1790]. [Paris: Imp. de Marat, 1790]. 8°. The New York Public Library, Rare Books and Manuscripts Division, Talleyrand Collection.

29. Marat, Jean-Paul. *Opinion de Marat, l'ami du peuple . . . sur le jugement de l'ex-monarque.* [Paris: Imp. Nationale, 1792]. 8°. The New York Public Library, General Research Division.

30. Mirabeau, Honoré-Gabriel de Riqueti, comte de. *Sur la liberté de la presse, imité de l'anglais, de Milton.* London, 1788. 8°. The New York Public Library, Rare Books and Manuscripts Division, Talleyrand Collection. *(64)*

31. Moulins (sénéchaussée). Tiers-état. *Cahier général des plaintes et doléances du Tiers-état de la province du Bourbonnais.* N.p., [1789]. 8°. The New York Public Library, Rare Books and Manuscripts Division, Talleyrand Collection.

32. *Observations patriotiques sur la prise de la Bastille, du 14 juillet 1789, et sur les suites de cet événement.* Paris: Debray, 1789. 8°. The New York Public Library, Rare Books and Manuscripts Division, Talleyrand Collection.

33. Parlen, Pierre-Mathieu. *Les Crimes des parlements, ou les horreurs des prisons judiciaires dévoilées.* Paris: Girardin, Lesclapart, 1791. 8°. The New York Public Library, General Research Division.

34. *Le Patriote français, ou Journal libre, impartial et national; par une société de citoyens. Prospectus.* Ed. Jacques-Pierre Brissot de Warville. [Paris, 1 avril 1789]. 8°. The New York Public Library, Rare Books and Manuscripts Division, Talleyrand Collection. *(160)*

35. *Plan et représentation exacte de la salle de Bourbon au Louvre, où se tint l'assemblée des Etats-généraux en 1614, gravé d'après un exemplaire de la biblio-*

thèque du roi, avec le cérémonial qui y fut observé, pour donner une idée de ce qui sera pratiqué dans la salle de Versailles, où doivent être assemblés les Etats-généraux en 1789. Paris: Nyon, l'aîné & fils, 1789. 4°. The New York Public Library, Rare Books and Manuscripts Division, Talleyrand Collection. *(Pl. 2)*

36. "Prise de la Bastille par les Gardes françaises. . . ." Engraving. 9¾ × 10¾ (25 × 27). In *Gravures historiques des principaux événements depuis l'ouverture des Etats-généraux de 1789.* Paris: Janinet & Cussac, 1789. The New York Public Library, The Miriam and Ira D. Wallach Division of Art, Prints and Photographs.

37. *Récit fidèle et complet de tout ce qui a précédé et suivi la découverte du testament de la reine.* Paris: Imp. de Mme. Vve. Perronneau, [1793?]. 8°. The New York Public Library, General Research Division.

38. *Réflexions, sommaires et impartiales, sur l'effet que le décret de l'Assemblée nationale relativement à la destruction de la féodalité, doit produire dans la province d'Alsace.* N.p., n.d. 8°. The New York Public Library, General Research Division.

39. *Rendez-nous la Bastille.* [Paris]: Hôtel de la mairie, rue des Capuchins, [1789]. 8°. The New York Public Library, Rare Books and Manuscripts Division, Talleyrand Collection.

40. *Requête des femmes, pour leur admission aux Etats-généraux.* N.p., [1788]. 8°. The New York Public Library, Rare Books and Manuscripts Division, Talleyrand Collection.

41. Sieyès, Emmanuel-Joseph. *Qu'est ce que le Tiers-état?* 2d ed., corrected. N.p., 1789. 8°. The New York Public Library, Rare Books and Manuscripts Division, Talleyrand Collection.

42. Common Press, British. Early eighteenth century [replica]. 78 × 36 × 60 (31 × 14 × 24). Property of Clinton Sisson.

43. Stone from the Bastille, executed under the direction of P.-F. Palloy, serving as a frame for a "Plan de la Bastille," color aquatint by J.-B. Chapuy after Palloy. 1790. Stone: 32 × 20 × 3 (82 × 50 × 7); aquatint: 22 × 14 (56 × 36). Musée de la Révolution Française, Vizille, France. *(Pl. 3)*

44. Vieilh de Varennes, Raymond-Augustin. *Collection entière des drapeaux de l'Armée nationale parisienne.* [Paris, 1790?]. Color engravings. 11 × 8¾ (27 × 22). The New York Public Library, Spencer Collection. *(Pl. 4)*

45. *Vive la République. La Guerre est déclarée aux oppresseurs du monde.* N.p., 1793. Broadside. 7½ × 6¼ (19 × 16). The New York Public Library, Rare Books and Manuscripts Division. *(Pl. 12)*

Section I: Printing Shop

46. Composing table. Eighteenth century. 36½ × 48½ × 28¾ (93 × 123 × 73). American Antiquarian Society, Worcester, Massachusetts.

47. Lead, molds, and utensils used in the fabrication of typographical characters. Eighteenth century. Imprimerie Nationale, Paris.

48. The Isaiah Thomas Printing Press. 1747. Press: 72 × 33 × 59 (183 × 84 × 150); pedestal: 2½ × 36 × 72 (6 × 91 × 183). American Antiquarian Society, Worcester, Massachusetts. (*Pl. 7*)

49. Type stand and type cases. Seventeenth century. Stand: 64½ × 59½ × 22¾ (164 × 151 × 58). Yale University Library, Arts of the Book Collection.

Section II: Bookshop

50. Baritel. Letter to the Société typographique de Neuchâtel, 19 septembre 1774. Manuscript. 9⅛ × 7⅜ (23 × 19). Bibliothèque Publique et Universitaire de Neuchâtel, Archives de la Société Typographique de Neuchâtel, Switzerland. (*43*)

51. Bergeret. Letter to the Société typographique de Neuchâtel, 11 février 1775. Manuscript. 10 × 7⅜ (25 × 19). Bibliothèque Publique et Universitaire de Neuchâtel, Archives de la Société Typographique de Neuchâtel, Switzerland. (*45*)

52. "Ce Visage vaut mieux que toutes vos chansons." Engraving by N. Le Mire, after H. Gravelot. 1762. 5½ × 3 (14 × 8). In Pierre Corneille, *Théâtre*, vol. 11, ed. Voltaire, 1764. Musée de la Révolution Française, Vizille, France. (*143*)

53. Grasset, Gabriel. Account with the Société typographique de Neuchâtel. [Août 1775]. Manuscript. 14½ × 9⅜ (37 × 24). Bibliothèque Publique et Universitaire de Neuchâtel, Archives de la Société Typographique de Neuchâtel, Switzerland. (*34*)

54. Grasset, Gabriel. Letter to the Société typographique de Neuchâtel, 25 avril 1774. Manuscript. 9 × 6½ (23 × 17). Bibliothèque Publique et Universitaire de Neuchâtel, Archives de la Société Typographique de Neuchâtel, Switzerland. (*35*)

55. Grasset, Gabriel. "Note de livres philosophiques." [1774]. Manu-

script. 6¼ × 4⅛ (16 × 11). Bibliothèque Publique et Universitaire de Neuchâtel, Archives de la Société Typographique de Neuchâtel, Switzerland. *(35)*

56. Hardy, Siméon-Prosper. "Mes Loisirs." Manuscript journal for 3 février 1789. [Paris, 1789]. Folio. Bibliothèque Nationale, Paris, Cabinet des Manuscrits. *(19)*

57. "Une Marchande de journaux. Fragment d'un almanach pour 1791." 1791. Color engraving by Philibert-Louis Debucourt. 13 × 16½ (33 × 42). Bibliothèque Nationale, Paris, Cabinet des Estampes, Collection Hennin. *(Pl. 5)*

58. "Les Métiers de Bologna: Vendeur de tableaux et de livres pour les enfants." N.d. Engraving by Simon Guillaume, after Carraccio. 10 × 6 (26 × 16). Musée de l'Imprimerie et de la Banque, Lyon, France. *(204)*

Section III: Printing and Publishing Books

59. "A. F. M. Momoro, premier imprimeur de la liberté nationale." N.d. Engraving. 5½ × 4 (14 × 10). Musée de la Révolution Française, Vizille, France. *(103)*

60. Archives de la Chambre syndicale de la librairie et de l'imprimerie de Paris. *Registre de la communauté des libraires et imprimeurs de Paris.* 14 juillet 1789. Manuscript. Folio register. Bibliothèque Nationale, Paris, Cabinet des Manuscrits. *(75)*

61. Boulard, Martin-Silvestre. *Le Manuel de l'imprimeur, ouvrage utile à tous ceux qui veulent connaître les détails des ustensiles, des prix, de la manutention de cet art intéressant, & à quiconque veut lever une imprimerie.* Paris: Boulard, 1791. 8°. The New York Public Library, General Research Division. *(110)*

62. Buffon, Georges Louis LeClerc, comte de. *Histoire naturelle, générale et particulière.* New ed. 127 vols. Paris: F. Dufart, an VIII (1799–1800). 8°. The New York Public Library, General Research Division. *(183)*

63. "Charles Guillaume LeClerc, libraire, ancien Juge consul, Député de Paris." Engraving. [1790?]. 7⅞ × 6¼ (20 × 16). Bibliothèque Nationale, Paris, Cabinet des Estampes, Collection de Vinck.

64. *Club typographique et philanthropique.* No. 1, 1 novembre 1790. [Paris]: Roux. 8°. Bibliothèque Nationale, Paris, Département des Imprimés. *(121)*

65. Communauté des libraires & imprimeurs de Paris. *Code de la librairie*

et imprimerie de Paris, ou Conférence du règlement, arrêté au Conseil d'état du roi le 28 février 1723, et rendu commun pour tout le royaume, par arrêt du Conseil d'état du 24 mars 1744, avec les anciennes ordonnances, édits, déclarations, arrêts, règlements & jugements rendus au sujet de la librairie & de l'imprimerie, depuis l'an 1332, jusqu'à présent. Paris, 1744. 8°. The New York Public Library, General Research Division. *(71)*

66. Condillac, Etienne Bonnot de. *Oeuvres de Condillac, revues, corrigées par l'auteur, imprimées sur ses manuscrits autographes, et augmentées de La Langue des calculs, ouvrage posthume.* Paris: Imp. de Ch. Houel, an VI, 1798. 8°. The New York Public Library, General Research Division. *(185)*

67. Decremps, Henri. *La Science sans-culotisée. Premier Essai sur les moyens de faciliter l'étude de l'astronomie, tant aux amateurs et aux gens de lettres, qu'aux Marins de la République française, et d'opérer une révolution dans l'enseignement.* 8 vols. Paris: l'auteur, an II (1793–94). 8°. The New York Public Library, Science and Technology Research Center. *(192)*

68. Diderot, Denis, et al. *Encyclopédie, ou Dictionnaire raisonné des sciences, des arts et des métiers, par une société de gens de lettres. Mis en ordre & publié par M. Diderot . . . & quant à la partie mathématique, par M. d'Alembert. . . .* Paris: Briasson, 1751–65. Folio. The New York Public Library, General Research Division.

69. *Faillite de sieur Debure-d'Houry, libraire-imprimeur à Paris.* 26 juillet 1790. Demi-folio manuscript notebook. Archives de Paris. *(87)*

70. Florian, Jean-Pierre Claris de. *Galatée, roman pastoral; imité de Cervantes.* Paris: Defer, 1793. 4°. The New York Public Library, Spencer Collection. *(Pl. 9)*

71. France. Assemblée nationale constituante. *Loi [de l'Assemblée nationale du 2 mars 1791] portant suppression de tous les droits d'aides, suppression de toutes les maîtrises & jurandes, & établissement de patentes. Donnée à Paris, le 17 mars 1791.* [Paris: Guilhemat, 1791]. 8°. The New York Public Library, Rare Books and Manuscripts Division, Talleyrand Collection. *(81)*

72. Graffigny, Françoise d'Issembourg d'Happoncourt de. *Lettres d'une péruvienne.* New ed. Paris: P. Didot l'aîné, an V, 1797. 8°. The New York Public Library, Spencer Collection.

73. Jean-Baptiste [pseud., "Anacharsis Cloots"]. *Discours prononcé à la barre de l'Assemblée nationale, au nom des imprimeurs, par Anacharsis Cloots, orateur du genre humain, le 9 septembre 1792.* [Paris: Imp. Nationale, 1792]. 8°. Archives Nationales, France.

74. La Fontaine, Jean de. *Les Amours de Psyché et de Cupidon, avec le poème d'Adonis par Lafontaine*. With figures by Moreau le jeune, engraved under his direction. Paris: Didot, le jeune, an III (1794–95). Folio. The New York Public Library, Spencer Collection.

75. Lapérouse, Jean François de Galaup, comte de. *Voyage de La Pérouse autour du monde, publié conformément au décret du 22 avril 1791, et rédigé par M. L. A. Milet-Mureau*. Paris: Imp. de la République, P. D. Duboy-Laverne, an V (1796–97). 4°. The New York Public Library, Rare Books and Manuscripts Division.

76. Lottin, Augustin-Martin. *Catalogue chronologique des libraires et des libraires-imprimeurs de Paris, depuis l'an 1470, époque de l'établissement de l'imprimerie dans cette capitale, jusqu'à présent*. Paris: Lottin, 1789. 4°. The New York Public Library, Rare Books and Manuscripts Division. *(100)*

77. *Manuel de l'auteur et du libraire*. Paris: La Veuve Duchesne, [1777]. 12°. The New York Public Library, General Research Division. *(18)*

78. Marchand, Prosper. *Histoire de l'origine et des premiers progrès de l'imprimerie*. La Haye: La Veuve le Vier et Pierre Paupie, 1740. 4°. The New York Public Library, General Research Division. *(Pl. 6)*

79. Momoro, Jean-François. *Traité élémentaire de l'imprimerie, ou le manuel de l'imprimeur*. Paris: Veuve Tilliard & fils, 1796. 8°. The New York Public Library, General Research Division. *(111, 112)*

80. Monge, Gaspard, comte de Péluse. *Géométrie descriptive. Leçons données aux écoles normales, l'an 3 de la république*. Paris: Baudouin, an VII (1798–99). 4°. The New York Public Library, Science and Technology Research Center. *(198)*

81. Piis, Pierre-Antoine-Augustin de. *Hymne à l'imprimerie par le citoyen Piis, chanté à la section des Tuileries, le décadi 30 pluviôse*. N.p., [1793–94]. 8°. Bibliothèque Nationale, Paris, Département des Imprimés. *(254)*

82. St-Pierre, Jacques Henri Bernardin de. *Paul et Virginie*. Paris: Imp. de Monsieur, 1789. 18°. The New York Public Library, Spencer Collection. *(Pl. 10)*

83. Engraved woodblock used to print *Paul et Virginie*. By engraver of the school of Bewick. Eighteenth century. 5¾ × 4 (15 × 10). Musée de l'Imprimerie et de la Banque, Lyon, France.

Section IV: Journals and Pamphlets

84. *Les Actes des apôtres.* Ed. Antoine-Joseph, comte de Barruel-Beauvert. Prospectus and no. 1. [Paris: Imp. des Actes des apôtres, 1796]. 8°. The New York Public Library, Rare Books and Manuscripts Division. *(163)*

85. *L'Ami du peuple, ou le Publiciste parisien, journal politique, libre et impartial, par une société des patriotes. Et rédigé par M. [Jean-Paul] Marat.* No. 81, 29 décembre 1789. Paris: Imp. de M. Marat. 8°. The New York Public Library, Rare Books and Manuscripts Division, Talleyrand Collection. *(155)*

86. *L'Ami du peuple, ou le Publiciste parisien, journal politique, libre et impartial, par une société des patriotes. Et rédigé par M. [Jean-Paul] Marat.* No. 103, 20 janvier 1789 [sic for 1790]. Paris: Imp. de M. Marat. 8°. The New York Public Library, Rare Books and Manuscripts Division, Talleyrand Collection.

87. *L'Ami du roi, des français, de l'ordre, et surtout de la vérité. Par les continuateurs de Fréron.* No. 1, 1 juin 1790. Paris: Crapart et Artaud. 8°. The New York Public Library, General Research Division. *(148)*

88. Portrait of Jacques-Pierre Brissot. Engraving by N. F. Maviez, after F. Bonneville. From *Portraits des personnages célèbres de la Révolution,* F. Bonneville and P. Quénard. Vol. 2. 1796. 8¾ × 5½ (22 × 14). Musée de la Révolution Française, Vizille, France.

89. Cérutti, Joseph-Antoine-Joachim. *Lettre de M. Cérutti, adressée au café de Foix, au sujet d'un écrit de M. Schmits, membre de l'Assemblée nationale.* Paris: Desenne, 1789. 8°. The New York Public Library, General Research Division.

90. *La Chronique du mois, ou Les Cahiers patriotiques de E. Clavière, C. Condorcet, L. Mercier, M. E. Guadet, J. Oswald, N. Bonneville, J. Bidermann, A. Broussonet, A. Guy-Kersaint, J. P. Brissot, J. Ph. Garran, J. Dussaulx, Th. Paine et F. Lanthenas.* Paris: Imp. du Cercle Social, 1793. 8°. The New York Public Library, General Research Division.

91. Club des Jacobins. *Bordel national sous les auspices de la reine, à l'usage des confédérés provinciaux.* Cythère, 1790. 8°. Bibliothèque Nationale, Paris, Département des Imprimés, Enfer. *(174)*

92. Portrait of Georges-Jacques Danton. Engraving by Claessens. From *Tafereelen van de Staatsomwenteling in Frankrijk.* Amsterdam: J. Allart, 1794–1801. 8¾ × 6¼ (22 × 16). Musée de la Révolution Française, Vizille, France.

93. Desmoulins, Camille. *Discours de la lanterne aux Parisiens. En France, l'an premier de la liberté.* [Paris: Le Jay fils, 1789]. 8°. The New York Public Library, Rare Books and Manuscripts Division, Talleyrand Collection.

94. "Les Ecrivains de la patrie française." N.d. Detail of "La Révolution française." Engraving by A. Duplessis. 20½ × 25¾ (52 × 65). Musée de la Révolution Française, Vizille, France.

95. *Etats-généraux.* Ed. Honoré-Gabriel de Riqueti, comte de Mirabeau. No. 1, 2 mai 1789. [Avignon]. 8°. The New York Public Library, General Research Division.

96. *Gazette nationale, ou Le Moniteur universel.* No. 1, 5 mai 1789. Reprint. Paris: H. Agasse, an IV (1795–96). Folio. The New York Public Library, General Research Division. *(152)*

97. La Motte, Jeanne (de Luz de Saint-Rémy de Valois), comtesse de, purported author. *Adresse . . . à l'Assemblée nationale, pour être déclarée citoyenne active.* [Londres, le 20 mai 1790]. London, 1790. 8°. The New York Public Library, Rare Books and Manuscripts Division, Talleyrand Collection.

98. Marat, Jean-Paul. *Appel à la nation.* N.p., [1790]. 8°. The New York Public Library, General Research Division.

99. Portrait of Jean-Paul Marat. N.d. Engraving by Jean-Baptiste Vérité. 20 × 14½ (51 × 37). The New York Public Library, The Miriam and Ira D. Wallach Division of Art, Prints and Photographs.

100. *Mercure de France.* 3 janvier 1789. Paris: Bureau du Mercure. 8°. The New York Public Library, General Research Division. *(146)*

101. "Mirabeau arrive aux Champs-Elysées." N.d. Engraving by Marquelier, after Moreau le jeune. 9 × 12½ (23 × 32). Musée de la Révolution Française, Vizille, France. *(65)*

102. Morande, Charles Théveneau de. *Le Gazetier cuirassé: Ou Anecdotes scandaleuses de la cour de France.* [London?]: Imprimé à cent lieux de la Bastille à l'enseigne de la liberté, 1771. 8°. The New York Public Library, General Research Division. *(30)*

103. "Motion faite au Palais royal par Camille Desmoulins le 12 juillet 1789." Engraving by Pierre-Gabriel Berthault, after Prieur. 7⅛ × 9½ (18 × 24). Bibliothèque Nationale, Paris, Cabinet des Estampes, Collection Hennin.

104. "Les Motionnaires au café du caveau [5 août 1789]." Engraving. 5¾ × 13⅛ (28 × 34). Bibliothèque Nationale, Paris, Cabinet des Estampes, Collection Histoire de France. *(144)*

105. *Nouveautés du Palais royal, ou Livres nouveaux des charlatans, des roués, &c. de la France, accompagnés de notes impartiales.* Par M.G.C.D.C. [Paris?]:

Imp. de la Vérité, et se trouve au Palais royal, chez Madame l'Ironie, 1789. 8°. The New York Public Library, Rare Books and Manuscripts Division, Talleyrand Collection.

106. "Les Nouvellistes dans un jardin." [1796]. Drawing with wash. 12 × 18 (31 × 46). Bibliothèque Nationale, Paris, Cabinet des Estampes, Collection Hennin.

107. *L'Orateur des Etats-généraux, pour 1789.* N.p., n.d. 8°. The New York Public Library, General Research Division.

108. "Ordre du cortège pour la translation des mânes de Voltaire le lundi 11 juillet 1791." 1791. Color etching. 13 × 20 (33 × 50). Bibliothèque Nationale, Paris, Cabinet des Estampes, Collection Histoire de France. *(249)*

109. *Le Patriote français, ou Journal libre, impartial et national; par une société de citoyens.* Ed. Jacques-Pierre Brissot de Warville. [Paris]: Imp. du Patriote Français, 1790. 8°. The New York Public Library, General Research Division.

110. "Presse de cabinet" (clandestine press). Eighteenth century. 63 × 43 × 26 (160 × 110 × 65). Musée de l'Imprimerie et de la Banque, Lyon, France. *(Pl. 8)*

111. *Révolutions de Paris.* No. 1, 17 juillet 1789. Paris: Imp. de P. de Lormel. 8°. The New York Public Library, General Research Division. *(153)*

112. Robespierre, Maximilien. *Prospectus. Le Défenseur de la Constitution.* N.p., [1792]. 8°. The New York Public Library, General Research Division.

113. Portrait of Maximilien Robespierre. Color engraving. In *Portraits des députés,* Jean Urbain Guérin. [Paris, 179–]. 4°. The New York Public Library, The Miriam and Ira D. Wallach Division of Art, Prints and Photographs.

114. *Le Vieux Cordelier: Journal.* Ed. Camille Desmoulins. 20 frimaire, an II. [Paris: Imp. de Desenne, 1793]. 8°. The New York Public Library, General Research Division.

Section V: Revolutionary Government and Printing

115. *Almanach royal, année M.DCC.LXX. Présenté à sa majesté pour la première fois en 1699.* Paris: Le Breton, [1769]. 8°. The New York Public Library, Rare Books and Manuscripts Division. *(10)*

116. Arbogast, L. F. A. *Rapport et projet du décret sur la composition des livres élémentaires destinés à l'instruction publique.* Paris: Imp. Nationale, [179–]. 8°. The New York Public Library, General Research Division.

117. Archives de la Chambre syndicale de la librairie et de l'imprimerie de Paris. *Rapports des censeurs sur les ouvrages soumis à leurs examens pour l'obtention des privilèges ou permissions.* 1769–88. Manuscript. Folio register. Bibliothèque Nationale, Paris, Cabinet des Manuscrits. *(15)*

118. Archives de la Chambre syndicale de la librairie et de l'imprimerie de Paris. *Registre des privilèges et des permissions simples de la librairie (1788– 1789).* Manuscript. Folio register. Bibliothèque Nationale, Paris, Cabinet des Manuscrits. *(8)*

119. Archives de la Chambre syndicale de la librairie et de l'imprimerie de Paris. *Répertoire des livres prohibés par ordre alphabétique.* N.d. Manuscript. Folio register. Bibliothèque Nationale, Paris, Cabinet des Manuscrits. *(4)*

120. Baudin, P. C. L. *Rapport et projet du décret sur la propriété des auteurs dramatiques, présenté au nom du Comité de l'instruction publique.* Paris: Imp. Nationale, n.d. [1791–92]. 8°. The New York Public Library, General Research Division.

121. Beaumarchais, Pierre Augustin Caron de. *Pétition à l'Assemblée nationale contre l'usurpation des auteurs.* Paris: Imp. Dupont, [1791–92]. 8°. The New York Public Library, Rare Books and Manuscripts Division.

122. Billaud-Varenne, Jacques Nicolas. *Rapport de Billaud-Varenne, au nom du Comité de salut public, sur un mode de gouvernement provisoire & révolutionnaire, fait à la séance du 28 brumaire, l'an second de la République française [18 novembre 1793].* [Paris: Imp. Nationale, 1793?]. 12°. The New York Public Library, General Research Division.

123. *Catéchisme français, à l'usage des gens de la campagne.* N.p., [1789]. sm. 8°. The New York Public Library, Rare Books and Manuscripts Division, Talleyrand Collection.

124. Condorcet, Marie Jean Antoine Nicolas Caritat, marquis de. *Rapport et projet du décret sur l'organisation générale de l'instruction publique, présentée à l'Assemblée nationale au nom du Comité d'instruction publique . . . le 20 & 21 avril 1792.* [Paris, 1792]. 8°. The New York Public Library, General Research Division.

125. *La Constitution française, et les droits de l'homme, chanson patriotique.* Paris: Garnéry, l'an premier de la liberté (1791?). 8°. The New York Public Library, Rare Books and Manuscripts Division, Talleyrand Collection. *(261)*

126. *La Constitution française, présentée au roi par l'Assemblée nationale, le 3 septembre 1791, & acceptée par sa majesté le 14 du même mois.* Paris: Imp. de Baudouin, 1791. 8°. The New York Public Library, General Research Division.

127. *Contre la multiplicité et le danger des brochures, par l'auteur de l'écrit intitulé: Je ne suis point de l'avis de tout le monde.* N.p., 1789. 8°. The New York Public Library, Rare Books and Manuscripts Division, Talleyrand Collection.

128. "Déclaration des droits de l'homme et du citoyen." Engraving. 15¼ × 10½ (39 × 27). Musée de la Révolution Française, Vizille, France.

129. *Déclaration des droits et des devoirs de l'homme et du citoyen.* [Paris]: Imp. du Directoire Exécutif, an III (1794–95). 8°. The New York Public Library, General Research Division.

130. *Declaration of Rights/Déclaration des droits.* London, 1789. 8°. The New York Public Library, General Research Division.

131. *Déclaration solennelle des droits de l'homme dans l'état social.* N.p., 1793. 8°. The New York Public Library, General Research Division.

132. *Description d'une nouvelle presse exécutée pour le service du roi; et publiée par ordre du gouvernement.* Paris: Imp. Royale, 1783. 4°. Imprimerie Nationale, Paris. *(116)*

133. "Droits de l'homme et du citoyen." Engraving. In *Collection complète des tableaux historiques de la Révolution française,* vol. 3. Text by Claude Fauchot, Sébastien R. N. Chamfort, Pierre L. Ginguené, and F. X. Pagès. Paris: P. Didot l'aîné, an VI (1797–98). Folio. The New York Public Library, The Miriam and Ira D. Wallach Division of Art, Prints and Photographs. *(281)*

134. "Extrait du registre des délibérations . . . de Toulon [interdiction de la presse royaliste]." 9 août 1792. Manuscript. 13⅛ × 9 (34 × 23). Musée de la Révolution Française, Vizille, France.

135. France. Assemblée nationale. Déclaration des droits de l'homme et du citoyen. *Projet de déclaration des droits de l'homme en société, présenté le 17 août 1789, par MM. du comité chargé de l'examen des déclarations de droits.* [Paris: Baudouin, 1789]. 8°. The New York Public Library, Rare Books and Manuscripts Division, Talleyrand Collection.

136. France. Constitution. *Constitution of the Republic of France, Completed on the 26th June, 1793, and Submitted to the People by the National Convention. (Translated from a French copy, direct from Paris).* New York: Thomas Greenloaf, 1793. 12°. The New York Public Library, Rare Books and Manuscripts Division.

137. France. Consulat. *Constitution de la République française, représentée par figures, gravées par F. A. David.* Paris: David, an VIII (1799–1800). 12°. The New York Public Library, General Research Division.

138. France. Statutes. *Décret de la Convention nationale du 19 juillet 1793 sur la propriété littéraire des auteurs.* Paris: Imp. Nationale, 1793. 4°. Archives Nationales, France.

139. France. Statutes. *Décret de la Convention nationale du 2 septembre 1793 . . . portant que tous les imprimeurs de Paris sont en état de réquisition pour le service public. . . .* Paris: Imp. Nationale, 1793. 8°. Archives Nationales, France.

140. France. Statutes. *Décret de la Convention nationale, du 18 germinal, an III [7 avril 1795]. . . .* Paris: Imp. de la République, an III (1794−95). 8°. The New York Public Library, General Research Division.

141. France. Statutes. *Décret du 12 mars 1793 . . . qui ordonne l'envoi du Bulletin de la Convention aux sociétés patriotiques.* Marseilles: Mossy, 1793. Broadside. 15½ × 11½ (39 × 29). The New York Public Library, Rare Books and Manuscripts Division.

142. France. Statutes. *Journal des débats et lois du Corps législatif, arrêté du 27 nivôse, an VIII [16 janvier 1800].* Paris: Baudouin, 1800. 8°. The New York Public Library, General Research Division.

143. France. Statutes. *Loi qui ordonne que les libellistes seront poursuivis. Donnée à Paris, le 21 juillet 1792.* Aix: Veuve André Adibert, 9 août 1792. Broadside. 15 × 11¼ (38 × 29). The New York Public Library, Rare Books and Manuscripts Division.

144. France. Statutes. *Procès-verbal de la Convention nationale. Décret du Directoire du 15 vendémiaire, an IV, contre la liberté de la presse.* Paris: Imp. Nationale, an IV (1795−96). 8°. The New York Public Library, General Research Division.

145. France. Statutes. *Procès-verbal de la Convention nationale. Décret du Directoire du 24 vendémiaire, an IV, contre la liberté de la presse.* Paris: Imp. Nationale, an IV (1795−96). 8°. The New York Public Library, General Research Division.

146. *Le Front de Robespierre et de sa clique, ou la nécessité de la liberté de la presse.* Paris: Imp. des Patriotes, [an II (1793−94)]. 8°. The New York Public Library, General Research Division.

147. Gouze, Marie, called "Olympe de Gouges." *Droits de la femme, à la reine.* N.p., [1791]. 8°. The New York Public Library, Rare Books and Manuscripts Division.

148. Grégoire, Henri. *Rapport sur la nécessité & les moyens d'anéantir le patois, & d'universaliser l'usage de la langue française.* Paris: Imp. Nationale, n.d. 8°. The New York Public Library, General Research Division.

149. "Institutrice républicaine." [1793]. Engraving. 7⅞ × 6 (20 × 15). Bibliothèque Nationale, Paris, Cabinet des Estampes, Collection Hennin. *(284)*

150. *Je suis le véritable père Duchesne foutre.* No. 334. [Paris: Imp. de la rue Neuve de l'Egalité, 1794]. 8°. The New York Public Library, General Research Division.

151. Type characters called "les romains du roi," spelling out "Père Duchesne." Imprimerie Nationale, Paris. *(149)*

152. La Chabeaussière. *Catéchisme français, ou principes de philosophie, de morale et de politique républicaines, à l'usage des écoles primaires.* Paris, an IV (1795–96). 8°. The New York Public Library, General Research Division.

153. Manuel, Pierre. *La Police de Paris dévoilée.* 2 vols. Paris: J. B. Garnéry, l'an seconde de la liberté [1791?]. 8°. The New York Public Library, General Research Division. *(12)*

154. *Manuel du républicain.* Paris: Imp. Nationale Executive du Louvre, an II (1793–94). 12°. Bibliothèque Nationale, Paris, Département des Imprimés.

155. Panckoucke, Charles-Joseph. "Sur les chambres syndicales." *Mercure de France.* 23 janvier 1790. Paris: Bureau du Mercure. 8°. The New York Public Library, General Research Division.

156. Paris. Printers. *Pétition présentée aux consuls de la République par les imprimeurs de Paris soussignés.* Paris: Imp. de Stoupe, 1799. Folio. The New York Public Library, Rare Books and Manuscripts Division.

157. Sieyès, Emmanuel-Joseph, comte. "Projet de loi contre les délits qui peuvent se commettre par la voie de l'impression et par la publication des écrits et des gravures, etc., présenté à l'Assemblée nationale le 20 janvier 1790, par le Comité de Constitution." In *Procès-verbal de l'Assemblée nationale.* Vol. 12. Paris: Baudouin, 1790. 8°. The New York Public Library, General Research Division.

158. United States. Declaration of Independence. *Acte d'indépendance des Etats-unis d'Amérique, et constitution des Républiques française, cisalpine et ligurienne, dans les quatres langues française, allemande, anglaise et italienne.* N.p., [17—]. 8°. The New York Public Library, General Research Division.

Section VI: Printing in Everyday Life

159. *Almanach du père Gérard pour l'année 1792.* Ed. J.-M. Collot d'Herbois. Paris: Au secrétariat de la Société des Amis de la Constitution, 1792. 12°. Bibliothèque de l'Arsenal, Paris. *(211)*

160. *Almanach républicain chantant, pour l'an 2ᵉ de la République française, commençant le 22 septembre 1793, et finissant le 21 septembre 1794; avec la Déclaration des droits de l'homme et le maximum. Par le citoyen B***.* Paris: Lallemand, [1793]. 32°. The New York Public Library, Rare Books and Manuscripts Division. *(209)*

161. *Assignats* of 1792: (a) 400 livres, série 1213. 4½ × 7½ (11 × 19). (b) 50 livres, série 4127. 6¼ × 8¼ (16 × 21). Musée de l'Imprimerie et de la Banque, Lyon, France. *(275)*

162. *Assignats:* (a) 50 sous, janvier 1792. 3⅛ × 3½ (8 × 9); (b) 10 sous, mai 1793. 2¼ × 2½ (6 × 7). Bibliothèque Municipale de Lyon, France. *(Pl. 17)*

163. *Assignats,* Commune d'Avignon: (a) 1 sou, 6 deniers. 2 × 1½ (5 × 4); (b) 1 sou, 12 deniers. 2 × 1½ (5 × 4). Bibliothèque Municipale de Lyon, France. *(Pl. 17)*

164. *Assignats,* Département de Côte d'Or: 5 sous en échange d'assignats de 100 livres jusqu'en janvier 1793. 2 × 2⅜ (5 × 6). Bibliothèque Municipale de Lyon, France. *(Pl. 17)*

165. *Assignats,* Commune de Montpellier: 6 deniers. 2 × 1½ (5 × 4). Bibliothèque Municipale de Lyon, France. *(Pl. 17)*

166. *Assignats,* Nîmes: billet d'un sou avec crocodile et palmiers. 2⅜ × 1½ (6 × 4). Bibliothèque Municipale de Lyon, France. *(Pl. 17)*

167. Engraved plate used for the printing of *assignats.* Eighteenth century. 6½ × 10¼ (17 × 26). Musée de l'Imprimerie et de la Banque, Lyon, France.

168. Aubry, Charles Louis. *Le Système des nouvelles mesures de la République française, mis à la portée de tout le monde, et sa nomenclature restreinte aux seize mots génériques du décret.* . . . Paris: Imp. de Pain, 1797. 8°. The New York Public Library, Rare Books and Manuscripts Division.

169. *Avis sur le maximum. Aux citoyens et citoyennes qui veulent l'unité et l'indivisibilité.* Paris: Charpentier, Imp. de la Section des Amis de la Patrie, [1793]. Broadside. 20½ × 16½ (52 × 42). The New York Public Library, Rare Books and Manuscripts Division.

170. Blondel, C. M. "Un Vieillard lisant avec un lorgnon une affiche ainsi conçue: Ordonnance de police qui défend de porter l'épée à tous les vagabonds et gens sans aveu." 1789. Engraving. 8½ × 11½ (22 × 29). Bibliothèque Nationale, Paris, Cabinet des Estampes, Collection Hennin.

171. "Bon pour huit livres de pain pour deux jours à délivrer au citoyen ———." Engraving. 5 × 8 (13 × 21). Bibliothèque Municipale de Lyon, France.

172. Burial announcement. An X (1801–2). Broadside. 10¼ × 15½ (26 × 40). Musée de la Révolution Française, Vizille, France.

173. "Calendrier national calculé pour 30 ans et présenté à la Convention nationale en décembre 1792." 1792. Engraving by J. F. Lefèvre. 22 × 15½ (56 × 39). Bibliothèque Nationale, Paris, Cabinet des Estampes, Collection Hennin.

174. *Carte de la France divisée en départements et districts vérifiée au Comité de la Constitution dédiée et présentée à l'Assemblée nationale, au roi et à M. le dauphin.* 1790. Color engraving. 21½ × 25 (55 × 63). The New York Public Library, Map Division. *(Pl. 18)*

175. *Catéchisme français, républicain. Des sociétés en général.* [Paris]: Imp. de la Municipalité, [1792?]. Broadside. 21 × 17 (53 × 43). The New York Public Library, Rare Books and Manuscripts Division. *(287)*

176. Cérutti, Joseph-Antoine-Joachim, ed. *La Feuille villageoise, adressée, chaque semaine, à tous les villages de la France, pour les instruire des lois, des événements, des découvertes qui intéressent tout citoyen: proposée par souscription aux propriétaires, fermiers, pasteurs, habitants & amis des campagnes.* Paris: Desenne, 1790. 8°. The New York Public Library, General Research Division. *(159)*

177. Chemin-Dupontès fils, J.-B. *L'Ami des jeunes patriotes, ou Catéchisme républicain.* . . . Paris: Imp. de l'auteur, an II (1793–94). 16°. Bibliothèque Nationale, Paris, Département des Imprimés. *(286)*

178. Letterhead, Commission des subsistances. Engraving. 17¾ × 11½ (45 × 29). Musée de la Révolution Française, Vizille, France.

179. Convocation, Société des amis des noirs. Engraved invitation. 4⅛ × 6½ (11 × 17). Musée de la Révolution Française, Vizille, France.

180. "Les Délassements du père Gérard. La Poule de Henri IV. Mise au pot en 1792. Jeu national" (Board Game). N.d. Engraving. Color proof. 17¾ × 23½ (45 × 60). Bibliothèque Nationale, Paris, Cabinet des Estampes, Collection Hennin. *(Pl. 16)*

181. Dezauche, M. *Carte de Paris, divisée en ses 48 sections.* 1790. Color engraving. 25 × 40¾ (63 × 103). The New York Public Library, Map Division. *(Pl. 19)*

182. Du Saulchoy de Bergemont, Joseph-François-Nicolas. *Almanach du peuple pour l'année 1792[–1793].* 2 vols. Paris: Au bureau des Révolutions de France, n.d. 8°. Bibliothèque Nationale, Paris, Département des Imprimés. *(215)*

183. *Fête à l'Être suprême. Strophes chantées à la fête du 20 prairial, an second de la République une et indivisible.* Blois: Billault, [1794]. 8°. The New York Public Library, General Research Division. *(263)*

184. France. Conseil d'état. *Arrêt qui suspend l'exportation des grains à l'étranger. Du 7 septembre 1788.* [Paris: Imp. Royale, 1788]. 8°. The New York Public Library, Rare Books and Manuscripts Division, Talleyrand Collection.

185. *Hommage aux bons citoyens ou catéchisme des démocrates.* N.p., n.d. 8°. The New York Public Library, General Research Division.

186. L'Epithète, M. de [pseud.]. *Dictionnaire national et anecdotique, pour servir à l'intelligence des mots dont notre langue s'est enrichie depuis la révolution, et à la nouvelle signification qu'ont reçue quelques anciens mots. Enrichi d'une notice exacte et raisonnée des journaux, gazettes et feuilletons antérieurs à cette époque. Avec un appendice contenant les mots qui vont cesser d'être en usage, et qu'il est nécessaire d'insérer dans nos archives pour l'intelligence de nos neveux.* N.p., 1790. 8°. The New York Public Library, General Research Division.

187. "La Liberté patronne des Français." 1789–90. Fan, with color engraving. 5½ × 20 (14 × 51). Musée de la Révolution Française, Vizille, France. *(Pl. 14)*

188. Revolutionary playing cards. Designed by the comte de St. Simon; manufactured by V. Jaume and J.-D. Dugourc, an II (1793–94). 3½ × 2⅜ (9 × 6). Albert Field Collection of Playing Cards, Astoria, New York. *(Pl. 13)*

189. Playing cards: "Jeu de cartes des grands hommes." Edited by Chassoneris. Paris, 1793. 3¼ × 2¼ (8 × 6). Musée de la Révolution Française, Vizille, France.

190. Pleyel, Ignace. *Hymne à la liberté.* London, 1792. 4°. The New York Public Library, Music Division. *(263)*

191. *Proclamation du roi, sur le décret de l'Assemblée nationale du 1 juin concernant la forme, la valeur et le nombre des assignats.* Amiens: Imp. Caron, 1790.

Broadside. 7¾ × 19 (20 × 48). The New York Public Library, Rare Books and Manuscripts Division.

192. Restif de la Bretonne, Nicolas-Edmé. *L'Année des dames nationales.* 1794. Frontispiece. 6½ × 4 (17 × 10). Musée de la Révolution Française, Vizille, France. *(208)*

193. Four sectional identity cards. Engravings. (a) 2¼ × 2¾ (6 × 7); (b) diameter: 3½ (9); (c) diameter: 2⅛ (5); (d) 3½ × 2¾ (9 × 7). Musée de la Révolution Française, Vizille, France. *(276–77)*

194. Engraved woodblock used to print a sectional identity card. 1½ × 2 (4 × 5). Imprimerie Nationale, Paris.

Section VII: Distant Echoes

195. *A l'Assemblée nationale. Supplique et pétition des citoyens de couleur des îles et colonies françaises, sur la motion faite le 27 novembre 1789, par M. de Curt, député de la Guadeloupe, au nom des colonies réunies, tendante à faire nommer un comité des colonies, composé de vingt membres, mi-partie de députés des villes maritimes & des manufactures, et mi-partie de députés des colonies, pour préparer toutes les matières qui peuvent être relatives à ces possessions importantes (1) du 2 décembre 1789.* [Paris, 1789]. 8°. The New York Public Library, General Research Division.

196. *Aanmerkingen over de staats-omwentelingen, van Engeland, in den jaare 1688. En van Frankryk, op den tienden van oogstmaand, des jaars 1792.* Haarlem: J. Tetmans, [1792?]. 8°. The New York Public Library, General Research Division.

197. *Annuaire du Jura, pour l'an VIII de la République française, contenant les foires et marchés des départements du Jura, du Doubs, de Saône-et-Loire, de l'Ain, du Léman: La taxe des barrières, les nouvelles mesures de la République, la nomenclature des départements, le tableau des principaux fonctionnaires publics, etc. etc.* Ed. Jomaron. Lons-le-Saulnier: Imp. J.-E. Gauthier, an VII (1798–99). 12°. Bibliothèque Nationale, Paris, Département des Imprimés. *(137)*

198. Bonneville, B. *Ce que Speravian pas, ou Jean-Pierre vengu de Brest, intermède provençal. . . .* Marseilles: Hermitte, 1790. 8°. Musée de la Révolution Française, Vizille, France.

199. Bourdon de la Crosnière, Louis-Jean-Joseph-Léonard. *Collection of the Heroic and Civic Actions of the French Republicans Laid before the National Convention, in the Name of Its Committee of Public Instruction.* Translated by

H. P. Nugent. Philadelphia, 1794. 8°. The New York Public Library, Rare Books and Manuscripts Division.

200. Burke, Edmund. *Reflections on the Revolution in France*. London: J. Dodsley, 1790. 8°. The New York Public Library, Rare Books and Manuscripts Division.

201. Committee of Constitution. *The New Constitution of France Literally Translated from the Original Copy. Presented to the People of France for Their Consideration.* London: James Ridgway, 1793. 8°. The New York Public Library, General Research Division.

202. *Complot infernal exécuté à Quincey: Affreux Désordres en Franche-Comté & en Bourgogne.* Paris: Gueffier, [1789]. 8°. The New York Public Library, General Research Division. *(129)*

203. *Costituzione della Repubblica Ligurge.* [Ligurge], 1797. 8°. The New York Public Library, Rare Books and Manuscripts Division.

204. Cousin d'Avallon [pseud.] (Charles Yves Cousin). *Histoire de Toussaint-Louverture, chef des noirs insurgés de Saint-Domingue.* Paris: Pillot, 1802. 12°. The New York Public Library, Schomburg Center for Research in Black Culture.

205. *Dialogo sul dangé de la patrio et de la countro-rebouluciou.* Toulouse: Viallanos, [1790]. 8°. The New York Public Library, General Research Division.

206. France. Convention nationale. *Adresse de la Convention nationale au peuple français décrété dans la séance du 18 vendémiaire, an III*ᵉ *de la République française, une et indivisible, traduite en arabe par P. Ruffin.* Paris: Imp. de la République, an III (1794–95). Folio. The New York Public Library, Oriental Division. *(Pl. 11)*

207. Arabic type characters used to print the preceding work. Imprimerie Nationale, Paris.

208. France. Statutes. *Loi portant que tout homme est libre en France, & que, quelque soit sa couleur, il y jouit de tous les droits de citoyen, s'il a les qualités prescrites par la Constitution.* Paris: Imp. Royale, 1791. 4°. The New York Public Library, Schomburg Center for Research in Black Culture.

209. Grégoire, Henri. *Motion en faveur des juifs.* Paris: Belin, 1789. 8°. The New York Public Library, Jewish Division.

210. Karayev, Nikolai Ivanovich. *A History of Western Europe.* N.p., 1913. 9 × 6 (23 × 15). The New York Public Library, Slavic and Baltic Division.

211. Lequinio de Kerblay, Joseph-Marie. *Adresse populaire aux habitants des campagnes*. Nîmes: C. Belle, 1791. 8°. The New York Public Library, General Research Division. *(136)*

212. *Lettres-patentes du roi, sur un décret de l'Assemblée nationale, portant que les juifs, connus en France sous le nom de juifs portugais, espagnols et avignonnais, y jouiront des droits de citoyen actif.* Nancy, 1790. 4°. The New York Public Library, Jewish Division.

213. *Massacre of the French King! View of the Guillotine; or the Modern Beheading Machine at Paris.* London: William Lane, [1793]. Broadside. 20¼ × 15 (51 × 38). The New York Public Library, Rare Books and Manuscripts Division.

214. *Die national Versammlung an die Franzosen.* Strasbourg, 17 février 1790. 8°. The New York Public Library, General Research Division.

215. Noclauf [pseud.] and Ingitalg [pseud.]. *Au coq qui chante, sur les hommes de couleur libres.* Paris: L. M. Collot, 1791. Broadside. 20¾ × 15½ (53 × 39). The New York Public Library, Rare Books and Manuscripts Division.

216. Paine, Thomas. *Rights of Man: Being an Answer to Mr. Burke's Attack on the French Revolution.* London: J. S. Jordan, 1791. 8°. The New York Public Library, Rare Books and Manuscripts Division.

217. *Traduction de la Déclaration bretonne de l'ordre de la noblesse, envoyée aux Paroisses qui ne parlent pas la langue française.* N.p., [1789]. 8°. The New York Public Library, General Research Division.

218. *Victoire remportée par les patriotes de la ville de Nîmes, sur les soi-disants catholiques, le 14 du mois.* [Nîmes?]: Imp. L. L. Girard, [1789?]. 8°. The New York Public Library, General Research Division. *(133)*

219. Wollstonecraft, Mary. *A Vindication of the Rights of Woman; with Strictures on Political and Moral Subjects.* London: J. Johnson, 1792. 8°. The New York Public Library, Rare Books and Manuscripts Division.

NOTES

Roche: Censorship and the Publishing Industry

This essay is a revised version of Daniel Roche's contribution to *Histoire de l'édition française: le livre triomphant, 1660–1830* (Paris: Promodis, 1984), vol. 2, pp. 76–91.

1. M. Cerf, "La Censure royale à la fin du XVIIIe siècle," *Communications* 9 (1967): 2–28.

2. The principal works consulted are H. D. Macpherson, *Censorship under Louis XIV* (New York, 1929); A. Bachman, *Censorship in France from 1715 to 1750: Voltaire's Opposition* (New York, 1934); D. T. Pottinger, *The French Book Trade in the Ancien Régime* (New York: 1944); J. P. Belin, *Le Commerce des livres prohibés à Paris de 1750 à 1789* (Paris, 1913); N. Hermann-Mascard, *La Censure des livres à Paris à la fin de l'Ancien Régime (1750–1789)* (Paris, 1968).

3. H. J. Martin, *Livre, pouvoirs et société à Paris au XVIIe siècle, 1598–1701*, 2 vols. (Paris, 1909), 1: 460–466; 2: 764–768.

4. H. Beaumont de la Bonninière, "L'Administration de la librairie et la censure des Livres, 1700–1750" (Master's thesis, Ecole des Chartes, 1975); Françoise Bléchet, "L'Abbé Bignon et son rôle" (Master's thesis, Ecole des Chartes, 1974); J. Lebrun, "Censure préventive et littérature religieuse en France au début du XVIIIe siècle," *Revue d'histoire de l'Eglise de France* (1975): 201–25.

5. Catherine Blangonnet, "Recherche sur les censeurs royaux et leur place dans la société au temps de M. de Malesherbes" (Master's thesis, Ecole des Chartes, 1975).

6. Martin, *Livre, pouvoirs*, 1:440–44; Beaumont, "L'Administration de la librairie," 7–9, 339–40; for a celebrated seventeenth-century case, see F. Lachèvre, *Le Procès du poète Théophile de Viau* (Paris, 1909).

7. Madeleine Ventre, *L'Imprimerie et la librairie en Languedoc au dernier siècle de l'Ancien Régime, 1700–1789* (Paris / The Hague, 1958), 78–86.

8. Michel Antoine, *Le Conseil du Roi sous le règne de Louis XV* (Geneva, 1970).

9. Beaumont, "L'Administration de la librairie," 360–61.

10. Daniel Roche, *Le Siècle des Lumières en Province: Académies et académiciens provinciaux, 1660–1783*, 2 vols. (Paris / The Hague, 1978).

11. Blangonnet, "Recherche sur les censeurs," 40–63.

12. D. Ozanam, *La Disgrâce d'un premier commis, Tercier et l'affaire de l'Esprit, 1758–59* (Bibliothèque de l'Ecole des Chartes, 1955), 140–70; Pierre Grosclaude, *Malesherbes, témoin et interprète de son temps* (Paris, 1961).

13. Two vols. (Paris, 1792).

14. (Paris, 1789).

15. Cerf, "Censure royale," 7–8.

16. Robert Estivals, *La Statistique bibliographique de la France sous la monarchie* (Paris / The Hague, 1964); Lebrun, "Censure préventive," 203–06.

17. Belin, *Le Commerce des livres prohibés*, 21–33; Blangonnet, "Recherche sur les censeurs," 162–70.

18. Martin, *Livre, pouvoirs*, 1:442–43, 462–66.

19. Ventre, *L'Imprimerie*, 112–41; Hermann-Mascard, *La Censure*, 59–96.

20. Jean Quéniard, *L'Imprimerie et la librairie à Rouen au XVIIIᵉ Siècle* (Paris, 1969), 172–75.

21. Ventre, *L'Imprimerie*, 116–17.

22. Hermann-Mascard, *La Censure*, 88–96; Isabelle Lehu, "La Diffusion du livre clandestin à Paris de 1750 à 1789" (Master's diss., Université de Paris, I, 1979), 23–24.

23. M. Champeaux, "Recherche sur le livre clandestin à Paris au XVIIIᵉ siècle" (Master's diss., Université de Paris, VII, 1978), 50–51; Frantz Funck-Brentano, *Les Lettres de cachet à Paris, 1659–1789* (Paris, 1903).

24. J. L. Flandrin and Marie Flandrin, "La Circulation du livre dans la société du 18ᵉ siècle, un sondage à travers quelques sources," François Furet, ed., *Livre et société en France au XVIIIᵉ siècle*, vol. 2 (Paris / The Hague, 1970), 39–73; R. C. Darnton, *The Great Cat Massacre* (New York, 1984), 145–89.

25. Ventre, *L'Imprimerie*, 120–37.

26. Jacques Billioud, *Le Livre en Provence du XVIᵉ au XVIIIᵉ siècle* (Marseilles, 1962), 45–47.

27. Ventre, *L'Imprimerie*, 118.

28. Martin, *Livre, pouvoirs*, 2:695–97.

29. Robert Mandrou, *Louis XIV en son temps* (Paris, 1973), 161–68.

30. (Paris, 1937), 66–67.

31. Hermann-Mascard, *La Censure*, 112–13.

32. R. C. Darnton, *The Business of Enlightenment: A Publishing History of the "Encyclopédie," 1775–1800* (Cambridge, 1979; French trans., Paris, 1982); R. C. Darnton, "Le Livre à la fin de l'Ancien Régime," *Annales: Economies, Sociétés, Civilisations* 3 (1973):735–44.

33. Lehu, "La Diffusion," 37; see also Archives of the Bastille, Arsenal, 12392, "fraude aux barrières," 12476, and 12951, "affaire de la Théodoron et de Thérèse philosophe"; see also R. Bontoux, "Paris janséniste au XVIIIᵉ siècle, les *Nouvelles Ecclésiastiques*," *Mémoires de la Fédération des Sociétés historiques et archéologiques de Paris et de l'Ile de France* 7 (1956), 205–20.

34. Raymond Birn, "Les Colporteurs du livre et leur culture à l'aube du siècle des Lumières: les pornographes du Collège d'Harcourt," *Revue Française d'Histoire du Livre* (1982).

35. Lehu, "La Diffusion," 7; Champeaux, "Recherche sur le livre clandestin," 10–11.

36. Martin, *Livre, pouvoirs,* 2:765–69; Mandrou, *Louis XIV,* 167.

37. Ventre, *L'Imprimerie,* 165–205; Quéniard, *L'Imprimerie,* 171–226.

38. R. C. Darnton, *Business of Enlightenment,* 387–407; S. Tucoochala, *Charles Joseph Panckoucke et la librairie française, 1736–1798* (Paris, 1977), 392–95.

39. P. Chauvet, *Les Ouvriers du livre en France des origines à la Révolution* (Paris, 1959).

40. *De la Bible aux larmes d'Eros, le livre et la censure en France* (Paris, 1987), pref. by R. Badinter (catalogue of the exhibition "Censorship," BPI, Paris; directors, M. Poulain and F. Serre).

Darnton: Philosophy Under the Cloak

1. The calculation is my own, based on the material on annual condemnations of books in the appendix of Félix Rocquain, *L'Esprit révolutionnaire avant la Révolution, 1715–1789* (Paris, 1878). A large proportion of the condemned works were only topical pamphlets. Instead of being burned, most were merely "suppressed" by an edict of the Conseil d'Etat or the Parlement de Paris, which meant they would be confiscated if seized by the police, and the dealer who sold them might be fined or imprisoned. In my own research in the archives of publishers and the police, I have compiled a list of 720 highly illegal books that were circulating in the underground trade during the twenty years before the Revolution, but there could have been many more.

2. The fullest list compiled by the officials in charge of the book trade can be found in the Bibliothèque Nationale, ms. fr. 21928–21929, which contains 1,563 titles for all sorts of works, many of which were never printed, from 1696 to 1773. But this list is not very accurate and does not represent the literature in circulation during the prerevolutionary years. The inspector of the book trade, Joseph d'Hémery, took notes on all the books that came to his attention. Although his journal is another valuable source of information, it covers only the years 1750–69, and it can be read as testimony to the vastness of the corpus of forbidden books and the inability of the police to bring it under control: Bibliothèque Nationale, ms. fr. 22156–22165 and 22038. See Nelly Lhotellier, "Livres prohibés, livres saisis. Recherches sur la diffusion du livre interdit à Paris au XVIIIe siècle" (Master's diss., Université de Paris, I, 1973), and Marlinda Ruth Bruno, "The 'Journal d'Hémery,' 1750–1751: An Edition" (Ph.D. diss., Vanderbilt University, 1977).

3. Hans-Christoph Hobohm, "Der Diskurs der Zensur: Über den Wandel der literarischen Zensur zur Zeit der 'proscription des romans' (Paris, 1737)," *Romanistische Zeitschrift für Literaturgeschichte* 10 (1986):79.

4. Bibliothèque Nationale, ms. fr. 21933–21934. The earlier registers, mss. 21931–21932, cover the period 1703–1771 but do not usually give the reasons for the confiscations. The later registers give too many reasons, hence the confusion.

But, as I hope to show in a later work, the most illegal and most dangerous books can be winnowed out from all the verbiage, and so these manuscripts are a valuable source for identifying forbidden literature.

5. Jean-François Pion of Pontarlier to the Société typographique de Neuchâtel, 21 November 1771, with the text of the note from M. Petit, the *buraliste* at the customs office in Frambourg; papers of the Société typographique de Neuchâtel (cited henceforth as STN), Bibliothèque publique et universitaire, Neuchâtel, Switzerland.

6. Poinçot to STN, undated letter received 22 September 1781, and Poinçot to STN, 1 June 1781.

7. Veuve Baritel to STN, 9 September 1774, and "Livre de Commissions" of the STN, entry for Baritel's order of 9 September 1774.

8. On 24 September 1768 the Parlement of Paris condemned Jean-Baptiste Josserand, a grocery boy; Jean Lécuyer, a dealer in secondhand goods; and Lécuyer's wife, Marie Suisse, for selling *Le Christianisme dévoilé, L'Homme aux quarante écus, La Chandelle d'Arras,* and similar works. They were exposed in chains for three days on the Quai des Augustins, Place des Barnabites, and Place de la Grève, wearing a sign saying "Purveyor of impious and immoral libels." The two men were then branded on their right shoulders with the letters GAL and sent to the galleys, Lécuyer for five years, Josserand for nine years, followed by perpetual banishment from the kingdom. Mme Lécuyer was sent to prison in the Maison de force of the Salpetrière for five years. The punishments were softened by *lettres de grâce,* but the letters arrived too late. Bibliothèque Nationale, ms. fr. 22099, folios 213–21.

9. Charpentier, *La Bastille dévoilée, ou recueil de pièces authentiques pour servir à son histoire* (Paris, 1789), 4:119.

10. A.-F. Momoro, *Traité élémentaire de l'imprimerie, ou le manuel de l'imprimeur* (Paris, 1793), 234–35. Momoro specified that this "term from the Old Regime" covered "libels, works against the state, morals, religion, the ministers, the king, magistrates, etc."

11. STN to J. Rondi, 9 September 1773.

12. The quotations, in the order of their appearance in the text, come from P. J. Duplain to STN, 11 October 1772; Manoury to STN, 4 October 1775; Le Lièvre to STN, 31 December 1776; Blouet to STN, 30 August 1772; Audéart to STN, 14 April 1776; Billault to STN, 10 September 1776.

13. Patras to STN, 6 June 1777; Rouyer to STN, 9 June 1781; Regnault le jeune to STN, 19 September and 28 December 1774.

14. Jean-Elie Bertrand of the STN to Frédéric-Samuel Ostervald and Abram Bosset de Luze in Geneva, 19 April 1777.

15. STN to Téron, 6 April 1774; Téron to STN, 14 April 1774; Téron to STN, 23 April 1774; Téron to STN, 10 June 1777.

16. Gabriel Grasset to STN, 19 June 1772, and 25 April 1774.

17. Grasset's catalogue is in his letter to the STN of 25 April 1774; the catalogues of Chappuis et Didier are in the firm's letter of 1 November 1780.

18. The STN's secret catalogues, along with a half-dozen copies of its standard, legal catalogues, can be found in a dossier labeled "Société typographique de Neuchâtel" in the papers of the STN. The catalogue confiscated with the Veuve Stockdorf's papers is in the Bibliothèque Nationale, ms. fr. 22101, folios 242–249. The

remark regarding Wittel appears in Quandet de Lachenal to STN, 6 May 1781. A full account of the intrigues connected with the remark about keeping the catalogue "mum" can be found in the dossier of Noël Gille, Bibliothèque Nationale, ms. fr. 22081, folios 358–366, quotation from folio 364 recto. Poinçot reported on his interview with Martin, the secretary and right-hand man of Le Camus de Néville, the director of the book trade, in a letter to the STN of 31 July 1783.

19. STN "Copie de lettres," entries from 12 August to 19 September 1776.

20. Laisney to STN, 26 July 1777; Prévost to STN, 11 May 1783; Malassis to STN, 27 June 1775. See also Teinturier of Bar-le-Duc to STN, 2 September 1776, and Guichard of Avignon to STN, 16 April 1773.

21. STN to Bergeret, 6 July 1773; Bergeret to STN, 7 August 1773; and STN to Bergeret, 17 August 1773. See also the similar exchange between the STN and Prévost of Melun: Prévost to STN, 10 April 1777, and STN to Prévost, 15 April 1777.

22. In sending its latest catalogue of philosophical books to Cazin of Reims on 24 September 1775, the STN regretted its inability to set stable prices for such works: "The prices of books in this genre are, as you know, very irregular in general and depend on all kinds of different circumstances."

23. Grasset to STN, 25 April 1774.

24. The catalogues can be found in Décombaz to STN, 8 January 1776; Chappuis et Didier to STN, 1 November 1780; and the papers confiscated in Stockdorf's bookshop in Strasbourg in 1773; Bibliothèque Nationale, ms. fr. 22101, folios 242–49.

25. Malherbe to STN, 13 August 1774.

26. Favarger to STN, 16 August 1776, and 4 September 1776.

27. For example, Barret of Lyons to STN, 10 April 1772; Mossy of Marseilles to STN, 12 March 1777; Gay of Lunéville to STN, 19 May 1772; Audéart of Lunéville to STN, 8 April 1775; and Le Baron of Caen to STN, 24 December 1776.

28. Manoury to STN, 24 June 1783; Desbordes to STN, 12 January 1773; Malassis to STN, 15 August 1775; Baritel to STN, 19 September 1774; Billault to STN, 29 September 1776; Charmet to STN, 1 October 1774; Sombert to STN, 25 October 1776.

29. Bergeret to STN, 11 February 1775; Charmet to STN, 30 September 1775; STN "Livre de Commission," entry for 24 April 1776, based on an order from Malherbe of Loudun. The clerks were to lard sheets of pornographic and irreligious books into those of devotional works. *La Fille de joye* was the French translation of *Fanny Hill*, John Cleland's pornographic novel, which originally appeared under the title *Memoirs of a Woman of Pleasure*.

30. Regnault to STN, 6 July 1774; Favarger to STN, 15 November 1778, reporting the instructions given by Nubla; Jacquenod to STN, September 1775 (exact date missing); and Bornand to STN, 16 October 1785, reporting the instructions given by Barrois.

31. Blouet to STN, 10 September 1773.

32. Guillon to STN, 6 April 1773, and STN to Guillon, 19 April 1773.

33. François Michaut of Les Verrières to STN, 30 October 1783.

Birn: Malesherbes and the Call for a Free Press

1. C.-G. Lamoignon de Malesherbes, *Mémoires sur la librairie et sur la liberté de la presse* (Paris: H. Agasse, 1809), 307.

2. The standard biography of Malesherbes is Pierre Grosclaude, *Malesherbes, témoin et interprète de son temps* (Paris: Fischbacher, [1961]).

3. Announcement of the convening of the Estates General was made on 5 July 1788. Malesherbes composed his *Mémoire sur la liberté de la presse* during the winter of 1788–89.

4. Bibliothèque Nationale, Fonds Français 22102, fols. 51–58. Condemnations by the Council of State, Parlement of Paris, and Châtelet Court of Paris from 14 July 1788 through 6 April 1789.

5. Ibid., fol. 47, 4 September 1787. Arrêt du Conseil d'Etat du Roi concernant le commerce de librairie dans les lieux privilégiés. (Order of the Royal Council of State concerning the book trade in privileged locales.)

6. Frantz Funck-Brentano, *Les Lettres de cachet à Paris, étude suivie d'une liste des prisonniers de la Bastille (1659–1789)* (Paris: Imprimerie Nationale, 1903), nos. 5247, 5250, 5251, 5252, 5254; April–June 1788.

7. Arrêt du Conseil d'Etat du Roi. Qui ordonne la suppression des trente premiers volumes de l'ouvrage ayant pour titre *Oeuvres complètes de Voltaire*, de l'imprimerie de la Société typographique, 1784, 3 June 1785. (Order of the Royal Council of State. Which orders the suppression of the first thirty volumes of the work called *Oeuvres complètes de Voltaire*, from the printshop of the Société typographique, 1784, 3 June 1785.) Copy in The Newberry Library, Chicago.

8. Malesherbes, *Mémoire sur la liberté de la presse*, in *Mémoires*, 302–07. *Histoire de l'édition française*, 4 vols., ed. Henri-Jean Martin and Roger Chartier (Paris: Promodis, 1984), 2:74, 78–81.

9. Isabelle Lehu, "La diffusion du livre clandestin à Paris de 1750 à 1789" (Thesis U.E.R. d'Histoire, Université de Paris I, 1979), 135–40.

10. F.-A. Isambert, A.-J.-L. Jourdan, and Decrusy, eds. *Recueil général des anciennes lois françaises, depuis l'an 420 jusqu'à la Révolution de 1789*, 29 vols. (Paris: Belin-Leprieur, 1821–1833), 22:272–74.

11. Robert Darnton, *The Literary Underground of the Old Regime* (Cambridge: Harvard University Press, 1982).

12. Malesherbes, *Mémoire*, 287–88. "What will an assembly of the Estates be? A great and solemn court of pleas, where the interests of the nation will be discussed. Will this liberty accorded by judges to every individual be denied the nation? Or will it be refused out of fear of the very inconveniences which, until now, have not seemed sufficient to restrain the freedom of the courtroom?"

13. Henri-Jean Martin, "La direction des lettres," in *Histoire de l'édition française*, ed. Martin and Chartier, 2:65–75, and "La prééminence de Paris," 2:263–81.

14. Eric Walter, "Les auteurs et le champ littéraire," in ibid., 2:391.

15. Chartier and Roche, "Les Pratiques urbaines de l'imprimé," in ibid., 2:403–29.

16. René Moulinas, "La Contrefaçon avignonnaise," in ibid., 2:294–301. Christiane Berkvens-Stevelinck, "L'Edition et le commerce du livre français en Europe"

and "L'Edition française en Hollande," in ibid., 2 : 305–25. Bernard Lescaze, "Commerce d'assortiment et livres interdits: Genève," in ibid., 2 : 326–33. Raymond Birn, "Le Livre prohibé aux frontières: Bouillon," in ibid., 2 : 334–41. Robert Darnton, "Le Livre prohibé aux frontières: Neuchâtel," in ibid., 2 : 343–59.

17. Jean Quéniart, "L'Anémie provinciale," in ibid., 2 : 282–93.

18. Lehu, "La Diffusion du livre clandestin." Important collections of documents pertaining to government condemnations of books and punishments of publishers are in the Bibliothèque Nationale (Collection Anisson-Duperron) and Bibliothèque de l'Arsenal (Archives de la Bastille) in Paris. An idea of the magnitude of the industry of suppression may be obtained from the printed catalogue of the Anisson-Duperron collection available at most major research libraries: Ernest Coyecque, *Inventaire de la Collection Anisson sur l'Histoire de l'Imprimerie et la Librairie* 2 vols. (Paris: Leroux, 1900). In considering the evolution of public opinion after 1750, illegally printed and sold remonstrances of the sovereign courts of France against so-called ministerial despotism are very important. Malesherbes himself composed two of the most significant remonstrances. See *Les "Remonstrances" de Malesherbes, 1771–1775*, ed. Elisabeth Badinter (Paris: U.G.E., 1978), and Keith Michael Baker, "Politics and Public Opinion Under the Old Regime: Some Reflections," in *Press and Politics in Pre-Revolutionary France*, ed. Jack R. Censer and Jeremy D. Popkin (Berkeley and Los Angeles: University of California Press, 1987), 204–46.

19. *Mémoire*, 314–15.

20. René-Louis de Voyer de Paulmy, marquis d'Argenson, *Journal et mémoires*, ed. E.-J.-B. Rathery (Paris: Veuve Renouard, 1859–67), 7 (1753) : 424: "Président de Malesherbes sets about matters pleasantly enough. He tolerates everything that is presented. . . . Then, once he receives superior orders prohibiting books, he has them [the orders] printed and proceeds to return to his policy of toleration, so that more passes in literature than anywhere else."

21. *Troisième mémoire sur la librairie*, 105–06.

22. Malesherbes began writing his five memorandums in 1758. In an addendum to the first memorandum, he dated its composition as between the denunciations of *De l'Esprit* and the *Encyclopédie* issued in the Parlement of Paris on 23 January 1759 and the subsequent judgment of 5 February. On 8 March the *arrêt* of the Royal Council revoked the letters of privilege for the *Encyclopédie*, and Malesherbes himself had to write the revocation order.

23. *Second Mémoire sur la librairie*, 61.

24. *Troisième Mémoire sur la librairie*, 72.

25. Ibid., 93.

26. Ibid., 101.

27. *Quatrième Mémoire sur la librairie*, 144–45.

28. Ibid., 155.

29. Ibid., 171–72.

30. Grosclaude, *Malesherbes*, 389–649.

31. *Catalogue des livres de la Bibliothèque du feu Chrétien-Guillaume Lamoignon-Malesherbes* (Paris: J.-L. Nyon, l'aîné, 1797).

32. Here is a breakdown by field of aristocratic libraries in eighteenth-century Paris, including Malesherbes's:

	Religion	Law	History	Letters	Sciences/Arts
			(in percentages)		
Nobles (1750–89) (50 libraries)	10	4	25	49	12
Parlementaires (1734–95) (30 libraries)	12	18	31	24	15
Malesherbes	2.4	0.7	32.7	29.5	34.7

Data from Chartier and Roche, "Les Pratiques urbaines de l'imprimé," in *Histoire de l'édition française,* 2:407.

33. Isambert, Jourdan, Decrusy, *Recueil général,* 25:108–12. Authors obtaining the privilege to their books won the right to sell them and to pass the privilege on to their heirs in perpetuity. If an author ceded the privilege to a publisher, the publisher's right to it would cease upon the author's death.

34. *Mémoire,* 430–31.

35. Victor de Riquetti, marquis de Mirabeau, *Sur la liberté de la presse, imité de l'anglois de Milton* (London, 1788). Marie-Joseph Chénier, *Dénonciation des inquisiteurs de la pensée* (Paris: Lagrange, 1789).

Hesse: Economic Upheavals in Publishing

1. See, for example, Eugène Hatin, *Histoire politique et littéraire de la presse en France* (Paris: Poulet Malassis, 1860) vol. 5; Alma Söderhjelm, *Le Régime de la presse pendant la Révolution française* (1900–1901; Paris: Slatkine Reprints, 1971); Claude Béllanger et al., eds., *Histoire générale de la presse française* (Paris: Presses universitaires de France, 1969) vol. 1.

2. Restif de la Bretonne, *Les Nuits révolutionnaires* (1789; Paris: Livre de Poche, 1978), 79. I would like to thank Frederick Tibbetts for his translations of the French citations.

3. Marie-Joseph Chénier, *Dénonciation des inquisiteurs de la pensée* (Paris: Lagrange, 1789), 41.

4. Kéralio, *De la liberté d'énoncer, d'écrire et d'imprimer la pensée* (Paris: Imprimerie de Potier de Lille, 1790), 51; Archives Nationales (hereafter A.N.), ser. ADVIII, cart. 38.

5. Kéralio, 52.

6. *Moniteur,* 24 August 1789.

7. A.N., ser. V1, 552, undated report by Thiebault, cart. June–October 1789.

8. A.N., V1, 549, undated letter from Fouquet, January–February 1789; V1, 549, undated letter from Toulouse guild, January–February 1789; V1, 550, March 1789, *Mémoire* of the Paris Book Guild; V1, 551, undated letter from Toulouse guild, April–May 1789; V1, 551, letter from Maissemy to Latourette (Lyon), 30 May 1789; V1, 553, letter from Marin (Marseille) to the bureau, 26 June 1789; V1, 552, letter from Chenu (Metz), 11 July 1789, and Maissemy's response; V1, 552, letter from Houvin (St. Malo) and response, undated [11–28 July?] 1789; V1, 552, report from Royez (Nîmes), 14 August 1789; V1, 553, letter from the office of the "sénéchaussée

du siège présidial et de la police de La Rochelle" to the bureau, 9 June 1789; V1, 553, letter from the general tax farmers (Nantes), 9 October 1789; V1, 553, letter from Chassel (Nancy), 12 November 1789; V1, 552, letter from Maissemy to Villeneuve (Paris), 22 July 1789; V1, 552, his last letter as director dates from 28 July 1789, to Villeneuve, announcing his resignation; Bibliothèque Nationale, mss. fr. 6687, Siméon-Prosper Hardy, "Mes loisirs," journal of the Paris publisher, vol. 8, 396. His entry for 18 July 1789 notes the resignation of Barentin, the keeper of the seal.

9. A.N., V1, 553, letters from Sélis, 11 August and 9 September 1789; V1, 553, letter to Panckoucke, 12 November 1789; V1, 552, letter from Dietrich, and response, 13 August 1789; V1, 552, correspondence between Thiebault and vicomte de Toustain (*Journal Encyclopédique*) for 18 September, 10 and 25 October 1789; V1, 552, letter from De Gaigne, 22 October 1789; V1, 553, letter to the abbé Gentry, 17 November 1789; V1, 553, report from Thiebault, re: LeRoy, Demeunier, and Béranger, 12 November 1789; Kéralio, *De la liberté d'énoncer, d'écrire et d'imprimer la pensée* (Paris: Imprimerie de Potier de Lille, 1790); ser. ADVIII, cart. 38; V1, 553, letter from the bishop of Boulogne, 3 February 1790; for Bondy and Moreau, see Bibliothèque Nationale (hereafter B.N.) mss fr. 6687, Hardy "Mes loisirs," 8:424, entry for 6 August 1789.

10. For Cicé's appointment, see B.N., mss. fr. 6687, "Mes loisirs," 8:422, entry for 5 August 1789; A.N., V1, 552, letter from Villeneuve to Thiebault, 24 October 1789; V1, 553, letter from Havras, 22 October 1789; V1, 552, letter from Houvin, 6 October 1789; V1, 552, letter from Grélier, September 1789; V1, 553, letter from Dietrich, 9 September 1789; V1, 553, correspondence with the general tax farmers, 17 September and 9 October 1789. For the registers of *privilèges* for 30 September–October 28, 1789, see A.N., V1, 552.

11. A.N., F17 1258, doss. 2, "Loi relative à la dépense publique," 10 August 1790. Article XIII reads, "La dépense de douze mille livres affectée au bureau de la librairie sera supprimée à compter du 1e janvier 1791."

12. A.N., V1, 553, "De la librairie," n.d. [1790], in Thiebault's hand.

13. B.N., mss. fr. 21861, "Registre de la Communauté des Libraires et Imprimeurs de Paris," entry for 14 July 1789.

14. William Sewell, Jr., *Work and Revolution in France* (London: Cambridge University Press, 1980), 86; for the Assembly's discussion, see M. J. Madival, *Archives Parlementaires de 1787 à 1860* (Paris: Dupont, 1878), 8:349.

15. *Révolutions de Paris* no. 4, 6 August 1789, 30–31.

16. For his conversations with the new keeper of the seal, see A.N., 144 AP 134, *Papiers Ormesson*, letter from d'Ormesson to Champion de Cicé, the keeper of the seal, concerning Maissemy, 22 September 1789. For his activities in the Commune, see Sigismond Lacroix, ed., *Actes de la Commune de Paris pendant la Révolution*, 7 vols. (Paris: LeCerf, 1895), 1e sér., 1:562–63 (20 October 1789).

17. P.-J.-B. Buchez and P.-C. Roux, eds., *Histoire parlementaire de la Révolution française*, 40 vols. (Paris: Paulin, 1834), 2:191, 246; and Lacroix, *Actes de la Commune*, 1:82.

18. This interpretation is confirmed by a report on the policing and registering of *privilèges* by the Chambre syndicale, in the papers of the Office of the Book Trade, A.N., V1, 553, 3 November 1789.

19. *Révolutions de Paris*, no. 4, 3 August 1789, 10.

20. Ibid., 9–11.

21. Ibid., 43–44.

22. Ibid., no. 10, 13 September 1789, 11.

23. A.N., V1, 553, report from Thiebault to the keeper of the seal, 12 November 1789.

24. Ibid.

25. *Procès-verbal de l'Assemblée Nationale* (Paris: Baudouin, 1790), vol. 12, 20 January 1790.

26. A.N., ser. DXIII, 1, doc. 12, Committee of Agriculture and Commerce, letter from the Paris Book Guild, 24 February 1790, signed Knapen, *syndic*, and Cailleau, Merigot jeune, Nyon l'aîné, and Delalain, *adjoints*.

27. Ibid., *Mémoire*, fol. 3, recto.

28. A.N., ser. AFI: *Procès-verbal du Comité d'Agriculture et de Commerce*, fifty-first sess., 5 March 1790. For copy sent to Committee on the Constitution, see A.N., ser. DIV50, Committee on the Constitution, doc. 1452.

29. A.N., ser. DXXIX *bis* 32, 334, 1. 17, Committee of Investigations, letter from the keeper of the seal, 22 June 1790.

30. Ibid., 1. 16, letter from the keeper of the seal to the Committee of Investigations, 28 June 1790; 1. 13, letter from the keeper of the seal to the Committee of Investigations, re: meeting between the guild and the committee, 10 August 1790; 1. 12, report from the guild to the Committee of Investigations, 11 August 1790; 1. 11, report from the guild to the Committee of Investigations, 13 August 1790; 1. 10, report from the guild to the Committee of Investigations, 13 August 1790.

31. See *Révolutions de Paris*, no. 15, 17 October 1789, 2–6; "Conjurations contre la liberté de la presse"; *Révolutions*, no. 21, 28 November 1789, 28; and no. 24, 19 December 1789, 30.

32. A.N., ser. AFI, *Procès-verbal du Comité d'Agriculture et de Commerce*, 124th sess., 6 September 1790.

33. A.N., ser. DXXIX *bis* 16, 1. 7, letter from the keeper of the seal to the president of the Committee of Investigations, 9 January 1791.

34. Ibid.

35. A.N., ser. AFI, *Procès-verbal du Comité d'Agriculture et de Commerce*, 12 January 1791.

36. A.N., ser. DXXIX *bis* 16, 182, 1. 10, letter from the Committee of Agriculture and Commerce to the Committee of Investigations, 13 January 1791.

37. A.N., ser. AFI, *Procès-verbal du Comité d'Agriculture et de Commerce*, 224th sess., 23 May 1791.

38. A.N., ser. ADVIII 16, *Rapport fait à l'assemblée nationale par M. Hell, député du Bas-Rhin, sur la propriété des productions scientifiques ou littéraires* (Paris: Imprimerie Nationale, 1791).

39. Decree of the National Assembly of 17 March 1791, *Collection Générale des Décrets rendus par l'Assemblée Nationale* (Paris: Baudouin, 1791), 52–62.

40. For a textual analysis of the provenance of the *projet*, see M. J. Guillaume, *Procès-verbaux du Comité d'Instruction Publique de la Convention Nationale*, 7 vols. (Paris:

Imprimerie Nationale, 1894), 2:80. Guillaume shows that crucial phrases of the proposal presented by Lakanal were drawn from the Baudin proposal, suggesting that the Lakanal version was drafted from both the Chénier proposal (not extant) and that of Baudin. My hypothesis is that Chénier is perhaps responsible for both laws and did not present them himself for political reasons. In both the contemporary press and the committee's proceedings, Chénier is assumed to be the author, and the proposals conform exactly to his views as expressed in his petition of 18 September 1792. This theory is also supported by Alfred Jepson Bingham, *Marie-Joseph Chénier, Early Political Life and Ideas (1789–1794)* (New York: Privately printed, 1939), 123. It should be noted, however, that Lakanal later claimed credit for the proposal. See his *Exposé sommaire des travaux de Joseph Lakanal* (Paris: Didot frères, 1838), 9–12.

41. For the stipulations of the *règlement* of 1777, see Jourdan, Decrusy, and Isambert, eds., *Recueil général des anciennes lois françaises*, 29 vols. (Paris: Belin-Leprieur, 1826), 25:108–23. For the law of 19 July 1793 concerning literary property, see *Archives parlementaires de 1787 à 1860,* ed. Jérôme Madival and Emile Laurent, 1ᵉ sér., 71 vols. (Paris: Dupont, 1906), 69:186–87.

42. B.N., mss. fr. 21861, entry for 18 March 1791.

43. Henri-Jean Martin, *Livre, pouvoirs et société à Paris au XVIIᵉ siècle* (Geneva: Droz, 1969), and esp. "La pré-éminence de la librairie parisienne," in *Histoire de l'édition française*, ed. Chartier and Martin, 4 vols. (Paris: Promodis, 1984), 2:262.

44. Roger Chartier, "La Géographie de l'imprimerie française au XVIIIᵉ siècle," in *Histoire de l'édition*, 2:290–91. The figures for 1701 are 51 printing shops in Paris to 30 in Lyon (nearest competitor) and, for 1777, 36 for Paris and 12 for Lyon (nearest competitor).

45. See Martin, "La pré-éminence," and Jean Queniart, "L'anémie provinciale," in *Histoire de l'édition*, 2:262–84.

46. See Robert Estival, *La Statistique bibliographique de la France sous la monarchie, au XVIIIᵉ siècle* (Paris: Mouton & Co., 1965); François Furet, ed., *Livre et société dans la France du XVIIIᵉ siècle*, I (Paris and the Hague: Mouton & Co., 1965).

47. Of central importance are Etienne Martin–St. Léon, *Histoire des corporations de métiers* (Paris: Alcan, 1909); William Sewell, Jr., *Work and Revolution in France* (London: Cambridge University Press, 1980); Louis Radiguer, *Maîtres imprimeurs et ouvriers typographes* (Paris: Société nouvelle de librairie et d'édition, 1903), and Paul Chauvet, *Les ouvriers du livre en France* (Paris: Presses universitaires de France, 1964).

48. B.N., mss. fr. 21896, *Registre des déclarations pour la contribution patriotique,* Pierres, entry 111, 11 May 1790; A.N., V1 552, letter from Valleyre to Maissemy, 19 August 1789, and letter from Godefroy to the Office of the Book Trade, 11 September 1789; B.N., mss. fr. 21896, Gueffier, entry 10, *Contribution patriotique,* 24 November 1789, B.N., mss. fr., 21896, Debure l'aîné, entry 34, *Contribution patriotique,* 24 December 1789, B.N., mss. fr. 21896, Merquignon, entry 79, *Contribution patriotique,* 12 March 1790, B.N., mss. fr. 21896, Gobreau, entry 108, *Contribution patriotique,* 7 May 1790; Panckoucke, in *Mercure de France,* "Avis sur l'Encyclopédie par ordre de matières," 27 February 1790, 155; Grangé, cited in Radiguer, *Maîtres imprimeurs,* 143.

49. A.N., ser. DIV 50, doss. 1452, Committee on the Constitution, letter from Langlois fils (n.d. [1790–91]); Charles de Lameth, "Speech to the National Assem-

bly," 12 January 1790, in *Histoire parlementaire*, ed. Buchez and Roux, 4:270. Proceedings of the National Assembly, 12 January 1791; A.N., BB 16 703, doss. 17, minister of justice, letter from Moutard to Laporte, 11 May 1793; A.N., F 17 1004c doss. 650, Committee of Public Instruction letter from Nyon l'aîné to the minister of the interior, 30 June 1793; A.N., F 17 1008a, doss. 1374, Committee of Public Instruction, letter from Nyon le jeune, 8 frimaire, an II (28 November 1793).

50. See B.N., mss. fr. 21896, *Contributions patriotiques*, entries 10 (24 November 1789), 34 (24 December 1789), 79 (12 March 1790), and 108 (7 May 1790).

51. See A.N., BB16, 703, doss. 17, minister of justice, letter from Moutard to Laporte, 11 May 1793.

52. See A.N., ser. DIV 50, doss. 1452, Committee on the Constitution, letter from Langlois, fils, n.d. [1790–91]; A.N., F17, 1004c, doss. 650, Committee of Public Instruction, letter from Nyon l'aîné, 30 June 1793; and 1008a, doss. 1374, Committee on Public Instruction, letter from Nyon le jeune, 8 frimaire, an II (28 November 1793).

53. See, for example, *Révolutions de Paris*, no. 23, 12–19 December 1789, 17.

54. See fig. 1.

55. See fig. 1.

56. This estimate is based on a computation of the individual declarations of bankruptcy extant in the Archives de Paris. Radiguer gives an estimate of the *passif* in 1790 of thirty million livres but gives no indication as to how he arrived at that figure. Nonetheless, it suggests my own estimate is probably extremely conservative. See Radiguer, *Maîtres imprimeurs*, 143.

57. B.N., mss. fr. 6687, Hardy, "Mes loisirs," vol. 8, entry for 21 January 1789.

58. His bankruptcy papers are found in Archives de Paris (hereafter A.P.), D4 B6, cart. 105, doss. 7454, 30 March 1789.

59. For the Debure-d'Houry bankruptcy, see A.P., D4 B6, cart. 110, doss. 7844, 26 July 1790. The papers of the Durand bankruptcy are no longer extant, but evidence of its occurrence can be found in B.N., mss. fr. 21896, entry 34, 24 December 1789.

60. B.N., mss fr. 21896, *Contributions patriotiques*, entry 34, 24 December 1789.

61. A.P., D4 B6, cart. 110, doss. 7844; D4 B6, cart. 109, doss. 7739; and D4 B6, cart. 111, doss. 7944.

62. This estimate is based on a computation of the declared debts of members of the Paris Book Guild in the accounts of the bankruptcies found in the Archives de Paris, *fonds faillites*.

63. A.N., ser. DIV 30, doss. 728, Committee on the Constitution, "Liberté de la presse, commerce de la librairie, réhabilitation des faillites, fév. 1790–jan. 1791 (7 pièces)," esp. letters from Toulouse decrying the collapse of the book trade and an increase in bankruptcies. See also B.N., mss. fr. 11708, *Procès-verbal des délibérations du Bureau de Paris*, 8 June 1790.

64. B.N., mss. fr. 11708, *Procès-verbal des délibérations du Bureau de Paris*, 8 June 1790.

65. Ibid.

66. The actual documents of these negotiations were removed from the king's *Armoire de Fer* in 1793 by the Committee of Domains and have since been lost. At the

time of their removal, however, the following inventory of their contents was prepared by the committee, still extant in the *Inventaire des papiers saisis aux Tuileries: Armoire de Fer*, A.N., C 183, laisse 107, nos. 384–93.

67. Ibid., nos. 386, 387.

68. Ibid., no. 393.

69. For royal approbation of Nyon's initiation of the timely publication of the *Tableau des droits réels et respectifs du Monarque et de ses sujets, depuis la fondation de la monarchie jusqu'à nos jours, ou théorie des lois politiques de la monarchie française*, see A.N., V1 552, Office of the Book Trade, letter from Nyon, and response, 25 September 1789. This edition ultimately received a royal subsidy.

70. *Révolutions de Paris*, no. 56, 4 August 1790, 172.

71. A.N., AF I, *Procès-verbal du Comité d'Agriculture et du Commerce*, 179th sess., 24 December 1790.

72. Ibid.

73. Ibid.

74. B.N., mss. fr. 21896, *Contributions patriotiques*, entry 34, 24 December 1789.

75. A.P., D4 B6, cart. 110, doss. 7829.

76. A.N., ser. DIX 81, no. 623, "Adresse à l'Assemblée Nationale au nom et par les chargés du pouvoir des Libraires et Imprimeurs propriétaires des privilèges des différentes liturgies de France," 10 January 1791; see also ADVIII 20, *Mémoire présenté à l'Assemblée Nationale au nom des Imprimeurs et Libraires, propriétaires des privilèges des diverses liturgies de France* (Paris: Nyon, 1790).

77. A.N., F17 1008a, doss. 1347; letter from Nyon le jeune, 8 frimaire, an II (29 November 1793).

78. B.N., Nouv. acq. fr. 12684, feuilles 12, 23–24, letter from Pierres, and bibliographic note.

79. A.N., V1, 552, letter from Anisson-Duperron to the Office of the Book Trade, and response re: Baudouin's purview.

80. A.N., BB16 703, doss. 17, May–August 1793, and ADVIII 20, *Pétition des Créanciers-Fournisseurs d'Anisson-Duperron*.

81. A.N., F 17 1199, doss. 1, Temporary Commission on the Arts, 20 germinal, an III (9 April 1795).

82. A.N., F 17 1204, doss. 7, *Mémoire* from Knapen fils, employee in the fourth division of the Ministry of the Interior, n.d. [1800?], to the Committee of Public Instruction.

83. A.N., V1, 553, report of Thiebault, 16 January 1790.

84. A.N., V1, 553, reports of Thiebault, 12 December 1789, 16 January and 11 February 1790.

85. A.N., ser. ADVIII, cart. 20, doc. 2.

86. A.N., V1, 549, doss. from January to February 1789.

87. Robert Darnton, *The Business of Enlightenment: A Publishing History of the "Encyclopédie"* (Cambridge: Harvard University Press, 1979), 481–87.

88. For his negotiations with the Paris Commune, see Lacroix, ed., *Actes de la Commune*, 2:656–57, 671–72; 4:13, 385; and 5:60 (May–June 1790). For a list of some of his *livres embastillés*, see his declaration of bankruptcy, Archives

de Paris, *fonds faillites*, D. 4 B6, cart. 109, doss. 7739, Claude Poinçot, 16 March 1790.

89. Brissot, cited in Hatin, *Histoire politique et littéraire*, 5:22–23.

90. A.N., V1, 553, letter from LeRoy, *libraire*, Paris, 20 October 1789; V1, 553, letter from Valade, *libraire*, Paris, 15 November 1789; V1, 553, letter from Crapart, *libraire;* V1, 553, letter in favor of Langlois fils, *libraire*, Paris, 19 January 1790; Paris, 12 December 1789; Boulard, B.N., nouv. acq. fr., 2666, fol. 6 [1790]; Momoro, cited in *Actes de la Commune*, ed. Lacroix, 1ᵉ sér., 3:16, 340, 574, 719, 768, 771; 4:460; 5:391, 432, 485; 6:99–100, 105, 648, 658; 7:29, 48, 50, 643; 8:621; Plassan, A.N., F18, cart. 11A, plaque 1, letter to the Ministry of the Interior detailing his career since 1789, 28 January 1810; Gillé fils, A.N., F18, cart. 11A, plaque 1, letter from Gillé to the minister of the interior detailing his career since 1789, 11 January 1810; Mérigot l'aîné, cited in *Actes de la Commune*, ed. Lacroix, 1ᵉ sér., 1:386 (25 November 1790). Mérigot l'aîné proposes the establishment of a new printing shop; Guillaume le jeune, A.N., Y 15021, doss. Bossange, 14 February 1790. Guillaume was charged with printing *contrefaçons;* Cussac, A.N., F18, cart. 25, "Notes sur les imprimeurs ci-après désignés," [1811]; Belin, ibid.; Colas, ibid.; DeHansy, ibid.; for information on LeNormant and Dentu, see A.N., F18, cart. 25, "Notes sur les Imprimeurs ci-après désignés" [1811]; for information on the career of Chambon, see A.N., F18, cart. 11A, plaque 1, report from Chambon, printer in Paris, 27 April 1810.

91. See, for example, *Histoire générale de la presse française*, ed. Béllanger et al., 1:434–36.

92. Paul Delalain, *L'Imprimerie et la librairie à Paris de 1789 à 1813* (Paris: Delalain frères [1900]). For the Napoleonic surveys, see A.N., F18, cart. 25. For an extensive discussion of these sources, their strengths and weaknesses, as well as a full presentation of the statistical data, see Carla A. Hesse, "Res Publicata: The Printed Word in Paris, 1789–1810," Ph.D. diss., Princeton University, 1986.

93. See, for example, A.N., C 356, 1883, "Réponse de l'agence de l'envoi des lois aux mémoires et pétitions adressés à la Convention Nationale par plusieurs imprimeurs de Paris sur les prétendus inconvénients et dangers des imprimeries exécutives," n.d. [1795].

94. Béllanger et al., eds., *Histoire générale*, 1:436.

95. Ibid.

96. Ibid., 435.

97. See Delalain, *L'Imprimerie et la librairie*, and A.N., F18, cart. 25, "Notes sur les Imprimeurs ci-après désignés" [1811].

98. Ibid.

99. Ibid.

100. Ibid.

101. See the observations to this effect in A.N., F18, cart. 11A, plaque 1, Bruysset, *libraire*, "Observations," 29 September 1810.

102. B.N., Archives Modernes, CXXIX: "Dépôt légal des livres imprimés, registre 1793, an VII (September 1799)."

103. Robert Estivals, *La Statistique bibliographique de la France sous la monarchie au XVIIIᵉ siècle* (Paris: Mouton & Co., 1965), 415.

104. Ibid.

105. Ibid.

106. Angus Martin, Vivienne G. Milne, and Richard Frautschi, *Bibliographie du genre romanesque français* (Paris: France Expansion, 1977; London: Mansell, 1977), xxxvi–xxxix. New titles for 1794 were 16; for 1795, 41; 1796, 54; 1797, 73; 1798, 96; 1799, 174.

107. See his essay in this volume.

108. See B.N., nouv. acq. fr. 9193, feuille 49. "Collection Ginguené: Compte sommaire des dépenses de la Commission de l'Instruction Publique, an II–IV." Over the course of years II through IV, the Commission of Public Instruction poured more than 2.5 million livres into cultural patronage and extended credit for another 16.25 million livres!

109. Smits and Maradan, Decree of the National Convention, 1ᵉʳ jour complémentaire, an III (17 September 1795); Haubout, A.N., F18 565, 15 ventôse, an IV (5 March 1796); Stoupe and Servière, A.N., F17 1306, doss. 10255, 13 messidor, an III (31 July 1795); Rousseau, B.N., nouv. acq. fr. 9193, feuille 117, 16 brumaire, an III (6 November 1794); Poinçot: A.N., AA 56 (1524), letter from Poinçot fils, *libraire*, to the Corps Législatif, 17 floréal, an VI (6 May 1798). The edition was begun in the Year III (1794–95); Agasse, A.N., F4 2554, doss. 4, 15 thermidor, an III (2 August 1795); Rondonneau: A.N., F4 2554, doss. 3, Rondonneau, Paris, 25 fructidor, an II (11 September 1794); Sciences, A.N., F4 2554, doss. 4, Bernard and Regence, *libraires*, Paris, 13 thermidor, an III (1 August 1795), arithmetics, geometries, and algebras by Bézout; A.N., F4 2554, doss. 4, Barrois l'aîné, *libraire*, Paris, 16 messidor, an II (4 July 1795), works on metrology; A.N., F4 2554, doss. 3, Goujou, *libraire*, Paris, prairial–messidor, an II (May–June 1794), maps and geographical dictionaries.

110. The publishing history of these editions is documented in the correspondence and business records of the publisher Maginel and the printer Loret, both of Paris. See A.N., AQ 24, cart. 26, *papiers privés*, Maginel, *libraire*, doss. "C. Loret, imprimeur à Paris, an VII" (1798–99).

111. A.N., F4 2554, doss. 4, Citoyen Say, *Imprimeur*, Paris, 19 floréal, an III (8 May 1795); F4 2554, Lefebvre, directeur de l'Imprimerie de la *Feuille du Cultivateur*, Paris, 1 fructidor, an III (18 September 1795); F4 2554, doss. 5, Reynier, imprimeur de la *Feuille villageoise*, 30 brumaire, an III (20 November 1795), and 12 frimaire, an III (2 December 1795); F4 2554, Dupont, imprimeur du *Journal des Mines*, 23 messidor, an III (11 July 1795); F4 2554, doss. 4, Goujet-Deslande (*Républicain Français*), 5 messidor, an III (23 June 1795); education, A.N., F4 2554, Dupont, imprimeur, *La Nouvelle Instruction sur les poids et mesures*, 23 messidor, an III (11 July 1795); F4 2554, doss. 4, Bodesère, 28 vendémiaire, an III (19 October 1794).

112. See these names in Delalain, *L'Imprimerie et la librairie*, 6, 15, 68–70, 73, 86, 102, 126, 141.

113. A.N., F18, carton 11A, plaque 1, Lamy, publisher in Paris, 8 May 1810.

114. A.N., F18, carton 11A, plaque 1, Bruysset, "Observations," 29 September 1810.

115. Cited by Hatin, *Histoire de la presse*, 5:24.

Casselle: Printers and Municipal Politics

1. Pierre Casselle, "Imprimeurs et publications des administrations parisiennes, XVIème–XIXème siècle," *Paris et Ile-de-France* 37 (1986): 185–245.

2. Maurice Tourneux, *Bibliographie de l'histoire de Paris pendant la Révolution française*, esp. vol. 2 (Paris: Imprimerie Nouvelle, 1894); André Martin and Gérard Walter, *Catalogue de l'histoire de la Révolution française. Ecrits de la période révolutionnaire*, vol. 4 (Paris: Bibliothèque Nationale, 1955).

3. *Hôtel de Ville. Du 13 juillet 1789, ce jour, lundi . . .* , 4 pp. in-4°, Bibliothèque Nationale, Lb⁴⁰ 1184.

4. The handwritten records of the debates of the City Board, from 1499 to 1782, are kept in the Archives Nationales. The records for 1499 to 1632 were published in the series entitled *Histoire générale de Paris* (Paris: Service des travaux historiques, 1883–1986).

5. Sigismond Lacroix, *Actes de la Commune de Paris pendant la Révolution* (Paris: Quantin, 1894), 1: 1, 121; Tourneux, *Bibliographie de l'histoire*, 2: 37–39. It appears that Lottin had already printed, in July or August 1789, a *Recueil complet de tous les arrêtés, délibérations et autres actes émanés, tant des comités de l'Hôtel de Ville que de l'Assemblée des électeurs* (Tourneux, *Bibliographie de l'histoire*).

6. Lacroix, *Actes de la Commune*, 6: 434, 445; 7: 200.

7. Archives de Paris, VD* 222–23.

8. *Archives parlementaires* (Paris: Paul Dupont, 1893), 43: 593. *Procès-Verbaux de la Commune de Paris, 10 août 1792–1er juin 1793*, ed. Maurice Tourneux (Paris: Société de l'histoire de la Révolution française, 1894), 12, 15.

9. Archives Nationales (hereafter A.N.), F⁷ 4774⁶⁴.

10. Ch.-L. Chassin, *Les Elections et les cahiers de Paris en 1789 . . .* , vol. 2 (Paris: Quantin, 1888), 235; vol. 3 (Paris: Quantin, 1889), 554–56.

11. *Archives parlementaires*, 11: 454.

12. A.N., F⁷ 4774⁶⁴. Patris was called as a witness of the Champs de Mars fusillade at the trial of Jean-Sylvain Bailly, first mayor of Paris, in November 1793 (A.N., W 294 B).

13. Paul Robiquet, *Le Personnel municipal de Paris pendant la Révolution* (Paris: Quantin, 1890), 472.

14. F.-A. Aulard, *La Société des Jacobins* (Paris: Quantin, 1892–), 1: LXVI; 3: 24, 277, 566–70. Patris published his justification, *A Camille Desmoulins* (n.p., n.d.), in-8°, 8 pp., Bibliothèque Nationale, Ln²⁷ 15879.

15. Robiquet, *Personnel municipal*, 486–88.

16. Frédéric Braesch, *Papiers de Chaumette* (Paris: Société de l'histoire de la Révolution française, 1908), 34–38.

17. A.N., F⁷ 4774⁶⁴.

18. Tourneux, *Bibliographie de l'histoire*, 2: 39–41.

19. *Archives parlementaires*, 49: 601; A.N., F⁷ 4774⁶⁴.

20. A.N., F⁷ 4774⁶⁴.

21. Ibid., and F⁷* 2514, 26 September 1793. For Poiret, see Albert Soboul and

Raymonde Monnier, *Répertoire du personnel sectionnaire en l'an II* (Paris: Publications de la Sorbonne, 1985), 508.

22. A.N., F⁷ 4774⁶⁴; F⁷* 2516 (1–4 germinal, an II [21–24 March 1794]); W 126. Albert Soboul, *Les Sans-Culottes parisiens en l'an II*, 2d ed. (Paris: Clavreuil, 1962), 843.

23. *Recueil des actes du Comité de salut public* (Paris: Imprimerie Nationale, 1918), 25:727–28. Martin and Walter, *Catalogue de l'histoire*, vol. IV-2, 13325–29.

24. A.N., F¹⁸ 25 (the same report of the imperial police notes: "Former school master; was charged with sodomy; was going to be prosecuted") F¹⁸ 1808; F¹⁸ 2087ᴬ.

Minard: Agitation in the Work Force

1. Arlette Farge, *La Vie fragile: Violence, pouvoirs et solidarités à Paris au XVIIIème siècle* (Paris: Hachette, 1986), 142, 151; Robert Darnton, *The Great Cat Massacre* (New York: Basic Books, 1984), 78–79; Michael Sonenscher, "Les Sans-culottes de l'an II: repenser le langage du travail dans la France révolutionnaire," *Annales: E.S.C.* 40 (September 1985): 1087–1108.

2. Louis Sébastien Mercier, *Le Tableau de Paris, extraits* (Paris: Maspero/La Découverte, 1982), 317–18.

3. Claude Béllanger et al., eds., *Histoire générale de la presse française* (Paris: Presses universitaires de France, 1969), 1:434–36.

4. David Bellos, "La Conjoncture de la production," and Frédéric Barbier, "L'Economie éditoriale" in *Histoire de l'édition française* (Paris: Promodis, 1984), 2:552, 558. Frédéric Barbier, *Trois Cents Ans de librairie et d'imprimerie: Berger-Levrault, 1676–1830* (Geneva: Droz, 1979), n. 924.

5. Expression quoted in "L'Ancien Régime typographique," *Annales: E.S.C.* 36 (March 1981): 191–209. For an overview, see William Sewell, Jr., *Gens de métier et révolutions. Le langage du travail de l'Ancien Régime à 1848* (Paris: Aubier, 1983).

6. M. D. Fertel, *La Science pratique de l'imprimerie* (Saint-Omer: Fertel, 1723; facs. ed., Gregg International, 1971); *Encyclopédie ou dictionnaire raisonné des sciences, des arts et des métiers* (Paris: Lebreton, 1771–72); L. A. Castillon, *L'Art de l'imprimerie dans sa véritable intelligence* (Paris: Castillon, 1783); *Encyclopédie méthodique*, "Arts et métiers mécaniques" (Paris: Panckoucke, 1784), 3:591–618; M. S. Boulard, *Le Manuel de l'imprimeur* (Paris: Boulard, 1791); A. F. Momoro, *Traité de l'imprimerie* (Paris: Momoro, 1793); Bertrand-Quinquet, *Traité de l'imprimerie* (Paris: Bertrand-Quinquet, 1798); Couret de Villeneuve, "Barême typographique," Bibliothèque Nationale, mss. NAF 4664, 1797–99 (?); Gillé le jeune, *Prospectus d'un nouveau manuel typographique, ou traité des moyens mécaniques qui concourent à la confection physique des livres* (Paris: Gillé, n.d.), 4 pp., Archives Nationales, AD VIII 20.

7. For Benjamin Franklin, see Ronald Clark, *Benjamin Franklin* (Paris: Fayard, 1986); Nicolas Restif de la Bretonne, *Monsieur Nicolas* (Paris, 1794–97; rpt. in 10 vols., Paris, 1883); Nicolas Contat, *Anecdotes typographiques* (1762; Oxford: Oxford Bibliographical Society, 1980), ed. Giles Barber. On the Société typographique de Neuchâtel, see Jacques Rychner, "Running a Printing House in 18th-Century Switzerland: The Workshop of the Société typographique de Neuchâtel," in *The Library*, 6th ser., 1 (1979): 1–24; and Robert Darnton, "A Printing Shop Across the

Border," in *The Literary Underground of the Old Regime,* ed. Robert Darnton (Cambridge: Harvard University Press, 1982).

8. For a detailed account of working conditions in printing shops, see Jacques Rychner, "Le Travail de l'atelier," in *Histoire de l'édition française,* 42–61; and Philippe Minard, *Typographes des Lumières* (Paris: Seyssel, Champ Vallon, forthcoming).

9. Bibliothèque Nationale, mss. Joly de Fleury, 1682, f. 347, report of Chénon, 28 December 1785.

10. Bertrand-Quinquet, *Traité de l'imprimerie,* 49; Momoro, *Traité de l'imprimerie,* 210.

11. Fertel, *La Science pratique,* 263.

12. Ibid., 259.

13. Momoro, *Traité,* 35, 83, 107, 229, 254; Bertrand-Quinquet, *Traité,* 264, 274.

14. Robert Darnton, *L'Aventure de l'Encyclopédie* (Paris: Perrin, 1982), 180–82.

15. Cf. Contat, *Anecdotes typographiques,* and Rychner, "Le Travail de l'atelier."

16. The "monkey" is the compositor who works at the type-cases assembling the letters and setting up the pages; the "bear" works at the press. See Contat, *Anecdotes typographiques,* 33.

17. Boulard, *Le Manuel,* 24. See also Jacques Rychner, "Running a Printing House" as well as "A l'Ombre des Lumières: coup d'oeil sur la main-d'oeuvre de quelques imprimeries au XVIIIème siècle" in *Studies on Voltaire and the Eighteenth Century* 155 (1976): 1925–55.

18. Bertrand-Quinquet, *Traité,* 62–63; Darnton, *Literary Underground,* chap. 5; D. F. McKenzie, "Printers of the Mind: Some Notes on Bibliographical Theories and Printing-house Practices," *Studies in Bibliography* 22 (1969): 1–75; W. B. Todd, "Bibliography and the Editorial Problem in the Eighteenth Century," *Studies in Bibliography* 4 (1951–52): 20–53.

19. Bertrand-Quinquet, *Traité,* 64–65.

20. Bibliothèque Nationale, mss. F.F. 22 188, letter to Anisson, December 1785–April 1786, f. 207–217.

21. Bertrand-Quinquet, *Traité,* 173. See Barbier, "Les innovations technologiques," 545–51.

22. A. G. Camus, *Histoire et procédés du polytypage et de la stéréotypie* (Paris, brumaire, the Year X).

23. Bibliothèque Nationale, mss. F.F. 21861, Archives of the Association of Publishers and Printers, decree of the Council, 9 December 1787.

24. *Journal de Paris,* 1786, 482, 502; Momoro, *Traité,* 293; *Mercure de France,* 25 March 1786; *Journal polytype des Sciences et des Arts,* 1786, no. VII, 129.

25. Camus, *Histoire et procédés,* 90–115.

26. J.G.A. Stoupe, *Réflexions d'un ancien prote d'imprimerie sur un prospectus ayant pour titre "éditions stéréotypes"* (Paris, Year VII), 12 pp.; see also Paul Dupont, *Histoire de l'imprimerie* (Paris: Dupont, 1854), 422.

27. *Description d'une nouvelle presse exécutée pour le service du Roi et publiée par ordre du gouvernement* (Paris: Imprimerie royale, 1783), Bibliothèque Nationale, mss. F.F. 22188, with ms. note by Anisson le jeune, f. 24–25.

28. Momoro, *Traité,* 281; Boulard, *Le Manuel,* 43; Bertrand-Quinquet, *Traité,* 100.

29. Ph.-D. Pierres, *Description d'une nouvelle presse d'imprimerie* (Paris: Pierres, 1786), 26–33.

30. Wilhelm Haas, *Beschreibung und Abrisse einer neuen Buchdruckerpresse erfunden in Basel, 1772* (Basel: 1790).

31. Barbier, "Les Innovations technologiques," 551.

32. Rychner, "Running a Printing House," and Darnton, "Printing Shop Across the Border."

33. Grangé, *Mémoire présenté à l'Assemblée Nationale pour le corps des Libraires et Imprimeurs de l'Université de Paris* (Paris, 1790), 4, Bibliothèque Nationale Q 6574; Bertrand-Quinquet, *Traité*, 258.

34. *Mémoire des imprimeurs contre les imprimeries officielles*, c. 22 pluviôse, Year III (1795), Bibliothèque Nationale, Reserve F. 719.

35. Archives Nationales, AD VIII 20, Report of 16 floréal, Year V (1797), 20 pp.; *Almanach du commerce de Paris*, Year VII (1798–1799); Bibliothèque Nationale V 27655; *Almanach typographique*, Year VIII (1799–1800), Bibliothèque Nationale, Reserve p. Q739. Jacob l'aîné in 1806 put forward a figure of eight hundred shops (*Idées générales des causes de l'anéantissement de l'imprimerie* [Orléans, June 1806], Bibliothèque Nationale, Reserve F 719) in the early years of the Revolution. In 1806 there remained only ninety-five, and in 1810 a decree dated 5 February limited the number of printing shops in Paris to sixty; the figure was raised to eighty on 11 February 1811.

36. Grangé, *Mémoire*.

37. Archives Nationales, T 546(1), Royou-Fréron papers, bill of the cabinet-maker Lafond for a press, 8 February 1791; Bibliothèque Nationale, mss. F.F. 22066, "Prix d'une petite imprimerie," April 1765; Boulard, *Le Manuel*, 91–93.

38. Bibliothèque Nationale, mss. F.F. 21819, f. 66–68, 6 June 1743.

39. *Club typographique et philanthropique* (Paris), 30, 24 May 1791, 240.

40. Bertrand-Quinquet, *Traité*, 109.

41. Couret de Villeneuve, *Barême typographique*, 8–9.

42. Robert Darnton, "L'Imprimerie de Panckoucke en l'an II," *Revue française d'histoire du livre*, no. 23 (1979): 359–69; F. A. Duprat, *Histoire de l'Imprimerie Impériale de Paris* (Paris: Duprat, 1861).

43. Honoré de Balzac, *Les Illusions perdues*, rpt. (Paris, 1982), 29–39; Jules Michelet, *Ma jeunesse* (Paris, 1884), 24.

44. *Encyclopédie méthodique, Manufactures*, 3: xxii; *Mercure de France*, "Sur l'Etat actuel de l'imprimerie, lettre de M. Panckoucke à MM. les libraires et imprimeurs de la capitale," 6 March 1790, quoted by Robert Darnton in "L'Imprimerie de Panckoucke."

45. Grangé, *Mémoire*, 5; Momoro, *Traité*, 211. Boulard advises against ever giving raises, "especially since the Revolution, since there is now no means of penalizing the worker who does not act in good faith. True, he can perhaps be barred from working in Paris, but he is free to go to the provinces, where there is at present a shortage of workers; or he may even find employment with a clandestine printer, and there is no way of preventing this." Boulard, *Le Manuel*, 96, 124; Bertrand-Quinquet, *Traité*.

46. Biliothèque Nationale, ms. F.F. 22123, F°208–217; Boulard, *Le Manuel*, 59,

68–73; Paul Chauvet, *Les Ouvriers du livre en France de la Révolution à nos jours* (Paris: Presses universitaires de France, 1956), chap. 1; Louis Radiguer, *Maîtres imprimeurs et ouvriers typographes* (Paris: Rousseau, 1903), 141–63.

47. *Orateur du peuple* no. 43, 1790, Bibliothèque Nationale, 8° Lc² 390; *Confédération nationale, ou récit exact et circonstancié de ce qui s'est passé à Paris le 14 juillet 1790*, 5, Bibliothèque Nationale LB³⁹ 3767.

48. British Museum, brochure R 379; cf. Chauvet, *Les Ouvriers du livre*, which gives the text on pp. 637–43, and Haïm Burstin, *Le Faubourg Saint-Marcel à l'époque révolutionnaire* (Paris: Société d'études robespierristes, 1983).

49. Bibliothèque Nationale, 8° Lc² 2438.

50. Bibliothèque Nationale, Ms. F.F. 21861, 20 August 1788.

51. Chauvet, *Les Ouvriers du livre*.

52. Bibliothèque Nationale, mss. F.F. 21861, 9 and 10 May 1790.

53. On the "Encyclopedic Assembly," see Bibliothèque Nationale, mss. NAF 2654, 7 January 1791: "Comprising all the artists, proprietors, workmen and suppliers met in session at the Grands Augustins," this "Assembly" denounced the organization of the workers in a "Typographical Society" in the following terms:

> They issue decrees such as these: that no workman in a Paris printing house may undertake a task for lower pay than that arbitrarily determined for another worker who has already begun it . . . that any worker who agrees to such lower rates shall be forbidden by the Society to continue with the task; that if he ignore this prohibition, the other workers shall hold no communication with him; that if he remain unmoved by this further rebuke, they shall threaten to lie in wait for him on a street corner. . . .

For the complaint of April 1791, see *Club typographique* 25 (19 April 1791), which reproduces the following letter: "Sir, I am advised that there is, on the rue de la Huchette, an association of printers, whose Committee meets on Tuesdays and Fridays; that the members of this Committee enter into printing houses, to compel the workers to leave their employment if they are working for lower wages than those they have fixed."

54. Archives Nationales, AD VIII 20, 1790; such claims may be found in the *Club typographique*, notably nos. 1 and 7.

55. Archives Nationales, AD VIII 20, *Discours prononcé le 10 août 1790 à la Fête célébrée en l'honneur de Benjamin Franklin par la Société des ouvriers imprimeurs de Paris;* cf. also *Club typographique* 3, 15 November 1790.

56. *Club typographique* 9, 28 December 1790, 70.

57. *Club typographique* 6, 6 December 1790, 43. On the climate of opinion among the workers, William Sewell, Jr., delivers an ill-judged polemic (based on a misinterpretation) against Albert Soboul: Sewell, *Gens de métier,* 155–58. In contrast, Michael Sonenscher offers some pointed criticism of the way in which Soboul, like George Rudé, has taken revolutionary rhetoric at its face value, resulting in a confusing picture of the shop floor: see Sonenscher, "Sans-culottes," and "Journeymen, the Courts and the French Trades, 1781–1791," *Past and Present* 114 (February 1987): 77–109.

58. Archives Nationales, C 177, 24 November 1791; AD VIII 20, various items from Year II (1793–94) and Year III (1794–95) C 356, file 1883; F 7 4646/3, report

on Citizen Chevalier, who tried to settle a strike on 12 messidor, Year III (30 June 1795).

Vernus: A Provincial Perspective

1. On the printing establishments and the bookshops of Franche-Comté, see Michel Vernus, *La Vie comtoise au temps de l'Ancien Régime,* vol. 2 (Lons-le-Saunier: Marque-Maillard, 1985), chap. 10, and Vernus, "Une page de l'histoire du livre dans le Jura, les Tonnet imprimeurs libraires," *Revue française d'histoire du livre* 27 (1980): 271–95.

2. Vernus, *La Vie comtoise,* vol. 2, chap. 8.

3. Michel Vernus, "Les Sires de Salins, ouvrage de l'abbé Guillaume," *Le Jura français* 176 (1982): 1–5.

4. Robert Darnton, *The Business of Enlightenment: A Publishing History of the "Encyclopédie," 1775–1800* (Cambridge: Harvard University Press, 1970).

5. Michel Vernus, "Le Livre à Dole aux XVIIe et XVIIIe siècles," in *L'Histoire du livre en Franche-Comté* (Dole: La Nouvelle Revue Franc-comtoise, 1984), 121–57; as well as Paul-Marie Grinevald, "Essai sur les bibliothèques privées de Besançon" (Thèse de doctorat de troisième cycle, Université de Paris, I, 1981).

6. Quoted in *La Vie comtoise,* chap. 9., 190–97.

7. Bibliothèque municipale de Besançon, Périod. 6210.

8. Maurice Gresset, *Gens de justice à Besançon, 1674–1789* (Paris: Bibliothèque nationale, 1978).

9. Michel Vernus, "La Lecture des romans dans le Jura au XVIIIe siècle," *La Revue française d'histoire du livre* (forthcoming).

10. Archives du département du Jura, C 957.

11. According to Louis Maggiolo, *Statistique de l'enseignement primaire* (Paris: Imprimerie Nationale, 1880), the following are the percentages of husbands and wives in 1789 who knew how to sign their names:

Department	Husbands	Wives
Jura	88.88	24.77
Doubs	80.71	39.65
Average for the whole of France	47.05	24.87

12. Michel Vernus, "La Diffusion du livre de piété et de la bimbeloterie religieuse," *Actes du 105e congrès des sociétés savantes* (Paris: Comité des travaux historiques et scientifiques, 1980), vol. 1, Histoire moderne, 127–41.

13. J.-B. Bergier, *Histoire de la communauté des prêtres missionnaires de Beaupré* (Besançon: Cyprien Monnot, 1853).

14. Bibliothèque Nationale, Ms. fr. 22019.

15. Michel Vernus, *Le Presbytère et la chaumière* (Cromary: Togirisc, 1986).

16. Michel Vernus, "Les Marchands merciers, pionniers de la diffusion du livre," in *Histoire du livre en Franche-Comté* (Dole: Nouvelle Revue Franc-comtoise, 1984), 153–60.

17. Archives du département du Doubs, 1 C 1284.

18. Ibid., L 53 ff.

19. Michel Vernus, "Le livre et la lecture dans la région de Lons-le-Saunier du XVIIᵉ siècle à 1850," *Travaux de la Société d'émulation du Jura*, 1987.

20. Archives du département du Jura, L 1237 and 1 J 196.

21. Ibid., L 870.

22. Ibid., L 128.

23. Ibid., vol. 2, L 870.

24. Jules Sauzay, *Histoire de la persécution révolutionnaire dans le département du Doubs de 1789 à 1801*, vol. 2 (Besançon: Turbergue, 1867).

25. Sauzay, *Histoire de la persécution*, vol. 2.

26. Archives du département du Doubs, L 1305.

27. Ibid., L 1305.

28. Sauzay, *Histoire de la persécution*, vol. 2.

29. Archives du département du Doubs, délibérations du conseil du département, L 56.

30. See, for example, Archives du département du Doubs, L 72 (21 March 1796).

31. Vernus, *La Vie comtoise*, vol. 1, chap. 3.

32. Sauzay, *Histoire de la persécution*, vol. 2.

33. Henri Libois, "Extraits des délibérations de la société populaire de Lons-le-Saunier," in *Société d'émulation du Jura, 1895–1896*, 207 ff.

34. Archives du département du Jura, L 128.

35. Archives du département du Doubs, L 1296.

36. J.-M. Lequinio, *Voyage pittoresque et physio-économique dans le Jura* (Paris, 1801; Marseille: Lafitte reprints, 1979).

37. Archives du département du Doubs, L 2673.

38. Ibid., L 1662.

Popkin: Journals

1. *Patriote françois*, 30 July 1789.

2. The most recent overall survey of the French press during the revolutionary era is Jacques Godechot, "La Presse française sous la Révolution et l'Empire," in *Histoire générale de la presse française*, ed. Claude Béllanger et al. (Paris: Presses universitaires de France, 1969), 1:403–567, which includes a comprehensive bibliography. There have been a number of recent monographs on various aspects of the revolutionary press. Among the most important are Jack R. Censer, *Prelude to Power* (Baltimore: Johns Hopkins University Press, 1976); Jeremy D. Popkin, *The Right-Wing Press in France, 1792–1800* (Chapel Hill: University of North Carolina Press, 1980), Jean-Paul Bertaud, *Les Amis du Roi* (Paris: Perrin, 1984), Gary Kates, *The 'Cercle Social,' the Girondins, and the French Revolution* (Princeton: Princeton University Press, 1985), and William J. Murray, *The Right-Wing Press in the French Revolution: 1789–92* (London: Royal Historical Society, 1986).

3. Pierre Rétat, "Forme et discours d'un journal révolutionnaire," in *L'Instrument périodique*, ed. Claude Labrosse and Pierre Rétat (Lyon: Presses Universitaires de Lyon, 1985), 142.

4. J. P. Brissot de Warville, *Mémoire aux Etats-Généraux: Sur la nécessité de rendre dès ce moment la presse libre, et surtout pour les journaux politiques* (Paris, 1789), 10. On the importance of the notion of public debate and the sovereignty of public opinion in eighteenth-century political thought, see the fundamental work of Jürgen Habermas, *Strukturwandel der Öffentlichkeit* (Neuwied: Luchterhand, 1962).

5. Pierre Rétat, "La diffusion du journal en France en 1789," in *La diffusion et la lecture des journaux de langue française sous l'ancien régime*, ed. Hans Bots (Nijmegen: forthcoming). The pressruns of the most successful daily newspapers during the Revolution seem to have been in the neighborhood of ten thousand to fifteen thousand. A few nondailies, such as Hébert's *Père Duchesne*, lavishly subsidized by the authorities in 1793, may have had higher pressruns, at least for some issues.

6. M. S. Boulard, *Le Manuel de l'Imprimeur* (Paris: Boulard, 1791), 59, 91–92.

7. Robert Darnton, "L'Imprimerie de Panckoucke en l'An II," *Revue française d'histoire du livre* 9 (1979): 365.

8. P.-A. Dumont-Pigalle to J. Valckenaer, letter of 21 August 1792, in Leiden University Library, ms. 1031(I); report of police commissioners, sec. Théâtre-français, 9 March 1793, in Bibliothèque historique de la Ville de Paris, ms. 749, no. 100; William J. Murray, "The Rightwing Press in the French Revolution, 1789–92" (Ph.D. diss., Australian National University, 1972), 330.

9. *Gazette universelle*, 6 January 1790.

10. "Sur l'état actuel de l'imprimerie," in *Mercure de France*, 6 March 1790.

11. *Courrier républicain*, 16 thermidor, an III (3 August 1795).

12. Béllanger et al., eds., *Histoire générale*, 3:141.

13. Ibid., 1:436.

14. A police list from early 1798 gives 107 Paris papers. In addition, there were fifty to sixty papers published in the provinces at any one time. Archives Nationales, F 7 3448B.

15. Prospectuses for Vaufleury's *Cabinet littéraire national* and Varin's *Chambre patriotique et littéraire*, both 1791, in Newberry Library, French Revolution Collection.

16. Michael Kennedy, *The Jacobin Clubs in the French Revolution* (Princeton: Princeton University Press, 1982), appendix E.

17. Stanley Morison, *The English Newspaper* (Cambridge, 1932), 184–85.

18. Panckoucke, "Sur les journaux et papiers anglois," in *Mercure de France*, 30 January 1790.

19. Rétat, "Forme et discours," 141–42.

20. Prospectus, *Journal logographique* (n.d. [1790]).

21. *Journal de Perlet*, 22 messidor, l'an III (10 July 1795).

22. Jeremy D. Popkin, "The Pre-Revolutionary Origins of French Political Journalism," in *The French Revolution and the Creation of Modern Political Culture*, ed. Keith Baker (Oxford: Oxford University Press, 1987).

23. Charles Lacretelle, *Dix années d'épreuves pendant la Révolution* (Paris: Allouard, 1842), 30–31.

24. Prospectus, *Journal Logographique* (n.d. [late 1790]).

25. "Avis" to "Discours préliminaire," (n.d. [October 1789]) in *Journal des Décrets de l'Assemblée nationale, pour les habitans des Campagnes*, vol. 1.

26. *Feuille villageoise*, 7 April 1791.

27. Ibid., 20 December 1792.

28. Melvin Edelstein, *La Feuille villageoise: Communication et modernisation dans les régions rurales pendant la Révolution* (Paris: Bibliothèque Nationale, 1977), 68.

29. *Patriote françois*, 28 July 1789.

30. Ibid., 1 August 1789.

31. Ibid., 5 September 1789.

32. *Publiciste parisien* (initial title of *Ami du peuple*), 13 September 1789.

33. Ibid., 12 September 1789.

34. *Ami du peuple*, 22 November 1789; 3 May 1792.

35. *Ami du roi*, 1 June 1790.

36. *Actes des apôtres*, vol. 1, no. 11.

37. J.-B. Louvet, *Discours sur la nécessité de mettre actuellement à exécution l'article 355 de la Constitution, en ce qui concerne la presse* (Paris: Imprimerie Nationale, 1796), 5–6.

Baecque: Pamphlets

1. Christian Jouhaud, *Mazarinades: La fronde des mots* (Paris: Aubier, 1983).

2. Vincent Milliot, "Les 'Cris révolutionnaires': mots d'ordre et réflexion politique dans les titres de la littérature pamphlétaire de 1788 à 1800" (Paper presented at the colloquium on Books and the Revolution, Bibliothèque Nationale [hereafter B.N.], May 1987 [proceedings to be published]).

3. *La Restauration de l'Etat* (n.p., n.d., but identified as 1789), B.N., Lb (39) 1301.

4. Raoul Girardet, *Mythes et mythologies politiques* (Paris: Le Seuil, 1986).

5. Robert Darnton, *Bohème littéraire et Révolution. Le monde des livres au XVIIIème siècle* (Le Seuil / Hautes Etudes, 1983).

6. *Les Tableaux de moeurs du temps aux différents âges de la vie* (Amsterdam, n.d.), B.N., Enfer (306).

7. *Art de foutre en quarante manières, ou la science pratique des filles du monde* (Amsterdam, 1789), B.N., Enfer (154).

8. *Les Amours de Charlot et Toinette* (n.p., n.d.), B.N., Enfer (145).

9. *Bordel apostolique institué par Pie VI en faveur du clergé de France* (Paris, 1791). B.N., Enfer (602).

10. *Requête et décret en faveur des putains, des fouteuses, des macquerelles et des branleuses: contre les bougres, les bardaches et les brûleurs de paillasse* (Gamahuchons, Second Year of the Copulatory Regeneration), B.N., Enfer (762).

11. *Bordel apostolique*.

12. Antoine de Baecque, "Les Soldats de papier. La Figure du soldat de l'armée émigrée dans la caricature révolutionnaire," *Les Nouvelles de l'estampe. Revue de la Bibliothèque Nationale* (January–February 1988).

13. *Les Délices de Coblentz, ou anecdotes libertines sur les émigrés français* (n.p., 1791). B.N., Enfer (1428).

14. Ibid.

15. Ibid.

16. Mlle Théroigne, *Catéchisme libertin à l'usage des filles de joie, et des jeunes demoiselles qui se décident à embrasser la profession* (Paris, 1792), B.N., Enfer (51).

17. There were very many projects, dating from the end of the eighteenth century, for organizing prostitution. The best-known is still *Le Pornographe* by Restif de la Bretonne, but the genre also influenced Sade: "There will, then, be places set aside for immorality under the protection of the government" (*Les instituteurs immoraux—Français, encore un effort* . . . [Editions U.G.E.], 237). See also E.-M. Benabou, *La Prostitution et la police des moeurs au XVIIIème siècle* (Paris: Perrin, 1987).

18. *Catéchisme libertin.*

19. *Bordel national à l'usage des confédérés provinciaux* (Cythera, 1790), B.N., Enfer (603).

20. *Requête et décret.*

21. *L'Echo foutromane, ou recueil de plusieurs scènes lubriques* (Démocratis, 1792), B.N., Enfer (70).

22. *Bordel patriotique pour le plaisir des députés à la nouvelle législature* (At the Tuileries, n.d.), B.N., Enfer (604).

23. *L'Echo foutromane.*

Dhombres: Books

1. "Every day the Committee of Public Safety stands in need of much material on physics, mechanics, etc. The need of the hour is for the Proceedings of the Royal Society in London." (Archives nationales, F^{17}, case 1306, quoted by G. Pouchet, *Les sciences pendant la Terreur* [Paris: Société de l'histoire de France, 1896]). On 25 floréal, the Year II (14 May 1794) the Commission for the Arts arranged for the completion of the committee's scientific library. A year later, following a similar request on 17 pluviôse (15 February) (Archives Nationales, F^{17}, case 1319), the Arts Commission had within three days dispatched "as quickly as possible to the information office of the Committee of Public Safety a complete set of the fourth edition of Fourcroy's *Eléments d'histoire naturelle et de chimie*" (cf. L. Tuetey, *Procès-verbaux de la Commission temporaire des arts*, 3 vols. [Paris: 1912]).

2. Related by E. de las Casas in his *Mémorial de Sainte-Hélène*, published two years after Napoleon's death. Attacks on Bernardin de Saint-Pierre were frequent; see, for example, a virulent attack by J. B. Biot, a physicist of some fame, in the *Mercure de France* 39 (December 1809): 393–407, or bitter remarks by P. J. Lancelin, Stendhal's professor of philosophy in Grenoble, in his *Introduction à l'analyse des sciences*, vol. 5 (Paris: Bossange, Masson, Besson, an IX [1801–1802]), 195.

3. For statistical sources, please refer to n. 5 below; the figures are all drawn from *Journal général de la littérature de France, ou répertoire méthodique* (Paris: Treuttel & Würtz, Year VII [1798–1799]).

4. We are speaking here only of titles, not of the size of their impressions. No

account is taken of the length of the works, nor are we concerned with daily or weekly periodicals.

5. For production of books in general during the eighteenth century, see R. Estivals, *La statistique bibliographique de la France sous la monarchie au XVIIIème siècle* (Paris: Mouton, 1965) and F. Furet, "'la librairie' du royaume de France au 18ième siècle," in *Livre et société dans la France du XVIIIème siècle*, ed. François Furet (Paris: Mouton, 1975), 1–32. See also Delalain, *L'Imprimerie et la librairie à Paris, 1789–1813*. For production of scientific books between 1798 and 1825, see Jean Dhombres, "French Mathematical Books from Bézout to Cauchy," in *Historia Scientiarum* 28 (1985):91–137. The universe for this latter study was provided by booksellers' advertising leaflets, rather than by the depository-library lists furnished in the abovementioned work by Estivals. The reason for this choice is self-evident: unlike the lists, booksellers' and publishers' advertising breaks titles down into categories. But we will not make use of such sources here as there is no way for the moment of comparing the two sources. The data for the years 1790–97 are still to be collected—the most important statistical shortcoming of the present chapter.

6. This figure was empirically deduced from the statistical material in Furet, "'la librairie.'" We had to average the percentage given in the sciences for the years 1786–88 and concerning some kinds of books (public permissions) with the other percentages for 1780–89 (tacit permissions). In his *Literary Underground of the Old Regime*, R. C. Darnton used a lower estimate (8 percent), which reinforces our picture of a large scientific production after 1797.

7. See Dhombres, "Mathématisation et communauté scientifique française, 1775–1825," in *Archives Internationales d'histoire des sciences* 36 (December 1986):249–93.

8. After *Journal général de la littérature de France ou répertoire méthodique* (Paris: Treuttel & Würtz, Year VII [1798–1799]).

9. Jean Dhombres and Nicole Dhombres, *Sciences, idéologies et pouvoirs de la Révolution à la Restauration* (Paris: Payot, 1988).

10. Publisher's description of the work in *Journal général*.

11. On syphilis and the treatments for it, see L. Fleck's remarkable *Entstehung und Entwicklung einer wissenschaftlichen Tatsache, Einführung in die Lehre von Denkstil und Denkkollektiv* (Basel, 1935; English trans., University of Chicago Press, 1979).

12. *Mémoire de F. A. Mesmer sur ses découvertes*, 130 pp. (Paris: Fuchs, Year VII).

13. Chaussier, *Table synoptique du plan général . . . du cours d'anatomie* (Paris: Barois); *Tableau synoptique des propriétés caractéristiques et des principaux problèmes de la force vitale*, (Paris: Barois, Year VII [1798–99]).

14. Paris: Croullebois, Year VII [1798–99], 70 pp.

15. Foucault, *Naissance de la clinique* (Paris: Presses Universitaires de France, 1963).

16. The *Flore Françoise* first appeared in 1779 in three volumes. The concern here was a new method of identifying plants, different from both Linnaeus's artificial system and the allegedly "natural" system put forward by Jussieu and Adanson. The book enjoyed great popularity.

17. The *Encyclopédie méthodique* is studied in Robert Darnton, *L'Aventure de l'Encyclopédie*, French trans. (Paris: Librairie Perrin, 1979), 295–341.

18. By A. P. Ventenat, 4 vols., published by Fuchs at twenty-four francs.

19. *Journal typographique et bibliographique* 47, second year (1799):369 (Paris: Roux).

20. "Séances des écoles normales recueillies par des sténographes et revues par les professeurs" (Paris: Régnier, Year III [1793–94]), 1:391.

21. Edition from the Year VII of *Mécanique Céleste*, 1:30.

22. *Oeuvres de Condillac*, 23 vols. (Paris: Batillot frères, beginning in Year VII [1798–99]).

23. A posthumous work at an elementary level, *La langue des calculs* (Paris: C. Houel, Year VI [1797–98]); octavo, 484 pp. A critical edition recently appeared, by S. Auroux and A. M. Chouillet, *La langue des calculs de Condillac* (Lille: Presses de l'Université de Lille, 1980).

24. *La Langue des calculs,* 226.

25. *Journal typographique* 47 (1799):369.

26. Gudin, *L'Astronomie, poème en trois chants* (Auxerre: L. Fournier, Year IX [1801–2]).

27. See, for example, the differential proof offered by Laplace (pp. 6–9, 1st ed.) on the composition of mechanical forces. It is analyzed in J. Dhombres, "Quelques aspects de l'histoire des équations fonctionnelles liés à l'évolution du concept de fonction," *Archive for History of Exact Sciences* 36 (1986):91–181.

28. There were three English translations of *Mécanique Céleste*. The one by N. Bowditch, 4 vols. (Boston, 1829–39), is enriched with commentary (the fifth vol. of Laplace was not translated). A German translation of vols. 1 and 2 appeared as *Mechanik des Himmels* (Berlin, 1800–02).

29. P.-S. Laplace, *Exposition du système du Monde* (Paris, Year IV [1794–95]).

30. S. F. Lacroix, *Essai sur l'enseignement en général et celui des mathématiques en particulier* (Paris: Courcier, 1805).

31. F. Berkeley, *The Analyst, or a discourse addressed to an infidel mathematician* (London: J. Tonson, 1734).

32. This quotation is most probably apocryphal. Arago, that eulogist of the learned, claimed to have found it on the flyleaf of a mathematics handbook by Garnier. See F. Arago, *Histoire de ma jeunesse* in *Oeuvres complètes* (Paris: Baudry, 1854) 1:5.

33. Foreword, *Réflexions sur la métaphysique du calcul infinitésimal* (Paris: Duprat, Year VII [1798–99]), octavo.

34. *Introductio in analysin infinitorum* (Lausanne: Bousquet, 1748); French trans. by J. B. Labey, *Introduction à l'analyse infinitésimale* (Paris, 1797). Another French translation had appeared some years before, proof (if it were needed) of the wide use made of the work for instruction in analysis. Euler's Latin original partook of the nature of a textbook and did credit to the category.

35. From the text of the book; a second edition appeared in 1813.

36. A. L. Cauchy, *Cours d'analyse de l'Ecole royale polytechnique, Analyse Algébrique* (Paris: de Bure, 1821).

37. M. J. Brisson brought out a second edition of his *Traité élémentaire, ou principes de physique fondés sur les connaissances les plus certaines tant anciennes que modernes et confirmés par l'expérience*, 3 vols. (Paris, Year III [1794–95]).

38. The point is made in a recent study by D. Roncin, "Mise en application du

système métrique (7 avril 1795–4 juillet 1837)," *Cahiers de métrologie* 2 (Paris: Institut d'Histoire Moderne et Contemporaine, CNRS).

39. Translations from the Latin suggest the increasing disuse of that language; in Year V (1796–97) Baudeux translated Newton's *Arithmetica Universalis*, first published by W. Whisten (Cambridge) in 1707 from the manuscript of Newton's lectures.

40. Pelletier, Brasdor, and Biron, "Rapport fait à la Société de Médecine de Paris, pluviôse, an X [January–February, 1803], sur l'application des nouveaux Poids et Mesures dans les usages de la médecine" (Paris: Imprimerie des sourds-muets, Year X [1803]).

41. Dhombres and Dhombres, *Sciences, Idéologies et Pouvoirs*.

42. Guyton de Morveau, Berthollet and Fourcroy, with, naturally, the master hand of Lavoisier, had published their *Méthode de nomenclature chimique* in 1787, with "a new system of chemical symbols adapted to the nomenclature" by Messrs. Hassenfratz and Adet (Paris: Cuchet, 1787), octavo, 314 pp. with 5 plates.

43. *Décade philosophique* for the ten days beginning 20 brumaire, Year VI (Friday, 10 November 1797): 1–10.

44. Lacroix, *Essai sur l'enseignement*.

45. *La genèse de la science des cristaux* (Paris: Alcan, 1918; facsimile ed., Paris: Blanchard, 1969), 206.

46. L. S. Mercier, *Satires contre les astronomes* (Paris: Terrelongue, Year VII [1798–1799]).

47. Chateaubriand, *Le Génie du Christianisme* (Paris, 1802).

48. "Rapport sur la situation de l'Ecole polytechnique, présenté au ministère de l'intérieur par le Conseil de perfectionnement (an IX [1801–2])." Quoted by Jean Dhombres in *Histoire de l'Ecole Polytechnique*, ed. A. Fourcy (Paris: Belin, 1986), p. 98 of the notes.

49. On 10 brumaire, Year VII (October 31, 1798), Duprat published S. F. Lacroix's *Cours de mathématiques à l'usage de l'Ecole centrale des Quatre Nations*, 4 vols. Later expanded to seven volumes (to be had separately), it went through several editions.

50. In Year IX (1801–2) Coucier brought out "the Bézout" in seven volumes in a new edition by Garnier. He had already edited Bézout's *Mécanique* (the section containing differential calculus), published by Duprat in two volumes on 25 vendémiaire, Year VIII (October 16, 1799). On 25 pluviôse (February 13, 1800) Louis released an adaptation by Peyrard of the *Algèbre* section of Bézout's courses.

51. Report by Fourcroy to the Convention, 7 vendémiaire, an III (28 September 1794), and draft of a decree for the establishment of L'Ecole Centrale for public works, issued by the National Convention on 25 ventôse (March 15, 1793). (Paris: Imprimerie du Comité de salut public, 1794).

52. Ibid., 3, 4.

53. The dissertation by C. Richard, *Le Comité de salut public et les fabrications de guerre sous la Terreur* (Paris: F. Rieder, 1921), is still the best source.

54. J. B. Biot, *Essai sur l'histoire des sciences pendant la Révolution française* (Paris: Duprat, 1803).

55. Published in Tours, 1794.

56. Paul Dimoff, ed., *Oeuvres complètes de André Chénier*, vol. 2 (Paris: Delagrave, 1922), 71.

57. Dimoff, ed., *Oeuvres complètes*.

Andries: Almanacs

1. Quoted by John Grand-Carteret, *Les Almanachs français (1600–1895)* (Paris: Alisie et lie, 1896), xxii.

2. The almanacs in question are those preserved in public collections. In André Martin and Gérard Walter, *Catalogue de l'histoire de la Révolution française* (Paris: éditions des Bibliothèques nationales, 1936), Martin lists 389 titles of almanacs and annuals of the Revolution preserved in the Bibliothèque Nationale. This list has served as the basis for my study, and all the books listed have been consulted. The estimate given below, that 73 percent of the almanacs from 1793 to 1796 were political in character, is based on this list. I completed my research by studying the revolutionary almanacs in the collections of the Bibliothèque Historique de la Ville de Paris, the Bibliothèque du Musée des Arts et Traditions Populaires, and the Bibliothèque Municipale de Troyes.

3. Emile Socard, "Etudes sur les almanachs et les calendriers de Troyes, 1497–1881," *Mémoires de la société académique des sciences, arts et belles-lettres de l'Aube* 18, (3d ser., 1881), 326–35.

4. *Chronique de Paris*, no. 276 (24 September 1792). I wish to thank H. J. Lüsebrink for having called my attention to this text.

5. *Almanach républicain* by Henri Blanc and P.F.X. Bouchard, *Almanach des républicains* (Paris: Sylvain Maréchal, 1793).

6. See Christian Jouhaud, *Mazarinades: La Fronde des mots* (Paris: Aubier, 1985), 87: "Mr. Petit . . . has sown many elements of dangerous vanity, as if they meant the ruin of royalty and the subversion of the state. . . . The Cardinal de Retz, the co-assistant of Paris, was an associate of the aforementioned Petit." (Jean Petit was an old editor of almanacs in Troyes.)

7. See n. 2 for a discussion of these figures.

8. Société populaire de l'Harmonie Sociale. Quoted by Albert Soboul in *Paysans, Sans-Culottes et Jacobins* (Paris: Clavreuil, 1966), 220.

9. J. R. Hébert, *A mes concitoyens*, 27 May, the Year II (1793).

10. According to this law, "All those are considered suspect who in their writings have shown themselves to be partisans of tyranny, federalism, or enemies of society."

11. I have drawn this Paris report from the police archives of the revolutionary sections, which have been preserved in the Archives historiques de la Préfecture de police.

12. Quoted by Soboul, *Paysans, Sans-Culottes*, 215.

13. Archives de police, AA 80, piece 66, prairial, the Year II (May–June 1794).

14. Henri Wallon, *Histoire du Tribunal révolutionnaire de Paris avec le journal de ses actes*, 6 vols. (Paris: Hachette, 1880), 4:185–86.

15. C. Pierre, *Les Hymnes et chansons de la Révolution* (Paris: Imprimerie Nationale, 1904), 3 ff.

16. Archives de police, AA 240, piece 159. Section du Temple. Search of the premises of the citizens Aubert.

17. A copy of the letter written by the citizen Couroux-Cluseaus to citizen Dameron, deputy to the National Convention, Donzy, 11 pluviôse, the Year II (January–February 1794), Bibliothèque Nationale, Lb⁴¹ 3760.

18. M. A. Edelstein, *La Feuille villageoise, Communication et modernisation dans les régions rurales pendant la Révolution* (Paris: Publications de la Bibliothèque Nationale, 1977).

19. Archives Nationales F¹⁷, Département des Landes, 28 vendémiaire, the Year VII (September–October 1798), kindly brought to my attention by Martine Sonnet.

20. See Bronislaw Baczko, "Le Calendrier républicain," in *Les Lieux de mémoire*, ed. Pierre Nora (Paris: Gallimard, 1984), vol. 1.

21. Romme, *Rapport sur l'ère de la République* (séance du 10 septembre 1793), Imprimerie Nationale, 2.

22. Ibid., 5.

Reichardt: Prints

This essay has grown out of research in progress on the political and social imagery of the "Bastille" in France and Germany from 1715 to about 1900. This research is being done in collaboration with Hans-Jürgen Lüsebrink and with the support of the Volkswagen Foundation.

1. Bibliothèque Nationale, Département des Estampes. François-Louis Bruel et al., *Un siècle d'histoire de France par l'estampe, 1770–1871. Collection de Vinck. Inventaire analytique*, 8 vols. (Paris: Bibliothèque Nationale, 1909–21), vols. 1–3.

2. Maurice Tourneux, "Les Tableaux historiques de la Révolution et leurs transformations. Etude iconographique et bibliographique," *La Révolution française* 15 (August 1888): 123–61.

3. Emile Dacier, "Les Gravures historiques de Janinet," *L'Amateur d'estampes* 31 (1928): 161 ff.; *L'Amateur d'estampes* 32 (1929): 14 ff., 44 ff.

4. Jack R. Censer, "The Political Engravings of the 'Révolutions de France et de Brabant,' 1789 to 1791," *Eighteenth-Century Life* 5 (1979): 105–22.

5. Pierre-Louis Duchatre and René Saulnier, *L'Imagerie parisienne. L'imagerie de la rue Saint-Jacques* (Paris: Grand, 1944); *Populäre Druckgraphik Europas. Frankreich vom 15. bis zum 20. Jahrhundert* (Munich: Callwey, 1968), 88–93.

6. Brigitte Schlieben-Lange, *Traditionen des Sprechens* (Stuttgart: Kohlhammer, 1983), 64–77.

7. François-Alphonse Aulard, ed., *La Société des Jacobins. Recueil de documents pour l'histoire du Club des Jacobins de Paris,* 6 vols. (Paris: Johans and Cerf, 1889–97), 3:263.

8. Jacques-Marie Boyer-Brun, *Histoire des caricatures de la révolte des Français,* 2 vols. (Paris, 1792), 1:préface.

9. See Louis-Sébastien Mercier, "Caricatures, folies," in *Le Nouveau Paris* (Paris: Fuchs, Pouglas, and Cramer, an VII), 1:164.

10. Unpublished research by the author. See also F.-A. Aulard, *Etudes et leçons sur la Révolution française,* 9 vols. (Paris: Alcan, 1893–1924), 1:241–67.

11. Jean-Nicolas Trouille, *Discours prononcé en faisant hommage d'une estampe à la gloire de la Liberté triomphante, ouvrage postum de Vincent Vangélisty* (Paris: Imprimerie Nationale, an VII [1799]), 3.

12. Rolf Reichardt, "Mehr geschichtliches Verstehen durch Bildillustration? Kritische Überlegungen am Beispiel der Französischen Revolution," *Francia. Forschungen zur westeuropäischen Geschichte* 13 (1985):511–23. Michel Vovelle succeeds only partially in freeing himself from this tradition in *La Révolution française, Images et récit,* 5 vols. (Paris: Livre Club Diderot & Messidor, 1986).

13. Lynn Hunt, *Politics, Culture, and Class in the French Revolution* (Berkeley and Los Angeles: University of California Press, 1984), 87–119; Klaus Herding, "Visuelle Zeichensysteme in der Graphik der Französischen Revolution," in *Die Französische Revolution als Bruch des gesellschaftlichen Bewußtseins,* Bielefelder Tagungsakten, ed. Reinhard Koselleck and Rolf Reichardt (Munich: Oldenbourg, 1987), 513–52.

14. See also the comparative literary-historical study by Hans-Jürgen Lüsebrink, "'Die zweifach enthüllte Bastille?' Zur sozialen Funktion der Medien Text und Bild in der deutschen und französischen 'Bastille'-Literatur des 18. Jahrhunderts," *Francia* 13 (1985):311–31.

15. André Basset, *Jeu national instructif, ou leçons exemplaires et amusantes données aux bons citoyens par Henri IV et le père Gérard* (Paris: Basset, 1791), color etching 505:735 mm, Bibliothèque Nationale, Coll. de Vinck, no. 4295.

16. For a full discussion of this idea, see Rolf Reichardt, "Revolutionäre Mentalitäten und Netze politischer Grundbegriffe in Frankreich 1789–1795," in *Die Französische Revolution,* ed. Kosselleck and Reichardt, 185–99.

17. For more on the journalistic and political context of the Bastille myth, which can only be touched on here, see my article "Bastille," in *Handbuch politisch-sozialer Grundbegriffe in Frankreich, 1680–1820,* ed. Rolf Reichardt and Eberhard Schmitt, Heft 9 (Munich: Oldenbourg, 1988), 7–74.

18. H.-J. Lüsebrink and Rolf Reichardt, "La 'Bastille' dans l'imaginaire social de la France à la fin du XVIIIᵉ siècle (1774–1799)," *Revue d'histoire moderne et contemporaine* 30 (April–June 1983):198–214.

19. See the letter of 16 May 1789 from the directeur-général de la librairie to the lieutenant-général de police in Paris, Archives Nationales, V² 551.

20. Jean-Pierre Seguin, "Les Feuilles d'information non périodiques ou 'canards' en France," *Revue de synthèse* 78 (July–September 1957):391–420.

21. *Les Lauriers du Faubourg Saint-Antoine, ou Le Prix de la Bastille renversée,* 8 pp. (Paris: Gueffier, 1789). For more detailed information on and analyses of the two *canards* discussed below, see H.-J. Lüsebrink and Rolf Reichardt, "Oralität und Textfiliation in rezeptionspragmatischer Perspektive. Sozio-kulturelle Fallstudien zur Konstitution populärer Druckschriften und zur Rezeption der 'Mémoires' von Latude in den Jahren 1787–93," in the conference volume *Zur Geschichte von Buch und Leser im Frankreich des Ancien Régime,* ed. Günter Berger (Rheinfelden: Schäuble, 1986), 111–43.

22. Auguste Martin, *L'Imagerie orléanaise* (Paris: Duchartre & Van Buggenhondt, 1928), 12–14, 79–107.

23. See the portrayal of the victors of the Bastille carrying aloft two impaled heads in the anonymous etching *C'est ainsi qu'on se venge des traîtres*, Bibliothèque Nationale, Coll. de Vinck, no. 1605).

24. Cf. the very perceptive study by H.-J. Lüsebrink, "Die Vainqueurs de la Bastille: Kollektiver Diskurs und individuelle 'Wortergreifungen,'" in *Die Französische Revolution*, ed. Kosselleck and Reichardt, 321–57.

25. Cf. the oft-copied, anonymous color etching of this title from July 1789, Bibliothèque Nationale, Coll. de Vinck, no. 1674.

26. Cf. the account in the anonymous pamphlet *Le Moine qui n'est pas bête* (n.p., n.d.), 1.

27. See the series of copperplate engravings, Bibliothèque Nationale, Coll. de Vinck, nos. 1150–57.

28. Of the many reports see, for example, the anonymous pamphlet *Paris sauvé, ou Récit détaillé des événements qui ont eu lieu à Paris depuis le 12 juillet 1789, une heure après midi, jusqu'au vendredi suivant en soir*, 34 pp. (n.p., n.d.).

29. Thus the title of another version of the broadside, Bibliothèque Nationale, Coll. de Vinck, no. 1696.

30. Cf. the anonymous documentation, partially attributed to Louis-Pierre Manuel, *La Bastille dévoilée, ou Recueil des pièces authentiques pour servir à son histoire*, 4ᵉ livraison (Paris: Desenne, November 1789), 132.

31. *Le Comte de Lorges, prisonnier à la Bastille pendant trente-deux ans*, 16 pp. (n.p., September 1789). For more on this problem see Lüsebrink and Reichardt, "La 'Bastille,'" 216–23.

32. Cf. the anonymous pamphlet, *La Bastille* (Paris, 1789), 6–7.

33. *Révolutions de Paris*, no. 1 (12–17 July 1789), 23.

34. Thus the title of a color etching published by Jacques François Chereau of the rue St. Jacques at the end of July 1790, Bibliothèque Nationale, Coll. de Vinck, no. 3855.

35. Speech by Jean Lambert Tallien, printed in the anonymous collection *Fête civique sur les ruines de la Bastille, le 14 juillet, l'an troisième de la Liberté* (n.p., n.d. [Paris, 1791]), 3–4.

36. Cf. the analysis of Fourteenth of July commemorative speeches in Lüsebrink and Reichardt, "La 'Bastille,'" 228–34, and in H.-J. Lüsebrink and Rolf Reichardt, "La Prise de la Bastille comme 'événement totale,'" in the conference volume *L'Evénement* (Aix-en-Provence: Université de Provence, 1986), 78–102.

37. Mona Ozouf, "Le cortège et la ville: les itinéraires parisiens des fêtes révolutionnaires," *Annales: Economies, sociétés, civilisations* 26 (September–October 1971): 889–916.

38. *Journal de Paris*, no. 192 (11 July 1791).

39. "Sur un étendard déployé on voyait l'image de la Bastille; cette forteresse représentée au relief suivoit ensuite . . . ," *Détail exacte et circonstancié de tous les objets relatifs à la fête de Voltaire, extrait de la Chronique de Paris* (n.p., n.d. [Paris, July 1791]), 2.

40. For more on this, see Lüsebrink and Reichardt, "La 'Bastille,'" 224–28.

344

41. On the lasting effect of Bastille symbolism in the nineteenth and twentieth centuries, see Rosemonde Sanson, *Les 14 Juillet, fête et conscience nationale, 1789–1975* (Paris: Flammarion, 1976); Christian Amalvi, "Le 14 Juillet: Du 'Dies irae' à 'Jour de fête,'" in *La République*, vol. 1 of *Les Lieux de la mémoire*, ed. Pierre Nora (Paris: Gallimard, 1984), 421–72.

Mason: Songs

1.
> By your means each idea
> is changed into metal bits;
> Through your eyes each is placed
> one by one, into an ordered spot;
> By your arms each is pressed
> to double its power and its price;
> By your hands it is sent
> to reach everyone's thoughts.

Piis, "Hymne à l'imprimerie." Bibliothèque historique de la Ville de Paris, #960 349.

2. *Histoire générale de la presse française* (Paris: Presses Universitaires de France, 1969), 436.

3. The increased production of songs was the more striking because royalist songwriters, who had been responsible for almost a third of the songs written in 1790 and 1791, had almost entirely disappeared by 1792. The percentage of songs that was royalist is a rough estimate based on the figures in Constant Pierre, *Hymnes et chansons de la Révolution française* (Paris: Imprimerie Nationale, 1904). From his totals for the years between 1791 and 1795, I subtracted those songs that appeared in newspapers or song collections that were avowedly hostile to the Revolution.

4. In a short comic piece written in 1789, a marketwoman is offered a song on the taking of the Bastille, four months after the event. She refuses by snapping at the songseller, "La Bastille, ça fait raisoir? [*sic*] On scait tout ça à present" ("The Bastille, that's a bore. Everyone knows all about that by now"). *Gazette de Paris*, 20 November 1789.

5. Among these were the opera aria "Où peut-on être mieux qu'au sein de sa famille?" ("Where is one better off than in the bosom of his family?"), played in honor of the royal family and of the mayor of Paris, and the popular song "Vive Henri IV," which was sung as a means of comparing Louis XVI to his beloved ancestor.

6. Abbé Fauchet, in *Journal de Paris*, 19 May 1790.

7. *Révolutions de France et de Brabant*, no. 8 [January 1790].

8. *Chronique de Paris*, 9 July 1790.

9. "Ça ira" is a colloquial phrase, meaning roughly: "Things will work out."

10.
> Oh! things will work out
> Let's rejoice that the good times have come
> The marketpeople, once down and out
> Can sing Hallelujah.

Journal des Halles no. 1 [July 1790].

11. *Chronique de Paris*, 10 July 1790.

12. *Mercure de France* [July 1790], 214–16.

13. *Chronique de Paris*, 3 November 1790.

14. *Dictionnaire laconique* ("A Patriopolus: l'an 3eme de la prétendue liberté" [1792]).

15. Later printed versions and parodies of "ça ira" were not hopeful and conciliatory; instead they expressed the growing social and political tensions of the Revolution. See, for instance, Ladré's "Ah! Com' ça va" [1791?] (Bibliothèque Nationale: Ye 35763[7]), or the version of "ça ira" in the *Nouveau chansonnier patriote*, Year II (1793–94).

16. *Chronique de Paris*, 6 April 1792; *Courrier des 83 départements*, 7, 24, 27 April 1792.

17. Michel Vovelle, "La Marseillaise," in *Les Lieux de la mémoire*, 3 vols., ed. Pierre Nora (Paris: Gallimard, 1984), vol. 1, *La République*; Pierre, *Hymnes et chansons*, entry for "The Marseillaise."

18. Vovelle, "La Marseillaise," *Courrier*, 28 July 1792.

19. *Chronique de Paris*, 29 August 1892.

20. Ibid., 19 October 1792.

21. See, for instance, *Chronique de Paris*, 29 October 1792; *Chansonnier de la Montagne* (Paris: Chez Favre, an II [1793–94]).

22. Pierre, *Hymnes et chansons*, entries for "ça ira" and the "Marseillaise."

23. Although just what those possibilities might have been is hard to imagine. Even with the text as firmly established as it was, at least 250 parodies of the "Marseillaise" were written during the Revolution. On this point, regarding one parody in particular, see H. Hudde, "Le Jour de boire est arrivé," *Dix-huitième siècle* 17 (1985): 377–95.

24. Archives Nationales (hereafter A.N.), F17 1004c, no. 700.

25. A.N., F17 1004a, no. 395.

26. *Feuille de la République*, 9 thermidor, an II (27 July 1794); A.N., AFII67, nos. 15, 19, 65.

27. Pierre, *Hymnes et chansons*, 34, and see n. 3.

28. This does not mean that spontaneous singing in the street stopped. Although accounts of such activity receded from printed sources, they continued to appear in the reports submitted by police spies who wandered the streets of Paris. See A.N., F7 3688 (3) and F1c III Seine 27.

29. A.N., DI§2(1), no. 41.

30. There was a great deal of singing of the "Marseillaise" in Paris as well, but it was usually on the part of a group singing for itself or for a sympathetic audience, rather than against an enemy.

31.   Frenchmen, brothers,
                    can you see without shuddering in horror
                    crime raising the standard
                    of carnage and of Terror?

32.   What! this cannibalistic mob
                    that Hell has vomited from its bowels

preaches murder and bloodshed!
and is covered with your blood!

33. *Messager du soir*, 1 pluviôse, an III (20 January 1795).

34. The *jeunesse d'orée*, meaning literally "gilded youth," were young men of middle-class origins who carried out the Thermidoran reaction in the streets. Although they helped to defend the National Convention during the demonstrations of prairial, Year III (May 1795), they were also responsible for violence and terrorism against those they believed to be Jacobins.

35. Alphonse Aulard, "La Querelle entre la 'Marseillaise' et le 'Réveil du peuple,'" in Alphonse Aulard, *Etudes et Leçons sur la Révolution française*, 3eme sér. (Paris: F. Alcan, 1902–04).

36. *Annales patriotiques*, 7 germinal, an III (26 March 1795).

37. See, for instance, the report of the events preceding the closing of the Jacobin Club in *Annales patriotiques*, 3 brumaire, an III (24 October 1794).

38. This decree was part of the larger project of the Convention's efforts to dissociate itself from the *jeunesse d'orée* and the reaction of the streets, from which it had drawn the benefits it sought and whose activity it was now seeking to curb. See Aulard, "La Querelle"; François Furet and Denis Richet, *La Révolution française* (Paris: Hachette, 1965); François Gendron, *La Jeunesse D'Orée* (Quebec: Presses de l'Université du Québec, 1979).

39. *Courrier de Paris*, 27 messidor, an III (15 July 1795).

40. *Courrier de Paris*, 28 messidor, an III (16 July 1795).

41. *Annales patriotiques*, 3 thermidor, an III (21 July 1795).

42. *Courrier républicain*, 2 thermidor (20 July); *Annales patriotiques*, 3 thermidor, an III (21 July 1795).

43. *Courrier de Paris*, 30 messidor (18 July); *Courrier républicain*, 2, 5 thermidor (20, 23 July); see also comments in *Annales patriotiques*, 3 thermidor, an III (21 July 1795).

44. *Moniteur universel*, 15 thermidor, an III (4 August 1795).

45. A.N., F7 3688(5), doss. 3, 14 ventôse, an IV (4 March 1796).

Leith: Ephemera

1. Marshall McLuhan, *Gutenberg Galaxy: The Making of Typographic Man* (Toronto: University of Toronto Press, 1962).

2. Brevet de vainqueur de la Bastille . . . Nicolas invenit, gravé par Delettre. Bibliothèque Nationale (hereafter B.N.), Estampes, Coll. de Vinck, t. 10, no. 1643.

3. Brevet de Garde Nationale, B.N., Estampes, Coll. Hennin, t. 129, no. 11392.

4. Jean Lafaurie, *Les Assignats et les papiers-monnaies émis par l'Etat au XVIIIe siècle* (Paris: Le Léopard d'Or, 1981).

5. James A. Leith, "Symbols in the French Revolution: The Strange Metamorphoses of the Triangle," in *Symbols in Life and Art / Les Symboles dans la vie et dans l'art*, ed. James A. Leith (Montreal and Kingston: McGill-Queen's University Press, for the Royal Society of Canada, 1987), 105–117.

347

6. Auguste Boppe, *Les Vignettes emblématiques sous la Révolution. 250 reproductions d'en-têtes de lettres* (Paris and Nancy: Berger-Levrault, 1911).

7. The *Bulletin des lois* began publication on 22 prairial, an II (10 June 1794). The central figure was changed on 26 fructidor, an II (12 September 1794), between 1ère sér., no. 57, Loi 310, and no. 58, Loi 311.

8. The entire heading and seal change again with *Bulletin* no. 127 on 14 prairial, an V (2 June 1797). The decision to change the heading and seal had been made by the executive of the Directory a year earlier. Evidently, it took time to make and approve the engravings.

9. *Au Français libres et leurs amis par un helvétien non dégénéré*, B.N., Estampes, Coll. de Vinck, t. 25, no. 4221.

10. Chemin fils, *L'Ami des jeunes patriotes, ou catéchisme républicain* (Paris: Imprimerie de l'auteur, an II).

11. François-Marie Quéverdo, *Maximes du jeune républicain gravé* (Paris: Quéverdo, n.d.) B.N., Estampes, Coll. de Vinck, t. 25, no. 4214. The catalogue of the collection identifies the central figure as the Republic, although she has none of the usual features and wears the luminous eye usually associated with Reason.

12. *Sur l'ère, le commencement de l'année et sur les noms des jours,* loi du 4 frimaire, an II (24 November 1793).

13. A good example is the calendar engraved by Quéverdo, B.N., Estampes, Coll. de Vinck, t. 44, no. 6100.

14. J.-J. Rousseau, *Oeuvres Complètes*, 3 vols. (Paris: Pléiade, 1964), 3:955.

15. Baron de Vinck, *Iconographie du noble jeu d'oye. Catalogue descriptif et raisonné* (Brussels: F. J. Olivier, 1886).

16. *Jeu de la Révolution française tracé sur le plan du jeu d'oye renouvelé des Grecs* (Paris, n.d.), B.N., Estampes, Qb¹ 1789, 14 juillet.

17. *Les Délassements du père Gérard, ou la poule de Henri IV. Mise au pot 1792. Jeu national* (n.p., n.d.), B.N., Estampes, Coll. Hennin, t. 126, no. 11126.

18. Athanase Détournelle, *Aux armes et aux arts! Peinture, sculpture, architecture, gravure. Journal de la Société républicaine des arts séant au Louvre* (Paris: Détournelle, n.d.), 155–57.

19. *Nouvelles Cartes à jouer de la République française* (Paris, n.d.), B.N., Estampes, Coll. Hennin, t. 134, no. 11839.

20. C.-A. Helvétius, *De l'homme, de ses facultés intellectuelles et de son éducation,* 2 vols. (London, 1771), in *Oeuvres complètes* (Paris: P. Didot l'aîné, 1795), 12:71 (sec. 10, chap. 1).

CONTRIBUTORS

LISE ANDRIES is chargée de recherche at the Centre National de la Recherche Scientifique. She is also an associate of the research center XVIIe–XVIIIe Siècles, Université de Paris, IV. She has published two books, *Robert le Diable et autres récits* (1981) and *Les Contes bleus,* with G. Bollème (1983).

ANTOINE DE BAECQUE is assistant-normalien at the Université de Paris, I. He has written several articles on political imagery during the Revolution and published *La Caricature révolutionnaire* (1988).

RAYMOND BIRN is professor of history at the University of Oregon. His publications include *Pierre Rousseau and the Philosophes of Bouillon* (1964) and *Crisis, Absolutism, Revolution: Europe, 1648/1789–91* (1977). He has edited *The Printed Word in the Eighteenth Century* (1984) and has written numerous articles in European cultural history.

PIERRE CASSELLE is conservateur at the Bibliothèque administrative de l'Hôtel de Ville de Paris. He is a contributing author to the *Histoire de l'édition française,* vol. 2 (1984) and coauthor of the *Dictionnaire des éditeurs d'estampes à Paris sous l'ancien régime* (1987).

ROBERT DARNTON is Shelby Cullom Davis Professor of European History at Princeton University. His publications include *Mesmerism and the End of the Enlightenment in France* (1968), *The Business of Enlightenment: A Publishing History of the Encyclopédie, 1775–1800* (1979), *The Literary Underground of the Old Regime* (1982), and *The Great Cat Massacre and Other Episodes of French Cultural History* (1985).

349

JEAN DHOMBRES is professor of mathematics at the Université de Nantes and Directeur d'études at L'Ecole des Hautes Etudes en Sciences Sociales. He recently published the *Histoire de l'Ecole polytechnique* and was supervising editor of *Mathématiques au fil des âges*.

CARLA HESSE is assistant professor of history at Rutgers University and research curator for The New York Public Library's exhibition "Revolution in Print: France, 1789." She is completing a book entitled *Res Publicata: Paris Publishers and Revolutionary Politics, 1789–1810*.

JAMES LEITH is professor of history at Queen's University in Kingston, Ontario, Canada, and a fellow of the Royal Society of Canada. He has published extensively on the use of the media in various revolutionary and totalitarian regimes. He has recently completed a book, *Space and Revolution: Projects for Monuments, Squares and Public Buildings in France, 1789–99*.

LAURA MASON is a doctoral candidate at Princeton University. Her dissertation, *Singing the French Revolution: Popular Songs and Revolutionary Politics, 1789–1799*, is a study of the relationship between revolutionary politics and Parisian popular culture.

PHILIPPE MINARD is assistant-doctorant at the Université de Lille, III. He has published *Typographes des lumières, essai sur le travail et la culture ouvrière au XVIIIe siècle* (1988).

JEREMY D. POPKIN is professor of history at the University of Kentucky. He is the author of *The Right-Wing Press in France, 1792–1800* and has published numerous articles on journalism before and during the French Revolution.

ROLF REICHARDT is history bibliographer at the University of Mainz. He is the editor of *Handbook on French Historical Semantics, 1680–1820* and of the *Bielefeld Colloquium on the French Revolution* (1988). He is the author of two forthcoming books, one on the prints of the French Revolution and another on the political symbolism of the Bastille in France and Germany (1989).

DANIEL ROCHE is professor of modern European history at the Université de Paris, I, and at the European Institute at Florence. His publications include *Le Siècle des lumières en province, 1660–1789* (1978), *Le Peuple de Paris* (1981; English trans., 1987), *Le Journal de ma vie par Jacques Louis Ménétra*, *vitrier compagnon parisien au XVIIIe siècle* (1982; English trans., 1987), and *Sociétés et cultures dans la France d'ancien régime* (1985).

MICHEL VERNUS is maître de conférences at the Université de Dijon. He has published *La Vie comtoise au temps de l'ancien régime* (1984) and *Le Presbytère et la chaumière* (1986). He is a specialist on the Franche-Comté and the social and cultural life of Old Regime France.

Designer: Sandy Drooker
Compositor: G&S Typesetters
Text: 10/13 Baskerville
Display: Caslon Open Face and Baskerville
Printer: Malloy Lithographing, Inc.
Binder: John H. Dekker & Sons